Almost Over

Almost Over
Aging, Dying, Dead

F. M. KAMM

OXFORD
UNIVERSITY PRESS

OXFORD
UNIVERSITY PRESS

Oxford University Press is a department of the University of Oxford. It furthers
the University's objective of excellence in research, scholarship, and education
by publishing worldwide. Oxford is a registered trade mark of Oxford University
Press in the UK and certain other countries.

Published in the United States of America by Oxford University Press
198 Madison Avenue, New York, NY 10016, United States of America.

Library of Congress Cataloging-in-Publication Data
Names: Kamm, F. M. (Frances Myrna), author.
Title: Almost over: aging, dying, dead / F.M. Kamm.
Description: New York, NY, United States of America:
Oxford University Press, 2020. | Includes index.
Identifiers: LCCN 2019047219 (print) | LCCN 2019047220 (ebook) |
ISBN 9780190097158 (hardback) | ISBN 9780197764107 (paperback) |
ISBN 9780190097172 (epub) | ISBN 9780190097189
Subjects: LCSH: Death. | Aging.
Classification: LCC BD444 .K315 2020 (print) | LCC BD444 (ebook) |
DDC 306.9—dc23
LC record available at https://lccn.loc.gov/2019047219
LC ebook record available at https://lccn.loc.gov/2019047220

Paperback printed by Marquis Book Printing, Canada

In memory of Robert Nozick and Derek Parfit.
With gratitude.

Table of Contents

Introduction

Overview of the book. This book deals with philosophical, legal, and medical issues related to aging, dying, and death that face a society and people in it as a matter of advance planning as well as in clinical care.[1]

Chapter 1 considers different views about what makes death bad for the person who dies (its intrapersonal badness) and what could be done to reduce or eliminate its badness. It also considers how death compares with prenatal nonexistence and whether factors that make death bad for a person also bear on whether extinction of humanity (or other types of persons) would be bad. Given this as background, Chapters 2 and 3 begin consideration of when it could make sense to die rather than live on because death is preferable to living on for the person who would die. Chapter 2 focuses on the views of Shelly Kagan about (i) when ending or not ending one's life does or does not make sense and (ii) how to decide. It considers whether his views about the worth of living on are consistent with his views about when it makes no sense to end one's life. It also examines whether the way in which he adds the negative and positive aspects of life to decide whether to live on gives sufficient weight to context-dependent values and to the reasonableness of not going through great suffering for the sake of an even greater good to oneself.

Chapter 3 focuses on the views of Atul Gawande about the process of dying and the possible conflict between trying to live on by way of medical treatment and retaining meaning at the end of life. It considers how his views relate to Bernard Williams' distinction between categorical and conditional desires and how they bear on when it makes sense not to resist the end of one's life. There is critical discussion of Gawande's conception of meaning in life and the importance he attributes to endings. Chapter 4 considers attempts to help the general public plan in advance for the end of life. Possible conflicts are identified between the aim of respecting people's preferences and meeting objective standards of best practices, family preferences, and requirements of informed consent. The chapter also locates imprecision, nudging, and framing effects in the questions recommended

Almost Over. F. M. Kamm, Oxford University Press (2020) © Oxford University Press.
DOI: 10.1093/oso/9780190097158.001.0001

by conversation guides for eliciting people's preferences as well as tendencies of the questions to promote specific values.

Chapter 5 begins consideration of aging per se by reflecting (with the help of a work of fiction) on hypothetical possibilities for the direction and distribution of goods and bads in life. It first distinguishes qualitative aging from becoming older in years by considering the fictional case of Benjamin Button. It then considers the significance of death in lives with different aging trajectories, better and worse distributions of goods and bads within lives, and tradeoffs between quantity and quality of life. Chapter 6 considers a type of view about aging and death exemplified in the work of Ezekiel Emanuel (a prominent bioethicist and architect of public health policy). It examines Emanuel's reasons for thinking that after a "complete life" (by around 75) it can be reasonable (at least for some) to omit easy preventive measures (e.g., flu shots) that would extend life even when such life would not be worse than death. To better understand such a position the chapter makes use of the views of Susan Wolf and Bernard Williams on meaning in life and reasons to go on living, and also considers different ways of judging the worth of activities. It further compares Emanuel's views with those of Atul Gawande, B. J. Miller, and Douglas MacLean. Finally, it considers whether Emanuel's argument also supports the moral permissibility of suicide and assisted suicide.

Chapter 7 presents arguments in favor of the moral permissibility of, and even a duty to engage in, physician-assisted suicide. It considers objections to these sorts of arguments presented by David Velleman from a Kantian perspective and by Neil Gorsuch (now associate justice of the U.S. Supreme Court) who argues against intending death. The chapter considers how to identify such an intention, the significance of the intention for moral and legal permissibility, and the role of the Doctrine of Double Effect in arguments about assisted suicide. Chapter 8 considers how one should reason about assisted suicide as a matter of public (and legal) policy in the absence of a constitutional right to it by critically examining Emanuel's anti-legalization views. The chapter considers the role of (i) rights and wronging of people and how they come about as well as (ii) harms and benefits and how to aggregate them. The bearing on these issues of arguments for the distinctive role of the state in enabling or interfering with behavior is considered by critically reviewing some arguments for and against capital punishment. Finally, in the light of empirical data about effects of legalizing physician-assisted suicide and given what else he believes, the chapter considers whether Emanuel should no longer oppose legalization. In connection with issues raised in Chapters 4 and 8, an appendix considers whether using cost-effectiveness analysis to determine what health procedures to use can involve unfairness. Different views of fairness are considered as well as such possible sources of unfairness as not giving priority to the worse off and discrimination against the disabled. The views of Daniel Hausman and Peter Singer, among others, are critically examined.

Origins of the book. More than my other books, it is events—ones in which I was an invited participant as well as public events—and their upshots that have led to this book. I came to write the article that served as the basis for Chapter 1 as a result of being invited to a conference on death in Norway in 2015. Since I had not worked on the topic of death itself since writing *Morality, Mortality*, vol. 1, I read Shelly Kagan's (at the time) new book *Death* to prepare. At about the same time the Museum of Modern Art (MOMA) in New York invited me to serve on a panel with Atul Gawande to discuss his book *Being Mortal*. (Though he was ultimately unable to participate, I participated in another MOMA panel, "Modern Death," which took its place.) I was struck by differences in the way Kagan and Gawande approached some similar issues and this led to writing the article that was the basis for Chapters 2 and 3. I also became interested in the questions asked of patients that Gawande described as being used to determine appropriate end-of-life care, and Dr. Lachlan Farrow provided some references to read on this topic. My published article about these questionnaires is the basis for Chapter 4. Chapters 6 and 7 are the result of having been invited to debate Ezekiel Emanuel, a major figure in U.S. health policy, on a panel about death and dying at the thirtieth anniversary of the Edward J. Safra Center for Ethics at Harvard University. Emanuel and I had different views about assisted suicide in the past and in preparation for that panel I read more of his work on that topic and on also his views on aging. It was writing Chapter 6 that triggered my consideration in Chapter 5 of a short story by F. Scott Fitzgerald because of the different way it presents aging, growing old, and the distribution of goods and bads in life. It is a speculative chapter less connected to real life issues than other chapters. Chapter 7 was prompted by the appointment of Neil Gorsuch to the Supreme Court, an event that made it especially important to examine his views on assisted suicide. Parts of that chapter served as my Lanson Lecture in Bioethics at the Chinese University of Hong Kong and my Lecretia Seales Memorial Lecture at the Victoria University of Wellington Law Faculty.

Acknowledgments. For comments on drafts of Chapter 1, I am grateful to Espen Gamlund and Carl Tollef Solberg. Chapters 2, 3, 6, and 7 were fruitfully discussed with Shelly Kagan, Jeff McMahan, Larry Temkin, and others mentioned in the individual chapters. Temkin also provided comments on Chapters 1, 4, and 8 when he attended my graduate seminar at Rutgers University's philosophy department in spring 2017. For their detailed written remarks, I am grateful to Larry Sager and Seana Shiffrin who commented on Chapter 8 when it was delivered at the UCLA Law and Philosophy Colloquium, and to Dr. Chun-Yan Tse, who was my official commentator on my Lanson Lecture. For the opportunity to discuss their work and their continuing support of my own efforts I am grateful to Thomas Nagel and Susan Wolf. I also thank for their comments audiences at the Australian National University, NYU, Brandeis, Syracuse University, MOMA, the Columbia University Seminar on Death, the Chinese University of Hong Kong, the Victoria University Law Faculty, UCLA, UCSD, UCI, and students in my seminars at Harvard and Rutgers Universities. Throughout the time I worked on this book I was the beneficiary of help for which I am very grateful from Lily Safra and the Edmond J. Safra Ethics Center at Harvard University, the Harvard Kennedy School, Sharon Street, Maria Twarog, Agnes Mosejczuk, and Hubert Mosejczuk. Finally, I am indebted to Jenn Valois for deciphering and typing, to Margaret Collins, Christopher Fruge, and James Goodrich for editing, and to Rhys Southan for the index. They made possible a more readable book.

Note

1. Though this book deals with death, the last word in its subtitle is not "death" but "dead" as in "you are aging, you are dying, you are dead."

Almost Over

Chapter 1

The Badness of Death and What to Do About It (if Anything)

In this chapter I will consider certain views about why death per se (as opposed to the process of dying) is bad for the person who dies.[1] Given these views about what makes a death bad, I will consider (1) what might help to avoid or minimize the bad aspects of death and (2) whether these things should be done.[2] I briefly consider whether and how factors analogous to those that make death bad for a person would make the end of all persons bad.

1. Preliminary Remarks

The standard contemporary view about why death is bad for the person who dies is called Deprivationism.[3] On this view death, assumed to involve irreversible nonexistence after life, is bad only because it deprives one of goods and the more deprivation, the worse the death.[4] Hence, the badness (or goodness) of death for a person is discovered by comparing the life he could have had if death did not occur at a certain time to the life he will have if it occurs at that time. Alternatively, we might determine how bad (or good) death is for a person by comparing his nonexistence after a certain point in time where the event of death occurs with what his life would have been like from that point in time onward if he had not died then. These are comparisons between actual and counterfactual lives and states. Figure 1.1 shows both comparisons.

On the alternative view, if only things worse than nothing (involved in nonexistence) are to come, then death that prevents them from coming would not be bad and an earlier death would be better than a

Almost Over. F. M. Kamm, Oxford University Press (2020) © Oxford University Press.
DOI: 10.1093/oso/9780190097158.001.0001

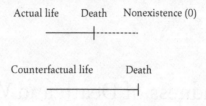

Figure 1.1

later death. On this view, sometimes one could be better off dead but only in a sense that it would be better to have a shorter rather than longer life. This sense is still compatible with one not being in a better state once dead since death is assumed to involve our nonexistence. Deprivationism so understood takes a forward-looking, consequentialist view of the badness or goodness of death; death is bad or good depending on whether its consequence is no more good or no more bad life.

I have concerns about Deprivationism as an adequate theory of the badness of death. First, I think that how good or bad one's life will have been (or how much good or bad one will have had) by the time one dies could be a better indication of how bad one's death is for one than how good or bad one's life would be in the future. It is worse to die at 20 than at 50 (holding quality of each year constant) even if the 20-year-old is deprived of only 5 additional good years of life and the 50-year-old is deprived of 20 additional good years of life (holding quality of each year constant). Call this view about the badness of death *Willhavehadism*. In a sense it is a "backward consequentialist" view since how much one will have had is an effect of death.

Second, it might be better for us all to put off the time at which our conscious life as a person will be all over even holding constant the assumed good contents of our life overall as well as its beginning point. One way of doing this is by going into an unconscious limbo state for a long time and then returning to consciousness for a significant period. This "Limbo Man Case" indicates that one's life as a conscious and self-conscious person being all over is a bad aspect of death independent of its depriving us of additional goods. Indeed, I think it is the aspect of death that we find most terrifying. Call this view *Alloverism*.

Third, because death takes from us a life, thought of as a thing that we have already had, it exhibits what I call *Insult Factors* (such as decline from a higher point and vulnerability). These Insult Factors do not apply to nonexistence prior to the beginning of life, a state which can only prevent us from having goods sooner rather than take them away. Call this view Insultism.

2. More on Deprivationism

2.1. The idea of deprivation

Some object to the term "deprivation" on the grounds that not getting more of something is not always to be deprived of it. Further, some would say one can only be "deprived" of something that one has a right to in the first place.[5] However, it can be bad for one not to receive more of some good even if one has no right to it. In addition, death does not involve merely the nonprovision of some period of life; it is the interruption of life that would continue on without it. This is analogous to the distinction between not helping someone have more time at a park and interfering with their having more time at a park that they would have had without your help. The term "Preventionism" might also strictly be better than "Deprivationism" because one does not usually speak of being deprived of something bad and death could interfere with forthcoming life worse than death. I will continue to use the term deprivation but these points should be kept in mind.

2.2. Deprivationism and the past

Deprivationists should be aware that how good or bad the future will be for someone could depend on their past. If someone has already had a very good life there might be something like diminishing marginal utility (DMU) in having ten more good years by comparison to someone who has had a bad life having ten more good years.

2.3. Deprivationism and future goods

It could make sense to consider whether future additional goods might even make our life overall (including past and future) be worse than death if it continues; or conversely, whether additional bads might make our life overall better than death if it continues. The former could occur, for example, if going downhill while still getting goods were worse for one than ending at a peak.[6] Having future goods could make one's life overall worse, it is sometimes said, because it is only being deprived of more goods by death that makes us appreciate the limited amount of goods we do have. However, even if this were true, it would not show that losing out on more goods is not bad, only that one bad is necessary to avoid a (possibly) greater bad. There is also little reason to think this claim is true. After all, shortening a life span from 70 to 20 years is not thought necessary to increase appreciation of goods of youth and even if there were less appreciation of such goods without shortening, it is compensated for by having more goods from 20 to 70 years.

In any case, a version of Deprivationism that considers whether goods or bads that we could have in future life would deprive us of a better life overall (so we will be living a worse life overall) will not face a possible objection to the version of Deprivationism that just compares the possible future (and goods or bads in it) with death. This indicates that these two versions are not merely different ways to say the same thing.

It may also be important to distinguish between types of future goods since it may be bad to be deprived of only some types by death. Bernard Williams distinguished two types of desires connected with two types of goods.[7] Conditional desires have as objects things it is good for us to have if we are alive but getting them does not give us a reason to go on living. For example, not being bored and not being in pain seem to be objects of only conditional desires. By contrast, categorical desires have as objects things that give us a reason to go on living (e.g., completing certain projects). We could also move beyond Williams' talk of desires and just speak of the things (whether desired or not) that are conditional goods and others that are categorical goods. If death would deprive us of only conditional goods then Deprivationism would imply that death would not be bad for us since death would also remove the condition (life) on which the goodness of these things depends. They would not be needed to make life bearable if there was no life. By contrast, suppose we would have categorical goods if we continued living; then death would deprive us of the condition (life) which is needed in order to bring about these goods which give us a reason to go on living. Deprivationism would then imply that death would be bad for us only when it deprives us of categorical goods.[8]

It may also be necessary to consider the distribution and not just the overall quality and quantity of categorical goods to decide if death is bad for someone. For example, suppose someone must suffer a significant period of only intense pain and suffering before going on to get categorical goods in life whose quality and quantity are greater than those bads. Death before the period of suffering would prevent an overall positive future life. Nevertheless, it may not be unreasonable to choose death at that time if it is the only way to avoid the concentrated suffering. By contrast, it may not be reasonable to choose death at that time if the same amount of suffering were dispersed over the entire future.[9]

2.4. Deprivationism and the Principle of Irrelevant Goods

One way to deal with the bad aspect of death on which Deprivationism focuses is to extend life so long as it provides (roughly) life whose content makes it worth having. This could be a combination of categorical goods and conditional goods needed once one must stay alive to achieve categorical goods. We also deal with the bad aspect of death on which Deprivationism focuses if we save lives whose continued existence would involve a future that is better than nothing (or contributes to making the lives overall better than if they had ended earlier). If someone will have a better future (or one that contributes more to his life overall) than someone else, saving the first person would prevent the worst death on the Deprivationist view.

However, saving the first person rather than the second when we cannot save both may be morally ruled out by what I have called the *Principle of Irrelevant Goods*. That is, if the difference between the first and second person's future goods is not significant relative to the good each could achieve, it would be wrong to deprive each of an equal chance to survive merely to prevent what Deprivationism implies is the worst death. However, a difference in goods that would be irrelevant interpersonally in choosing between people could be relevant intrapersonally (in choosing whether to give one person only a slightly better or worse future).[10] What if the difference between individuals' futures is significant (e.g., one person will be fully capable and the other a paraplegic) and we cannot save both? I have argued that while each may reasonably *care to have* the better future if this were possible, a person could *reasonably care about* keeping his significantly less good prospects as much as the other person cares about keeping his better prospects. This is some reason to give each an equal chance to be saved rather than simply deciding to prevent what is the worst death according to Deprivationism (i.e., the death that deprives someone of a future that would be better than someone else's without making his life overall worse than someone else's).[11]

2.5. Deprivationism and senseless deaths

In the intrapersonal case, the Deprivationist view (that focuses on comparing futures) is that if one's future life would be worse than or no better than death, that will make death less bad for one than if one's future life would have gone on to be wonderful. So it might seem that another way of diminishing the badness of death itself is to make future life equal to or worse than death. Suppose one could cause the deprivation of the goods of life without death (e.g., by a permanent coma). Then death itself would come too late to cause the deprivation; one would still suffer the bad of deprivation but not as a bad aspect of death. (There could also be bads of life that are unlike the bads of death, e.g., great suffering. Those bads could also deprive someone of the same goods as death, thus robbing death of its sting.) Yet these are not reasonable ways to make death less bad, only ways to make alternatives to it worse or as bad.

But what if life could not turn bad and so would never deteriorate if it did not end? According to Deprivationism, someone's death gets worse for them the better their future would be (or the more it contributes to the goodness of their life overall). If this is so, we could actually have reason to welcome someone's death becoming worse for him and more rather than less senseless (Kamm 2013, 57) for it would be better if more life would always be good life. We should not resist creating lives that would always be good (e.g., by new improvements in quality of life) just to make it the case that some deaths will not be bad on a Deprivationist view.

However, it would not be reasonable to pay much to make life such that it could never deteriorate from within if we could not also eliminate death, since many of the goods thereby possible would never be attained by mortal individuals.

2.6. Deprivationism and priority to the worst off

If it is morally more important to help people who will have had less good in their lives if they die at t_1 rather than those who will have had more good (other things equal), then it may be morally wrong to decide whom to help at t_1 merely by seeing who would lose a better future (or lose a future that would make their overall life better than someone else's) if they are not saved. It may be morally right (or have greater moral value) to give a smaller benefit to the person who would die having had least.[12] This implies that sometimes when we can help one person rather than another to avoid more of what Deprivationism claims makes death bad, we should not do so. This directly connects with the next section's discussion. Additional conceptual and moral concerns about Deprivationism are also raised in what follows.

3. More on Willhavehadism

3.1. Willhavehadism and the worst off

According to Willhavehadism, Deprivationism is wrong to claim that considered *interpersonally* person A's death is worse for him than person B's death is for him just because person A would lose out on a better future than would person B. (This is so even if A's life would also be made better than B's would be made by their respective futures.) Suppose person A has lived a long good life and if he didn't die at t_1 he would go on to live a good life for a long time. Person B has lived a short, not very good life and if he didn't die at t_1 he would go on to live a moderate period of good life. B's death at t_1 could be worse for him than A's death at t_1 would be for him because although A would lose out on more goods than B overall, A will have already had more goods of life than B will have by t_1. This point could be raised as an objection to the view that it was worse for Mozart to die when he did (given all he could still do) than for an ordinary unaccomplished person to die at the same age.

When helping the worst off is morally correct, this can *conflict* with saving a person from what Deprivationism says as a conceptual matter is the worst death but be consistent with saving a person from what Willhavehadism says as a conceptual matter is the worst death. So we could have a moral reason to save B from what Willhavehadism implies is his worse death rather than A from his less bad death when we cannot save both. The moral and conceptual conclusions will here coincide. Note that this could be true even if the person who will have had much less by the time he dies would die *later* than the person who will have had more by the time he dies. Suppose that A in our previous case would die at t_1 if he is not saved now but B in our previous case would die a year later at t_2 if we do not provide him with a treatment now and we cannot help both. According to Willhavehadism, if B will have had a shorter and worse life by the time he dies than A, we should provide B with the treatment now even though he will not die now rather than save A from death now.

Considered intrapersonally, Willhavehadism would determine the badness of someone's death by considering how much good he will have had if he dies at a certain point rather than by considering how much he would lose out on. Death at 20 is worse for someone though he could otherwise live on only 5 more years than death at 50 would be for that same person though he could then otherwise live on for 20 years (holding constant the value of each year of life). Intrapersonally, if there is a reason to focus resources on saving people when they will have had fewer rather than more goods of life, then we would have a reason to save a person from what Willhavehadism implies is a worse death (e.g., saving him when he is younger rather than older holding constant the value of each year of life).

The approach to rationing of medical resources for which I have argued elsewhere (Kamm 2013, Chapter 12) suggests the Willhavehadist way of thinking about the badness of death and what to do about it. I distinguished how bad someone's death will be for him from how much good he could get in the future or overall if he avoided death. This distinction, I believe, is important in general, not just for a theory of rationing, and it is not recognized in Deprivationism, which may be one of its faults. Suppose that two people would die without a scarce medicine but with it, one person would live for 5 more years and the other for 20 (holding value per year constant). We may after all decide that we should give the medicine to produce the best outcome in terms of future goods but that is different from thinking that death would be worse for the person who would lose out on the best outcome. For if the person who would get only 5 years will die at age 20 if he does not get the medicine, his death would arguably be worse for him than death would be for the person who could gain 20 more years with the medicine but would otherwise die at age 50.

I believe there is a sense of how much one "needs" the medicine that depends on it being worse to die if one will have lived only 20 rather than 50 years at death. We could also say that the person who would die younger needs 5 years more than the person who would die older needs 20. Considered intrapersonally, the person at 20 also needs the additional 5 years more than he would need the additional 20 years if he were 50. That is why we can call this view of the badness of death *Needism* (for life) as well as Willhavehadism. The less one has had of goods, the more one needs more.

Might the moral correctness of saving the younger person depend on the fact that the more good years of life one will have had at death, the more there is DMU of additional years? So perhaps the 20 additional years that would go to the person who will have lived 50 is a smaller good than the 5 additional years that would go to a person who will have lived only 20. If this were so, helping the 20-year-old could also accord with a Deprivationist account of the badness of death since preventing the death of the person who will have had much would involve preventing the lesser future loss. However, it is hard to believe there is so much DMU of years of life. Rather, it seems that there is *diminished moral value* (DMV) in giving a bigger benefit to someone who will have had more (even without the additional good) than someone else rather than giving even a smaller benefit to someone else who will otherwise have had less. Likewise, intrapersonally there could be DMV in giving a bigger benefit to someone at a time when he will have had more already (e.g., when he is older) rather than giving him a smaller benefit at a time when he will otherwise have had less (e.g., if he would otherwise have died young).

3.2. Willhavehadism and not diminishing the badness of death

One reason not to give 1 additional year to the person who will otherwise have had only 20 at death (rather than giving 20 years to the 50-year-old) is that we can do very little to remedy the badness of his death, given that dying at 21 is not much better than dying at 20 and we would omit giving a big benefit to someone else. This conclusion is consistent with the view that it is morally wrong to always maximize the situation of the worst off if the gain to them is too little and the cost to others is too great. Sometimes we should not diminish the badness of death by saving the person for whom death would be worst according to Willhavehadism. In such cases, the moral view about what to do and conceptual views about the badness of death will pull apart. (The ratio between what one will already have had and the possible gain may be important in this regard: the more one will have had, the greater the gain may have to be in order to morally outweigh a gain to the worst off.)

Similarly, intrapersonally it may be wrong to focus resources on saving someone from death at 20 when she would live only a few additional months rather than focus on saving her at 50 (if she gets to 50) when she could live another 20 years.

Furthermore, it is false that focusing resources on those who will have had a worse death than others according to Willhavehadism always involves aiming to avoid what is the worst death. Here is why: Suppose someone who would otherwise die at 25 risks dying at 20 by undergoing surgery that may extend his life to 50 if it succeeds. He risks the worst death (at 20) but he does not necessarily act imprudently in not assuring himself 25 years. If the only reason people ever died at 20 was due to such surgery, it would not necessarily be wrong (for such people themselves or we who would help them) to do what will (over time) increase the badness of some people's deaths.

3.3. Willhavehadism, Deprivationism, and persons' rights

Doing what would prevent the worst death according to either Willhavehadism or Deprivationism may be morally wrong because it is contrary to the *rights* of persons. Suppose someone's health insurance scheme explicitly promises that so long as he is under 80, the fact that he will have had a greater number of good years will be irrelevant to a decision whether to save his or another's life. Then he may have a promisee's right that takes precedence over preventing the worst death. If there were a human right (independent of any agreement) to certain forms of assistance in living to a certain number of years, then how much or little of that number of years one has had (or if helped would get to have) could be irrelevant to a decision about whose death to prevent.

3.4. Some problems with Willhavehadism

Willhavehadism (aka Needism) may have faults as an account of the badness of death. First, it seems to imply that the death of an infant is worse for that infant than the death of a 20-year-old is for him. (Deprivationism can also have this implication: assuming equal possible lengths of life, an infant has more future to lose out on than someone older.) Intuitively, to many this implication seems wrong. One way to try to account for its being wrong is that there is much less psychological connectedness between the infant and her possible future years hence than between the 20-year-old and his possible future years hence, and losing a future with which one is less psychologically connected is said by some to be less bad for one than losing a future with which one is more connected.[13] Perhaps a Willhavehadist can use this claim to argue that what the person (who the infant, by assumption, already is) will have had if she goes on living is not much better than what she will have had if she dies as an infant since her "unconnected future" does not satisfy what is in her interest as an infant and so is not of much benefit to her. This proposal seems implausible for suppose we could cure a mentally disabled person even overnight (rather than gradually as an infant changes into an adult). That he will have a type of life that does not satisfy interests he had when mentally disabled does not show that it would not be better for him to be cured. Furthermore, even if this proposal offered an account of why the infant's fate cannot be much improved by living on, it would not explain the intuition that her death is not as bad for her as the death of the 20-year-old is for him in a way that is consistent with Willhavehadism.

Another way Willhavehadism might account for the common intuition about an infant's death emphasizes the sort of entity to which so little good will have accrued in its short life. To understand this approach, it helps to imagine a hypothetical case in which humans are born functioning at an adult level (complete with self-consciousness and language). The death of such newborns does seem worse for them than the death of adults who will have lived 20 years is for the adults.[14] If this is so, how little good actual infants will have had at death may matter less because they are still underdeveloped as persons in certain important respects.

Now consider a second concern. Willhavehadism implies that death itself is not worse for someone merely because it comes before future goods rather than before future bads worse than death. (Strictly, this is consistent with a Willhavehadist accepting that (1) death could be more worth avoiding if life would have future goods than if it would have future bads worse than death and (2) that it is more important to die before life becomes permanently worse than death than before it becomes good.) In the case where death comes before future bads worse than nothing, death is instrumentally good in preventing great bads and it seems problematic to exclude that from our evaluation of the goodness or badness of someone's death. The tension between backward-looking Willhavehadism and forward-looking Deprivationism is especially clear in comparing a 20-year-old who will die before his life gets worse than death with a 50-year-old who will die before many more good years. In one sense death is worse for the 20-year-old than for the 50-year-old but in another sense (forward instrumental) it is better. Suppose one would rather be the person who dies at 50 than the one who dies at 20 even though the 20-year-old's death is forward instrumentally good and the 50-year-old's death is forward instrumentally bad. Does this suggest that the 20-year-old's death is still worse for him than the 50-year-old's death is for him or only that his life (which is what it is because of his death) was worse but his death itself was less bad? Combining the relative badness of the life with the relative instrumental goodness of the death in the 20-year-old case could give an overall value that is still less than living to 50 and dying before 20 years of life. However, one could also just say that the 20-year-old's death is worse for him than the 50-year-old's is for him, even though the 20-year-old's death is still better for him than the alternative he has of living a life worse than death.[15]

Compare a 20-year-old who will die before his life becomes worse than death with a 20-year-old who will die before many more good years of life. In one sense death is equally bad for each (assuming their lives will have had equivalent amounts of good and bad) but in another sense (forward instrumental) death seems better for the first person and worse for the second. Even if what one will have had by the time one dies were more important in judging the badness of death than what one would have had in the future, when what one will have had by the time one dies is held constant, it seems the forward instrumental factor becomes salient in regard to the badness of death. However, it might be better to say that death is equally bad for each but just better for the first 20-year-old than the even worse alternative he alone faces. As noted above, one should not accept a conclusion that implies that one could make someone's death better for him by arranging for his life to go worse if he were to survive.

Perhaps a Willhavehadist could also note about such a case that if one 20-year-old died at 25 after 5 more years of life worse than death, he will have had a worse life than he would have had after only 20 years. Preventing him from having had a worse life overall by the time he dies accounts for the way in which his death is better than the second 20-year-old's. This shows that we are concerned with determining how bad someone's death is by comparing the goodness or badness of what he will have had by the time of death. However, such an approach seems to overlap with a version of Deprivationism. This is because it looks at what the person would come to have but uses it to describe what he will have had by the time of death.

An additional concern is whether Willhavehadism is distinct from the version of Deprivationism that considers the effect of future good or bad on one's overall life and so could also exhibit concern about what one will have had overall by the time one dies. However, unlike Willhavehadism this version of Deprivationism is not specifically concerned with raising the minimum one will have had rather than with maximizing what one will have had or avoiding the biggest negative impact on what one will have had. So according to this version of Deprivationism the death of a 30-year-old who could have lived to 40 may be worse than the death of a 20-year-old who could have lived to 25 because the first death has a greater impact on what someone will have had at death. One might say it is the Needism (help the worst off) aspect of Willhavehadism that distinguishes it from the overall-life version of Deprivationism.

Morally (rather than merely conceptually) speaking, helping the person who will have had least could imply that when we cannot do both, we should (1) end the first 20-year-old's life before he will have an additional 5 years worse than death rather than (2) give 10 more good years to the second 20-year-old. Doing this results in both people having had 20 good years whereas helping the second person would result in his having had a much better outcome than 20 years while the other person will have had a much worse outcome than 20 years.

What if one 20-year-old could live another 5 years in a coma state and this involves his not having had a worse life than if he died at 20? Willhavehadism implies that what this person will have had if he died at 20 is no worse than what he would have had if he died at 25 and so the deaths are equally bad for him. By contrast, another 20-year-old who could have had more good years will have had less if he dies earlier rather than later and so his earlier death is worse for him than his later death. In a forced choice, we should try to prevent the second death rather than the coma since only this will reduce how bad someone's life will have been.

4. More on Alloverism

4.1. The Limbo Man

I have described a version of Deprivationism that is a future-looking consequentialist evaluation of the badness of death, and Willhavehadism which is a backward-looking consequentialist evaluation of the badness of death. But is there a less consequentialist approach to the badness of death that focuses less on what it causes and more on what it intrinsically involves? Imagine that we all had a choice between acquiring the same goods (including the order in which they would come) by one of two different methods: (1) either by beginning at t_1 and living life continuously (including sleep) and ending at t_2 (as is true currently); or (2) by beginning at t_1 but living on much further to t_3 by interrupting our continuous life with long periods in a limbo state (a coma-like state involving suspended animation) followed by return for significant remaining goods of life.[16] Someone who preferred the latter Limbo Man existence (Kamm 2013, 19, 49–53) would not choose to avoid an earlier death because a later one would provide more goods of life (or mean he will have had more goods by the time of death) since it would not do this. Rather, he might choose it to avoid the goods of life and their possibility—in particular goods that come from conscious experience and action—being all over for as long as possible from the point of his life's beginning. He might also choose to put off further the bad factor of Extinction of himself as a conscious and self-conscious being that is involved in death. A concern to avoid Extinction might be distinguished from the concern to avoid goods being all over since it is specifically a concern that oneself as a conscious person not be all over. (However, being a conscious person might be considered a particular good in itself independent of objects of consciousness.)

It might be said that since being in limbo still involves being a person (i.e., someone having the physical capacity, even if unexercised, to be conscious and self-conscious) and it's good for someone to be a person, even if not conscious, the Limbo Man would get *more* goods of life. He would also avoid Extinction of himself for longer than if he lived continuously to t_2. However, I do not think that being a person in limbo is in itself a good for that person and being in such a state permanently would be no better than death with respect to having more goods or avoiding Extinction of himself as a conscious person.

Yet it seems to me that there is some reason to go into temporary limbo if one is concerned about death. If so, this suggests that death is bad for some reason other than that it interferes with more goods of life (or means one will have had fewer of those) and supports the view that I earlier called Alloverism. On the other hand, even though one never experiences long gaps between events in one's life as a Limbo Man, it might be a countervailing, nonexperienced negative aspect of such a life that, for example, completion of some of one's projects or even thoughts begun before limbo will actually not come until millions of years later. Another objection is that putting off goods in one's life by going into limbo is not consistent with really appreciating goods (as would be shown by finding them irresistible). Then one would have to choose or find a good balance between the advantage of going into limbo as a way to diminish to some degree the bad aspect of death identified by Alloverism, and its disadvantage with respect to some other things. Further, suppose the Limbo Man might not unreasonably give up some quantity of the goods of life in order to further extend the overall period of his life. This is consistent with his not reducing the goods by too much for this purpose.[17] Having goods matters greatly and the fact that extending his life from its beginning to its end will not eliminate death altogether may also make it unreasonable to give up too many goods for the sake of merely putting off his end.

On the other hand, even though going into limbo does not eliminate but only puts off a bad aspect of death—being all over as a conscious person—there can be reason to go into limbo. There can be reasons to put off bads that will come at some time anyway and putting off death does increase the amount of time during which there is the potential of one's existence as a conscious person which seems to be a (nonexperienced) good. Further, suppose merely putting off a bad were not a reasonable way to mitigate a bad. Trying to do so would still show that one thought that one was dealing with some bad, and that bad would not be deprivation of more goods of life. This is because going into limbo would clearly not increase the goods of life but only put off their being all over.[18]

4.2. How not to show that being all over per se matters

It might be thought that the following example also supports the view that death is bad not only because of the goods of which it deprives one: Small Pains Man would rather stay alive as a conscious and self-conscious being even though all that will occur in his life are small pains. Death may not seem to deprive him of goods of life but he prefers to suffer small ills rather than not exist as a conscious and self-conscious being. His preference does not seem unreasonable.

The Limbo Man and Small Pains Man hypotheticals suggest that no longer being a conscious and self-conscious being is at least one negative factor about death for the person, no matter what the further content of his life would be. That factor may be overridden by bad enough content so that overall death is welcome, but it has a residual negative factor to be regretted nevertheless. However, for purposes of showing that the end of oneself as a conscious and self-conscious being is a negative aspect of death there is a crucial difference between the Limbo Man Case and the Small Pains Man Case. This is because Small Pains Man might be accounted for by Deprivationism and Willhavehadism if simply being conscious and self-conscious is a good.[19] After all, Small Pains Man would both get more and will have had more of such conscious and self-conscious time alive if he dies later rather than sooner. By contrast, Deprivationism or Willhavehadism cannot account for there being a reason to deal with death by becoming a Limbo Man as this is accounted for by Alloverism. This is because the Limbo Man does not increase the quantity of consciousness and self-consciousness in his life by going into limbo.

This is also why cases in which we think both that death is overall good for someone who will otherwise suffer greatly, and that there is yet something to be regretted for his sake in his death, cannot be used to show that Deprivationism is flawed. For a Deprivationist could say mere consciousness and self-consciousness are goods and that the negative factor we regret in these cases is that the person will not get more of these goods and not that he will merely be all over as a conscious and self-conscious being. It is the latter that the Limbo Man Case is supposed to show.

4.3. Goods relative to time of existence

Consider choosing between starting someone's life earlier in the history of the universe or later in the history of the universe, holding content, shape, and length of the life constant. On behalf of the person created, I think one could reasonably prefer the later creation because it means his life and the goods it would contain will be over later and the possibility of his being a person and having goods of life (consistent with his having them at some point) will be present longer.[20] (Unlike the Limbo Man Case, this hypothetical does not involve the person's life ending later by being extended forward from the point of his beginning to his end. It involves his beginning later.) If this is so, where one exists in time could have significance because it helps deal with the negative factor focused on by Alloverism (since being all over is put off and the possibility of one's self-conscious life which will eventually exist is present longer). However, it seems that one should not deal with the "all over" bad aspect of death by moving the creation of persons forward in time if this diminishes the goods in their lives.

5. More on Insultism

5.1. Prenatal deprivation of goods

A worry about Deprivationism that was raised by Robert Nozick[21] builds on (what is said to be) Lucretius' objection to concern about death: We do not exist prior to our commencing to exist (called prenatal nonexistence or previtalism) just as we will not exist after death. Why, therefore, are we concerned about the goods of which death deprives us and not about those of which prenatal nonexistence deprives us? This is known as the Asymmetry Problem. Thomas Nagel's answer was that any person who began much earlier than we did could not be us whereas it could be consistent with constant personal identity that we live longer. But Robert Nozick imagined that a particular egg and sperm determine someone's identity, and he considered a hypothetical case in which that combination as a spore could have been triggered into developing into a person long before it actually was. Given that personal identity would then be preserved, someone would have lost out on many goods in her life by not starting to exist earlier given that she will die at the same time as in her actual life. Should such prenatal deprivation reasonably evoke the same response as deprivation due to death because they are equally bad? If not, how can Deprivationism account for the badness of death?

5.2. Intuitive responses to different deprivations

Suppose our intuitive responses to these two deprivations are different. I suggested one explanation and justification of this that is consistent with Deprivationism (Kamm 1993, 37): Someone's beginning earlier, through a possible extension back in time, would have altered the actual life that he has lived with its actual commitments and relationships. A longer possible future added to his actual life need not do this. That is a reason for his now not preferring that his life had been longer by backward extension while preferring that it be longer by dying later. However, I also counterargued to this proposal (37): One's actual life, including its commitments, relationships, and memories of the past, could be exactly the same even if many more good years of one's life had preceded one's actual life. This is so if we assume that the earlier years would have been, in some respects, like the earliest years of our actual childhood: namely, good for us to have had though forgotten and even (unlike childhood) having no lasting impact on later life.[22] (Alternatively, we can imagine that this past that we have forgotten actually occurred and made us what we are now.) If this response to the proposed explanation of the asymmetry is correct, we will still need to explain and perhaps justify the asymmetrical responses to the deprivations caused by prenatal nonexistence and death.

5.3. Parfit and Future Deprivationism

Derek Parfit offered another possible answer to the Asymmetry Problem and the challenge it poses to Deprivationism by connecting it with similar asymmetrical attitudes toward past and future bads from the perspective *within* a life. For example, one prefers (not unreasonably, it seems to many) that it is the day after a very painful surgery (with no future aftereffects) rather than the day before a slightly painful surgery.[23] Caring less about the real deprivations due to prenatal nonexistence (as Nozick imagined it) than those to come through death might be part of a general differential and possibly reasonable attitude to past and future ills (and goods), caring less about the former than about the latter. If this were an explanation and justification of the asymmetrical attitude to death and prenatal nonexistence, Deprivationism should be renamed *Future Deprivationism*. The Parfitian approach is consistent with there being a perspective from *outside* a life from which a life with more pain in it (including pain in the past) is worse than one with less pain. The same would be true for a life with fewer good years in it even if this were due to prenatal nonexistence.

5.4. Different past bads and insults

I raised the following concerns (in *Morality, Mortality*, vol. 1) about the Parfitian approach as applied to the Asymmetry Problem: (i) As Parfit himself recognized, unlike pains, other past bads and goods do not always count for less than future bads and goods from the perspective within life. Would one now reasonably prefer that it be true that (a) one has had a long life filled with good achievements and relationships but one will die shortly or that (b) one has just recently come into existence as an adult and will live for one good year but with no significant achievements or relationships? Presumably, it would be a mistake to prefer (b). It would also make sense now to prefer (c), that one's life will have some physical suffering in the future, if this is a necessary concomitant of its being true that one had good achievements and relationships in the past. This is so even if it doesn't make sense now to prefer future suffering if this suffering is a necessary concomitant of its being true that one did not have greater physical suffering in the past. This may be because having had even great physical suffering does not reflect negatively on oneself and one's life as does the absence of good achievements or relationships.[24]

This suggests that not having come into existence earlier than one did could be worse than death if it deprived one's life of having significant achievements in it that will not be present if one puts off death. However, we can recreate the Asymmetry even with achievements by holding constant the quantity and types of achievements possible if one does not die and if one started life earlier. A preference for the achievements being in the future would exhibit the asymmetrical attitude to past and future.

(ii) If there are factors seen from the perspective outside the life that make death worse than prenatal nonexistence, then it will not be merely that prenatal nonexistence has the same bad factor that death has (deprivation of additional goods) but we just care less about it from the perspective within one's life (the Parfitian approach). These additional bad factors about death that Deprivationism (or Future Deprivationism) fails to capture could be, in part, what I called the Insult Factors[25]: (a) destruction of the person occurs in death, not in the failure to exist earlier; (b) death happens to a person, not existing earlier does not happen to a person[26] though it affects him once he exists (by his being someone who did not exist before a certain point); (c) death but not prenatal nonexistence takes away what we have had already (one's life thought of as an entity), though prenatal nonexistence makes it true that one has not always had what one comes to have; (d) the characteristics of death in (a)–(c) signify the vulnerability of a person that is not signified by prenatal nonexistence—not coming into existence sooner is not due to vulnerability of an entity since it is then nonexistent; (e) death can be seen as a decline from a good life to zero whereas prenatal nonexistence can be seen as an incline if it is followed by any life with positive value relative to nonexistence; inclines are narratively preferable to declines holding content constant, perhaps because they exhibit rational change (moving toward what is better). The badness of death due to the Insult Factors is the focus of the view about the badness of death that I called *Insultism*.

I also argued that the Extinction Factor in death (discussed in connection with the Limbo Man Case) ends the possibility of more of oneself as a conscious person, whereas prenatal nonexistence still leaves open the possibility of such a life.[27] Prenatal nonexistence can make impossible one's earlier life but it is only in conjunction with death that all possibility of more of one's life is gone. Giving greater weight to the temporally definitive element implies that one takes seriously that the "passage of time" creates an earlier and later boundary to life rather than merely two differently-located boundaries.

5.5. Death(2) and pre(2)

One can construct a hypothetical case that eliminates some of the Insult Factors in order to see which ones are most important: Suppose one had always existed as a person and one will always exist as a person. However, except for some period in one's existence, one would be in an unconscious limbo state while retaining the neural capacities for self-consciousness and consciousness (or for whatever else was needed to make one a person). Then the end of the conscious person would not involve the destruction of the person, just the end of his life of consciousness and self-consciousness. Call this death(2). Furthermore, there would be no prenatal nonexistence, only preconsciousness; call this pre(2). Pre(2), like death(2), would involve the absence of more goods of experience and action happening to a person who exists both before and after his conscious life and it, like death and death(2), would involve vulnerability to consciousness-impeding forces. However, in death(2) but not in pre(2) there would be loss of a conscious life (conceived of as something one already had), decline (if conscious life has been good) to nothing, and no more possibility of conscious personhood.

Death(2) seems to be no better than death. Hence, we should not focus on avoiding the destruction of the person unless this means consciousness and self-consciousness will continue. Also, as judged from a perspective outside the life, death(2) seems worse than pre(2), though pre(2) shares some of the Insult Factors present in death (e.g., bad things happening to a person and the person's vulnerability). Hence, it may be that only some of the Insult Factors (e.g., decline and loss of conscious and self-conscious life once had) and Extinction (of oneself as a conscious person) which is part of Alloverism help to explain the badness of death and should be dealt with if possible to reduce the badness of death.

The Extinction Factor and the decline to nothing could be avoided by immortality as a conscious and self-conscious being. However, immortality or even a very long life might be incompatible with the life being good and so have its own negatives (in which case goods of life besides being a conscious person would be all over anyway).[28] Avoiding these negatives could outweigh avoiding some of the negatives of death emphasized by Alloverism and Insultism. It is important to remember that if worse things than death can happen to people, then avoiding some bads of death could give one a worse fate.[29] Extending life to the point where it is still good enough and creating invulnerability to death (except by a person's own choice) during that period seems a good compromise.[30] (A Willhavehadist might argue for the importance of creating such invulnerability to death in those who would die having had least. A Deprivationist might argue for the importance of creating such invulnerability to death in those who would lose the greatest future goods.)

It might be suggested that one could diminish the badness of decline and loss of a life one has had by making one's life very bad. That way the decline to death is minimal (or death is an improvement) and the loss of life is arguably at least overall good. But this is a bad solution to some concerns of Insultism. It is manifested in the view that it is better if death at t_2 ends a decline within life from t_1 to t_2 than if death at t_2 ends a life that is still on an incline from t_1 to t_2. We should not refrain from making the time before death (and a possible future) as good as possible just to reduce the badness of death per se (if it did this).

The problems in someone's mortality to which Alloverism and Insultism point could also be avoided by not creating that person. (Strictly speaking, it is also true that no one would be deprived of more goods of life or will die having had too few goods if they are not created. However, if one's only concern with death were that there will be no *more* goods for someone or that there will have been *too few* goods for someone, it seems odd not to provide any such goods by not creating.) It is because of the bad factors that Alloverism and Insultism identify that one might, I think, decide not to create even someone who would have only a great many goods worthy of him in his life.[31] Nevertheless, not creating would be a bad solution because the goods of life can compensate for these bads of death. Table 1.1 summarizes some of the points we have considered.

6. No More Persons Forever

Now consider whether and how the four factors I have discussed in connection with the death of a person might bear on the end of humanity (or any other types of persons) as a whole.

(1) Suppose the continued existence of persons would involve more overall future categorical goods. Then the Deprivationist view could imply that the end of persons would at least be an impersonally bad thing to happen. (This is on the assumption that future goods did not make the history of persons overall worse.) This is so even if the end of humanity did not involve any individual living a shorter life than she otherwise would have.[32] Suppose being created to a good life is also good for the people created even if it isn't better for them to be created than not (because they would not be in a worse state if they were never created). Then in an extended sense, the end of all persons would also eliminate goods *for* persons and so be more than merely impersonally bad.

Table 1.1 A summary of some of the points we have considered.

Factors Making Death Bad	Good and Bad Solutions or Ameliorations
A. *Deprives* of more goods of life (or deprives of better overall life)	a. Extend life (forward or backward) with good content (or content to make life overall better) (Bad solutions or ameliorations—arrange for life to have no future goods that can be lost; always select whom to save according to who will have a better future; ignore rights)
B. Puts limit on what one *will have had* of goods of life	b. Extend life with good content for those who will have had least otherwise (Bad solutions or ameliorations—give absolute priority to worse off regardless of ability to benefit; take no risks of worse death; ignore rights)
C. Goods of life being all over and being all over as a conscious person once begun; no more possibility of goods or existence as a person	c. (i) Extend life forward even via Limbo (Bad solutions or ameliorations—exchanging too many goods to get more extension of one's life and its possibility; extend life worse than death) (ii) Not create (Bad solution if goods in life would justify bads) (iii) Later creation (Bad amelioration if less good life)
D. *Insults* of vulnerability to loss of life one had and decline to nothing	d. (i) Extend life with good content (even via Limbo) (ii) Invulnerable periods of life (Bad solutions or ameliorations—extend life that is worse than nothing; make life so bad that death is incline; don't create even if goods in life would compensate for bads)

However, Deprivationism might also have to take into account the potential distribution of goods and bads that the end of all persons would prevent. Suppose that for the next million years all mortal persons would have lives of intense pain and suffering but for many billions of years after that completely different persons would have lives containing only enormously worthwhile categorical goods. Suppose the quality and quantity of the goods would outweigh the bads, but the only way to prevent the long period of suffering is to allow the existence of persons to end forever. Not allowing the end of persons forever for the sake of the eventual good to come seems to involve using the persons who will have to suffer as mere instruments both so that others will eventually live good lives and so that persons will not cease (or not as soon cease) to exist. Such a use of persons seems impermissible and for this reason it would be morally preferable for the end of persons to come about. (Suppose at least the early prehistory of human beings was qualitatively like the imagined bad million-year future. This raises the moral question about whether, had anyone had control over it, the better human history that came about should have been allowed to come about at the cost of that bad prehistory.)

(2) If the existence of persons were to come to an end, Willhavehadism suggests that it would worse for this to occur after a shorter rather than a longer history if that history were good. However, it would be better for the end to occur after a shorter rather than a longer history if that history were worse than nothing.

(3) Assume the existence of persons is good. Then Alloverism suggests that there being a time when persons will be all over is bad independently of its reducing the amount of good that their existence would involve over time. For example, suppose we could extend into the future the point at which humanity (and all other persons) would end if the existence of humanity (or any other persons) was not continuous but there were temporal gaps among periods where persons exist. The amount of good and bad in the universe due to the existence of persons is assumed to be constant in the discontinuous and continuous histories but all persons would be all over sooner in the continuous than in the discontinuous history. The concern that persons not be all over would be exhibited in favoring the extended "gappy" option.[33]

(4) Insultism suggests that the longer and better the existence of people has been the greater is the insult of their vulnerability and decline to nonexistence. From the point of view of Willhavehadism it is better that there have been greater value before the end but this is consistent with the insult of the end then also being greater.[34]

Notes

1. An earlier version of parts of this chapter appears in eds. S. Garland and C. T. Solberg, *Saving People from the Harm of Death* (Oxford University Press, 2019). I thank the editors of that volume for their comments.

2. In earlier work (primarily *Morality, Mortality*, vol. 1 [Oxford University Press, 1993]) I considered death and why it is bad and worse than prenatal nonexistence (assuming one doesn't exist prenatally). In this chapter, I briefly summarize (and in some ways) expand on some of what I said there. This leaves much to be made more precise.

3. An early form of this view is presented in Thomas Nagel's "Death," in *Mortal Questions* (Cambridge University Press, 1979), 1–10.

4. That death involves nonexistence is assumed only for argument's sake since the intellectual origins of Deprivationism lie in the attempt to show (despite significant deniers) that death can be bad for one even if it does not involve any bad afterlife or continued experience of any sort. Deprivationism does not really require this assumption, for suppose that death involved a pleasant afterlife. Deprivationism could still compare this afterlife with what continued life would have involved and then decide whether death was bad by comparison with continued life if the latter would have been better. What the goods of life are and whether they include merely being a conscious and self-conscious person is here left open. I discuss this further later in this chapter and in Chapter 2.

5. Galen Strawson (in his "I Have No Future," *The Subject of Experience*, Oxford University Press, 2017) and Douglas MacLean in his "Longevity" (unpublished) make these points.

6. Insofar as there is a distinction between what is good for a person and what is good for his life, it is possible that it will not be better for one if one's life gets better. We discuss this distinction between "me" and "my life" (raised by Shelly Kagan in his "Me and My Life," *Proceedings of the Aristotelian Society* 94 [1994], 309–24) in more detail in later chapters.

7. See Bernard Williams, "The Makropulos Case: Reflections on the Tedium of Immortality," Chapter 6 in his *Problems of the Self: Philosophical Papers 1956-1972* (Cambridge University Press, 1973), 82–100.

8. Williams himself argues that those who think death is never bad for us (e.g., Epicureans) must be denying that we even have categorical desires. (See his "The

Makropulos Case: Reflections on the Tedium of Immortality," 87-88.) We could also say that they are denying that any categorical desires we have are reasonable or that there are any categorical goods. For if Epicureans held that the absence of goods is bad only when it leads to bad experiences for us and death is nothing to us because we have no experiences at all when dead, then it is not bad to die regardless of the goods of which we are deprived. No goods would give us a reason to go on living on this view because their absence would not be experienced by us when we are dead.

9. I consider the case of concentrated suffering further in Chapter 2. Larry Temkin emphasizes the distinction between concentration and dispersal of goods and bads in his *Rethinking the Good* (Oxford University Press, 2015).

10. See my *Morality, Mortality*, vol. 1, for more on the Principle of Irrelevant Goods (there called the Principle of Irrelevant Utility).

11. For more on this argument see my "Aggregation, Allocating Scarce Resources, and Discrimination Against the Disabled," reprinted in my *Bioethical Prescriptions* (Oxford University Press, 2013). I also discuss cases where our causing a difference in prospects between people (by contrast to our taking advantage of a difference we did not cause) might make it permissible for us to prevent what is (according to Deprivationism) the worst death.

12. Saying that there is greater moral value in helping a person who will have least should not be interpreted to imply that we should maximize moral value in the world, for example, by creating less well off people whom we help rather than very well off people who do not need our help. Analogously, there may be more moral value in saving a life at great cost to oneself than at small cost to oneself but that is consistent with it being better if there is less moral value in the world because all rescues are easy rather than hard.

13. Jeff McMahan argues in this way in *The Ethics of Killing: Problems at the Margins of Life* (Oxford University Press, 2003). Connectedness is more than causal continuity as it involves overlapping psychological content.

14. I first discussed such remarkable newborns in "Ronald Dworkin's Views on Abortion," reprinted in my *Bioethical Prescriptions*. Note also that these remarkable newborns may not be as psychologically connected to their futures as the 20-year-old would be to his. That this does not reduce the badness of these newborns' deaths is a reason to think that psychological connectedness is not as important to the badness of the loss of one's future life as some think. In general, it seems that the current nature of a being does much more to determine whether it has a claim to some future independent of the character of the future that is in question. This is the correct response, I think, to those like Don Marquis (in his "Why Abortion is Immoral," *Journal of Philosophy*, 86:4 [1989], 183–202) who in discussing abortion focus on what would be lost and not on to whom or to what this loss would occur.

15. Michael Rabenburg favors this approach. He notes that being tortured for an hour can be equally bad for each of two people even if in the case of one person being tortured for that hour prevents the worse fate of being tortured later for

more hours. See his "Against Deprivationism" in his Ph.D. dissertation, *Matters of Life and Death*, Harvard University, 2018 (unpublished).

16. Returning for insignificant time and goods would not maintain the continuing possibility during limbo of a worthwhile life after limbo.

17. Finding the right balance attempts to deal with what are called the "scheduling" and "meagerness" problems in P. Greene and M. Sullivan's "Against Time Bias," *Ethics* 125:4 (2015), 947-970.

18. For more on these points see *Morality, Mortality*, vol. 1 (52, 59).

19. In his "Death," Nagel included consciousness itself as a personal good (2). Michael Rabenberg has suggested (in correspondence) the following as evidence that being a conscious person is a good in itself:

> "Suppose you can have one of the following two options: (a) a life with a 1,000-year limbo in the middle; (b) a life with a 1,000-year stretch of small pains in the middle. . . . it would be reasonable to pick (b) over (a). But neither (a) nor (b) does better than the other [in dealing with] the Extinction Factor. . . . This suggests that there's something good in the 1,000-year stretch in (b) that's absent from the 1,000-year stretch in (a), and a plausible candidate for that "something good" is the property of being a conscious person. . . . [Also,] compare option (a) with (c) a life with a 500-year stretch of small pains in the middle. (c) does *worse* than (a) [in dealing with the] Extinction Factor. . . . [If it still seems] reasonable to pick (c) over (a), this suggests that mere consciousness is [very] valuable."

20. See *Morality, Mortality*, vol. 1 (44–45).

21. Cited in Nagel's "Death," 8.

22. This proposal and response in *Morality, Mortality*, vol. 1, seem to anticipate and also respond to one of Elizabeth Harman's claims in her "Fischer and Lamenting Nonexistence," *Social Theory and Practice* 37 (2011), 129–42.

23. See Parfit's *Reasons and Persons* (Oxford University Press, 1986).

24. See *Morality, Mortality*, vol. 1 (31–32).

25. See *Morality, Mortality*, vol. 1 (Chapter 3).

26. This is so even in Nozick's hypothetical spore case since the sperm and egg are meant to determine which person will exist but are not themselves a person.

27. In this connection in *Morality, Mortality*, vol. 1, I quote Philip Larkin (from his poem "The Old Fools," in his *High Windows*, Gardners Books, 1978): "At death, you break up. . . / It's only oblivion, true: / We had it before, but then it was going to end, / And was all the time merging with a unique endeavor / To bring to bloom the million-petaled flower / Of being here. Next time you can't pretend / There'll be anything else."

28. Bernard Williams argued this in "The Makropulos Case and the Tedium of Immortality." I remain skeptical of his conclusion.

29. I discuss when it does and does not make sense to seek death including to avoid worse fates in "The Purpose of My Death: Death, Dying and Meaning" (*Ethics* [April 2017]), and in Chapters 2, 3, and 6.

30. See Kagan's *Death* (Yale University Press, 2012) for more on death-free zones.

31. A potential parent's grief at awareness that his precious child will someday die could inhibit procreation. That the child will die only after the parent's life is over does not diminish the significance of the child's eventual death to the parent.

32. Samuel Scheffler cites P. D. James' novel *The Children of Men* (Knopf, 1992) to describe how this might occur because mortal persons were no longer able to reproduce. See his *Death and the Afterlife*, Oxford University Press, 2013.

33. The view that it makes no sense to put off the end if it does not affect the goods and bads in the lives of persons is particularly hard to accept in the case of the end of all persons. (An asymmetry may exist with backward-extending gaps.)

34. Suppose the value due to persons' existence diminished gradually before they were all over. Then even if there will have been much of value before their ending, the insult of their ending might be diminished because they were no longer of great value when they succumbed. However, if this meant there was overall less value in their having existed, it would not be preferable to a more insulting end.

References

Harman, Elizabeth. 2011. "Fischer and Lamenting Nonexistence." *Social Theory and Practice* 37, 129–42.

James, P.D. 1992. *The Children of Men*. New York: Knopf.

Kagan, Shelly. 1994. "Me and My Life." *Proceedings of the Aristotelian Society* 94, 309–24.

Kagan, Shelly. 2012. *Death*. New Haven: Yale University Press.

Kamm, F. M. 1993. *Morality, Mortality*, vol. 1. New York: Oxford University Press.

Kamm, F. M. 2013. "Ronald Dworkin's Views on Abortion." In her *Bioethical Prescriptions*, 172–74. New York: Oxford University Press.

Kamm, F. M. 2013. "Aggregation, Allocating Scarce Resources, and Discrimination Against the Disabled." Reprinted in her *Bioethical Prescriptions*. New York: Oxford University Press.

Kamm, F.M. 2017. "The Purpose of My Death: Death, Dying, and Meaning." *Ethics* 127:3, 733–761.

Larkin, Philip. 1978. "The Old Fools," in his *High Windows*. Gardners Books.

Marquis, Don. 1989. "Why Abortion is Immoral," *Journal of Philosophy*, 86:4, 183–202.

McMahan, Jeff. 2002. *The Ethics of Killing: Problems at the Margins of Life*. New York: Oxford University Press.

Nagel, Thomas. 1979. "Death." In his *Mortal Questions*, 1–10. Cambridge: Cambridge University Press.

Parfit, Derek. 1984. *Reasons and Persons*. Oxford: Oxford University Press.

Rabenburg, Michael. 2018. *Matters of Life and Death*. Ph.D. thesis (unpublished).

Scheffler, Samuel. 2013. *Death and the Afterlife*. New York: Oxford University Press.

Strawson, Galen. 2017. "I Have No Future." In *The Subject of Experience*. Oxford: Oxford University Press.

Temkin, Larry. 2015. *Rethinking the Good: Moral Ideals and the Nature of Practical Reasoning*. New York: Oxford University Press.

Williams, Bernard. 1973. "The Makropulos Case and the Tedium of Immortality." In his *Problems of the Self*, 82–100. Cambridge: Cambridge University Press.

Chapter 2

The Purpose of My Death

Kagan on the Worth of Living On

My purpose in this and the next chapter is to consider some more views about death and also dying. I focus on those presented in two recent books: *Death*, by philosopher Shelly Kagan; and *Being Mortal*, by medical doctor Atul Gawande. I focus on their different views about when it does and does not make sense to die given the quality of one's life. In addition to what we can learn from examining the arguments in each book separately, I hope it will be enlightening to see how prominent figures in two different professional areas deal with the same problem.[1]

In this chapter to situate my discussion, I first briefly review some views about death discussed in greater detail in Chapter 1. I then argue that there is a tension between two views of Kagan's about when it could make sense not to go on in life and also between two of his views that bear on how to decide when it makes sense not to go on in life. I then argue for some other ways of deciding.

I. On Death: Deprivationism and Other Views

The standard contemporary view about why death is bad is called Deprivationism.[2] On this view death, assumed to involve irreversible nonexistence after life, is bad only because of the goods of which it deprives one, and the more deprivation, the worse the death. Hence, we might determine how bad death is intrapersonally by comparing what our life would look like if we die at a certain point with what our life would look like if we do not die then. Or we could compare our not existing after a certain point in time (death) with what our life would look like from that point in time onward (without death at that

Almost Over. F. M. Kamm, Oxford University Press (2020) © Oxford University Press.
DOI: 10.1093/oso/9780190097158.001.0001

point).[3] According to the latter view, if only things worse than nothing (involved in nonexistence) are to come, then death that prevents them from coming would not be bad comparatively, and death earlier would be better than death later. Furthermore, on this view one can say that sometimes one could be better off dead but only in a sense that is still compatible with one not being in a better state since death is assumed to involve our nonexistence. Deprivationism so understood seems to take a forward-looking, consequentialist, and comparativist view of the goodness or badness of death.

One might have the following concerns about Deprivationism so understood as an adequate theory of the badness of death. First, one might think that not getting more goods in life is only a case of "deprivation," strictly speaking, if one has some claim or right to more.[4] But even if this were the strict meaning of "deprivation," it could also be bad for one to have an event interfere with one's getting a gift (to which one has no right or claim) that would be very good for one to get. And it is the interference with getting goods with which Deprivationism is concerned.

Second, one might think that how good or bad one's life will have been (or how much good or bad one will have had) by the time one dies is a better indication of how bad one's death is for one than how much future good one will lose. For example, I think it is worse to for one to die at 20 than at 50 even if the 20-year-old is realistically deprived of only 5 additional good years of life and the 50-year-old is realistically deprived of 20 additional good years of life.[5] I call this view about the badness of death Willhavehadism.

Third, one might think that, holding constant the beginning point of our life and the assumed good contents of it, from the point of view of concern with death it would be better for us all to put off the time at which we and our conscious life will be all over. One way of doing this is by going into a limbo state for a long time and then returning to a significant period of consciousness. (I call this the Limbo Man Case.) If this is so, I think it indicates that one's being all over as a conscious person (what I call the Extinction Factor) is a bad aspect of death independent of its depriving us of additional goods since going into limbo does not increase goods but only puts off our and their being all over.[6] Indeed, I think it is this bad aspect of death, which I call Alloverism, that we find most terrifying.

Fourth, our not beginning to exist earlier than we actually did could arguably also deprive us of more good life so the worry arises that Deprivationism cannot account for asymmetrical attitudes to death (concern) and prenatal nonexistence (lack of concern). Perhaps, from the perspective within life we are merely less concerned with past bads than with future ones. However, some differential factors evident even from a third-person perspective outside a life might help explain and justify the asymmetry: Because death (but not nonexistence prior to our beginning) happens to us and takes from us a life conceived as a thing that we have already had, it exhibits what I have called Insult Factors (such as decline from a higher point and vulnerability to loss). These are not present if we are deprived of goods because we could have started life earlier. I call this view about the badness of death Insultism.[7]

One might construct a hypothetical case that eliminates some of these additional asymmetrical factors to see which ones are most important in accounting for the badness of death. Suppose one had always existed as a person and one will always exist as a person. However, except for some period of time in one's existence, one would be in a coma-like, unconscious, inactive (limbo) state though still a person because one had the physical (but unused) capacities for consciousness and self-consciousness (or for whatever else was needed to make one a person). Then the end of the conscious person would not involve the destruction of the person, just the end of his life of consciousness, self-consciousness, and activity. Call this death(2). Furthermore, there would be no prenatal nonexistence, only preconsciousness. Call this pre(2). Pre(2) like death(2) would involve absence of more goods of activity and consciousness (the Deprivationist Factor) but it would be happening to a person who exists both before and after his conscious life. Thus pre(2) like death(2) would involve vulnerability to consciousness-impeding forces. However, in death(2) unlike in pre(2) there would be loss of a conscious life (conceived of as a thing one already had), decline (if conscious life was good enough) to nothing of value, and no more possibility of conscious life as a person. Hence some asymmetry between pre(2) and death(2) exists. If death(2) is no better than death and also, as judged from a perspective outside the life, worse than pre(2), it may be that some of what I call the Insult and the Extinction

Factors, and, therefore, Insultism and Alloverism, play a distinctive role in making death bad for us.

II. *Dying and Reduced States*

Having briefly reconsidered death, we now focus on states that may precede it. Theoretically someone might be dying (i.e., in the process that leads to a not-distant death) without this in any way negatively affecting the quality of his capacities and life. I will call this a nonreduced or nondiminished state. On the other hand, the quality of someone's capacities and life may be reduced or diminished both when he is dying and when he is not dying. In this section, I mean to discuss living in a reduced state when it will but also when it will not, without further action, shortly lead to death and how such a reduced state bears on the sense it makes to end one's life. (Ending one's life need not involve suicide but merely refusing life-prolonging means.) In this chapter, I will consider the views on this matter of Shelly Kagan (in his *Death*) and in the next chapter those of Atul Gawande (in his *Being Mortal*). Kagan emphasizes (ix, 5)[8] that his book is an introductory survey of many topics related to death, and though it is excellent as such he recognizes that further refinements may be called for. Gawande does not aim for the rigor prized in philosophical discussion but provides detailed case discussions and some sensible advice. I find that both books present views that are contrasting and sufficiently important, even for public policy, that it is worth considering them in some detail.[9]

Kagan

1.—To consider Kagan's views on reduced states and ending life, it will be important to first consider some of his other views.

(a) Kagan argues that even if there were no change in personal identity and only gradual, continuous change in him over the course of an endless existence, he would have no interest now in living such an endless life because eventually that life would not have in it the memories, interests, and values he has now. He says (164): "The really crucial question is not 'Do I survive?' but 'Do I have what I wanted when I wanted to survive?' . . . I want to survive with the same personality." He goes on to describe what he calls his Methuselah case, in which Kagan lives not endlessly but for merely hundreds of years but gradually changes as a person. He says (167), "when I think about the Methuselah case I say, 'So what? Who cares? He doesn't remember growing up in Chicago. He doesn't remember my family. He has completely different interests and tastes and values.' I find myself wanting to say, 'It's me, but so what? This doesn't give me what I want. It doesn't give me what matters.'" In these cases even psychological *continuity* is preserved throughout by causal continuity, but eventually the person is no longer psychologically *connected* content-wise to the current (earlier) stage of his life.

Although he changes for the worse in his actual Methuselah case, Kagan's more general claim commits him to the reasonableness of not caring about a future life of hundreds of years even if he were to improve as a person when he would not have the interests, memories, and values he has now. I find his implied response in this case, in particular, implausible.[10]

In any case, we see that Kagan gives great weight—perhaps more than he should—to connectedness in the content of life's values (V), interests (I), and memories (M). Call this concern of his Connectedness VIM.

(b) Kagan argues that in addition to depriving us of goods, death is bad because it takes away all that we have already been in possession of, and in doing this it adds insult to injury. (So he is in part a Deprivationist about death, but here also accepts one of the Insult Factors I have described.) Comparing ordinary human life to a possible meal of which we are just given a taste, he says (278): "it adds insult to injury that we are offered just a whiff . . . and then they snatched the whole thing away. . . . The deprivation is a comparative bad, but it is not bad in and of itself. . . . To capture what's excruciatingly undesirable about being teased . . . you need to think about the two [the taste and deprivation] in combination. It's an interaction effect."[11] He goes on: "The second potential negative interaction effect . . . falls under the heading 'How the Noble Have Fallen.' . . . There's something horrifying about the thought that something as amazing as us . . . could end up . . . as a piece of rotting flesh" (279). He goes on to compare this second insult to someone who was once a king and becomes a waiter. He says (279): "If you just think about the life as a

ruler . . . in isolation—it is likely to seem pretty good. And even life as a waiter viewed in isolation, isn't all that bad. . . . . [I]f you want to notice the problem with this fate . . . you've got to think about . . . an entire package here being evaluated. . . . There is . . . something especially insulting about having gone from king to waiter." (This is like the Insult Factors of vulnerability and decline that I have described.) Call these concerns of Kagan's Insults.

2.—Now consider whether Kagan's concern with Connectedness VIM and Insults is consistent with his view about when ending one's life makes no sense from an intrapersonal point of view. (This means he is bracketing the issue of ending one's life merely for others' sake. Under "ending life" Kagan discusses suicide but also refusing life-saving means or otherwise not resisting the end of life. Indeed, we could just focus on whether someone's life-ending would make sense prudentially, abstracting entirely from whether and what someone will do about this. Hence, the issue of concern to us here is not anything about the ethics of suicide in particular.) He repeatedly makes the very strong claim that, at least so long as one can maintain control over when one's life ends, ending life "does not make sense" so long as life will have some goods in it (presumably not outweighed by bads) because that will make one's future better than nothing (i.e., better than one's nonexistence involved in death). He does not say it would always be senseless to end life while it will still have goods if this is the only time at which one still retains control over avoiding another period of forthcoming life that is worse than nothing. Unless otherwise noted, I will assume the presence of continuing control.

Note that Kagan's view on when ending one's life is senseless is consistent with his thinking that respect for autonomy, thought of as involving a negative right not to be interfered with, requires that people often be allowed to do what is senseless. Still, if someone's choice to end his life is senseless, it would be harder to argue that others should aid him, and so it may make it harder to argue for the legalization of physician-assisted suicide as a public policy. (Not aiding someone to end his life might not promote his autonomy thought of as a value but it would usually not interfere with it as a negative right.) Someone's choice to end his life being senseless also makes it conceptually impossible to claim that someone else who ends that life could be engaged in euthanasia since by definition that would have to involve aiming at a death that would be in someone's interests and so not intrapersonally senseless.

In particular, Kagan argues that while one's life may be worse than it was and not the sort of life one wanted, this is not a sufficient reason for ending it if there is still something good in it that makes the forthcoming period better than nothing. He plots on a graph what happens in lives. The x-axis represents time and the y-axis how good or bad the life is. Above the x-axis, life has positive value; at the axis, zero (as in being dead); and below the x-axis, negative value. He is open to the possibility that positive value resides not only in the contents of a life but in one's being a container (by which I think he means simply being a conscious person) (259). He says (328): "If the value of your life remains positive (it is always above the x-axis), things never become so bad that you would be better off dead so suicide doesn't make sense."[12] I take it that by "doesn't make sense" he means that there is a decisive reason against ending one's life (which is consistent with there being some but not a sufficient reason to end it).[13] It is also consistent with being willing to risk losing a remaining good thing by death in order to get something yet better. Hence, he says, it "makes no sense" to end a life that is diminished by total paralysis if one is still able to talk to one's family members, enjoy music, and so on (330), assuming this puts one above zero.

One concern I have with his view is that living just above zero does not seem to ensure that one's life is even moderately valuable or meaningful. While Kagan argues against the view that being hooked up to Nozick's Experience Machine[14] is an adequate substitute for real achievements and relationships, it remains true that mere pleasurable sensations (as would come from the machine stimulating neurons) could be something positive in a life. If something positive is better than nothing and so above zero and more valuable things are not available to someone, then it seems that ending a life with these good experiences makes no sense on Kagan's view; it seems to make no sense for a person to end his life (if he could) when its content is, it might be said, worthy of a rabbit but not of a person.[15]

It is also likely that a life just above zero would have very limited Connectedness VIM with most ordinary lives. Furthermore, consider the version of Kagan in a revised Methuselah case in which he is not bad and lives for hundreds of years. This life seems to be better than nothing if some nonoutweighed good things are going on in what

(he agrees) is still his life despite the absence of Connectedness VIM.
Even though these things are not what he wants, why would Kagan's
response of "who cares" to living on in this way (discussed earlier)
make sense? After all, he says that the fact that an ordinary reduced
life that is above the x-axis is "not what one wants" is not enough to
show that rejecting it and ending it (e.g., declining easy measures that
would keep it going) makes sense. Indeed, he says that being above
the x-axis provides a decisive reason against ending one's life but the
reasonableness of "who cares" implies that life above the x-axis sometimes provides no improvement over death and so no decisive reason
against ending one's life.[16]

The decline to a life much reduced from what it once was can
also be seen as an insult. However, Kagan seems to think that such
a diminishment is not as great an insult as moving to the total absence of all goods brought on by death (280). But perhaps having to
consciously live through reduced circumstances and being made to
confront them constantly could be more of an insult than the elimination of even more goods by death which also ends consciousness.[17]
(Conscious reduced living could also be more insulting in this way
than permanent coma, though living on in coma might have its own
distinctive insulting features.) In addition, being reduced to a form of
dementia that did not eliminate personal identity and still contained
overall pleasant experiences could be conceived as a greater insult to
a once-rational being than death because dementia involves a perversion of rationality as death does not.

So there seems to be tension and even an inconsistency between
Kagan's claim that very limited goods are enough to make ending life
senseless and some other things he says about Connectedness VIM
and Insults. Furthermore, I suggest that in one part of his discussion
he places too much emphasis on Connectedness VIM (as noted earlier)
and in another part he requires too little of a life in order that it make
no intrapersonal sense to end it. The tension or inconsistency alone
could be eliminated by rejecting one position or the other. However,
it seems neither position (Connectedness VIM nor the adequacy of
merely being above zero) is quite right.

3.—(a) Evaluating the significance of the insult of decline to a
reduced state also raises questions about Kagan's favored way of deciding whether a forthcoming period of life is better or worse than

nothing. Using his graphs, he determines that the goodness and badness of a particular time consists in what is going on in one's life at
that time considered in isolation and then he sums the values over
time. (Call this approach his Favored Way). He uses this additive aggregative method despite the fact that, as noted above, he understands
that something that does not seem bad in isolation (like being a waiter)
can be seen to be bad when we take account of interaction effects. And
despite the fact that he also at one point says (276–77): "One natural
thought . . . would be that when we want . . . the value of a compound,
we simply need to determine the value of its various component parts
and then sum these values. . . . This simple 'additive' approach to the
values of wholes will not always be correct. . . . You've got to think
about . . . the 'interaction effects.' "[18] Hence, there seems to be a tension in his support of two different methods of deciding about the
value of life stages. This raises the question of whether it is the additive approach of his Favored Way itself that is problematic or whether
it is what is added that is problematic. When Kagan criticizes "a simple
'additive' approach," he may be thinking that it is wrong to only add
the isolated value of forthcoming particular times (what he now calls
local value) as he does in his Favored Way and not also add the forthcoming interaction effects (what he now calls global values).[19]

Consider another example where his Favored Way of judging
whether a forthcoming period of life is better or worse than nothing
has questionable results. Kagan says about his figure 15.4 (333) that
the comeback at the end of life to a short period of positive life (Act 3
in the "play" of life) is not enough to justify going through a longer
period of life worse than death (Act 2) after already having had a
longer period than each of these of very good life (Act 1). (That is, Act
1 was high on the y-axis and long on the x-axis, Act 2 would be far
below zero on the y-axis and significant on the x-axis, and Act 3 would
be reasonably high on the y-axis but short on the x-axis.) But that
course of events could be compatible with the following reading: If
one didn't survive to finish some project (a book or experiment) in Act
3, what happens in Act 1 (writing most of the book or doing most of
the experiment) wouldn't even be ranked as high on the y-axis. That
is, that activity is rated higher because it bore fruit in Act 3 than it
would be rated just as the "local" activity of writing or experimenting
independent of completion. So when we would alter our evaluation

of Act 1 depending on what happens in Act 3, it's possible that the short comeback (to complete the project) could justify going through the period worse than death (Act 2). The focus of his Favored Way on "local" states independent of their role in the whole is not enough to give us true values and the correct decision about whether to end life.[20]

(b) Kagan does address another way of evaluating the goods and bads of life in order to decide whether ending life is senseless. Speaking of the sorts of graphs I described his using, he says (368):

> If you accept the possibility (mentioned in Chapter 13) that the value of a life can also be affected by its overall shape, then you would need somewhat different graphs to illustrate and discuss the points I am about to make. (Briefly, on these alternative graphs, the y-axis should represent how good or bad the overall value of one's life would be if it *ended* at a given moment, rather than how *well off* one is at any given moment; and being better off dead would then be represented by a line that dips *down*, rather than by one that crosses below the x-axis.) However, since the essential philosophical points I am making here wouldn't be affected, I won't pursue this alternative approach further.

The approach according to which one would be better off dead if living on meant that the overall value of one's life would go down would often claim (as we will see) that ending life is not senseless when Kagan's Favored Way says that it is, so one might wonder why Kagan thinks that "the essential philosophical points" he is making wouldn't be affected by using the second approach. I think what Kagan means is that the second approach is not in conflict with the *standard* underlying his Favored Way for deciding when it makes sense to go on—namely, is the forthcoming period worse than nothing—but only with how the approach decides whether that period of life is worse than nothing.

It may be that Ronald Dworkin favored something like the second approach.[21] He held that one's critical interests (or values) could be betrayed by living on in a state that was experientially good but not consistent with the life projects and goals with which one had identified. He held that life that involved experientially nonoutweighed goods considered in isolation (e.g., his example of demented Margo enjoying peanut butter and jelly sandwiches or getting pleasure from randomly picking pages in a book to look at) could ruin (something like) the narrative structure of one's life thus making it a worse life overall than if it had ended earlier.[22] It is especially this latter point that suggests something like the alternative graphs Kagan describes.

(c) This alternative may also exhibit the distinction Kagan once drew between how he is doing and how his life is doing, though not in the way he drew the distinction. In "Me and My Life"[23] Kagan distinguished between how "you" taken as subject may be faring and how "your life" taken as subject may be faring. He took the subject "you" to be made up of mental and (possibly) bodily states and how you are faring is a matter of your well-being. He said that pleasure and pain (on which hedonism focuses) are not usually thought to be the only ultimately good and bad mental states. However, according to the view he accepted at the time, well-being is limited to results of intrinsic changes in mental and bodily states, so it cannot involve states that must be related to nonmental things or events external to those states. Knowledge, friendship, and success do require relations of mental states to external things, events, or states. Without such relations, we have merely mental states of belief (rather than knowledge), friendly feelings (rather than friendship), and sense of success (not true success). It is not clear that these mere mental states can be added to pleasure and pain as nonhedonistic inherently good mental states.

The other possible subject he discusses, "your life," can fare well by including goods that require a relation of mental states to external states or even merely external states on their own. For example, it will help your life fare well if your friendly feelings are for real friends or unbeknown to you your experiments will succeed. And it may even be, he says, that what is good or bad for you could be at odds with what is good for your life (e.g., you are miserable while producing what you will never know is a great masterpiece).

However, Kagan seems to have changed his original position on the contrast between me and my life. On the new account, extrinsic factors rather than merely intrinsic properties of the person can contribute to what is true of the person (not just what is true of his life). For example, when doing a calculation in *Death* to see whether it makes sense for **someone [you]** to continue or end his life (e.g., 325) he says:

> If we are not hedonists we'll accept a more complicated theory of **well being**. So when doing the calculations we will need to take into account other things besides pleasure and pain. In evaluating what **your**

life would be like from here on out, we will need to **take into account not just what your mental states** would be like, but also **what your life would be like** in terms of the various relevant **external** goods and bads. For example, will you continue to accomplish things in your life . . . or will you be unable to achieve your significant aims? Will you continue to have friendships . . . or will others neglect you? Will you continue to learn and know about your place in the universe or will your future life be one of ignorance and illusion? . . . [W]e're going to want to add up all the various goods and bads—internal and external. . . . [I]f the good will outweigh the bads from here on out, then **your life** is worth continuing—**you** are better off alive. . . . [I]f the bad will outweigh the good, then **your life** is not worth continuing. **You** are better off dead.

Hence this quote shows that in *Death*, by contrast to what he does in "Me and My Life," Kagan (i) includes in well-being goods that require relations to external states and (ii) speaks interchangeably of what's good for you and what's good for your life. Similarly, on page 327 of *Death* in describing his graphs, Kagan says, "The *y*-axis represents how good or bad it is [for **you**] to be alive at a given time. (The higher up the *y*-axis the better **the life**.)"

However, in these calculations in *Death* what's good for your life is understood as what's good for your life from "here on out" (a stage of your life) by contrast with the contribution made by "here on out" to the goodness of your life overall. As already noted, it is in connection with the latter approach that (368, endnote 1) Kagan describes the alternative approach to doing calculations that accepts "the possibility . . . that the value of **a life** can also be affected by its overall shape . . . [On] these alternative graphs, the *y*-axis should represent how good or bad the overall value of **one's life** would be if it ended at a given moment, rather than how *well off one is* [**you are**] at any given moment." But on his Favored Way (rather than this alternative approach) the locus on the *y*-axis would, he says, represent how well **your life** is going at that point (including both experiential and externally related matters).

Hence, the contrast between his Favored Way and the alternative approach to calculation as described (in *Death*) is not really about the contrast between "you" and "your life" as described in "Me and My Life" but between (i) your life at a certain point or in the stage henceforth (including internal and external states) and (ii) your life overall. The latter approach allows that both "you" and "your life" going well from "here on out" could also make your life overall be worse. Consider someone who when demented at the end of life feels fulfilled only in painting over the great artwork she produced in the past and this new work still shows true but much diminished talent. She and her life in this stage would have internal and some external value. Nevertheless, if there were no other way to stop her overpainting, arguably an earlier death would prevent her from robbing her life overall of much value.[24] Dworkin (205–6) and also Kagan (*Death*, 271) use the analogy of a novel that has a final part that is overall good and that on its own might be an achievement but that makes the novel worse than if it ended before that final part. This is because it didn't live up to the rest or was inconsistent with it. (Of course, it may not be right to think of one's life as an achievement at which one aims or a thing that one judges in the way a novelist aims at or judges her work. Seeking achievements within life and trying not to have them undone [as in my example of the demented artist] is different from trying to make a unified achievement of one's whole life. Indeed deciding what to do at each point in one's life on grounds of what makes "one's story" go best may be the wrong way to decide what to do and so may actually make one's life worse overall [though this would not be the reason not to decide in this way]. More on this later.)

(d) Suppose it would be wrong to use Kagan's Favored Way to determine whether Margo's final period of life (described by Dworkin) is worse than nothing—that is, by considering the goodness and badness of only that period in isolation—rather than by comparing it with her past activities and values or by considering its contribution to her life overall. This still need not imply that every decline in value within a life makes the whole life decline in value so that it dips on a graph being used in the alternative way that Kagan describes (368).[25] Similarly, a good ending that is not as great as what preceded it need not always make a novel overall worse than if it had abruptly ended earlier.

On this view, it is not inappropriate to use some comparative judgments (e.g., with past achievements or values) to help decide whether a period of life is worse than nothing for a particular person.

If the additional life is deeply inconsistent with values and goals to which a person is or was committed (assuming these are not unreasonable) and does reduce the value of the life overall, ending life need not be senseless even if it contains what are, considered in isolation, nonoutweighed goods. (This might accord with the aspect of Kagan's view that emphasizes Connectedness VIM and that seems inconsistent with his Favored Way of calculating when it makes no sense to end life.)

4.—(a) A third approach which is different from both Kagan's Favored Way and the alternative he describes goes further. It does not commit one to reject continuing when this would cause one's life overall to dip (an indication that it *is* overall worse). After all, why must one maximize the overall goodness of one's life, especially when this will cost one goods that can make the period from here on out overall good even if they also bring down the overall value of the life? Still, even according to this third approach, ending life need not be intrapersonally senseless whenever there remains a nonoutweighed good in the life. I think this third approach may be better than the others we have considered.

(b) What if additional life would be deeply "inconsistent" with previous life or with past current reasonable values but it would be just as good or even a better life according to different reasonable values? (An example might be being an esthete and then being a monk.) This could yield an entire life with no connectedness between its past and its future. I do not think that continuing in such a life is necessarily worse than nothing for a person even though judged as a whole it may seem odd. I don't think it is necessarily senseless to choose such a life or to choose death in the absence of sufficient connectedness. There could be sufficient (just not decisive) reason to do either.[26] In judging a whole life, therefore, we should distinguish between one's future detracting from the whole because it fails according to one set of values (that one may still live by) and the same future not detracting from the whole because it is excellent according to some other new and reasonable set of values (that one may come to accept). If this is so, then the standard of "being worse than dead" used to judge one's life for purposes of deciding whether to end it need not depend on using a single standard of value. Nevertheless, ending life need not be senseless and there could be sufficient reason to do so even if continuing life is only worse than nothing relative to a set of reasonable values to which one is *not* rationally required, but to which one chooses, to remain committed. Even though the future life is worse relative to one set of values that one is not rationally required to maintain, one is also not required to change one's values merely to still get something sufficiently valuable in one's life according to another set of values.

5.—(a) So far I have discussed mostly whether it is senseless to end (or accede to the end of) one's life when it still has some (nonoutweighed) goods. Kagan also considers whether it is senseless to end one's life at a time when it is worse than nothing (according to his Favored Way of answering this question) if goods will come after this period that will make that later period better than nothing. He takes a temporally neutral view of the future, adding up the bads and goods to see whether they sum to an overall positive amount over the different future periods. If they do, he thinks it makes no sense to end the life during the bad period but if they do not, it is (at least) not senseless to end one's life. (The last two Acts of the 3-Act case discussed above, as he interprets it, provide an example of when they do not.) In this connection, he discusses the famous Texas Burn Victim Case involving "Dax" (335), who suffered severe burns over his entire body that were treated by extremely painful procedures. Kagan says that indeed it might not have made sense for Dax to go through the treatments that were imposed on him (against his will) for the sake of the good that would come after. However, in the actual case, Dax's life after his suffering from burns and treatments turned out to be a long and happy one (by his own account) despite his remaining handicaps; Dax presents the life he actually came to have as containing goods that when summed would outweigh the bads he had to go through. If Dax had had all this data at the time of deciding whether to continue treatments, Kagan would presumably say it would have made no sense for Dax not to have gone through all the suffering necessary in order to live on. By contrast, Dax himself thinks it would not have been senseless for him to die rather than go through the suffering and that is, in part, why he thinks it was wrong of medical professionals to treat him against his will. (Furthermore, I do not think he says this merely because at his actual decision time it was not reasonable for him to believe the future good would outweigh the bad he would have to go through.)[27]

I have (elsewhere) argued that it is just such a case that should lead us to believe there are some bads that it would be reasonable to refuse to endure even to get goods that are significantly greater than the bads.[28] This view, contrary to the standard view (adopted by Kagan), implies that it is not inconsistent with intrapersonal rationality not to maximize the overall good in one's life (including its future) when doing so would be very difficult; avoiding certain lesser bads is neither forbidden nor required by personal rationality. Hence, we can see this view as generating (what we can call) a Prudential Prerogative to go through the bad or not. If it is correct, it expands the range of cases from those Kagan accepts in which it would be false that it "makes no sense" to end one's life and expands the range of cases in which there is sufficient reason to do so.[29]

Notice also that the goods Dax eventually came to have were substantial ones distributed over the course of a remaining normal human life span. For example, his legal education, marriage, and children would have made many points on one of Kagan's graphs continuously quite high on the positive region of the y-axis for the entire length of the x-axis after Dax's time far below the x-axis during treatment. This contrasts with Dax suffering through treatment to have very small goods low on the y-axis continuously for a much longer time on the x-axis. However, Kagan's Favored Way of additive aggregation can yield the same overall sum for Dax's actual and this hypothetical life. But it seems even more obvious that it would not be unreasonable to refuse intense concentrated suffering for a significant period of one's life when it led to such a life barely above zero (represented by the x-axis) even if it lasted a very long time. Henceforth, I shall assume that it is the distribution of the greater good that could make it reasonable not to suffer lesser bad for its sake though that is not true in Dax's Case.[30]

(b) This is not the place to try to completely explain the idea of a Prudential Prerogative but it is worth noting certain of its characteristics: (i) Unlike a moral prerogative not to maximize the goodness of interpersonal outcomes by suffering personal costs for others' sakes, it seems that only very serious personal costs could reasonably stand in the way of getting a greater good for oneself. For example, for some amount of money x, morally one might permissibly refuse to give it up to produce great happiness for other people. However, it would not be reasonable to refuse to give x up to produce great happiness for oneself. (ii) This also shows that the Prudential Prerogative is not grounded in intrapersonal sufficientarianism, since there is no principled objection to maximizing one's good. Further, it is sometimes appropriate to exercise one's prerogative not to suffer a great bad even if this means one's life will not be a sufficiently good one, which also demonstrates that sufficientarianism is not at issue.[31] (iii) Not suffering some bad to produce greater good for oneself need not be unreasonable because there is an absolute threshold on bads such that at the threshold it could always be reasonable not to endure them regardless of the goods at stake. For example, it might not be reasonable to refuse a significant period of torture in hell if the gain is eternal life with God but not unreasonable to refuse the torture if the gain is a significantly greater period of goods of ordinary human life. (iv) There seems to be a distinction between suffering severe experiential bads to reduce the amount of other forthcoming severe experiential bads and suffering them to increase (or prevent the loss of) other forthcoming types of benefits. So to avoid 20 years of torture on one's left side, it would be unreasonable to refuse one year of torture on one's right side. However, it need not be unreasonable to refuse the year of torture to avoid losing out on 20 years of happiness, assumed to be a good greater than the bad of a year of torture.[32]

(v) Does the possibility of a Prudential Prerogative depend on taking a temporally nonneutral perspective on the future, giving greater weight to the bads one would have to go through first and discounting the goods that would come later? I do not think so. Consider another case Kagan discusses (illustrated in his diagram on 329) in which things go very well for a long stretch from Q to A, turn bad at B, and become worse than nothing from C to D. Using his Favored Way to determine when a period is worse than nothing, he says about this case (331): "But what if the last time that you are able to kill yourself is well before B? Would suicide still make sense? . . . Your life is going to have tremendous value for a very long time after Q which is the last time you could kill yourself. . . . You face a choice between having a good part and a bad part, or having neither. . . . The good part is significantly greater than the bad part. . . . Killing yourself at Q simply doesn't make sense." In this case you do not have to go through the part that is worse than nothing before the period of greater good, but you know the greater good will be followed by that bad part. The Prudential Prerogative could imply about this case that if you know you will definitely go through a significant period later that is worse than death, it is consistent with personal rationality to give priority to avoiding that bad period even if it means sacrificing the earlier period of greater good.

This would show that the Prudential Prerogative is consistent with temporal neutrality toward the future and depends on sometimes giving priority to avoiding the worst in the future rather than to having the best. It implies that it could be consistent with rationality not to allow one's future life to go below a certain level for the sake of even some greater future goods; "groveling for the good" might be rejected even if it is not morally or rationally prohibited.[33] If giving priority to avoiding certain states worse than death in one's own future life is not senseless, this would show that Kagan's claim that "killing yourself at Q simply doesn't make sense" is not true.[34] It would expand the range of cases in which it is not senseless to end one's life.

(vi) It might be suggested that the Prudential Prerogative depends on viewing the self at different times somewhat in the way nonconsequentialists view separate persons: imposing a small cost on one person for the sake of each of many others may be permissible, but not likewise imposing a large cost. Similarly, the Prudential Prerogative may view a person at one stage as separate from his other stages even though he is the same person, and so making small sacrifices but not great ones can be reasonable for him at one stage to benefit other stages. However, there are significant disanalogies: (1) Avoiding equal or worse bads in later stages *does* justify imposing a great bad on an earlier stage but avoiding such bads in each of several other persons need not justify imposing a great bad on one separate person; (2) Intrapersonal aggregation of great harms to separate stages is reasonable in deciding whether to impose great harm on one other stage to prevent the aggregate but it may be irrelevant interpersonally. So going through torture at t_1 seems reasonable to avoid one's being tortured from t_2-t_{10}. But it is not morally permissible to torture one person to save nine other people from being similarly tortured. These disanalogies may arise simply because the interpersonal judgments are about moral permissibility of harming and that is not what intrapersonal judgments should be about.

Does deciding whom to aid, when each will suffer equally if not aided and we cannot aid everyone, provide a closer analogy to the Prudential Prerogative? After all, in the aiding case, aggregation of the same or sufficiently similar bads to each of several people would be morally permitted and could determine that we help several people, leaving one other person to suffer as a side effect. However, we may not be permitted to allow the one other person to suffer as a mere means to help the others. In the intrapersonal case, by contrast, it could be permissible not merely to allow a bad to occur as a side effect at one stage for the sake of goods in other stages. It could be permissible to impose the bad and even do this as a mere means to help other stages avoid bads. So we may harm, or allow harm to, a stage as a mere means to help other stages but perhaps only allow someone to be harmed as a side effect of instead helping other people.[35]

(c) The view that there could be some bads that it is not senseless to avoid and which there is sufficient reason to avoid, even if this means one can't get greater goods, has the following implication: from an intrapersonal perspective, even when one will always have control, the best time to die might not be before the rest of one's life will be worse than nothing but rather before it will become unavoidable that one will undergo a period of life that is so bad that it is not senseless (and there is sufficient reason) to avoid going through it even if going through it would get (or have gotten) one life that amounts to a greater good. Suppose we combine this conclusion with the second and third approaches discussed earlier for determining when having a period of life is worse than having nothing. Then the implication is that sometimes turning down periods of greater good to avoid some periods of lesser bad that still have some nonoutweighed goods in them (and so are above the x-axis according to Kagan's Favored Way but worse than nothing on the other approaches) need not be senseless.[36]

In short, a sensible purpose of one's death could be to avoid such bad periods of life. Of course, it may be better still to reduce the time between the bad to be avoided and the time when one's life ends. One way to do this if one is not always in control is to make it possible for others to end one's life just before that bad begins. This is an alternative to ending one's life when one is still in control, and losing out on good times still possible before the bad occurs. However, it could be even better to make ending one's life lack the purpose of avoiding such bad periods, making it intrapersonally senseless to end one's life, because lives no longer had such bad periods in them to avoid. Hence, it is possible that improving the quality and length of lives without eliminating either mortality or the possibility of ill-chosen deaths could lead to only senseless deaths being chosen. This is not necessarily to be regretted if the alternative is there being more lives that it is not senseless to end.[37]

6.—We have been considering when ending one's life is and is not intrapersonally senseless. Among the points for which I have argued are: (1) There is at least a tension between Kagan's view that connectedness in one's values, interests, and memories is important in deciding whether it matters if one's life continues and his other views that so long as there will be some nonweighed good in one's life it does not make sense to end it. (2) There is another tension between his view that one needs to consider the interaction between individual factors to determine the value of a whole and the simple additive aggregative methods that he favors in deciding about the worth of periods of life. (3) Contrary to what is implied by Kagan's Favored Way of deciding, it may not be unreasonable to give priority to avoiding certain bads in life even if this interferes with having a life with greater goods.

In conclusion, it is worth noting that while Kagan thinks that it would make sense to end one's life when it will go on being worse than nothing, and so it is not only not senseless but there is sufficient reason to do this, he never insists that in this case staying alive is senseless and so there is a decisive reason not to do so.[38] But he does not explain why, if one's life is worse than death, it could still make sense from an intrapersonal point of view to stay alive. It may be that there is something about staying alive (at least as a person) that sometimes makes not ending one's life not senseless even while ending one's life would also not be senseless. This is an issue for any approach that determines that when a life is worse than nothing for a person on an absolute value standard (i.e., there is no value standard such that relativized to it the life is not worse than nothing for him), ending one's life is not senseless and there is sufficient reason to do so. If it were true that nevertheless it could also make intrapersonal sense to stay alive, then there would be sufficient reason for more than one option (life or death) both with a relativized value standard and with an absolute value standard for life "worse than nothing."[39]

Notes

1. This chapter and Chapter 3 are based, in part, on "The Purpose of My Death: Death, Dying, and Meaning," which appeared in *Ethics* (April 2017) as a review of Shelly Kagan, *Death* (New Haven, CT: Yale University Press, 2012) and Atul Gawande, *Being Mortal: Medicine and What Matters in the End* (New York: Holt, 2015). I am grateful for the comments of Shelly Kagan, Jeff McMahan, Larry Temkin, Douglas MacLean, attendees at the New York University Bioethics Colloquium, the Brandeis Conference on Death, the International Association of the Philosophy of Death and Dying Conference at Syracuse University, the Moral Philosophy Colloquium at Oxford University, and the Moral Theory Conference at Jagiellonian University. I also received helpful comments from an editor and an anonymous reviewer for *Ethics*.

2. An early form of this view is presented in Thomas Nagel's "Death," reprinted in his *Mortal Questions* (Cambridge: Cambridge University Press, 1979), 1–10.

3. See Chapter 1 on the differences between these two approaches.

4. This objection was raised by Douglas MacLean (based on one by Galen Strawson) in his comments on an earlier version of this chapter.

5. I assume same quality per year in the two lives.

6. The Limbo Man Case also shows that it is not any interruption in consciousness that is of concern since the Limbo Man willingly goes into a coma state to prevent his conscious life being all over sooner.

7. I discussed the roles of what one will have had, extinction and being all over, and the insult factors in *Morality, Mortality*, vol. 1 (New York: Oxford University Press, 1993). See also Chapter 1.

8. All citations in the text referring to Kagan's views are to pages in his *Death* unless otherwise noted.

9. Gawande's book was a bestseller in the United States and so has had general impact on the public as well as on those involved in end-of-life medical care. This is another reason for examining it carefully.

10. I find some other implications of his view implausible: (a) A child could reasonably say "who cares" to, and thus reasonably reject, growing to adulthood because his interests, memories, and values will most probably not include those he has now (given empirical facts about human development). (b) A person who faces death could reasonably reject a life-saving surgery because it will involve permanent amnesia and the development of new and even better interests and values that last for a normal human life span.

11. Notice that in prenatal nonexistence (not beginning earlier than one did) the taste of life comes after the absence of additional life. The order, not only the combination, of the two factors is significant.

12. This is meant to apply to ending one's life in other ways as well. Of course by "better off dead" he does not mean you will be in a better state when dead, just that a shorter life would be better for you than a longer one.

13. In the *Ethics* article on which this chapter is based I said: "I take it that by 'doesn't make sense' he means there is no sufficient reason to end one's life." While this is true, his claim seems to be stronger; there is decisive reason not to end one's life. (I owe this point to James Goodrich.) There being sufficient reason *not* to end one's life is compatible with there being sufficient reason *to* end it and so this would be too weak to capture Kagan's claim. Also as I shall use the term "sufficient reason," there being no decisive reason *against* ending one's life is not enough to imply that there is a sufficient reason to do so. That is, eliminating any objection to ending one's life does not provide a positive rationale for doing so.

14. Robert Nozick imagined a machine that could provide one with the illusion of life experience and activity in the absence of these really occurring. See his *Anarchy, State, and Utopia* (Basic Books, 1974).

15. Though he does not say so, perhaps it would also not make sense on Kagan's view to become so miserable due to one's limited goods that the negative value of this misery would outweigh the positive value of the limited goods, thus driving the life below the x-axis. That is, suppose it was not unreasonable for one's limited goods to elicit a response of misery to degree n. But insofar as misery is reasonable, Kagan might think that the prospect of nothing in death would merit more misery than the prospect of very limited goods in life (280). So it would at least be instrumentally bad to remain miserable on account of the limited goods if such misery made it reasonable to end one's life to avoid a condition made worse than nothing only by the misery. In this case, it seems that the continuance of an intrinsically appropriate response (misery) to a reduced state could be instrumentally inappropriate. (Analogously, suppose it would be appropriate to be unhappy about the loss of one's leg. However, if this unhappiness would cause the loss of one's remaining leg, one would have to decide whether to have the intrinsically appropriate response or control it to avoid its bad effect.)

16. Beth Holden has suggested that the implications of this for action might differ depending on how one would end one's life. Suppose Kagan is specifically discussing suicide and this involves some action (e.g., inducing one's death or putting oneself in the way of an easily avoidable oncoming threat) with the intention to die. Holden suggests that if a life and a death are both representable by zero at the x-axis, one would need a positive reason to move from the status quo of continuing alive to take the action involved in suicide. If there was no such positive reason, strictly speaking it still would not make sense to end one's life though there would be no decisive reason not to. (One such positive reason might be that life minimally above the x-axis was not worthy of a person.) However, if one had to actively take a medication in order to stay alive, the "status quo" would be one's life about to end and one would need a reason to act to save it. "Who cares" if justified implies there is no reason.

17. We have already noted that misery at one's reduced capacities could make continuing life worse than death.

18. He even considers the possibility that the negative interaction effect of declining from being a person to being a corpse could outweigh small enough

positive goods in some lives and that the "tease" of just getting a taste could outweigh a small enough good taste (279–80). Presumably, in his view these judgments are to be acted on only in deciding whether to create someone since he argues that once one is alive, becoming a corpse sooner rather than later is no solution to the problems of decline and teasing (280).

19. Indeed, this is what he suggested to me in fall 2017 in response to my earlier article on which this chapter is based.

20. Kagan has told (in conversation) of people who have decided to end their lives after drawing diagrams and following his advice about how to interpret them. Hopefully if they relied only on his Favored Way, they did not decide incorrectly.

21. See Ronald Dworkin, *Life's Dominion: An Argument about Abortion, Euthanasia, and Individual Freedom* (New York: Knopf, 1993). All citations in the text referring to Dworkin are to pages in *Life's Dominion* unless otherwise noted. I also described a version of Deprivationism according to which a forth-coming period with goods in it could make a life be overall worse than one that ended before those goods. See Chapter 1 and the beginning of this chapter.

22. Ibid., 221.

23. *Proceedings of the Aristotelian Society* 94 (1994), 311.

24. I discuss a similar case in a "Note on Dementia and End of Life," reprinted as Chapter 7 in my *Bioethical Prescriptions* (New York: Oxford University Press, 2013).

25. This point was emphasized to me by James Goodrich and corrects a claim in the *Ethics* article on which parts of this chapter is based.

26. It is possible that there is no decisive reason against doing either without there being sufficient reason to do either but there could be sufficient reason to do either (or one).

27. See the following documentaries: Robert White, director, *Please Let Me Die* (Galveston: University of Texas Medical Branch, 1974); Keith Burton, producer, *Dax's Case* (New York: Filmakers Library, 1984).

28. F. M. Kamm, *Morality, Mortality*, vol. 2 (Oxford: Oxford University Press, 1996), and "Four Step Arguments for Physician-Assisted Suicide and Euthanasia," in *Bioethical Prescriptions*, 53–83. To determine that it is a greater good and a lesser bad that are at stake rather than a lesser good and a greater bad, it helps to imagine the good and the bad separately without thinking that to have the good it is necessary to have the bad. It seems to me that when I consider a person going through some bad, I can rate its degree of badness and when, separately, I consider him having some good, I can rate its degree of goodness. I can also decide that on the scale of bads, his bad is lower on the scale of bads than his good is on the scale of goods and yet think (when only these factors are relevant to a decision) that he might have sufficient reason not to go through the bad to have the good. (Kieran Setiya [in conversation] has suggested that this view is in tension with the so-called "buck passing" view of goodness in which to say that something is good is to say there is a reason to choose it for its own sake and

to say that something would maximize the good in one's life is to say there is the most reason to choose it [when all that is relevant to a decision is one's own interests]. I am not sure that this tension exists, but if it does, it may reveal a problem with the buck-passing view.)

29. See F. M. Kamm, "Non-consequentialism," in *The Blackwell Guide to Ethical Theory*, ed. Hugh LaFollette and Ingmar Persson, 2nd ed. (Malden, MA: Blackwell, 2013), 261–86, for more about a prerogative not to maximize one's own good when only one's own interests are at stake rather than a side-constraint (prohibition) on doing so. Samuel Scheffler introduced the idea of a moral prerogative not to maximize impartial good in his *The Rejection of Consequentialism* (Oxford University Press, 1982). Note that even though it would not be senseless to end one's life to avoid lesser pain needed for a greater good, going through greater pain to get a lesser good (such as a small achievement) may have little negative weight in evaluating a person's life from the outside. This is because undergoing pain need not reflect badly on one's life as a person by contrast with lacking achievements or being morally bad. (This may connect with the distinction some psychologists draw between the "experiencing" and the "remembering" self that I discuss in Chapter 3.)

30. Could it be reasonable to refuse the same significant period of suffering for the sake of an equally long period of intense ecstasy (or any other extreme concentration of goods)? Consideration of these issues accords with ideas argued for by Larry Temkin in his *Rethinking the Good: Moral Ideals and the Nature of Practical Reasoning* (Oxford University Press, 2012, Chapter 4) that how goods and bads are distributed within a person's life matters as well as how goods are distributed between separate persons. In particular, Temkin emphasizes that the concentration of bads (as in Dax's treatment period) may be more significant than the same total amount of bad distributed over a much longer period of time. (This too would not be captured by simple additive aggregation. Temkin is primarily concerned with how distribution affects the goodness of outcomes rather than with whether it is morally permissible to bring about the good outcomes.)

31. I owe this point to Shelly Kagan.

32. This claim seems related to the distinction drawn by Seana Shiffrin in "Wrongful Life, Procreative Responsibility, and the Significance of Harm," *Legal Theory* 5 (1999), 117–48. She argues that we may not impose on others without their consent "harmed states" to achieve greater "pure" benefits for them, but we may impose such states to minimize their harmed states. If there is a place for a comparable distinction in the case of the Prudential Prerogative, it would not generate a side constraint on what one may do to others (as in Shiffrin's view) or to oneself but the lifting of a requirement of personal rationality to produce one's own good greater "pure" benefits at the cost of some "harmed states."

33. However, temporal neutrality toward parts of the future is not the same as temporal neutrality with respect to past and future. (This point was emphasized by Michael Rabenberg.) Following Parfit's discussion of asymmetry between our attitudes to past and future (described in Derek Parfit, *Reasons and Persons*

[Oxford: Oxford University Press, 1985 and in Chapter 1 this volume]), it might be that it is not unreasonable to prefer it to be true that (1) it is the day after a period in one's life worse than death and before a period of greater good rather than that (2) one had no such bad period in the past but will also not have the future period of greater good.

34. This conclusion could be further supported by considering what preceded Q in Kagan's case: Suppose one will have had a long and happy life already before Q. Then there might be some diminishing value to getting more goods (reducing the positive value they add to a calculation) from Q on relative to avoiding the great bads after Q. If so, then isn't it wrong of Kagan not to consider the quality of that antecedent period in deciding on the rationality of ending one's life at Q even on his purely additive approach to goods and bads? Relatedly, Kagan says that if one has already undergone most of the great bads that it would have made no sense (on a purely additive view) to go through to get some lesser future goods, it now makes no sense not to go through a few more for the sake of those future goods that outweigh those few more bads (334). However, might there not be a straw that reasonably breaks the camel's back? Might it not be that given that one has already undergone so many bads, one more (that in isolation would be tolerable for the future greater goods) is not tolerable, and so it would not be senseless to refuse to undergo it? What seems to be going on here is what I would call increasing marginal disutility (or nonmoral disvalue) of a harm (e.g., the more torture one has had, the worse is the next instance of torture for one). It has its opposite in diminishing marginal utility (or nonmoral value).

35. Is the notion of parity of use in understanding the formal structure of a Prudential Prerogative and also in understanding that there is no absolute threshold on bads it makes sense to suffer? (I owe the suggestion to Michael Rabenberg.) While a greater good is an improvement over a lesser good, this is consistent with both being on a par with some bad and so not trumping it. Nevertheless, there could be some much greater good which is no longer on a par with the bad and outweighs it. However, this parity approach implies that while the greater good is greater than some other good that is on a par with the bad, it is not greater than the bad but on a par with it. This is a denial of the original assumption in a case like Dax's that it is achieving a greater good that is being trumped by avoiding a lesser bad. (On the contrast between parity and equality (or "being on a par versus being equal"), see Ruth Chang, *Incommensurability, Incomparability, and Practical Reason* (Cambridge, MA: Harvard University Press, 1998), 1–34.

36. A possible concern here is that these bads be consistent with the view (stated earlier) that it is only serious bads that it makes intrapersonal sense to avoid at the cost of losing greater good for oneself.

37. I discuss it being an improvement to have more senseless natural deaths in *Morality, Mortality*, vol. 1, and in Chapter 1 this volume. A similar conclusion seems to apply to deaths that are voluntary.

38. This is not just because there are some cases in which staying alive and being dead are both at zero on his graph since he is discussing cases in which life would be worse than nothing for the person. It is also not because he is considering moral objections to ending one's life even when it is worse than death. The discussion of his we have considered abstracts from moral considerations and is only about what makes sense prudentially.

39. Philippa Foot seems to have believed (see her "Euthanasia," *Philosophy & Public Affairs*, 6 [1977], 85–112), that it makes sense to live with much less than Kagan thinks is sufficient to make ending one's life not senseless and indeed reasonable. She thinks that people typically want to go on in life (even in the Gulag) so long as they have certain "necessaries" (some rest, some food, some privacy) regardless of whether these goods outweigh the bads during a relevant period of time. She does not give the impression that she thinks this is unreasonable. Another way of putting this view is that so long as certain bads—for example, no rest, no food, no privacy—are not present, that one's life is overall bad does not make going on unreasonable. Perhaps Foot is really including being a conscious and self-conscious being as a good in which case the goods may actually outweigh the bads. If not, her view may support the reasonableness of an intrapersonal prerogative to undergo greater bad either (i) for the sake of lesser goods, or (ii) so long as one retains certain goods, or (iii) to avoid extinction of oneself as a conscious person independent of whether this is good for one. A prerogative to undergo certain greater bads so long as one retains or can achieve certain lesser goods could complement the Prudential Prerogative I discussed to refuse to undergo a lesser bad for the sake of a greater good.

Chapter 3

Death, Dying, and Meaning

Gawande on Choosing How to Die

We have considered some of Kagan's views[1] on when it is and is not senseless to end one's life and possible objections and alternatives to his views. Let us now consider Atul Gawande's views on diminished life, dying, and death (in his *Being Mortal*),[2] comparing them with Kagan's when this seems illuminating. My primary purpose is to see whether Gawande's views have different implications for when it is and is not senseless from an intrapersonal perspective to accede to the end of one's life and when there could be sufficient reason to actually end it (e.g., by refusing life-prolonging measures or committing suicide).

Gawande

1.—The title of Gawande's book suggests that he will be discussing what occurs in our lives because we are mortal. However, the first five chapters of the book discuss declines in abilities and achievements as one ages, and theoretically these declines could also occur in beings who were immortal.[3] Furthermore, Gawande discusses declines in mortal beings independently of whether they constitute the stage of dying that occurs close to death. Whereas it is commonly said that each of us does not take seriously that he or she will die, Gawande argues that each of us does not take seriously that he or she will decline in capacities and quality of life probably long before a dying stage and death. Our illusion is that we will continue to be on an incline or at least on a good plateau in terms of capacities and quality of life and then suddenly drop off to death. He says that this may have been an appropriate conception before modern medicine, but now

Almost Over. F. M. Kamm, Oxford University Press (2020) © Oxford University Press.
DOI: 10.1093/oso/9780190097158.001.0001

the trajectory is more likely one in which we decline from a medical emergency, medicine returns us to a point somewhat below the pre-emergency level, and severe decline occurs by way of repetition of such intermediate moves until death.

Gawande thinks we should aim to manage inevitable increasing dependency on the help of others through this decline while retaining autonomy. He thinks we can do this by being in control of the form dependency will take. In this way one's life can remain connected to the type of person one has been and the values one has and still tries to live by. Furthermore, he claims, deciding on and maintaining projects that give meaning to one's life is what is most important in the period of decline even if this comes at the expense of both personal safety and extending life itself, two goals typically emphasized by those caring for dependent people.[4]

(a) My focus in what follows will be on Gawande's discussion of dying that takes up the remaining parts of his book and what we can learn from that discussion about when it can make sense not to resist death (i.e., there is no decisive reason for resisting and a sufficient reason to not resist).[5] Gawande gives no precise characterization of when the dying stage begins, and there is very little discussion of its end point—death—itself. Though at one point Gawande describes (182) a palliative care professional who seeks to help people deal with "anxiety about death" among other anxieties, he never discusses people's conceptions of death or what gives rise to anxiety about it. Whereas Thomas Nagel said that he "should not really object to dying if it were not followed by death,"[6] Gawande's discussion gives the impression that people would not mind death if it were not preceded by dying.[7]

Part of what complicates this contrast is that when end-of-life medical professionals speak of death they are often speaking about what philosophers would call dying. So when they speak of having a "good death" they mean what philosophers would call a "good dying period" that precedes death understood as the event that ends life and begins the period of postexistence irreversible physical nonexistence (known as "being dead").[8] By contrast, by "a good death" philosophers have traditionally meant death that is in the interests of the person who dies (e.g., if death is the least bad alternative to a life worse than death). So, strictly speaking, it seems that as one's dying period becomes better, one has a "good death" in end-of-life professionals' terms but one's ceasing to exist (and so one's death, strictly speaking) can be worse for one. This is because nonexistence (rated at zero) and a shorter life is not better for one than the continuation of the good dying phase of one's life if that were possible. Comparably, as one's dying is worse (and so one has a "bad death" in end-of-life professionals' terms), ceasing to exist can be in one's interest (when nonexistence and a shorter life is the best alternative to continuation of the bad dying) and so death strictly speaking is better for one than any realistic alternative. This is the basis for the term "euthanasia," which is used only when death is overall the best option for the person who dies.

Suppose now that Nagel and the people Gawande discusses agreed on the distinction between dying and death. Despite the contrast I have drawn between their concerns, I think both would often agree (1) to go through even a bad period whose content is identical with a bad dying but that is followed by good continuing life rather than (2) to live without such a bad period—even having a good period of identical length substituted for it—and then die when more life would be good. This agreement would show that the people Gawande discusses also care about avoiding death and not just about avoiding bad dying. The problem is that patients who are truly dying do not have option (1) that includes continuing life. Hence they may focus on the quality of dying because unlike death it could involve bad experiences[9] that they may still be able to avoid.

Similarly, Nagel may overstate his position, for there could be dying periods whose contents were bad enough that he would prefer death; he would here mind dying more than death. This could even be true if a bad dying-like period ("dying") were very long and continued life that came after it was very short and not part of a meaningful life. In such cases, Nagel might also mind "dying" even if it would not be followed by death.

Nagel may also prefer a bad period of "dying" worse than the nonexistence involved in death if this meant he would never die. Given that his view is that no matter how old we are when we die, death could still be bad for us,[10] he may imagine not minding "dying" if he then would *never* have to die. Insofar as we agree that a good enough supernatural life with God could make even years of torture worthwhile, perhaps those going through bad "dying" might agree with

Nagel that it would be worth going through it to acquire a good natural immortal life. It is just that they do not have this option.

(b) One of Gawande's primary concerns is that medical care during
the dying phase focuses on extending a person's life even if there is
little chance of the treatments succeeding, or if the impact of care on
remaining quality of life would be very bad. He also complains that
focusing on achieving an improbable life-extending outcome often
interferes with preparing for the much more probable outcome of
death in the short run and deprives the patient of what he calls "the
dying role." The alternative he favors is the one recommended by the
hospice movement: first, ask patients with a life-threatening illness
what they fear and what they hope for and what they are prepared
to endure to avoid the first and to get the second. One specific question that is asked is: "How much reduction in quality of life are you
prepared to undergo to gain additional life?"[11] The answers to these
questions, it is said, help to locate the specific measures that can help
avoid or manage what is feared and achieve what is hoped for. One
possible measure is a form of hospice care in which the emphasis is
on maintaining the quality of the patient's life (including meaning in
life) and only pursuing treatments to extend life that are compatible
with maintaining that quality.

However, Gawande never emphasizes achieving such compatibility
by creating possible life-extending medical options that neither compromise the quality of one's remaining time alive nor reduce time
alive. In addition, just as palliative care may manage bad effects of
illness, it may also manage bad effects of possible life-extending
treatments.[12] Yet Gawande does not focus on its use in this connection. Finally, if not reducing acceptable quality of life is a condition
of employing possibly life-extending medical procedures, those who
are already in comas or otherwise immune to bad effects of treatment remain good candidates for procedures that could extend their
lives if this could also bring them back to consciousness. These people
have nothing to lose from the procedures in terms of quality of life
before death. Of course, these alternative options I have mentioned
are likely to be more expensive since they will not reduce use of
medical procedures as much as using only palliative care and hospice
will. However, Gawande says (157) that it is not in order to stem the
increasing costs of end-of-life medical care that he is emphasizing

palliative and hospice care. The alternatives I have described involving possibly life-extending treatments interfere with accepting a "dying role," and this may be why Gawande does not focus on them. (I shall discuss this aspect of his view further below.)

Gawande holds that acting on patients' answers to questions about what is feared and what is hoped for increases as much as possible a patient's control over his care, including how his life ends, and can give expression to the fact that patients "have priorities beyond merely being safe and living longer; that the chance to shape one's story is essential to sustaining meaning in life" (243). He here directly connects autonomy (in "the chance to shape one's story") and meaning in one's life.[13] However, when he considers what a patient hopes for after giving up on life-extending treatments he is referring to what still gives meaning to that person's life aside from autonomy itself. When he describes the minimum that someone is willing to live on with, Gawande calls it "drawing the line in the sand," which suggests it is both a necessary and sufficient condition for that person being willing to go on in life. But he also describes how that line can shift and how the things that once were crucial to someone can be forgone because another source of meaning is found (210).

Since Gawande emphasizes the importance of meaning in judging the quality of life, his view seems to go beyond a minimal hospice-provided good of no physical suffering. Also his view may imply that ending one's life (e.g., by refusing means that keep it going) is not senseless and there is sufficient reason to do so when there is no longer meaning in one's life even if there is no physical suffering and the life still contains some nonoutweighed goods (so one is above the x-axis on Kagan's Favored Way of deciding about ending one's life). He does not say this explicitly, but this conclusion is supported by his suggestion that helping people to continue to find meaning in their lives is an alternative to assisted suicide. The aim, he says, should not be a good death (by which he here seems to mean death that prevents prolonged suffering) but a good life (or dying period) to the very end in which suffering is prevented by means other than death and meaning is still found in life (245).[14] Finding "meaning in life," as Gawande here uses the term, I shall assume involves at least a belief or conscious attitude held during one's life about one's ongoing life. Similarly, having a "good life," in his sense, I shall assume involves at least awareness of what one takes to be goods in one's life.[15] If this is a life from which one would not need to escape if it could continue as such, then death that ends it is intrapersonally senseless. But this is preferable to a death that makes sense because it ends a life that is not worth continuing or would be worse than death.

On the other hand Gawande notes (176) that once patients see that the palliative care and other measures provided by hospice can maintain their quality of life, they will typically also give up on all medical treatments that have only a small chance of extending even this good-quality life.[16] Gawande notes that this good life will come to be characterized by what he calls "narrowed focus" due to limited time available; for example, one gives up on seeking many ordinary long-term goals as sources of meaning and focuses on meaning in relationships.[17] Hence, while there could still be pursuits that give one a reason to go on living, they are not the sort that require long life to be satisfied and so may not actually themselves give one reason to go on for long. (This helps reduce the senselessness of death in that it does not end the pursuit of goods that would provide meaning if life went on for long.) Drawing the line in the sand might then involve deciding what things can at minimum provide meaning in life, and different people could find (and fail to find) meaning in different things. Without this meaning, it would not be senseless (and there could be sufficient reason) to seek the end of one's life. If its absence were a line in the sand, giving up on life would alone make sense.[18]

The implied logic of this typical course of events seems to be that what patients most fear is the bad quality of life they will have during dying rather than highly probable death itself. What they hope for is to retain meaning in the life left to them. Once they find that to avoid what they most fear and get what they hope for it is not necessary to avoid death, they usually give up on treatments that have only a small chance of extending life (apparently even if the treatments would be consistent with an acceptable quality of life in what will probably be their dying stage). We might say that whereas those who keep on using possibly life-extending treatments *resist* death, and those who use assisted suicide *seek* death, those in hospice aim to *accept* (or accede to) death despite its ending a life still worth living.[19] However, in discussing the medical case of Stephen Jay Gould, Gawande concludes (171) that there is nothing wrong with not giving up hope that one will achieve a statistically unlikely life-extending outcome (as Gould did) "unless it means we have failed to prepare for the outcome that's vastly more probable."[20]

As already noted in Chapter 1, Bernard Williams called desires that give one reason to go on in life because life is needed to satisfy them "categorical desires." By contrast, he called desires that one has only because one is or must remain alive "conditional desires."[21] For example, the desire not to be in pain or not to be paralyzed does not give one a reason to go on living but it is important that it be satisfied if one will remain alive. The specific content of categorical and conditional desires could vary from person to person. Hospice and palliative care are commonly thought of in connection with comfort care and pain relief; and these would be objects of conditional desires. By contrast, it seems to me that my description of what Gawande and the current hospice movement (as he describes it) are trying to identify and provide are objects of categorical desires that still remain to people who are terminally ill. For the things that provide meaning in their lives are among those things that still give them reason to go on living at least in the short time remaining. One way to understand coming to accept death is that sometimes if one were to continue resisting it, one could no longer satisfy certain categorical (and even conditional) desires. To have good quality of life and pursue some meaningful relations or projects, one will have to give up on the pursuit of certain possibly life-extending treatments whose success, admittedly, would make possible the satisfaction of other categorical desires. Hence, having categorical desires will not always reasonably lead one to resist death (or seek much more life), and not resisting death need not mean that one no longer has categorical desires at least for the short run. Sometimes one does not resist death because doing so would make the longer period before death worse than much of it would otherwise be in terms of satisfying conditional and categorical desires. Sometimes one stops resisting death not because nonexistence is preferable to living on, but because continuing to resist makes living on worse than nonexistence.

2.—Given this presentation and interpretation of Gawande's views and before returning to our primary focus on when it is and is not senseless to seek, not resist, or accede to the end of one's life, it seems worth pointing to a related issue. Fear plays a large role in Gawande's account of dying, though it is fear of loss of control and loss of quality of life rather than of death. Is this perhaps because the people he discusses are certain their death is soon to occur and it makes no sense to fear what one knows is certain? Kagan argues that the fear of bad things that we believe or know will certainly occur is another thing that makes no sense (292–93).[22] He takes this view not only about death, which in his view is mostly a comparative bad when it deprives us of goods but about states that involve bad experiences (e.g., pain). However, though the things about dying that patients fear can often be made to disappear through palliative care, those who fear these things initially believe they are certain to occur. Hence, their fear would not necessarily go away if the bad things were truly certain to occur and they knew this. Unlike Kagan, Gawande is not puzzled by such fear of something one knows to be certain.

Is Kagan's view correct? I think that when we only say "I fear that something bad will happen" we mean to transmit uncertainty about the occurrence of the bad but when we say "I fear what will happen" (e.g., pain in surgery) the fear does not depend on uncertainty about the bad thing happening. Indeed, it could be reasonable for fear to become greater when one is certain the bad thing will happen. Kagan's contrasting view has the odd implication that as things get better because it is less certain that the bad thing will occur, it becomes reasonable to fear the bad thing. But as things get worse because it is certain that the bad thing will occur, it makes no sense to fear the bad thing. It may be that Kagan forms his view because he is thinking only about what we mean in saying "fear that" rather than "fear what."[23]

3.—Now return to the questions Gawande thinks patients should be asked. He describes (183) a daughter who would have to make health care decisions for her father, saying to him: "I need to understand how much you're willing to go through to have a shot at being alive and what level of being alive is tolerable to you."

(a) The father responded that he would go through quite a lot to get a life in which he could watch football and eat chocolate ice cream (though his response suggests certainty of getting this life rather than a "shot" at it). It is not clear that he thought these goods gave him meaning in life rather than being merely enjoyments that sufficed as a reason to go on living in the absence of meaning. If so, one's "line in the sand" might not involve meaning in life. Nor does it seem that Gawande thinks (or should think) that all enjoyments give meaning to life since he specifically says that the pleasures that give meaning are those associated with significant points in the narrative structure of one's life (239).[24] Yet, on one interpretation, the father did exhibit a categorical desire for the pleasures since he said he would go through quite a lot to live on to get them. An alternative interpretation is that continuing to just be a conscious person was the object of his categorical desire so long as life was "tolerable" and football and chocolate ice cream would be the conditional goods that made it so.[25] Perhaps in response to the father's answer, we should revise the view I attributed to Gawande that meaning in life is the line in the sand. He could instead say that in the absence of meaning in life, ending or acceding to the end of one's life is not senseless and there is sufficient reason to do so, but neither is it the only choice that can make sense (i.e., it is not a decisive reason against life). This is like the view mentioned in Chapter 2's discussion of Kagan, that there may be sufficient reason to stay alive even when there is also sufficient reason to end one's life. It is also consistent with this view that one needs more than any non-outweighed good (that puts one above the x-axis in Kagan's graph) to either give meaning to one's life or to suffice for going on in the absence of meaning.

(b) Gawande's own father, who had been a surgeon, held other responsible positions, and had been very physically active, said in response to the same (daughter's) question that a longer life with only football and chocolate ice cream would not be one he would prefer to death and that he would also prefer death to total paralysis. The fact that having such paralysis would put him below his line in the sand does not mean that not being paralyzed was the object of a categorical desire; that is, he did not want to go on in life in order not to be totally paralyzed. It is more like a necessary side constraint, a condition on the worth of his life rather than a goal, and it could be the object of a conditional desire.[26] Gawande's father's response provides reason to think that one's "line in the sand," at least as a necessary (if not sufficient) condition for life going on, need be neither meaning in life nor satisfaction of some categorical desire but the absence of some bad (e.g., total paralysis) whose presence would be a decisive reason not to go on. On the basis of these answers of his father, Gawande eventually decided to allow an ongoing operation on his father to continue when the operation turned out to be threatening his father's life (211–15).

He asked the surgeon whether proceeding with the surgery or stop-ping it was more likely to cause his father to be severely paralyzed. When the answer was stopping the surgery, he gave permission to proceed since his father prioritized not being paralyzed in this way over living.

While Gawande may have made this decision only out of respect for his father's autonomous choices, he nowhere indicates that he thinks the substance of his father's preference to die rather than be totally paralyzed was senseless and insufficiently justified or that the dif-ferent lines in the sand drawn by his father and the daughter's father could not be equally senseful. This is so despite the fact that Gawande thinks doctors should not merely take their patients' responses to life-and-death questions at face value but should rather discuss with them whether, for example, their stated preferences make sense in light of their second-order preferences (about what first-order preferences they want to have) (202).[27]

However, determining whether Gawande's decision about his father's operation was correct is complicated by the fact that his father's so-called line in the sand of no severe paralysis eventually shifted, at least as a bearable condition for his dying phase. This shift was in part due to palliative care's efforts to help him manage such paralysis when it was unavoidable and certain pleasures and mean-ingful relations remained. Suppose that at the time of the operation Gawande could have foreseen that the shift would eventually occur even in what was acceptable for longer-term life. Should he have made a different decision about the operation?[28] It seems that if his father's autonomy was a concern, he should have used information about an expected shift only if he first communicated it to his father and this, in essence, triggered a shift in his father's line in the sand at the earlier decision-making time. In some cases, such an earlier shift will not occur in response to information about predicted future shifts. This is because someone may reject and try to avoid becoming the sort of person who will shift the line later and adapt to less, whether this ad-aptation amounts to finding meaning in new things, living with what suffices in the absence of meaning, or jettisoning some side constraint on being alive. Even if a person's line in the sand may shift because he jettisons his values in order to get something good rather than nothing, Gawande need not (and does not) reason that it is always senseless to keep preferences or stick to values that lead to nothing (death) rather than some good that one finds insufficient. I am inclined to think this conclusion is on the right track.[29]

4.—So far I have emphasized the side of Gawande's focus on meaning in life that could accommodate differences among people's lines in the sand that make not resisting death a sensible option. I also amended my original interpretation to allow that while absence of meaning could make sense of acceding to or seeking the end of one's life, its absence need not imply that giving up on life alone makes sense. But there seems to be a less liberal side to Gawande's views that we will now consider.

(a) First, he emphasizes a particular rule for achieving meaning during a period in one's life. Gawande wants to make use of psychologist Daniel Kahneman's Peak-End Rule, according to which people remember episodes by the peak of good or bad in the episode and how the episode ends rather than by the total amount of time spent in a good or bad state.[30] One of Kahneman's examples is colonoscopy: people remember the worst part and how it ends. So they are more likely to repeat the procedure on the basis of more favorable recollections of colonoscopies that involve overall more pain but whose final moments are not as painful as they would be if the procedure ended earlier. Kahneman also describes an experiment in which people's hands are in painful ice water but only some have the painful experience extended so that the final period, while still painful, is less painful than it was. In retrospect, subjects prefer the experience with the better ending even though it involved more overall pain.

Whereas Kahneman's Peak-End Rule is an empirical report of retrospective evaluation and its effects on future choices, Gawande specifically asks (238): "Should we listen to the remembering—or in this case anticipating—self . . . or should we listen to the experiencing self?" So he suggests that the Peak-End Rule could also apply to the "anticipatory" (prospective) evaluation of events and experiences, and that deciding whether to apply it is a normative ("should") question. When the rule is used normatively, he thinks that it shows that in living and making choices, one should not merely be concerned with the average of good and bad in one's life; one should seek the meaning that may reside in the high points, for which one is willing to suffer greatly, and in the narrative structure of one's life that involves goals achieved and the character of endings.

In support of the significance of endings, he also points to the fact that we can have a wonderful experience at a ball game, but the crucial matter is how it ends, even if the amount of psychological pain at losing would be less than the great amount of enjoyment that preceded it. He says, "a football game is a story. And in stories, endings matter" (239). He thinks this is an appropriate analogy to a life.

Suppose that (intrapersonally) the presence of meaning in life was crucial to whether acceding to or seeking the end of one's life is or is not senseless, so that in the absence of meaning there is no longer a decisive reason against acceding to or seeking the end of one's life and there is sufficient reason to do so. Should the Peak-End Rule be used prospectively as a normative guide to achieving meaning in life as Gawande tries to use it? If so, this would imply that if a life or future relevant part of it would not satisfy the rule, it would not be senseless to accede to life's end or end it. A prospective use of the rule seems to recommend doing what will still allow for meaningful (high) points and a good end. One way of achieving this would be to have one's life end on a good peak itself. The fact that this is not Gawande's recommmendation suggests that he is not opposed to living through (and ending on) some declines from a good peak. However, the rule might still recommend bringing about some very good peak, even if it can only be followed by a lengthy bad experiential period that is worse than nothing, so long as one will then rise to a minimally less bad experiential ending. This does not seem like good advice (if the ending is not necessary to secure the goodness of the very good peak).[31] If the best that would follow the peak were such an ending, it does not seem senseless to seek or not resist death as soon as possible after the peak. And if someone were asked antecedent to a colonoscopy whether he would want to have it extended so that he will have overall more pain in order that it end with lesser pain, he should (and probably would) reject this if his concern were only about this colonoscopy. All this suggests that the Peak-End Rule is not useful as a normative guide to prospective choices.[32] Gawande himself quotes Kahneman, who observes, "a memory that neglects duration will not serve our preference for long pleasure and short pains" (239), and Gawande says: "We do not want to endure long pain and short pleasure. Yet certain pleasures can make enduring suffering worthwhile" (239). (The latter would be all too obvious were he not implying that because of some particular quality had by certain shorter pleasures they could trump longer suffering. I will return to this point.) But note that extending a bad experience only for the pleasure of remembering it more favorably is not like having a bad experience for the sake of some independent pleasure worth suffering for.

Furthermore, I doubt that a dying patient should significantly reduce the amount of time she still can live during which she has nonpeak good experiences in her life just in order to make its very end point better. For example, suppose a surgery were sure to make only her last few hours worse than they would otherwise be but would eliminate her nausea for weeks before that worse end. She might reasonably choose surgery. One point here is that as Kahneman presents the Peak-End Rule it applies to the very end point of what is identified as an episode, and as such this Nausea Case shows that the end part of the rule does not work well as a prospective guide. By contrast, Gawande most often thinks of "the end" as the entire dying period of someone's life that could go on for months. This leaves it open that one might average goods and bads within that last period (or do something else such as giving priority to reducing the badness of any forthcoming worst point in life, whether it would come before or at the very end point of life). Furthermore, Gawande speaks of peaks that can occur within the extended ending period of one's life, which help give meaning to it. Hence, the contrast between peak and end on which the Peak-End Rule depends is not maintained in his use of it.[33]

While it makes little sense for someone who will shortly die to focus on whether her memories of her dying period and end point will be in accord with a retrospective Peak-End Rule, Gawande also mentions the effect on relatives of memories of a good end for their loved one (e.g., 242). From the point of view of intrapersonal concerns, this raises the issue of whether it enhances the patient's own remaining life to know that she will affect the memories of her relatives in accord with the Peak-End Rule, giving them a good peak and a good very end point within the dying period to remember even at the expense of much misery to her in-between. It would certainly not be a sign of love on the part of those relatives to deny the dying person relief from nausea for weeks merely so that they have memories of a good peak (e.g., she

can go to a wedding) and do not have memories of the increased badness of her very end point if it would be caused by the procedure that
relieved weeks of nausea.

Suppose one should not use the Peak-End Rule prospectively. It is
hard to believe that all the lives whose ending period will then not
conform to the rule lack meaning in them because of this failure.
Certainly the ending period in which there is a narratively important
peak but whose very end point will be very bad needn't lack meaning.
If meaning can make suffering worthwhile (as Gawande claims) it is
unclear why one couldn't agree to unavoidably suffer greatly at one's
very end point rather than give up the earlier good peak.

Gawande's comparison of the end of a life with the end of a ball
game seems particularly inapt. First, the end of the game really is the
very end point by contrast to the longer dying phase. Second, since the
point of the ball game is to win, there is a definite final goal toward
which the players aim that (to a great degree) gives meaning to all the
efforts made in the game. The same is not true with life; all the time
before the end of a life (whether thought of as the very end point or
the more extended dying period) is not lived for the sake of having the
best possible end in terms of the evaluative factors Gawande might use
(e.g., continuation of meaningful [or enjoyable] activities). It would be
particularly pernicious, I think, to use the ball game analogy to try to
dissuade someone from using medical treatments that are the only
way to get a small chance of truly lengthy survival on the ground
that they will probably result in his life ending with a lot of physical
suffering. Telling him that he is thereby throwing away a "win" in
the game of "how one ends" or ruining a story, and that that matters
more than simply having additional merely adequate time alive (even
independent of the improbability of getting more time) is dangerous
advice.[34] It might also be wrong to try to reduce the number of people
who take a chance on treatments that could leave them in very bad
end states by eliminating the only option that could let them escape
such states if they come about (once it is too late for palliative care),
namely suicide or assisted suicide.

I do think that one merit of Gawande's example of the ball game
is that it shows that the meaning represented by an achievement
or relationship in life is not a matter of the amount of pleasure had
in or in response to it. One can suffer greatly to achieve something

meaningful without worrying whether the amount of pleasure had in, or in response to, it outweighs the suffering that makes possible what is meaningful.[35] This is because it is not in terms of pleasure that one evaluates meaningful events or things at all. However, this is a point Gawande does not quite see for, as noted above, in this section of his book he seems to identify meaningful events (such as winning a game) with a particular type of pleasure, a little bit of which can outweigh a greater quantity of pain (239). This view is like J. S. Mill's, who emphasized the quality of "higher pleasures" (in addition to the quantity of pleasures) instead of allowing that there simply were other goods apart from pleasure that matter. Because Gawande here thinks of meaningfulness in terms of a particular kind of pleasurable experience, he does not consider the intentionality of the response. That is, lying on the beach could give one experiential pleasure but it does not involve taking pleasure *in* something that is the object of one's positive attitude. He also does not consider whether this object is something correctly believed to have objective worth that merits one's taking such pleasure in it. Its objective worth is a condition that some place on an activity or relationship actually being meaningful and not merely feeling meaningful. (Merely feeling that something is meaningful could occur if one had an incorrect belief in the worth of the object of one's positive attitude.)[36] Finally, he does not consider that engaging with what gives meaning in life need not involve pleasure. As Susan Wolf points out, it may involve struggle to achieve and anxiety about the condition of some good.

Gawande also says (239) of watching the team that has performed beautifully and then loses: "We feel that the ending ruins the whole experience. Yet there's a contradiction at the root of that judgment. The experiencing self had whole hours of pleasure and just a moment of displeasure, but the remembering self sees no pleasure at all." But there is no contradiction. In focusing on the loss, the so-called remembering self need not forget all the prior experiential pleasure; it is just that it does not forget the point of the game, which is to win, and the point of the game is more important than the pleasure (or displeasure) the game produced (either during its course or in its end).

(b) A second less liberal side to Gawande's view is his insistence that one important source of meaning in the dying period with which medicine should not interfere is what he calls the "dying role." He says (249): "People want to share their memories, pass on wisdom . . . settle relationships . . . This role is, observers argue, among life's most important, for both the dying and those left behind. . . . The way we deny people this role . . . is cause for everlasting shame." Is it true that denying people this role is a shame? It may depend on the way we do this. Consider a hypothetical way in which medicine could deny people this dying role[37]: Instead of having the period now devoted to the dying role (as Gawande describes it) that would begin at t_1 and end at t_2 with death, a new lifestyle is developed whose result is that during the same temporal period one would instead be perfectly healthy and engaged in ordinary worthwhile projects, dying suddenly in one's sleep at t_2. Is it clear that one should not exchange the dying role for this alternative content of the period preceding death? I do not think so. If it is not senseless to do the exchange, then this also suggests that the dying role is not "among life's most important."

The dying role (as Gawande describes it) may also be more important for some people than others. For example, it may be more important for those who have lived badly than for those who have lived well to spend time making amends.[38]

All this is consistent with the dying role being worthwhile when one can no longer do other worthwhile things. It is also consistent with it being unwise to always pursue a slim chance of longer survival if it interferes with goods and meaningful activities available in what is most probably the dying phase. This may be all that Gawande needs to say, but it is a much weaker claim than that "the dying role is among life's most important."

(c) Finally, suppose we take seriously the importance to people of having meaning in their life even in its dying phase. One way of doing this that Gawande does not consider, thus making his conclusion less liberal than it might be, is to arrange for goals that could give meaning to one's death that will shortly occur or to one's suffering avoidable only by terminal sedation or death.[39] For example, suppose that my suffering much pain during my dying phase would provide evidence to researchers that helps bring a cure for cancer and that the only means to rid me of the pain would not allow me to engage in any personally meaningful activities because it involved terminal sedation. In this case, if I choose to suffer the avoidable pain, I would be suffering "on purpose" and intentionally connecting my suffering with a purpose I find meaningful, curing cancer.[40]

The good of helping cure cancer is unlike narrow-focused end-of-life personal goals (e.g., wrapping up one's relations with others, giving final advice to students), which might not be enough to make personal sense of going through such pain and so may not make the pain experience meaningful to me. Purposes that could make meaningful to me great suffering and death are often those that I could see as making sense of great supererogatory sacrifices (without making the sacrifices obligatory). Even if these purposes involve benefiting many other people, this would not make my death or suffering merely "other-regarding." This is because the emphasis is still on finding a purpose that makes my death and suffering meaningful to me, the person making the sacrifice.[41]

Now suppose my suffering were entirely unavoidable (because, e.g., terminal sedation and assisted suicide that alone could end it were not available). If I join a research project where scientists learn from my suffering, one might say that though I did not suffer on purpose and even would not have done so, my suffering became meaningful to me and would not have been so had I not intentionally connected it to the research effort.

Further suppose that, ignoring Gawande's counsel, I choose to pursue medical treatments because they have a small chance of extending my life, and these treatments introduce much pain and suffering in what is probably the last short part of my life. I certainly have a purpose in my life, but it may be that my purpose of getting more life does not help me retain meaning in my suffering life. However, suppose that new discoveries that will gradually increase the success rates of these treatments depend on people like me trying them when they are not yet so successful. Then helping to improve treatments is an effect of what I do for other reasons. Suppose that effect could make meaningful to me my pursuit of treatments that cause me suffering even if the chances of my cure alone could not. Here I do not intentionally connect my suffering to the good effect, it merely happens as a foreseen side effect of my action. Further, I would not suffer treatment only for that effect and would suffer without it for my own sake (though suffering might then not be meaningful). Still it seems to me that I could take comfort in the fact that what I do has this effect.

Perhaps this may be enough, independent of a purposive relation to the further good effect, to make personally meaningful what I do in my remaining life.[42]

Perhaps purposes (or effects) could be found to also make my unavoidable death meaningful to me so that though I do not die on purpose and wouldn't do so if I had a choice, I connect my death to a purpose (or my death has an effect) that I could accept as important enough so that it makes my death meaningful to me. This may already occur when people will their organs for transplantation after their deaths to save many lives.[43]

My point is that we could arrange to make almost anything that can occur in my dying stage meaningful to me, including the very things Gawande thinks interfere with retaining meaning in my dying stage such as pursuing certain burdensome medical treatments unlikely to save me. Indeed, we might broaden the idea of an (optional) dying role to include such ways of attaining meaning.[44]

Suppose I would freely agree to dedicate my suffering and death to such personally meaning-providing purposes at the end of my life. Is there something morally wrong with making sure that I know about the availability of such goals and effects so that I could then freely choose to make my death and suffering have a type of purpose that makes it meaningful to me? I do not think so. Is making it possible for me to do these things treating me as a mere means (in a supposedly objectionable Kantian sense), for example, by allowing me to choose to suffer when I could avoid it simply in order to benefit others? If this were done only when I identify with a goal that could reasonably make my suffering or death meaningful to me, then I do not think it would involve objectionably treating me as a mere means.[45]

In terms of meaningfulness, the best death is probably the one in which one dies to save something that one loves even more than one's continuing healthy life. Suppose, for example, that one faced the choice of either allowing the person one loves most to die or dying to certainly save that person's life. If fear were at issue, the fear of her dying would dwarf the fear of one's own death. If there is no question but that one "must" save her, one could even be glad that one's death could have this purpose. So if everyone's death were due to their dying to save the thing they loved more than their own life (even when it could otherwise continue), death would be much less hard to accept.[46]

Gawande describes how his father moved his line in the sand far enough that he was willing to stay alive paralyzed for the sake of small pleasures and meaningful personal relations so long as he didn't suffer. At a certain point, however, although he was not in physical pain, he said he was suffering from consciously enduring his increasing limitations, his worries about those he would leave behind, and the dying process. He preferred to sleep through it (257). Instead of terminal sedation, might one have tried to provide him with some sufficiently important goal that could make enduring the dying process meaningful to him? If having meaning in life is so important, providing a goal that could give meaning even to enduring dying rather than sleeping through it seems to be an option.

Nonetheless, suppose someone recognizes a goal that could give meaning to his suffering while dying, but he prefers to use terminal sedation though it gives no meaning to his remaining life. His choice to avoid the suffering rather than give meaning to it seems entirely reasonable as well. So it seems both that having mere enjoyment can sometimes make sense of continuing one's life even in the absence of meaning (as I argued earlier) and avoiding suffering can sometimes make sense of ending a conscious life that could still be full of meaning. This suggests that continuing to have meaning in one's life is not all it's cracked up to be. Nevertheless, we shall continue to discuss it, especially in Chapter 6.

Conclusion

Our discussion in Chapters 2 and 3 suggests that ending one's life (e.g., by refusing means to continue it) need not be senseless and could be sufficiently reasonable if (a) it is done because meaningful activities or relations are no longer present; (b) there is insufficient connectedness with, or comparative great decline relative to, one's past or values; or (c) one faces bads that one could reasonably refuse to go through even for greater goods. However, the presence of any or all of these things also need not imply that resisting death is senseless and that there is no sufficient reason to do so.

Notes

1. In his *Death* (Yale University Press, 2012). All citations in this chapter referring to Kagan are to pages in that book.

2. *Being Mortal: Medicine and What Matters in the End* (New York: Henry Holt, 2015). All citations in the text referring to Gawande are to pages in this book.

3. Most of the aged persons Gawande discusses in detail are in their nineties. If declining in a worrisome way did not occur until then, this would much reduce the significance of Gawande's points and concerns about aging (at least in those who cannot live much beyond one hundred).

4. Gawande gives examples of people who do not care to live on when their lives are safe but seemingly lacking in meaning. See the case of Alice Hobson in Chapter 3. I discuss this part of Gawande's book in more detail in Chapter 6 of this volume, "Death Wish."

5. Kagan does not shy away from discussing suicide or seeking one's death by other means, but Gawande's focus is on acceding to one's death or not resisting it by refusing certain medical interventions without necessarily intending one's death. I will distinguish (i) acceding to one's death, which connotes mere acceptance, (ii) not resisting, which involves a decision but possibly only foresight to death, and (iii) seeking one's death, which involves intending it with act or omission.

6. Nagel, "Death," in his *Mortal Questions* (New York: Cambridge University Press, 1979), 3.

7. His discussion of Tolstoy's novella *Death of Ivan Ilych* exhibits this focus: Gawande describes how much Ivan misses being understood by most of those around him as he is dying and how he finds solace only in a helpful and truthful servant. But Gawande does not focus as much on the parts of the novella in which Ivan worries about death annihilating him and whether he has lived his past life all wrong. These concerns of dying people about death itself and the value and shortcomings of their lives appear neither in Gawande's discussion nor in the cases of dying people he describes. Perhaps this is because these concerns do not, in fact, often arise; it would be good to have been told explicitly if this is so. I discuss the novella in "Rescuing Ivan Ilych: How We Live and How We Die," reprinted in my *Bioethical Prescriptions* (Oxford University Press, 2013), 3–32.

8. A doctor recently said to me that death has changed so one no longer needs to fear it. But he was probably referring to the dying period having changed with hospice care. That dying has changed need not mean that death is not still whatever it was before hospice care.

9. Assuming death involves total nonexistence, not a supernatural afterlife that could involve experiences.

10. See the conclusion of his essay, which I discuss in Chapter 5.

11. Note that Kagan seems to deal with this question, by implication, in only one limited context. That is, he considers whether it is prudentially senseless or not senseless to end a life of a certain quality. He does not (I think) consider whether it does or does not make sense to trade off some length of life for

quality of life or vice versa when either resulting life would be on his view, worth living. Kagan's views imply that it makes sense to exit what would be a long life worse than nothing. This implies that it makes sense to trade that longer life for a shorter life of higher quality because, on his view, it makes no sense to end the higher quality life. But does it make sense to move to a life that is quite long but at minimal good quality or rather to one that is shorter but of yet higher quality? Kagan's discussion does not deal with these questions.

12. Palliative care can be given at any time; hospice care is provided closer to the end of life.

13. He also assumes that meaning in life is connected to one's life being a story. This suggests that some pattern or unity to the whole rather than merely to individual activities is needed to have meaning in life. We shall consider whether this is so below.

14. Gawande faults countries that are permissive with regard to assisted suicide for not developing means of improving quality of life up to (what we might call) its "natural" end (245).

15. This may contrast with having "a meaningful life," for possibly one can have this even if one has never consciously found meaning or goods in life. For example, if one was never aware that one was doing something truly worthwhile one might still have a meaningful life though not meaning in life. I discuss this issue further in Chapter 6.

16. As noted above, hospice care is focused on the dying stage and involves palliative care, but the latter can be used on nondying persons as well.

17. Kagan notes (195–96) that empirical results show that after a near-death experience one tends to focus on relationships rather than the "rat race." Gawande cites evidence suggesting that it is only when the future does not open up again that one maintains this attitude (95–99). It is also worth noting that in his *When Breath Becomes Air* (Random House, 2016) Paul Kalanithi speaks of the importance of relationships when one finds one's life is coming to an end. However, in interviews his wife says that he spent most of his remaining time while dying of cancer writing his book contrary to the advice in the book itself! This shows that accomplishing a goal before dying can be extremely important to some people.

18. We can see this as a fourth position in addition to the three mentioned in Chapter 2 on when it is not senseless to accede to or seek the end of one's life. Perhaps it is one specification of the third position mentioned there, except stronger because it involves a "line in the sand."

19. Gawande says that patients who forgo the aim of extending their life and use only palliative care actually live 25 percent longer (about three months) on average than those who use medical means in a quest for life extension (177–78). He calls this a Zen phenomenon in that it is only when one does not aim at something that one achieves it. This suggests to him that the standard medical approach that focuses on never giving up on treatments that may extend life fails on its own terms; it may cause patients to die sooner and thus defeat its own goal. (One way to account for this is that spending one's days undergoing

medical treatments in a probably vain attempt to save one's life is not enough to give meaning to life. So one may lack something psychologically necessary to sustain life. Alternatively, the rigor of treatments and exposure to iatrogenic illnesses in medical facilities may reduce life span.) However, note that the statistics he presents are compatible with a few who pursue the medical options living much longer still. If we were evaluating the two approaches only by success at extending life (independent of quality of remaining life), one would have to decide whether it could be reasonable to give up the (assumed) extra length of life provided by palliative care for the small chance of getting much greater additional length of life that could be provided by the medical care. It would not necessarily be unreasonable to do the latter.

20. The object of hope here is living much longer. (It contrasts with the objects of hope that hospice is concerned with: things that one might still look forward to even if one has given up hope of living much longer.) Gawande seems to accept that it is not irrational to hope for what has only a small probability of occurring. Adrienne Martin argues for such a position in her *How We Hope* (Princeton University Press, 2013). She argues that so long as theoretical rationality is preserved in acknowledging the actual small probability, how one deals with the fact is a matter of practical rationality. The latter, she argues, licenses one to focus on the possibility of a cure if this helps one further one's other goals and projects. Such *hope* is consistent with preparing for failure (the more probable result) and differs, she thinks, from *faith* that the improbable will occur, which is inconsistent with preparing for failure.

21. See his "The Makropulos Case: Reflections on the Tedium of Immortality," in his *Problems of the Self* (Cambridge University Press, 1973).

22. This is not because he thinks that it is useless to feel fear when it will not help prevent a bad thing from happening, as he thinks that we may appropriately feel useless anger, sadness, etc., when we know the occurrence of bads is certain.

23. Kagan lists three conditions on the reasonableness of fear: (1) what one fears must be bad, (2) there is a nonnegligible chance of its occurring, and (3) one is not certain that it will occur (291-2). I have criticized (3). But an additional condition might also be suggested as necessary for the reasonableness of fear: one cares whether something bad happens (as not caring could sometimes not be unreasonable).

24. I discuss this further below.

25. In Chapter 6 I discuss Williams' objection to mere continuation as a conscious person being the object of a categorical desire.

26. Not all conditional desires need be for things that are requirements on one's staying alive. One could want certain things only if one is alive and yet be willing to go on without them.

27. Some would say that what occupies the second order are values (versus additional preferences). See Gary Watson's "Free Agency," *Journal of Philosophy* 72: 205-20. It is not clear that medical doctors (rather than psychologists or ethicists, for example) have any special expertise that qualifies them to have

these discussions with patients about consistency among preferences or among preferences and their values.

28. Gawande notes that shifts occur, but he does not discuss their possible role in either first- or second-person decision-making.

29. In addition, even if an earlier shift in his father's line in the sand toward accepting a longer term life with total paralysis were triggered by predictions of a later shift, Gawande (or his father) could still reasonably risk losing this tolerable minimum by death in surgery in order to achieve an even better, hoped-for (nonparalyzed) life. Hence, a foreseen "shifted" answer to the question, "What level of well-being is tolerable to you?" may not have given Gawande (or his father) information that determined whether to continue his father's surgery. This points to a problem with the daughter asking her father only "What is tolerable to you?" and "What are you willing to go through to get it?" rather than also asking "What do you hope for in a longer survival period and what are you willing to go through or risk to get it?" (The hospice question that asks "What do you hope for?" does at least capture the "hope" element though it does not pertain to longer continuing life.) There seem to be other problems with the questions suggested by end-of-life care professionals. Among the concerns I have about "How much reduction in quality of life are you prepared to undergo to get additional life?" is that it may be subject to what are called "framing effects." For example, the most likely interpretation of the question is "How much would you give up (lose) to get a benefit of additional life?" This question could also be captured with a different frame, namely, "How much would you give up (lose) to avoid losing additional life?" Psychologists Kahneman and Tversky report that people are willing to take greater risks to avoid a loss than to achieve a gain (see Daniel Kahneman and Amos Tversky, "Prospect Theory: An Analysis of Decision under Risk," *Econometrica* 47 [1979]: 263–91) and the benefit version of the question is a "gain frame." So phrasing the question as getting a benefit may lead patients to more often reject treatments that lower quality of life. If this is so, one should at least try to ask the question in both avoiding a loss and getting a gain ways (perhaps on different occasions) to avoid skewing the answers in one direction. I examine in greater detail the questions asked of people by those concerned with end-of-life care in "Advanced and End-of-Life Care: Some Cautionary Suggestions" (*Journal of Medical Ethics*, February 2017) and in Chapter 4, which is based on that article and my responses to commentaries on it.

30. D. A. Redelmeier and Daniel Kahneman, "Patients' Memories of Painful Medical Treatments: Real-Time and Retrospective Evaluations of Two Minimally Invasive Procedures," *Pain* 66 (1996): 3–8.

31. See Chapter 2 for my interpretation of a Kagan case in which the ending could play this role.

32. Daniel Kahneman did once suggest that since we spend more time remembering our experiences than having them, perhaps we should prospectively choose which ones to have on the basis of how we will remember them (in his "The Cognitive Psychology of Consequences and Moral Intuition,"

Tanner Lecture on Human Values, University of Michigan, October 21, 1994). Kahneman's suggestion would imply not having a very good experience if it were guaranteed not to be remembered while we are still alive and instead having a much less good one that would be remembered. For a criticism of this view about how we should decide prospectively what experiences to have, see my "Moral Intuitions, Cognitive Psychology, and the Harming/Not-Aiding Distinction," reprinted in my *Intricate Ethics* (New York: Oxford University Press, 2007), 422–49.

33. Gawande tries to use the Peak-End Rule to interpret the case of a terminal patient (232–42) by saying that she still hoped for high points of going to a wedding or being able to eat but also a nonterrible ending period of her life. He thinks the importance to her of how she ends accounts for her refusing surgery that might get her the high points but that also risks making her worse off than she is. In this respect she rejects trying for peaks (which might be very meaningful) to ensure an experientially not too bad end. He asks (236): "How do you weigh relief from nausea and the chances of being able to eat again, against the possibilities of pain, of infections, of having to live with stooling into a bag?" (if the surgery goes wrong). She and Gawande agree on a compromise: he will perform surgery up to the point where there is a significant risk of something happening that will leave her worse off than she is; at that point he will perform what he calls a "palliative operation" whose overriding priority will be to just make her feel better immediately (e.g., alleviate nausea but not make eating possible). I do not think the Peak-End Rule is helpful in understanding this case. Rather than see Gawande's patient's rejection of a bad end as part of her attempt to give a good narrative ending point to her life, it is better to understand her as giving priority to making the worst future state that could possibly occur in her remaining life (whether at the very end point or not) be above a certain level. She is not willing to risk it being lower even for the sake of a higher peak in, or for a higher average over, her dying period. In her case, as well, the quality of her very end point is conjoined with what the dying period before that very end point will be like. This is because if the surgery is calamitous, she will immediately start being worse off than she was and this will continue through to her very end point.

34. This criticism of the focus on good endings is consistent with thinking that how one ends in terms of moral goodness and understanding may be more important than having had such good qualities for an equal length of time earlier in life and then losing them. It may be hard to explain why this is so, aside from inclines in life being better than declines in general, perhaps because they represent a rational direction of change (e.g., stay where you are unless you can go to a better place). One possibility is that a moral decline shows that even at one's moral high point one was vulnerable to corruption but if one dies on a moral high point one is invulnerable to further corruption. However, the invulnerability to corruption due to death is only morally significant if one thinks that the good character one comes to have at the very end is stable and so would have continued without decline had one continued to live on (see my "Rescuing

Ivan Ilych," reprinted in my *Bioethical Prescriptions*, 3–32). That death makes one's corruption impossible is not the same as one's becoming incorruptible in a morally significant sense. In any case, this is a different issue about the significance of endings than the one with which Gawande is concerned. Giving up on an extended ending (or very end point) that would contain good relationships or experiences when this results from having suffered for a chance at longer life that did not succeed is not the same as giving up on a morally good character at the end by becoming corrupt in order to have a chance at longer life. The latter is a Faustian bargain, the former is not.

35. For the sake of argument here continue the assumption that meaning in life and meaningfulness are the same thing. Chapter 6 distinguishes them.

36. See Susan Wolf in *Meaning in Life and Why It Matters*, Princeton University Press, 2012, for a view of meaning in life that emphasizes these elements. In the earlier section of his book when discussing aging, Gawande emphasizes that meaning comes from focusing on something outside of and greater than oneself. However, it remains unclear whether this pursuit must be objectively valuable. I discuss this other view of his about meaning further in "Death Wish: Beyond End-of-Life Care," Chapter 6 in this volume. A different reason for a doctor not distinguishing a patient feeling that something is meaningful from its really being meaningful is that medical professionals should not impose a particular system of objective values on patients.

37. I considered this hypothetical way previously in "Rescuing Ivan Ilych."

38. See ibid.

39. In discussing non-terminally-ill aged people, he says, "The only way death is not meaningless is to see yourself as part of something greater" (127). However, this is not the same as seeing your death as part of something greater. It may seem that the latter is not necessary for a meaningful death because death could have a significant purpose if it only ended one's own great suffering or (as noted at the end of Chapter 2) if it prevented a bad one could reasonably wish to avoid even at the cost of death. However, I shall assume in what follows that more than such a useful purpose is needed for death to be meaningful. Still, helping just one other person, not something greater than oneself, might suffice (as Susan Wolf notes in her *Meaning in Life and Why It Matters*). We discuss this issue further in Chapter 6.

40. However, suppose that I would have "on purpose" brought on myself not only much suffering but also loss of meaningful goods for a few months in the midst of life in order to achieve some goal. If such a goal were available at the end of my life, I might reasonably not make the same sacrifices. This is because forgoing meaningful goods for a goal may have greater significance at the end of life when no more goods can come later than forgoing goods for a goal in the midst of life when more goods are to come later. Temporal location of forgoing meaningful goods seems to matter and this needs explanation.

41. Though the ultimate aim in such a case is not merely other-regarding it is also not best thought of as acting from self-interest since one's interests

overall can be set back in achieving something meaningful to one. Susan Wolf emphasizes this about achieving meaning in life in her *Meaning in Life and Why It Matters*.

42. This course of events has some similarity to the way Susan Wolf suggests (in response to a commentator) that we might rescue meaningfulness in someone's life when he does not succeed in the aim that in fact was necessary to motivate his activities. However, I am not sure that this approach is compatible with Wolf's original theory of meaning in life. I discuss this in Chapter 6.

43. By contrast, providing money in one's will so that many people can have painting lessons may be a good thing to do, but it would not, I think, be the sort of good that could make my death meaningful to me. Hence, I think the idea of making one's death be meaningful is not captured by the idea of "not dying in vain" since attaching any small good effect to a death or just finding it had such an effect (even not achievable without the death) could meet that condition. (However, the goal of providing painting lessons might make meaningful choosing to die a few days earlier than one otherwise would.)

44. I owe this last point about use of "dying role" to Jeff McMahan.

45. It is not always easy to volunteer for the sort of research projects that could make personally meaningful one's suffering or death. (The following remarks include excerpts from my "The Morality of Risks in Research: Reflections on Kumar" in the *Journal of Medical Ethics* 43 [2017], 128–31.) This is because it is commonly thought that there should be a favorable risk/benefit ratio (FRBR) for research subjects even when they volunteer. Some think this view is implied by the Kantian claim that we not treat people as mere means to the greater good, but is this so? (1) There is much debate about what this Kantian claim amounts to. For example, Derek Parfit distinguishes between "treating as a mere means" and "harming as a mere means." The former does not occur, he thinks, so long as we would constrain our behavior toward someone in some way (e.g., not kill him for research purposes) even if we would paralyze him as a mere means for research purposes. But this seems too weak a side constraint; that is, the condition of "not treating as a mere means" would be satisfied even when conduct is still morally objectionable. This suggests that moral theory should be concerned with not harming someone or not stopping a harmful condition to him as a mere means. However, it is not commonly true of research subjects that a bad condition due to harm, risk of harm, or not being aided is itself a causal means to the achievement of a good to others. A case in which it is could involve requiring that someone suffer through the course of a disease so that we can see what its worse aspects are in order to help others. This could come about either by making him sick (harming him) or by not giving him a drug to stop his illness (not aiding him). (This is commonly referred to as a Guinea Pig case.) (2) A broader notion of "using someone as a mere means" for the good of others would be that we causally require his involvement even when we merely foresee that he might suffer a side effect harm that has no useful causal role. (Warren Quinn for one suggested this extension. See his "Actions, Intentions,

and Consequences: The Doctrine of Double Effect," *Philosophy & Public Affairs* 18 [1989], 334–51.)

(3) In addition, a risk/benefit ratio (RBR) that involves possible benefit to the subject himself (intrapersonal RBR) seems not to involve harming someone as a mere means (either on the broader or narrower notion of this) even if the risk comes to fruition. All this is consistent with it being unwise intrapersonally to agree to research because there is no FRBR (e.g., risk of harm is great with low probability of benefit to the person harmed). This is one way that concern for intrapersonal FRBR can diverge from concern for not harming as a mere means since we can fail to provide FRBR and yet not harm as a mere means.

(4) Considered interpersonally, it is not necessarily unreasonable to consent to make the ends of others (e.g., their seeking an HIV cure) one's own ends. This can introduce meaning in one's life. Hence consenting to help others can make it the case that neither the research subject nor others are treating or harming the subject as a mere means even if there is no possible benefit to him in the research and even if there are no constraints on how he is treated. Achieving one's ends and achieving meaning in one's life does not always consist in benefiting oneself. Indeed, even if there is no interpersonal FRBR (because risk to oneself is great and possibility of benefit to others is low), sufficient concern for others could make it reasonable to consent to take great risks for a small chance of benefit to others.

Rahul Kumar says (in his "Contractualist Reasoning, HIV Cure Clinical Trials, and the Moral (Ir)relevance of the Risk/Benefit Ratio," *Journal of Medical Ethics* 43 [2017], 124-7) that when there isn't a FRBR either intrapersonally or interpersonally, the refusal to allow someone to be a research subject looks to be paternalistic (which does not imply that it is necessarily wrong). Paternalism is standardly thought to involve limiting someone's liberty, when he does not consent to such a limit at the time it takes place, for his own good understood as self-interest. If this special reason is not present, it is not a case of paternalism. So-called soft paternalism would involve limiting liberty for the sake of personal goods that the individual paternalized himself accepts as goods, while hard paternalism would involve limiting his liberty for the sake of an objective view of the person's good whether or not he endorses it. Furthermore, the person's own good is not to be identified with his getting whatever he desires, which could include the good of others; the good of others does not become his own good just because he adopts it as one of his ends. However, if he chooses to help others as a means to having meaning in his life, preventing him from doing this may be acting against rather than for his good even if seeking meaning in life is not an ordinary form of self-interest.

Nevertheless, I think that when a researcher refuses to allow someone to become a subject, because there is no FRBR she need not be acting paternalistically. First, she is not literally interfering with that person's liberty. Rather she is not helping him do something he wants to do; she is not enabling him to become a subject. Refusing to help someone to do what he wants may not be promoting his autonomy but it is not an interference with his liberty (especially in the sense relevant to standard paternalism). For example, if the person who wants to be her research subject could carry out the research on himself without the researcher's help, the researcher could agree that she would not be justified in interfering with his liberty to do so. Furthermore, there may be another reason besides the potential subject's own good why a researcher refuses to make him a subject: namely, the researcher does not want to be complicit in doing what may harm or interfere with aid to that subject at least when there is no FRBR. This is a non-paternalistic reason for not enabling someone to achieve meaning in his life (though it may sometimes not be a good enough reason).

46. Suppose we know that we will recover and be happy again even if we cannot save the person or things we love most. This does not show that it makes no sense to die to save them. This is because we are not saving them to avoid being unhappy without them, but to see to it that they will continue living. At funeral services in Reform Judaism, there is a recitation that presents death as something one would not want to avoid if it meant that there would be no future generations but only ourselves. The point is to frame our death as being the necessary means to other things we would care about more than our living on. However, the recitation seems unconvincing for several reasons: (1) In the Old Testament personal immortality is the favored option and death is a punishment for misbehavior. So it is odd for the same religious tradition to present death as better than personal immortality. (2) There is no reason to think that some number of people who were immortal would make it impossible for new people to be created, some number of whom would also not need to die to make it possible for some others to be created, etc. (3) The creation of anonymous future generations is not the sort of thing for which one would usually want to sacrifice a large part of one's life (as would be true if one gave up all the good years involved in possible immortality). Samuel Scheffler notes that the thought of there being no more people after our death strikes us as a worse thing to happen than our own death. See his *Death and the Afterlife* (New York: Oxford University Press, 2016). Part of his explanation of this is how bad it would be for us if no one could continue what we have begun. But this assumes we will die and if we were immortal, we could continue what we have begun (given that our capacities would also be immortal). Further, its striking us that no more future generations is worse than our own death (given that we must die), does not necessarily imply that we would give up a large part of even our mortal lives (e.g., 40 years of 80 or 500 of 1,000) to prevent it. Similarly, one can appreciate that many people dying is worse than our losing our life and yet not be willing to give up 40 years of our life to save them.

Chapter 4

Advanced and End-of-Life Care

Some Cautionary Suggestions

In Chapter 3, we framed consideration of Atul Gawande's views around the question when it makes sense to end (or not resist the end) of life. But, in doing this, we also considered his views about what form of end-of-life and end-of-life care is best. (He thinks it is the form that allows for continued meaning in life whose absence, I suggested, may make sense of seeking or not resisting the end of life.) I there briefly raised some concerns about some of the programs of end-of-life care that he supports. In this chapter, I deal in more detail with this issue.[1]

In particular, I consider some recent views about both advanced care (AC) and end-of-life care (EOLC). The former involves care of those who have "advanced illness" involving "multiple chronic conditions with declining function and poor prospects for full recovery."[2] It is said that "many established advanced care models seek to include people . . . who may be two to three years from end of life. A common goal . . . is to provide . . . care at a stage that is sufficiently 'upstream' from end of life . . . to significantly improve quality of life and to help avoid unnecessary acute spells and accidents resulting in hospitalization or emergency room use."[3] As such, AC is an attempt to prevent persons from becoming patients in many cases. EOLC deals with people much closer to death (often identified in studies by a physician saying she would "not be surprised" if the person died within the next year). While some refer to care in this period as helping people to *die* well, it is now common to speak of helping them to *live* a life acceptable to them until death.

The views on AC and EOLC I consider are represented in several public documents whose contents I will critically examine. In Section I, I focus on the report and recommendations of the Massachusetts Panel

Almost Over. F. M. Kamm, Oxford University Press (2020) © Oxford University Press.
DOI: 10.1093/oso/9780190097158.001.0001

on EOLC entitled "Patient-Centered Care and Human Mortality"[4] (henceforth 2010), while also considering positions taken by the Conversation Project (henceforth TCP)[5] and presented in a report of the Coalition to Transform Advanced Care (henceforth C-TAC). The focus of both TCP and C-TAC is on reaching people who are not yet and who may never become patients (if they decide to decline medical treatments). So these projects may be considered population-based rather than clinical projects. This contrasts with 2010's focus on patients. In Section II, I consider a particular way in which some recommendations like 2010's are made concrete by TCP and in a study conducted by members of Beth Israel Hospital in Boston (henceforth 2015).[6] In Section III, I conclude by considering a study entitled "Peace, Equanimity, and Acceptance in the Cancer Experience (PEACE)" (henceforth PEACE),[7] which is cited in 2015.

Overall, I argue: (1) While professionals involved in AC and EOLC typically begin with calls to attend to preferences and values of a person (who may or may not yet be a patient) to be provided with care, they seem to have aims beyond guiding care according to those preferences and values and view their aims as having objective value. In particular, while a ground given for attending to patients' preferences is that views on what constitutes a "good death" vary, many professionals have a particular view of what a good death is and hope to promote it for what they see as patients' own good. A "good death" as used by these professionals is defined not as a death that is in the interest of the person by contrast to his living on but rather as a good experience of dying and a good life leading up to and including the event of death. Having such aims is not necessarily wrong, but it is worth bringing them out clearly for the sake of full disclosure and also because conflicts could arise between those aims and patients' preferences and values. (2) The way in which some of the documents I will consider attempt to elicit a person's preferences often involve "nudging," imprecision, and "framing effects" that could produce skewed or biased results that prevent reliably eliciting preferences. (3) Professionals show markedly different views on whether persons must be well informed about their condition. Those who put least emphasis on it may find that it conflicts with patients achieving the sort of EOLC professionals think best. It may also lead to a greater role for professionals' own EOLC recommendations because of their superior knowledge about a person's condition. (4) Increasingly higher standards for a life before death that is acceptable to persons may be in tension with refusal by many EOLC professionals to support the option of assisted suicide.

This chapter has the limited focus of providing a philosophical perspective on the documents. I attend to whether they are consistent, contain logical gaps, and how the issues they deal with are connected with some problems dealt with by philosophers. It is not meant to describe my own views about many of the issues. Far from denying the importance and merit of the aims of professionals involved in AC and EOLC, one aim of this chapter is to be useful to such professionals by identifying potential pitfalls of the current approaches and providing suggestions to address them. Another aim is to suggest, by examining some documents, that philosophers might play a useful role during the process that produces official reports and research results.

An additional benefit of examining these particular documents is that to a significant degree they are the work of an overlapping group of physicians and researchers and so it may be possible to track some developments in a single intellectual community. TCP is located in Boston and Dr. Lachlan Forrow, lead author of 2010, is an advisor to that project. The study in 2015 was undertaken at Beth Israel Hospital in Boston where Dr. Forrow is in charge of the EOLC program. When I asked him what questions are used with patients in his program, he referred me to 2015, so it is possible that the questions in 2015 are used in that hospital. They were also the questions developed by Ariadne Labs, a project founded by Dr. Atul Gawande who is a coauthor of 2015.

Section I

A. Preferences, well-informed choices, and needs

2010 begins (in its introduction, henceforth Intro) by noting that people have varying views on how best to deal with death and dying.[8] This is the fundamental reason it gives for emphasizing "patient-centered" care; that is, care "anchored in the patient's own values and preferences and goals" (Intro).[9] Another fundamental concern of 2010 is that patients "be supported in making well-informed choices among the full range of options for their care—whether aggressively life-prolonging, or entirely comfort-based or some balance of the two" (Intro). It says, "For some people, end-of life care will include the use of advanced medical technology that attempts to extend life even if the burdens of treatments increase and the odds of success diminish. Others . . . prioritize comfort . . . many will choose aspects of both, varying over the course of their illness" (2). It claims that well-informed patient-centered care would offer "improved end-of-life care" (2) and "enable individuals to retain as much control as possible over their end-of-life experience . . . a good death according to their own definition" (29).[10] 2010 seems to emphasize cognitive awareness of prognosis and options as playing an important role in this improvement.

What prompted the report was concern that patients as of 2010 were not getting such a "patient-centered" end-of-life (EOL) experience. 2010 notes that 70 percent of Americans say that they want to die at home yet 70 percent die in the hospital (1–2).[11] However, 2010 goes on to interpret this expressed desire to die at home: "When people say they 'want to die at home,' almost all have more in mind than the physical location of their last breath" (2). Hence, in going on to describe what it believes people actually want and what the report is concerned that they are not getting, 2010 says (in part), "Regardless of their care setting, what people want and need at the end of life . . . that their wishes and values are respected, that their symptoms are well controlled, that their dignity is maintained, and that they can spend as much meaningful time as possible with those they most love" (2). It also says "Some . . . undergo more intensive medical interventions than they want, some less. . . . Too often there is a mismatch between what they want and what they get" (3). Notice that the idea of a mismatch is neutral as to the content of their preferences; it does not refer to specifics such as symptom control and meaningful time with loved ones as the earlier quote does.

B. Possible conflicts among preferences, objective goods, and well-informed consent

The 2010 paragraph quoted above shows, I believe, that 2010 is concerned with more than what patients want and value. First, the paragraph is also concerned with what patients *need*. One could need something one does not want, and one could want something that one does not need. Furthermore, needs are usually thought of as being determined on more objective grounds (or grounds intersubjectively agreed to be reasonable), unlike wants and preferences, which may not be reasonable.[12] 2010 might be concerned with the overlap of wants and needs or think that in most patients they do overlap, but this is not clear.

Second, the quoted paragraph seems to list control of symptoms, maintenance of dignity, and spending meaningful time with loved ones both as objects of people's preferences and as goods different from and in addition to satisfying people's preferences. If they are considered goods independent of being preferred by patients, achieving them may be an additional standard to be met in determining whether EOLC and quality of EOL is good. These factors all have to do with the patient's well-being or status, but they are outside of "patient-centeredness," which (as used in 2010) does not refer to concern with patients' well-being or status in general but to being "anchored in the patient's own values and preferences" (Intro).

Third, 2010 is concerned with more objective measures of improving EOLC and experience. For example, 2010 says well-informed consent requires that "evidence-based practices" (19) be among the options from which patients choose. Also, "because palliation provides proven benefit (by measure of longer life, better time alive, etc.) [it] should be included as an option" (4). It goes on to say that given these proven benefits, a choice "cannot be considered well-informed . . . unless [patients] have . . . understanding, as early . . . as possible" (4) of palliative care as an option, and for "choices to be well informed . . . [patients] must understand what hospice offers" (5).[13] There is also mention (e.g., see its Executive Summary) that these options include spiritual support.

This raises the fourth point: 2010 holds that for EOLC to improve by being driven by patients' own choices, the choices must be well informed. This means that there is certain information with respect to best practices that patients "must" have (4) whether they want the information or not. This is not an unreasonable view but it would be good for it to be made clear since it goes beyond doing what patients prefer and value, which might be interpreted to imply that their preferences about whether or not to receive full information should also be respected. (The latter position is taken in 2015 and in TCP, as we shall see.) Indeed, 2010 goes so far as to say that "payment for medical services requires adequate documentation that they are based on the well-informed wishes of patients (or appropriate surrogates) including understanding of life-prolonging and palliative care or hospice alternatives" (23). Hence, 2010 touches on an important and disputed philosophical issue about whether well-informed consent is an option that patients have a right to exercise or more like a duty that patients must perform.

Despite its emphasis on full information about options, 2010 never mentions physician-assisted suicide (PAS), available in some areas of the United States and foreign countries, as something about which patients should be informed. Though PAS was not offered in Massachusetts in 2010, it remained an option as some patients move residence to acquire PAS.[14] 2010 also does not mention suicide undertaken without physician assistance. I shall return to this issue below.

In any case the additional criteria for judging EOLC—meeting needs, employing evidence-based practices, and choices being fully informed—could potentially conflict with a person's preferences and values.

C. Possible conflicts between preferences and best practice standards

Conflicts might also be generated between 2010's (a) commitment to some choosing "medical technology that attempts to extend life even if the burdens of treatment increase and the odds of success diminish" along with its insistence that "[n]o patient is forced to decline life-prolonging measures in order to receive palliative care services that enhance quality of life" (23) and (b) its claim that "[f]rom time of diagnosis . . . the central responsibility of health providers . . . is to help ensure that patients and their loved ones make the most of whatever amount of time it is possible for them to have together" (11–12). Point (b) suggests that the focus is on quality of life but that may conflict with increasing burdens of treatments allowed by point (a). 2010 describes a palliative care physician saying to patients that "your oncology team is in charge of helping you live as long as possible. I am in charge of helping you live as well as possible. And we are working together" (12). However, living "as long as possible" may be inconsistent with living "as well as possible," and more likely there will be compromises with one or both goals. 2010's claim that "if an acceptable quality of life can be achieved, most patients will then of course want longer life in that condition" (12) seems to recognize that "acceptable quality" need not be "as well as possible."

Most importantly, the standard of "evidence-based best practices" that is used as grounds for including palliative and hospice care as options might not endorse the report's permission to pursue life-extending treatments that have "marginal or no benefit" (4) as "the odds of success diminish" (2). 2010 refers to a report that says about EOL medical treatments: "the extra care does not produce better outcomes overall or result in better quality of care" (14). So, it seems that 2010 does not require possibly life-extending medical treatments at EOL to meet a best practices standard that it requires of palliation and hospice. On one hand, this exhibits willingness to allow people to go on resisting death and unwillingness to deny payment for such treatments while, on the other hand, it raises the question of why a standard of provable benefit used to judge the inclusion of some options should not be used to judge them all.

D. Possible conflicts between patient preferences/needs and family preferences/needs

The measures of improved care in 2010 that we have considered so far all focus on the patient—what is thought to be best for the patient or satisfies the patient's preferences (even if conflict is possible between these measures). However, an additional measure of improved experience of death and dying in 2010 emphasizes effects on family members (3, 5). It speaks of seeking "lasting positive memories for family members after their loved ones have died" (7) independently of whether patients have this as one of their preferences. Indeed, a diagram providing a new model of planning care lists bereavement support for the family after the patient's death (13). This is another way in which it is suggested that EOL experience can be improved independent of merely following patients' preferences. Hence, the way is open for possible conflict between patients' preferences and their family's comfort.[15]

It is already well known that despite a person's having signed an organ donor card, doctors have often gone to family members to ask permission to take organs and desisted when they refused. It is not clear why family members should have such control, but a recommendation like 2010's to attend to the comfort of family members after their relative has died might be interpreted to support such practices. It should not have such a result for it should be possible for someone to place legal restrictions on family members overriding his wishes (especially when a potential organ recipient's life stands to be saved). There is a problem with such a legal restriction, however. In suggesting topics for conversation with relatives, TCP asks: "Are there any disagreements or family tensions that you are concerned about?" (4). And C-TAC notes that family members are increasingly involved in providing EOLC (4). While it is expected that conversations will smooth disagreements, there is a possibility that relatives will abandon a patient who insists on enforcing his preferences at odds with their own once they find out his preferences in a TCP-recommended conversation.

So far, we can see that given what 2010 recommends, there are at least three standards for improvement in EOLC and experience: (a) satisfying patients' preferences and values; (b) satisfying such objective values as well-informed consent, less pain and suffering, exposure to best practices, etc., and (c) family positive reactions. There is a possibility of conflict among these standards that 2010 does not seem to recognize.

E. Possible conflicts among preferences, cost-effective choices, and distributive justice

Is there another possible standard for judging EOLC (which could lead to further possible conflict among standards)? 2010 emphasizes that its proposals are not motivated by a desire to cut medical costs even though palliative and hospice care may cost less. However, it may seem that ensuring that patients are well-informed about more cost-effective EOLC options (i.e., ones producing equal or greater benefits at lower cost) may lead to patient choices producing results that other countries try to achieve by public rationing (such as practiced by the National Institute for Health and Care Excellence in the UK) to which there is often public resistance. However, rationing can often *sacrifice benefits* to those whose costs are cut. By contrast, 2010 claims that alternatives such as palliation and hospice can actually increase benefits to those whose costs are cut (e.g., improve the quality of life and length of life). So there is said to be no conflict between reducing costs and increasing benefits.

Nevertheless, C-TAC emphasizes that in its view when it comes to finances, changing AC and EOLC is a "population-based approach to care and coverage" (24) involving "population-based or value-based payments" (25) and "outcomes and successes are measured and valued at a population level rather than just service encounters between individual clinicians and patients' (9). The sense of "value" in play here is important. For example, prominent palliative care proponent Dr. Diane Meier (in a lecture at Mt. Sinai Medical School, July 21, 2016) used the formula Value = Quality/Cost (which she said ruled U.S. government healthcare programs under the Obama administration) to evaluate the worth of palliative care. This is a cost-effectiveness measure, but according to Meier, one could also directly read off of it ethical improvement: increasing quality represents increasing beneficence and decreasing costs represents more distributive justice (because money is not concentrated in one group where it does little good but is available for better use by others). However, it is not true that providing improved outcomes at lower cost is automatically a sign of more distributive justice or increased beneficence. This is both because *who* gets the cost-effective outcomes is crucial for distributive justice and how much moral value a benefit has is crucial for beneficence.

To understand this note that many moral philosophers, known as prioritarians, think that there is greater moral value and increased distributive justice in giving at least some priority to helping those who would be among the worst off without help.[16] On this view, there could be greater moral value and more distributive justice achieved in giving even a *smaller* benefit at *greater* cost to those who would be worse off without help than in giving a greater benefit at less cost to those who would be better off even without help. For example, home palliative care might produce more improvement at less cost if (a) given to the rich and educated who also have a relative caretaker than if (b) given to the poor who have little education and are living alone. Yet distributive justice and beneficence might be better served in (b) than (a). Seeking the biggest improvement at the lowest cost may be a mark of value interpreted as efficiency, but it is not necessarily a measure of value interpreted as beneficence or distributive justice. It would be unfortunate if this position in moral philosophy were ignored by those involved in AC and EOLC projects.[17]

Hence even if there were no conflict between cost effectiveness and giving palliative or hospice care to some people there might be such a conflict in giving it to other people instead. There could also be conflicts between cost effectiveness and satisfying patient's desires for other forms of treatment.

F. Conversation versus written documents and future versus current preferences

The ultimate recommendations of 2010 are that there be AC planning consisting of more than a living will and involving meaningful conversations with patients: "physicians . . . helping them understand their prognosis, explore options and evaluate the risks and burdens of their choices" (19) and to "reliably elicit patients' wishes" (Executive Summary). C-TAC emphasizes helping patients clarify their own values and goals through reflection over time (21), often revealing preferences they were unaware of before. 2010's listed goal to "elicit patients' wishes" suggests others becoming aware of wishes the patient already knows he or she has; by contrast TCP's suggestion is that a patient may for the first time come to know his own preferences through reflection. A process that seems to do the latter may actually be bringing people to have new preferences.[18] One should be sure they are authentic and not instilled by others through a suggestive process if one wants to be respectful of persons. In addition, 2010 and C-TAC emphasize that the results of conversations and medical orders for life-sustaining treatment should be recorded, retrieved, and respected by all caretakers. Conversations and recording of results are to be initiated earlier rather than later because patients may die much sooner than their own doctors predict (12) and because of the benefits to be achieved by earlier commencement of palliation or hospice (if chosen).

While 2010, C-TAC, and TCP all emphasize conversation with loved ones and professional caretakers, TCP seems to place less emphasis than the other two on creating a permanent and retrievable record of these conversations. This may be a crucial omission for though the project's title refers to "the" conversation, TCP specifically says, "having the conversation isn't just a one-time thing. It's the first in a series of conversations over time" (3). More than one conversation may be required with different people to clarify or change what was said first or to deal with questions that cannot be dealt with in one session. Though there is mention of someone being concerned about how he or she was interpreted and what people will remember of what he or she has said (11), no mention is made of recording the conversations so that there is a permanent record.

In general, one might wonder why person-to-person conversations rather than only a written record of one's preferences are necessary with those who are not to be designated proxy decision makers. Perhaps conversation is emphasized because written preferences require directives that are too precise to be useful in changing circumstances, whereas conversation allows communication of underlying values from which others can extrapolate decisions.[19] However, a written record of underlying values is also possible independent of a conversation and decisions could be extrapolated from it. It is possible that back and forth conversation could lead to useful examination of one's preferences and presentation of more information bearing on them, perhaps leading them to change. Perhaps conversation is emphasized because "90 percent of people say that talking with loved ones about EOLC is important [though only] 27 percent have actually done so" (2). However, these people may be wrong to think it is more important to speak to loved ones than to (a) write down either what one prefers or one's underlying values and to (b) make it legally impossible for loved ones to act contrary to these unless one wants them to have this option. However, without a legal restriction on loved ones' actions, an additional reason for having conversations appears: finding out if there will be opposition to one's wishes or underlying values and convincing loved ones not to override these.

2010, TCP, and C-TAC all emphasize that conversations should begin well in advance of a decision time so that people have time to reflect and discuss issues. But this may lead some to suggest that past preferences be given precedence over a competent patient's current ones just because the former were the result of longer reflection and more conversation. So it is worth emphasizing that if a patient is still competent at the time decisions must be made, his or her current wishes should take precedence over any past written or discussed ones.[20] At the time a decision must be made, even patients whose wishes are clearly inconsistent with their past wishes and past (and even present) deepest values typically have their current wishes honored out of respect for their personal sovereignty. The most famous cases of this sort involve Christian Scientists and Jehovah's Witnesses who request life-saving medical procedures (e.g., transfusions) contrary to their past instructions and even current deepest values. (This is a case in which someone exhibits "weakness of will" in carrying out his value-laden views of a good death. It suggests that the ground for respecting preferences may be personal sovereignty rather than that there are a variety of views about what is a good death as 2010 suggests.)[21]

Section II

Let us now consider two projects that can be seen as (in part) attempts to carry out recommendations like those in 2010 to engage in meaningful conversations that "reliably elicit patients' wishes." I will first consider TCP and then 2015.

A. The Conversation Project

TCP's questions are intended for anyone, not only patients, to help prepare for and then actually have a conversation with someone else whom one either wants to (a) know one's preferences for one's EOL or (b) encourage to tell their preferences. As such, it is a population-wide effort not limited to clinical relationships. I will briefly examine some of TCP's preparatory questions, prompts, and actual conversation suggestions, and point to some possible problems.

1. Imprecision in identifying "what one most wants" with one's minimal requirements

TCP first asks people to think about "what matters to me at the end of life," saying this "could help communicate . . . what abilities are most important to you—what's worth pursuing treatment for and what isn't" (4). Unfortunately, the second quote contains much more than a clarification of the first. This is because failure to get "what matters" or "what is most important" to one does not necessarily imply that one would not want treatment and it would not be worth pursuing. The problem is that when people are asked what matters to them at the EOL they are probably thinking of goods they hope to get, not the minimum without which they would not want treatment. For example, being with your child may matter to you at the EOL, but this does not imply that if your child is not available, then you would not want treatment. More precision is needed especially in introductory material for the general public who may otherwise be scared off.

2. Preference for limited information versus well-informed involvement in decisions

Some specific preparatory questions and prompts list possible answers on a scale (from 1 to 5). A set of answers is supposed to be the basis for deriving a more general conclusion—of which (as C-TAC suggests) one might not have previously been aware—about what one prefers. For example, for "As a patient, I'd like to know . . ." the answers range from ". . . only the basics" to ". . . all the details" (4), and for "If I had a terminal illness, I would prefer . . ." the answers range from ". . . not know how quickly it is progressing" to ". . . to know . . . [the] best estimation of how long I have to live" (5). Since these prompts allow persons to choose how much information they will get, patients will not necessarily wind up being well-informed. The prompts thus go counter to 2010's call for well-informed consent, but they are con- sistent with one interpretation of 2010's call for following a patient's preferences, here applied to preferences for amount of information. This makes clear how the two strands in 2010—following preferences and fully informed choices can come apart.

Between these two prompts is "As doctors treat me, I would like . . ." with the answers ranging from ". . . my doctors to do what they think is best" to ". . . to have a say in every decision." Following these three

prompts, the TCP asks, "Look at your answers. . . . what kind of role
do you want to have in the decision-making process?" It may become
clear to someone that "having a say in every decision" is problemati-
cally conjoined with declining best information about one's condition.
Thus, it could be a useful point of this exercise to clarify preferences
so that their consistency or inconsistency is clear.

3. Imprecision and nudging versus reliably eliciting preferences

Some concerns about the next set of questions in TCP are *imprecision*
and whether there is *nudging* by the use of non-neutral questions.[22]
The distinctive idea behind nudging is that there is a bias introduced in
one direction, though people remain free to ignore it and move in another direction at relatively low cost. However, the nudge is introduced
because it is assumed that there is "status quo bias" so people are
more likely to stay with the direction of the nudge. Imprecision and
nudging could interfere with reliably eliciting people's wishes as
recommended in 2010.

An example of imprecision is in the preparatory question, "How
long do you want to receive medical care?" The answer scale's #1 is
"Indefinitely, no matter how uncomfortable treatments are" and #5 is
"Quality of life is more important to me than quantity." This seems
to be a "trade off" question whose assumptions are that medical care
can extend quantity of life and that the most effective care provides
the lowest quality of life. A person who chooses #1 would presumably
agree that "Quantity of life is more important to me than quality" (the
contrast to #5), but #1 also suggests "No reduction in quantity is worth
an increase in quality." The contrast to this is "No reduction in quality
is worth an increase in quantity" (implying comfort care regardless of
how short this makes life). But this is stronger than "quality is more
important to me than quantity." So the options among answers don't
present fully contrasting attitudes, but it may mistakenly be thought
that assenting to #5 involves assenting to the strong contrast to #1.
More precision in phrasing questions seems advisable when dealing
with matters of life and death in EOLC discussions.

There is imprecision and nudging in the question dealing with
comparable subject matter that is suggested for the actual conversation: "When would it be okay to shift from a focus on curative care to

focus on comfort care alone?" (9). This question is imprecise because it seems to overlook the fact that giving up on a cure is not the same as giving up on extending life by medical care (for example, seeking a remission rather than a cure). In addition, the question involves nudging because it presupposes it would be okay to shift at some point (in use of "when"), thus introducing a bias in favor of shifting even though one may say "never." By contrast, "Would it ever be okay to shift . . .?" would be a neutral (unbiased) substitute question that also more clearly allows for "treatment indefinitely," which was the first possible answer to the preparatory questions (we examined earlier).

Other sets of questions and prompts whose specifics I omit raise similar concerns. But it is worth nothing that there seems to be a mismatch between the first question in the set dealing with loved ones, "How involved do you want your loved ones to be?," and the options given for possible answers to it, which focus on whether you want loved ones to do what you have said or what brings them "peace." Deciding *what* you want loved ones to do is not an answer to the question of "how involved" you want them to be, since their doing everything you want could still make them very involved.

B. *The Serious Illness Conversation Guides*

2015 can be seen as another attempt to carry out recommendations like 2010's to engage in meaningful conversations to "reliably elicit patients' wishes" based on information about prognosis and options for further care.[23] The study constructed and used (a) a Serious Illness Conversation Guide (henceforth SICG) for use between doctors and patients with a family member or other support person (see figure 1 in 2015) and (b) a preconversation list of questions (henceforth Pre) that patients should consider before the conversation (see figure 5 in 2015). The questions in Pre do not correspond exactly to those in SICG though they do bear on them. (It would be good to know why patients are not asked to reflect on the SICG's actual questions.) 2015's SICG is identical with the SICG developed by Ariadne Labs (date May 22, 2015).[24] Ariadne Labs is a project with which Dr. Atul Gawande, one of the coauthors of 2015 (and the author of *Being Mortal*, parts of which we considered in Chapter 3) is affiliated. Let us now consider the study in 2015 in more detail.

1. Nudging versus neutral questions in Pre

Do Pre questions "reliably elicit patients' wishes"? One concern is that phrasing nudges people to answer in a particular way and so may introduce a bias. Consider some questions: (a) "What are you afraid of about your illness?" is used rather than "Are you afraid of anything about your illness?" The first question assumes that there is something you are afraid of, so you may be less likely to answer "nothing" even if that is true.[25] The second question is neutral. (b) "What kinds of medical care do you not want?" is used rather than "Are there kinds of care (medical or non-medical) that you do not want?" Because the first question assumes that there are kinds of care (and that these are medical) that someone does not want rather than being neutral about this, it might make it less likely for someone to say "none" even if that is true. That there is a nudging effect is only a hypothesis, subject to testing..

2. Nudging, imprecision, and possible framing effects of questions in SICG

The questions in SICG evidence the same sort of nudging as well as some imprecision and *framing effects*. These problems could interfere with the aim of "reliably eliciting patients' wishes." Consider these questions: (a) "What are your biggest fears and worries about the future with your health?" is used rather than "Do you have big fears and worries about the future with your health?" The first question presupposes that there are biggest (and presumably big) fears and worries whereas the second question does not.[26] (b) "What abilities are so critical to your life that you can't imagine living without them?" is used rather than "Are there abilities so critical to your life that you can't imagine living without them?" Because the first question assumes there are such critical abilities rather than being neutral as to whether there are any, it may nudge toward the view that mere time alive is not enough. This question is also imprecise in not distinguishing living without certain abilities long term (which one might reject) from living without them short term in order to get more adequate long term life. Alternatively, one might reject living short term without certain abilities if this is all the time one will have but be willing to live without them long term because more time alive compensates for their absence. More precision in this question (or additional follow-up questions) seems crucial to avoid mistakes in EOLC decisions.

The next question (c) in SICG raises an issue that would be harder to fix: "How much are you willing to go through for the possibility of gaining more time?" According to behavioral economists Kahneman and Tversky, people will do more to avoid losses than to acquire gains even when the loss or gain would leave them in the same absolute position. Hence "framing" a question as acquiring a gain rather than as avoiding a loss (or vice versa) can lead to what is known as a framing effect.[27] The question in the SICG is framed as a "gain" and so people may not be willing to go through as much as if the question were framed as a "no loss" (e.g., "How much are you willing to go through for the possibility of not losing more time?"). Avoiding this possible framing effect is not easy since there does not seem to be a version of the question that is neutral between the gain and loss frames. It may be worth first asking the question in the two different ways to different audiences to see if a difference is produced by the frames. If there is, it may be worth asking the same person the gain and loss versions at different times and averaging results if there are different responses. (Then the issue is whether there is a "real" answer that has been elicited.)

Question (c) is also imprecise because no specific amount of time to be gained is mentioned; how much one might be willing to go through could depend on how much time is at stake and what the probability of gain (or no loss) is. In addition, no quality is attached to the time so it seems that "mere time" is at issue regardless of quality. Given that the preceding question asked what abilities one could not live without, responders may be primed to think that "mere time" cannot be that important or, alternatively, to assume that the time at issue in question (c) has those critical abilities. It is possible that the question is meant to trigger further "meaningful discussion" that will take up these issues, but, if not, the question should be made more precise.

In the same vein, there is no explicit recommendation in SICG to "push back" or investigate with the patient the reasons for their views about (a) fears, (b) critical abilities, or (c) trade-offs for more time; perhaps it is assumed the questions and answers will trigger more discussion. Suppose a patient said it was critical that he or she still be able to run a 3-minute mile, that his or her greatest fear was having to visit a doctor ten times, and that he or she would not be willing to trade an evening at the ballet for a year of life. Without doubting this person's legal competence, it would be odd to merely take such preferences at face value and act in light of them.[28]

3. Preferences for amount of information versus being well informed

Both Pre and SICG begin with questions about patients' knowledge of their illness and prognosis. However, rather than doctors "helping them understand their prognosis" in a way that requires that they be well-informed, as 2010 recommends, SICG asks, "How much information [about illness and prognosis] . . . would you like from me?" It directs interviewers to "Share information, tailored to information preferences" of the patients. (The corresponding Pre question asks, "What information would you want to help make decisions?") As in TCP, the goal is following patients' preferences for information rather than ensuring a well-informed patient. While this is consistent with one interpretation of 2010's focus on "patient-centered care," it does not meet 2010's (possibly philosophically conflicting) focus on well-informed consent. Patients may choose not to get information about prognoses that they would need in making decisions, even if they have full information about care options. (By contrast, PEACE—to which 2015 refers and which I shall discuss further below—says: "patients who have unrealistically positive views of their prognosis tend to choose invasive measures . . . instead of care directed at comfort . . . patients are the best individuals to make decisions for their care based on their personal values *when they have accurate knowledge about prognosis.* Therefore, prognosis communication has become a focus of palliative care" (2509).[29]

4. Enhanced role of professionals and conditional versus unconditional commitment

The SCIG that I have just discussed underwent changes and a "Redesigned Serious Illness Conversation Guide" (henceforth 2016) is posted at the Ariadne Labs website (dated March 9, 2016) along with a conversation about it with Dr. Susan Block.[30] It is said to be "the centerpiece of our Serious Illness Care Program" (2) and that "using the guide—as written—leads to rich, meaningful discussion with . . . patients" (4). The question concerning provision of information, one of whose aims is to "assess . . . information preferences" is still "How much information . . . would you like from me?" and the directions to the professional in sharing prognosis are still to "tailor information to patient preferences." The questions concerning fears, critical abilities, and what one is willing to go through to get more time are also unchanged and so still are imprecise, possibly nudging, and subject to framing effects.

There is one new question: "What gives you strength as you think about the future with respect to your illness?" It is phrased non-neutrally, by contrast to "Is there something that gives you strength?" In addition, the interviewer is now not only to ask questions but in concluding (a) show her understanding of what the patient has said and (b) affirm her commitment to the patient by saying "We're in this together" (2).

Another important addition coming between (a) and (b) has the professional say, "Given your goals and priorities and what we know about your illness . . . I recommend . . ." (2). No longer is the patient alone to combine his or her knowledge of his or her illness and options with his or her values and goals. The professional is given a role in doing this. However, given that the information provided to the patient about his or her illness will have been tailored to patients' preferences, it is not clear whether "what we know" here involves the best information available (presumably known by the professional) or only what the patient knows. But it is clear in what is said that it is the patient's goals and priorities that the professional should use to derive a recommendation. Since the recommendation is not an order, the patient may reject it. But this raises a question about the concluding interviewer statement "We're in this together" which is said to "affirm your commitment to the patient." Is "We're in this together" contingent on the patient having accepted the recommendation? If not, a patient's possible concern that there will be no commitment unless he accepts the recommendation could be avoided if the commitment were made before and not (as currently) after giving the recommendation.

5a. Dignity versus peacefulness?

While 2016 gives the professional an enhanced role it confines her or him to working within the values and "priorities" of the person deciding on care. Presumably this includes the person's views about what is a good death and EOL. However, other aspects of 2015 and PEACE do not seem to accept such restrictions as we shall now see. 2015 describes the goal of its SICG as "to optimize the alignment between patient goals and medical care . . . and to enhance quality of life and peacefulness" (2); and it says of its research that "the primary outcomes of the trial are patient receipt of goal-concordant care and peacefulness at the end of life" (7). "Peacefulness" seems to be a psychological state, not merely absence of physical suffering, and it is here listed as a good independent of achieving the patient's goals. Something can be good either in itself, for the sake of something else (instrumentally), or because of its relation to something else, while some things can be good in all these ways. Peacefulness seems to be thought of as good in itself in 2015. (As we shall see, it seems to be thought of as also instrumentally good in PEACE.)

Is peacefulness always a good state in itself? Considered on its own it may well be. But this does not settle the question of whether it is good to be in that state in the sense of "appropriate to have that attitude," whatever is happening to one. Recall that 2010 began by emphasizing that there was variation in belief about how to deal with death and dying and that was the reason it gave for the patient's own preferences and values having a dominant role in determining care. This variation in beliefs may apply to whether peacefulness at EOL is always appropriate. After all, Dylan Thomas wrote, "Do not go gentle into that good night. Rage, rage against the dying of the light."[31] (This need not mean that he thought that the intrinsic properties of rage were better than those of peacefulness. Only they were appropriate given what was happening.) Further, if one has lived incorrectly, it might be appropriate to struggle with this at the EOL (as Ivan does in the Tolstoy novella *The Death of Ivan Ilych*), forgoing peacefulness in most of one's final phase.[32] And if one believes punishment after death will come for wrongs one has done, it might also be appropriate not to be peaceful at the end of one's life.

My assumption here is that "appropriateness" of an attitude is a matter of its reasonableness and that it is not determined solely (or at all) by whether having the attitude is good for one or has good consequences for one. Rather, it is determined by the "fit" between the attitude and one's past and present (good or bad life), and one's future (e.g., nonexistence, heaven, or hell) and the attitude to it. That having an attitude would make one feel good does not show it is correct just as a belief's making one feel good does not show it is correct (true). Suppose one is told one has incurable cancer that will be very painful. If one feels happy in response to this news one will be in a pleasant psychological state, but this does not show the response is appropriate. In virtue of what it is a response to (an extrinsic property of the mental state), happiness may not be good to have. (Just as pleasure in even imagined pain of others may not be good to have.)

Furthermore, choosing a belief system (e.g., there is no hell for sinners) or way of reflecting on one's life on the basis of whether it allows for a peaceful end (because peacefulness would be an appropriate response to it) might conflict with the claim in 2010 that "What people want and need as the end of life approaches . . . that their dignity is maintained" (2).[33] It is not clear what a person's dignity is and whether it is to be "maintained" or rather respected. ("Maintained" suggests it could be lost, e.g., by occupying an "undignified" posture or through disrespectful treatment. By contrast, that the dignity of the person should be respected does not imply that it can be lost if it is not respected or that respect is needed to maintain it.[34]) One possibility is that a person's dignity is related to his or her capacity to form beliefs and attitudes and decide on conduct on the basis of reasons. This is presumably why palliative caregivers try to provide reasons for being at peace rather than merely injecting someone with a drug that would render him or her peaceful. However, philosophers typically distinguish (i) the reasonableness of a belief, which has to do with whether there is adequate support for its truth and one is in a position to know this, from (ii) the instrumental reasonableness of making oneself believe something (even something unreasonable) because doing so would promote one's self interest (e.g., taking a drug to believe that $2 + 2 = 5$ because someone will kill you unless you believe it). Making oneself have beliefs and attitudes that promote peacefulness, rather than having beliefs that are grounded in the truth of their content and to whose truth peacefulness may be a fitting response, seems inconsistent with a certain conception of dignity. It is possible that comfort should take precedence over dignity (so conceived), but then one may have to rethink one's commitment to dignity or what it involves.

5b. Professionals' conception of a good death versus patients' conceptions and rights

Suppose some professionals in EOLC believe a good death is a peaceful one and aim at this in using the SICG (as 2015 recommends). Then they would come to their mission with a particular view of what makes a death good and not be neutral among a variety of views. This raises the following issues. (i) As noted, 2016's revisions to the 2015 SICG has the professionals say to a patient, "Given your goals and priorities and what we know about your illness . . . I recommend . . ." It does not say "given your goals and priorities and my aim of achieving a peaceful death for you . . . I recommend . . ." So the revised SICG gives the impression that any favored view that the professional has about a good death will not play a role in the recommendation. If this is not so, then the phrasing should be changed for the sake of transparency to make clear that the professional's view is being incorporated (although this may raise the problem of nudging in virtue of perceiving the professional's status as an authority).

(ii) Suppose professionals make clear to those they are advising that they believe a good death (and dying experience) involves peacefulness and they aim to convince the person of this by giving reasons in conversation. I think this is not appropriately considered nudging. It is also consistent with their respecting and acting on the wishes of people who continue to adhere to different views.[35] This could be because professionals recognize that their holding one view does not necessarily make it more reasonable than someone else's. However, sometimes their ground for giving priority to another's wishes may have to be rights-based, namely that even if a person's views are idiosyncratic and not as reasonable as the professional's, the person should have final say over whether his or her EOL will be peaceful, and it could be wrong not to remain committed to helping him or her. As noted earlier, this rights-based ground for helping someone with a different view seems stronger than the ground given in 2010 for "patient-centeredness." It may be based on another sense of respecting the dignity of the person, namely respecting a person's sovereignty over decisions concerning important and intimate areas of one's life. This may include decisions to form beliefs independently of their truth and only for the sake of one's well-being which would supersede the sense of dignity I discussed earlier.[36]

There may be reasons for not acceding to people's preferences and values (such as economic constraints on funding or the failure of people to have well informed preferences), and it may be permissible to question people about the reasonableness of their choices. However, that professionals have a particular (possibly controversial) view about what is a good EOL does not by itself seem to be sufficient reason for not acceding to people's preferences about their own EOLC.[37]

Section III

A. EOLC and emotional versus mere cognitive acceptance

2015's discussion of peacefulness makes reference to PEACE, a study of different responses to knowledge of impending death that can help us to better understand some professionals' conception of a good death. PEACE begins by distinguishing between mere cognitive awareness of one's prognosis, the sort of understanding of information that 2010 emphasizes, and emotional response to that information. It claims that one possible emotional response is an "existential crisis" as "patients review their lives in light of illness and impending death" (2510). It distinguishes two particular types of responses (called "adjustments", 2515): (a) One type, called "peaceful acceptance" (henceforth Acceptance), is described in the words of Erik Erikson as involving "confronting one's own mortality— with integrity . . . an informed and detached concern with life itself in the face of death . . . finding meaning at the end of life (EOL) . . . main-tain their sense of dignity" (2510); it is seen as the "final stage of human development (typically occurring in late adulthood)" (2510). (b) The second type of adjustment (called Struggle) involves "despair, fear, and foreboding, injustice, anger . . . and the sense of a foreshortened future" (2510) and is more frequent in younger patients (2515).

The purpose of the study was to see the relation between Acceptance or Struggle and EOLC outcomes, in particular the relation to "location of death and use of invasive measures at the EOL" (2510). However, the authors also say, "This construct [Acceptance/Struggle] . . . may be an important target for clinical interventions aimed at improved well-being at the EOL" (2515). This might imply that Acceptance or Struggle in itself is a component of well- (or ill-) being independent of its effects. This would represent a view about the intrinsic value of these adjustments. Alternatively, it may merely imply that the effects of Acceptance or Struggle (e.g., certain locations of death and use of noninvasive means) are in themselves components of well- (or ill-) being at the EOL. Then Acceptance or Struggle would have only instrumental value or disvalue.

B. The contents of Acceptance and Struggle as the study describes them

1. Does peacefulness require detachment?

Acceptance is said to involve a "detached" attitude to one's illness and death, suggesting that one does not focus on "personal" loss to oneself (one is detached). But suppose that unexpectedly a good chance of long-term, high-quality survival returned. Presumably one would seek out the chance not because it was a good thing to happen from a detached (or impartial) perspective but because it involved avoiding a personal loss. Such a switch in perspectives might suggest that the detached attitude was only what is referred to as an "adaptive preference," a comforting way of dealing with outcomes one cannot change perhaps by seeing "sour grapes" in what one cannot have. Some might argue that a correct perspective on life should be constant through different circumstances, either detached or personal or some combination. And if one adopts the detached view only to get comfort, how does it represent "confronting one's own mortality—with integrity" (2510)? A better (re)description of Acceptance might be "a nondetached point of view that acknowledges personal loss but still allows for emotional acceptance." Such Acceptance might be based on appreciation of a personally meaningful life one has had.[38]

2. Acceptance of imminent death versus acceptance of probable death

"Acceptance" in PEACE is reserved for acceptance that death is certainly imminent but there could be peaceful acceptance of the high probability of imminent death and the low probability of successful life-extending treatments. Having hope only in proportion to the probability of successful treatment is also acceptance though it would not necessarily reduce an accepting person's use of expensive technologies with little probability of success. The ball would be in society's court to deny, perhaps on cost-effectiveness grounds, means it might not be unreasonable for such an accepting individual to choose.[39]

3. Acceptance of unfairness and appropriate struggle and fear

(a) As noted, PEACE finds Struggle more prevalent among younger people dying "before the age-appropriate time of confronting death" (2515). Perhaps, then, Struggle in younger people is not age-inappropriate and could be consistent with their integrity even within the researchers' own framework.

(b) With respect to the fear, foreboding, sense of unfairness, and anger said to characterize Struggle: (i) If one believed that death involved an afterlife where one would be punished for one's wrong acts, fear and foreboding could be appropriate at any age. Only a denial of the reasonableness or correctness of a particular belief system— which is not supposed to be a part of the therapeutic approaches I am considering—could imply that such fear and foreboding were unreasonable. (I have already argued that the reasonableness of a belief system should not be judged by whether it disturbs one's peace.) (ii) However, fear might reasonably vary with age if the old need not but the young can fear that they will have had very little time in their life. (If one is *certain* that one will have had very little time, one may not "fear that" one will have had little time because that phrase expresses uncertainty. But this is compatible, I think, with "fear of" the meagerness of one's life itself.) (iii) It is also possible to believe that one's dying young when others do not is "cosmically" unfair without reacting with anger to this; hence, one could have an accepting attitude to unfairness or injustice and this might not be inappropriate. Hence, 2015's claim that a sense of unfairness accompanies only Struggle and not Acceptance need not be true.

C. Problems of aiming at peaceful acceptance, noninvasive means, and spirituality

Now given PEACE's (debatable) conception of Acceptance, consider its ultimate conclusions: To improve well-being (an intrinsic good) in EOL one should seek (peaceful) Acceptance in patients. A prominent effect of Acceptance, the study says, is less use of invasive measures (e.g., feeding tubes) in EOL, while there is increased use of invasive measures with Struggle (2515). One interpretation of this is that not using (even minimally) invasive means is itself considered a component of well-being and an improvement in EOLC. But why is this true if the invasive means are life-sustaining and not major impositions on other activities?

With respect to caregiver action, PEACE says, "If acceptance and struggle . . . change over time, then they also may be targets for interventions to improve EOL care . . . This construct [Acceptance/Struggle] . . . may be an important target for clinical interventions aimed at improving well-being at the EOL" (2515). A prominent cause of Acceptance, it is reported, is a patient's sense of being "highly spiritual" (2515), though no details are given about what this spirituality involves.[40] With respect to caregiver action this could imply that "interventions" should be aimed at making people more spiritual because this would lead to Acceptance which would lead to reduced use of invasive means and hence, according to the study, a better EOL.

It seems that adding "peacefulness" as an independent factor worth achieving either intrinsically or instrumentally might lead some who begin with the aim of satisfying patients' preferences (because there are *varying* opinions about good EOL [2010]) to adopt different aims. In particular, they may come to aim at encouraging a *particular* world view or way of approaching reality (high spirituality) as a means to further *particular* views of a good EOL and good EOLC (e.g., peaceful one with no invasive means such as feeding tubes). I think such a change in professionals' aims is a matter for concern.

If evidence showed that mere knowledge of one's prognosis and options led to patients choosing the professionals' preferred EOL, patient knowledge and choice would be vindicated as a means to what professionals view as the best EOL (though not necessarily as valuable in their own right). However, according to PEACE, mere cognitive awareness does not always lead to choosing its favored EOL experience because Struggle can occur in response to knowledge. (Struggle and use of invasive care are also more likely if patients are allowed to reduce the information they are given as in SICG (2015 and 2016) and so do not know how bad their prognosis is.) Some might see this as an argument for also not providing information about invasive options or for society refusing to fund EOL invasive procedures. Rather than recommending such action, PEACE seems to suggest doing what will bring about the particular emotional adjustment (Acceptance) that will lead patients to choose non-invasive EOLC. The problem is that this may require encouraging "spiritual awakening" and such encouragement does not seem respectful of persons with different views.

D. Suicide, assisted suicide, and acceptable life to the end

Finally, PEACE's discussion of *Acceptance* of, and *Struggle* with, illness and death is not supplemented by discussions of *Seeking* death (as in suicide or physician assisted suicide [PAS]). PEACE says: "[P]atients with higher symptom burdens . . . [and] poorer functional status also had higher Struggle With Illness scores" (2515). This seems a reasonable patient response but one would have thought that in the absence of ability to lower symptom burdens and improve functional status, such patients might also want to be helped to seek death.

This brings us back to the declared aim of projects reported on in 2010, C-TAC, and TCP, which is to make life up to death acceptable to the person living it. One participant in a Petrie-Flom/C-TAC Harvard conference spoke about wanting to have a last phase of life leading to death that would be like jumping off Niagara Falls, implying that she wanted to avoid a long period of decline or of being at a low point before death.[41] However, this may not always be possible even if one avoids unlikely to succeed life-prolonging treatment and uses effective palliative care. For according to the projects I have discussed, a person is to determine what an acceptable EOL is for him or her and this may involve much more than simply avoiding physical suffering (e.g., having meaningful projects).[42] As we have already noted in Chapters 1 and 3, the philosopher Bernard Williams described what he called "conditional desires," the objects of which one would want if one is alive and must remain so. For example, for most people these include not being in pain and not being bored. Then there are other desires that Williams called "categorical," the objects of which make one want to go on living in order to get them. Not being in pain or bored are not usually the sorts of things which make one want to go on living in order to get them. When proponents of AC and EOLC talk about providing a life that is acceptable to a person, it seems that they seek to satisfy not only conditional desires but also some categorical ones and that a life without objects of categorical desires could be unacceptable. Persons not using life-support therapy cannot escape an unacceptable life (so understood) by being disconnected from life support (considered a form of letting die rather than killing).[43] Hence, a person's life may not end before it becomes unacceptable to him or her unless someone actually causes his or her death.

One may argue that inducing death differs from ending life support because only if life support is not ended will there be an imposition on someone's body contrary to his or her wishes. It is debatable whether this is a difference that morally rules out inducing death.[44] My concern now is only that those who support the aims of 2010, TCP, and C-TAC (i) do not oppose people ending life-saving treatment with the intention of avoiding what is a personally unacceptable life though it does not involve irremediable physical suffering;[45] (ii) they also want active interventions that will make life acceptable to the person whose life it is; and (iii) there are those—such as Atul Gawande (a coauthor of 2015)—who accept active intervention with PAS to end irremediable physical suffering,[46] implying that they think intentionally inducing death is not always a moral barrier to ending life. Holding these three views makes it harder to disallow PAS so that someone can avoid an EOL he or she finds unacceptable even if it does not involve irremediable physical suffering.[47,48]

Notes

1. This chapter is based in part on an article of the same name first published online in the *Journal of Medical Ethics* on February 7, 2017 (henceforth *JME*). It also incorporates my responses to commentaries on the article published as "Paternalism, Reasonableness, and Neutrality: Responses to Commentators" in the *Journal of Medical Ethics*, August 2017 (henceforth "Responses"). Shorter versions of parts of the original article appeared in my "End-of-Life Care and Assisted Suicide," *Boston Review*, October 2017.

2. Coalition to Transform Advanced Care (C-TAC). The Advanced Care Project, 4. http://www.thectac.org/wp-content/uploads/2015/06/ACP-Report-6-18-15-FINAL.pdf. References to pages in the Project's report are usually in the text.

3. C-TAC, 17.

4. L. Forrow, J. Conway, D. Kim, et al. "Patient-Centered Care and Human Mortality: The Urgency of Health System Reforms to Ensure Respect for Patients' Wishes and Accountability for Excellence in Care," October 2010. http://molst-ma.org/sites/molst-ma.org/files/2010ExpPanRep.pdf. References to pages in this report are in the text.

5. The Conversation Project and the Institute for Healthcare Improvement, "Your Conversation Starter Kit." http://theconversationproject.org/wp-content/uploads/2015/09/TCP_StarterKit_Final.pdf. I use "TCP" to refer to this document but also to the project itself. References to pages in the Project's written material are usually in the text.

6. R. Bernacki, M. Hutchings, J. Vick, et al., "Development of the Serious Illness Care Program: A Randomized Controlled Trial of a Palliative Care Communication Intervention," *BMJ* 5 (2015), e009032. References to pages in this article are in the text.

7. J. W. Mack, M. Nilsson, T. Balboni, et al. "Peace, Equanimity, and Acceptance in the Cancer Experience (PEACE): Validation of a Scale to Assess Acceptance and Struggle with Terminal Illness," *Cancer* 112 (2008), 2509–17.

8. The Conversation Project (TCP) also says: "Don't judge: A 'good' death means different things to different people" (9).

9. 2010 does not rely on more fundamentally rights-based reasons of personal sovereignty for emphasizing patients' preferences. Note that "person-centered" is now preferred by many to "patient-centered," because they aim to address people before they become patients. See Petri-Flom/C-TAC Conference on Advanced Care and Health Policy, "Aligning Policy and People: Why the Time is Right to Transform Advanced Care" (henceforth Petrie-Flom/C-TAC Conference) video at http://petrieflom.law.harvard.edu/events/details/aligning-policy-and-people. However, I will use 2010's locution in discussing 2010.

10. It has been noted (in D. L. Patrick, et al., "Measuring and Improving the Quality of Dying and Death," *Annals of Internal Medicine,* 139 [2003], 410–15) that quality of EOLC, end of life (EOL) quality, and quality of death as an event should be distinguished. (However, I will often follow a document's use of terms even when they do not distinguish these.)

11. It would be useful to know when people say they want to die at home since 2010 notes that preferences may change over time. Later preferences usually should take precedence.

12. This is consistent with objectively determining whether preferences are satisfied and with it being an objective good that they are. It is just that the object of the preference (what is preferred) may not be objectively reasonable (e.g., to drink one's urine).

13. Palliation and hospice differ. Palliation can be offered at any time during any illness; hospice is care once EOL is expected though 2010 also recommends it start much earlier than it does now for maximal benefit.

14. Bill Novelli, at the Petrie-Flom/C-TAC conferences, said C-TAC takes a "neutral position" on PAS because there is so much controversy about it that

it may interfere with their "larger agenda." See video at https://vimeo.com/175399098#t=16m04s.

15. Using family responses about EOLC as empirical evidence for how good the patient's EOLC was, as recommended by Dr. Forrow (see his video comments at https://vimeo.com/17539998#t=38m29s), may only work when preferences of the family and the person facing death did not conflict. Some hold that something worse happens to the people left behind when a loved one dies than happens to the person who dies because those left behind will experience suffering and the person who dies is beyond that. But suppose that instead of surviving their dead loved one these people had fatal heart attacks immediately after and due to his death. Presumably death would be worse for them than continuing on in life without their loved one. This implies that death is also a worse fate for their loved one than their continuing in life without him (at least assuming that his living on would have been good for him). Of course, we may attend to the relatives' loss rather than his (arguably greater loss) because we can still help them and can no longer help him.

16. Meier was not acquainted with prioritarianism.

17. For more on moral criticisms of cost effectiveness see Daniel Brock, "Ethical Issues in the Use of Cost Effectiveness Analysis for the Prioritization of Health Care Resources," in *Bioethics: A Philosophical Overview*, ed. George Khusfh (Kluwer, 2004) and the Appendix (this volume), which is based on my "Cost Effectiveness Analysis and Fairness" originally published in *Journal of Practical Ethics* 3, no. 1 (2015), 1–14.

18. Richard Moran argues that finding out what you think about a certain matter is not usually about becoming aware of a belief you already had but about forming a new belief. R. Moran, *Authority and Estrangement: An Essay on Self-Knowledge* (Princeton University Press, 2001).

19. Dominic Wilkinson made this point.

20. In TCP (10), a distinction is drawn between an Advance Directive (AD) ("a document that describes your wishes") and a Living Will (LW) (specifying "which medical treatments you want or don't want . . . if you are no longer able to make decisions on your own"). This implies that a person would be capable of overriding an AD but not a LW at the decision time.

21. Acts inconsistent with one's values are not necessarily indications of mental incompetence and may not even be unreasonable, for one can be inconsistent while making an objectively right choice. On the latter point see N. Arpaly, "On Acting Rationally Against One's Best Judgment," *Ethics*, 110(2) (2000), 488–513.

22. This term was made famous by Richard Thaler and Cass Sunstein in their *Nudge: Improving Decisions about Health, Wealth, and Happiness* (Penguin Books, 2009). Unlike these authors, I do not consider persuading by argument to be one type of "nudge."

23. I shall consider it at some length because (unlike TCP) it is a scholarly study.

24. Ariadne Labs SCIG. https://www.ct.gov/dph/lib/dph/molst/042715_most_serious_illness_conversation_guide.pdf.

25. However, the first question makes sense if there is pre-existing data that everyone does fear something about his or her illness.

26. What was said in Endnote 25 applies here as well.

27. Daniel Kahneman and Amos Tversky, "Prospect Theory: Analysis of Decisions Under Risk," *Econometrics* 47 (1979), 263–91.

28. In my Responses I noted that Schenker and Arnold in their commentary on *JME*, "Problems with Precision and Neutrality in EOL Preference Elicitation," *Journal of Medical Ethics* 433:589-590, 2017, claim that the sort of more precise and balanced questioning I suggest for end-of-life questionnaires "risks biasing preference elicitation." Specifically, their first concern is that "Kamm's model assumes that people have pre-formed preferences for end-of-life treatments." But I recognize that this is not true when I point to C-TAC's view that new preferences may arise from reflection. I relate this to Richard Moran's view that when people want to know what they think about something they are *not* aiming to uncover something they already believe but rather to form an opinion. These authors' second concern is that emotions are not revealed by precise, neutral questions; "inductive, interpretative conversational style" is required to "illuminate patients' emotional statements . . . [and] values." But I only considered questions in an existing guide for conversations, and these do not have an interpretive conversational style though they are meant to lead to actual freer conversations. So their complaint is really about the questions already in the questionnaires I am examining. Furthermore, "What are you afraid of?" does try to get at emotions. I only suggested that one could uncover fears without assuming there are any by asking the more neutral "Are you afraid of anything?" Schenker and Arnold also think that "more precise questions impose a pre-existing medical framework." For example, asking someone how much she is willing to do to get more time assumes she cares about time per se rather than certain accomplishments (e.g., going to her daughter's wedding) and so will fail to "elicit her true values." My concern about the time question was that persons could reasonably respond, "Well, that depends on how much time I will get." Only when the question becomes more precise (perhaps in conversation) can they give a useful answer (e.g., "for five months I would do x, for a year I would do more"). Schenker and Arnold are suggesting that another reasonable response to the question is, "Why do you assume I care about time per se rather than going to my daughter's wedding?" But putting the question in terms of time could capture the woman's concern if she said she would do a lot to get a time period that, in fact, sufficed for attending the wedding. In addition, questions that ask what particular project a person wants to achieve risk the mistaken implication that the person does not care about living except to achieve that project (a problem I noted in the Conversation Project's opening paragraph).

The authors note that the questions I criticize as imprecise were developed based on clinical experience. But is it the imprecision that makes them useful? Could they be improved, for example, by eliminating the suggestion that not wanting to satisfy relatives' wishes for one's end of life implies not wanting them to be involved in one's end of life, or by eliminating the suggestion that caring *only* about quantity and not quality is properly contrasted with caring *more* about quality than quantity (rather than with caring only about quality and not quantity)? Since my aim was to examine a limited number of documents whose authors were part of a particular intellectual community (as I noted at the beginning of this chapter), I did not consider Schenker and Arnold's own approach, which is to ask open-ended questions: "Who are you as a person? What do you hold dear? What gives your life meaning? What do you most want to avoid?" Their aim is "not an accounting of preferences but . . . understanding of patients' values and goals" to guide decisions by patients and doctors together. But notice that their first most general question, "Who are you as a person?," is made more precise by their follow-up questions, without which it is not clear how one should answer. Their approach differs from that taken by the Conversation Project and SICG, which ask specific questions in order to help people discover their position on more general ones. I agree that because values and goals most often ground preferences for specific courses of action, it is good to clarify and record them. But I also pointed to the case of the weak-willed Christian Scientist, competent at the time of decision-making, to show that if we looked at values, goals, and perhaps even preferences rather than to someone's actual choices (e.g., to have a blood transfusion), we would make a moral mistake.

Schenker and Arnold also object to my suggestion that questions be phrased neutrally so as not to "nudge" in one way. They claim that such neutrality is not possible either in forms of language or in human beings. But I argue in Responses that the view that neutral questions should be used does not "presume that it is possible for clinicians to be completely neutral" since clinicians can be neutral by presenting the option they favor and the one they oppose. Then others just cannot tell which option they favor by the way they present each.

Schenker and Arnold say, "every choice of words involves framing (. . . nudging) of some kind." Even if this were true it would not imply that some words are not closer to neutral than others. "Do you want to end your pregnancy?" is more neutral than "When do you want to end your pregnancy?" (though both assume pregnancy and the possibility of its being ended). Further, if framing and nudging involve choices intended to have a specific effect on people, they are not involved in "every choice of words" that have *unintended* effects. And some changes in preferences and values could be due to words that constitute a reasonable argument (i.e., so the patient decides to do something for the sake of the reasons that actually justify the decision), which (contrary to Sunstein and Thaler) is not a nudge.

Schenker and Arnold (and Wilkinson in his commentary on *JME* "What has philosophy got to do with it? Conflicting views and values in end-of-life care," *Journal of Medical Ethics* 43 (2017), 591–592) argue that neutrality is not desirable because it does not counteract pre-existing biases (favoring aggressive medical treatment). They say when we "know the direction of many biases . . . nudging may be helpful in counteracting such bias . . . and allowing people to express their true wishes" and "to redress the balance" (as Wilkinson puts it). In Responses I noted that this view itself assumes that one can tell when we are closer to neutrality (redress of bias) and that achieving it might be possible contrary to the claim that neutrality cannot be achieved. Further, if these authors truly aim to achieve neutrality in this way, they should favor a nudge toward medical treatment where there is a bias favoring hospice.

But is a skewed question (a) necessary to achieve neutrality; (b) does it even do so; and (c) might it be morally problematic for other reasons? Regarding (a), a more neutral question such as "Are there treatments you do not want?" (rather than "What medical treatments do you not want?") also undermines a pre-existing bias by implicitly denying the assumption that all treatments are wanted. Perhaps that suffices to level the playing field without assuming that some treatments are not wanted. (Analogously, compare countering a lie with its denial rather than with an opposing lie.) With respect to (b), rather than being left in neutral territory when a new nudge is introduced to neutralize a pre-existing one, a patient may merely act in the light of the most recent nudge. (This is subject to empirical test.)

With regard to (c), imagine a conversation in which a professional asks a Conversation Project question "When would it be okay to shift from a focus on curative care to focus on comfort care alone?" and the patient responds "Why do you assume I even want to do that?" To be transparent, the professional should say (something like) "I don't assume it. I just said it to counteract a pre-existing bias toward treatment," thus confessing to dishonesty and manipulation (even if for a good end). Is this the basis for meaningful conversations or "rational dialogue concerning the patient's best interest" (as Wilkinson wants) in which doctors present their actual, non-skewed reasons supporting their favored position and can openly discuss existing social biases? Asking the more neutral question prevents this moral problem.

29. However, the procedure used in 2015's study raises a question about its own adherence to informed consent. Under the topic of "Ethics," it says that it has participants' informed consent to the study (12). But it also says: "We measure depression. . . . If the patient answers 'more than half the days' or 'nearly every day' to the question, 'Thoughts that you would be better off dead, or hurting yourself?'. . . we notify the patient's NP or physician" (12). Were patients informed before participating that their physician could be notified? I think they should have been.

30. https://www.ariadnelabs.org/2016/03/09/redesigned-serious-illness-conversation-guide-supports-more-better-and-earlier-conversations-about-what-matters-most/.

31. Dylan Thomas, "Do Not Go Gentle into That Good Night," *Dylan Thomas Selected Poems 1934–1952* (New Directions, 1952), 122.

32. I discuss the novella in F. M. Kamm, "Rescuing Ivan Ilych: How We Live and How We Die," reprinted in my *Bioethical Prescriptions* (Oxford University Press, 2013).

33. Beth Israel Hospital's *Know Your Options* leaflet for patients also says "working to ensure your comfort and dignity."

34. For discussion of different views of dignity, see Michael Rosen, *Dignity: Its History and Meaning* (Harvard University Press, 2012). (Henceforth, *Dignity*.) I discuss this further in Chapter 6.

35. Dr. Dominic Wilkinson emphasized this last point to me. Though the question of professionals' conscientious objection to helping someone act on a view with which they disagree may arise.

36. In his *Dignity* Michael Rosen discusses the case of dwarf throwing, thought to be an undignified treatment of a person, that a dwarf wants to participate in for salary. Rosen thinks it would be a denial of the dwarf's dignity as an autonomous person to make the sport illegal. However, I believe someone could still refuse to throw the dwarf on the grounds that she would be treating him in an undignified manner. She is here not only acting on her own autonomous choice but arguing for a view of dignity beyond respect for autonomous choices. She can do so without denying him his dignity as an autonomous person to seek to be thrown. This suggests that two different senses of dignity are at issue in this case.

37. Robert Truog in his response to *JME*, "Patient autonomy and professional expertise in decisions near the end of life: commentary on Francis Kamm," *Journal of Medical Ethics* 43 (2017), 587–588 says that doctors can first emphasize patients' preferences but end by advocating what they think are objective goods because when patients' views are not knowledgeable, doctors see a conflict between respect for autonomy and beneficence (seeking the patients' good). To this, I counterargue that this conflict most clearly leads to permissible interference in cases involving what is known as "soft paternalism" where there is no disagreement between patients and doctors about whether an end is valuable but only about what is a means to achieving it. This is like Mill's case of someone who wants to get to the other side of a river but does not know that the bridge is broken. We may interfere with his using the bridge because this use would not achieve what he wants and achieve what he does not want (drowning). The case Truog goes on to discuss is like Mill's case in that both parents and doctors want an easy death for a child but only the doctor knows that what the parents want to do will not get them the child's easy death they desire. By contrast, the cases I am discussing in EOLC involve different opinions about ends rather than means. For example, I have argued that the view that peacefulness and hospice support constitute a good death and is the EOL at which we should aim is not the only reasonable view. When there are multiple reasonable views, a professional should not be as concerned that his involvement in doing what a patient wants is wrong. (In addition, some of patients' lack of knowledge that Truog points to it could be avoided if they were required to be fully informed and not just given as much information as they prefer [as in 2015]). Dominic Wilkinson argues that despite there being reasonable disagreement about what way of dying is

best, we should agree that some ways of dying are bad. He gives the example of death by torture undertaken for its own sake and claims that "deaths that occur in the setting of high technology medicine appear dangerously close to 'death by torture.'" He says that doctors should not be neutral toward treatments at the end of life that (a) "lack benefit" and (b) "risk substantial suffering." (See his "What has philosophy got to do with it?") I agree that treatments that are known to lack benefit should not be used at any point in life, not merely at its end (with the possible exception of research with consent). But a treatment that risks substantial suffering is not the same as one that has substantial risk of (substantial) suffering. Presumably we would not want to exclude a treatment at the end of life that has a high probability of big benefit and only a small risk of substantial suffering. And if one possible benefit is extension of worthwhile life, then it is not necessarily true that it would be a treatment "at end of life." Then the question is what probability of success is worth risking a "bad end." Should one element in this calculation be that it is the very end per se that may involve suffering rather than any time before? Suppose a treatment aimed at extending life given six months before expected death would cause the same degree of suffering but if it failed, death in six months would be peaceful. Could this treatment be reasonable but the one that causes suffering at the very end not be reasonable? Distinguishing these risks may give too much weight to endings (an issue I discussed in Chapter 3 in connection with Gawande's views). Furthermore, if a bad end results from a reasonable but failed effort to extend or improve life, that bad end occurs in a different context and so has extrinsic properties different from Wilkinson's example of torture undertaken for its own sake.

An example Wilkinson gives of what doctors should oppose despite a patient's preferences involves a man who had spinal surgery when he was terminally ill then dying in the intensive care unit. Assuming the surgery would not extend life, perhaps he chose it because it might improve the quality of his remaining life. We cannot know this is unreasonable without knowing the chances of such improvement and how important that was to him by contrast to assuring a better end. Note also that if assisted suicide or euthanasia were legally permitted, more terminal patients could reasonably risk such procedures because they could more easily exit the "torture" of unsuccessful outcomes.

38. As Willhavehadism (discussed in Chapter 1) suggests.

39. As noted in Chapter 3, in her *How We Hope* Adrienne Martin goes further in arguing for the reasonableness of hope. She suggests that so long as one accepts facts about probability of success, it is a matter of practical reasonableness how one deals with it (e.g., one may choose to hope if this helps in the pursuit of other aims).

40. Some spiritual views involve belief in a soul that is oneself and continues on after death of one's body. Other spiritual views (e.g., Buddhism) deny that there is a continuing self either during life or after death. Rather during life there is a stream of experience had by no separate self and that stream ends with death. Some spiritual views claim that there is no continuing self but a merger among all selves. PEACE does not speak to whether those who think they have lived

meaningful and fulfilling lives find it easier to accept death independent of their degree of spirituality (though differences in attitudes ascribed to age at death may suggest that).

41. Amy Berman in Petrie-Flom/C-TAC video. https://vimeo.com/175399097#t=11m55s.

42. For more on this issue see Chapter 3, this volume.

43. Andrew Dreyfus at the Petrie Flom/C-TAC Conference discussed how his father ended his life when he felt he was "fading" by having someone use a computer program to deactivate his heart pacemaker. (See video at https://vimeo.com/175399098.) This is an interesting form of ending life support since it involves stopping something that has become part of someone's body. It is not clear that it differs from stopping any other internal organ necessary for life if this could be done in the same way. Hence, it comes close to killing someone not dependent on technological life support.

44. We discuss this issue in greater detail in Chapters 6, 7, and 8. My earlier discussions of assisted suicide are reprinted in my *Bioethical Prescriptions* (Oxford University Press, 2013).

45. See generally *Being Mortal: Medicine and What Matters in the End* (Henry Holt & Co., 2014).

46. Gawande, *Being Mortal*, 245.

47. I provide a more complete argument for this conclusion in Chapter 7 (based on an argument for PAS first presented in my "A Right to Death" in the *Boston Review* (1998) and in my "Four-Step Arguments for Physician-Assisted Suicide and Euthanasia" reprinted *in Bioethical Prescriptions*).

48. I am grateful to Dr. Lachlan Forrow for directing me to many of the documents I discuss and for his comments on an earlier draft. I thank Dr. Dominic Wilkinson, an anonymous reviewer for the *Journal of Medical Ethics*, and Professor Glenn Cohen and his students at the Harvard Law School seminar on bioethics for comments on an earlier draft. Work on the article on which this chapter is based was supported by the Petrie-Flom Center for Health Law Policy, Biotechnology, and Bioethics at Harvard Law School.

Chapter 5

Direction and Distribution in Life

Lessons from Benjamin Button

In the previous two chapters, we focused to a great degree on death for those with terminal illnesses. However, the first part of Atul Gawande's *Being Mortal* is also concerned with aging as a problem in its own right,[1] and (as we will see) some others have come to see death as a way to avoid the bad aspects of aging as much as the bad aspects of terminal illnesses. In this chapter, we begin the discussion of the relation between aging and death in a highly speculative way that might be relevant to deciding how to change the human species. We will return to consider this issue more realistically in the next chapters.

Section I

A. Old and aged

There are two senses to the phrase "aging" with which we will be concerned in this chapter: one deals with the quantity of life, the other with quality. I shall use the term "getting older" to signify adding years (or other units of time) to one's life and, assuming mortality and ordinary human life span, getting closer to death (the end of one's life). Being old contrasts with being young, which involves having had less time alive. In this sense, greater age just amounts to being older.

By contrast to "getting older," in this chapter I shall use the terms "aging" and "being aged" to signify distinctive characteristics of life stages rather than the years of life one has had. After a certain point, normal human development is associated with a distinctive decline in many good personal capacities without compensation for this in the development of other good capacities. This is how I use "being aged."

Almost Over. F. M. Kamm, Oxford University Press (2020) © Oxford University Press.
DOI: 10.1093/oso/9780190097158.001.0001

Prior to that point, aging involves (roughly) either an overall increase in, or a plateauing of, good capacities. In this chapter, I shall use "aging" and "aged" in this way even though hypothetically it is possible that there could be distinctive qualities to all stages of aging that involve differences but not increases or diminishments in capacities.[2]

Given such senses of "old," "getting older," "aged," and "aging," getting older need not necessarily imply aging. For example, in F. Scott Fitzgerald's story "The Curious Case of Benjamin Button,"[3] Benjamin is aged when he is very young and becomes less aged as he grows older until he reaches a high point, plateaus, and then declines as he becomes older though not in the way typical of humans. Rather, he declines to lack capacities in the way normal humans lack them in infancy. At that point he is close to death (as I call his unusual exit from life). Fitzgerald calls this process "un-growth."[4]

Thomas Nagel argued[5] that while both an (ordinary) old person and an (ordinary) infant may require a diaper, this is not a ground for pitying the infant as it would be for pitying the old person. The same might be true for the lack of certain good capacities in the ordinary infant by contrast to the same lack in the ordinary old person (e.g., not being able to speak a language). Nagel's view here seems to be that we should evaluate a state not only by its occurrent characteristics but by whether it is a decline from a better state or precedes a better state to come.[6] (However, individuals who would never outgrow needing a diaper and would always lack other good capacities typical of humans would also be pitied, so such states need not be pitiable merely because they are part of a decline.) If Nagel is right about the ordinary infant and old person, then we should also not pity the (young) aged Benjamin Button at the beginning of his life if he needed a diaper but we would have reason to pity his (old) infant self. Seeing two indistinguishable qualitative infants and two indistinguishable qualitative aged people, we would have reason to pity only the old infant and the old aged person, not the young infant and the young aged person. (This assumes that we know that the young aged person will ungrow in the way Benjamin does. It is a surprising aspect of the Fitzgerald story that Benjamin's father, on seeing his aged newborn, does not think the infant will soon be dead as would realistically occur. If he would soon be dead, the young aged Benjamin would be pitiable.)

B. Ungrowth and predictability of quality and quantity

Benjamin's ungrowth is presented as unique among the people in his family, society, and the entire world. Some of the problems he faces are due to this uniqueness. For example, his wife ages as she gets older, but as he gets older he becomes less aged and this creates problems in their relationship that would not exist if they were on the same trajectory.[7] It is like someone beginning in the east and driving west when everyone else begins in the west and drives east though all are headed to death on one coast or another. They are not merely going in different directions: the many are going where the one has already qualitatively been and the one is going where the many have qualitatively been. This means they could learn from each other (in the way that those who are going in the same direction but starting off later than others could learn from those with a head start). However, it is never mentioned that such learning occurs. Importantly, those going in opposite directions meet on somewhat equal terms at certain points. For example, Benjamin has much in common with his father while they are both qualitatively fifty though they have different quantitative ages: they intersect when Benjamin has lived only twenty years, decreasing age-wise from his (described) birth age of seventy, while his father has lived the full fifty years (as he was thirty when Benjamin was born and got twenty years older in the normal aging fashion). Similarly, when Benjamin is fifty years old but age-wise at twenty he has a lot in common with his own son who is twenty in both years and age. But, to use another metaphor, these people are like ships passing in the night for in the story there are no friendships that are described as surviving these "age meetings."[8]

If we factor out the bad things in his life due to his going against the grain and being alone in doing so, it may seem that Benjamin and an ordinary person represent two different distributions in life of the same good and bad experiences and capacities. It may also seem that the same graph that represents one life could represent the other life (as in Figure 5.1 below). In the ordinary person, the graph rises from infancy to full capacities and then declines to agedness and death; in Benjamin, the graph rises from being aged to full capacities and then declines to infancy and death.

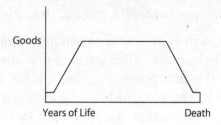

Figure 5.1

However, the background life each person brings to the identical point on the graph will be very different. When Benjamin and his father are "fifty" (in terms of years and qualitative characteristics for his father and qualitative characteristics alone for Benjamin), Benjamin only has life experience arising from twenty aged years whereas his father has life experience from fifty relatively youthful years. This could make the quality of experiences at their plateau different for each person. For example, Benjamin would have memories of having been slower as he becomes physically fitter in his prime. At the same point, his father (and other ordinary persons) would have memories of having been quicker and more energetic as a child and young adult. An aged old person (who is not demented) and Benjamin as an old child could both recall their plateaus of full competence. It might seem that in Benjamin's case, his (qualitatively speaking) young adult period should see him with an almost whole life of experience joined with a young person's physical strength. He would then be the answer to the wish that, "If youth but knew and age could do" (where "youth" is understood as non-aged and "age" is understood as many years of life).[9] He would know because he was old (in experience and years) but qualitatively had the capacities of youth. After a certain point at least, this is not how Fitzgerald represents things: he sees Benjamin as losing mental capacities as he ungrows (the college curriculum becomes harder and harder for him as he gets older and more childlike) so he may not retain all he has learned throughout his life.[10]

There are other problems with Figure 5.1. Not all aged old people "lose their minds" before dying, so they do not decline to the level of "mindlessness" (e.g., lacking language and understanding) that the beginning of normal infancy involves and that Fitzgerald describes as the end of Benjamin's life. And, indeed, Benjamin starts life as aged but mentally competent, and so he starts at a higher level than an ordinary early infant. Hence, in the case of both Benjamin and ordinary people, the graph at one end (aged, either young or old) might be qualitatively higher than at the other end (infancy, whether old or young). This seems to imply that Benjamin *must* decline to a lower functional point before death than that to which an ordinary person *must* decline (e.g., she might not be demented). This lower functional point would then certainly be Benjamin's near end period but only possibly the near end for ordinary old people. Some ordinary people who do face a certain decline to dementia before death arrange either to refuse life-extending care or for physician-assisted suicide. Given this, it would not be surprising if Benjamin, while still a competent adult and understanding the mindless near end that certainly awaits him, could in advance reasonably refuse life-extending care or seek assisted suicide for himself too before reaching infancy. If Benjamin's trajectory were typical for humans, child suicides or other willed deaths of children might not be unusual.

On the other hand, dying and death following Benjamin's infancy would probably involve less pain and suffering than some deaths after agedness in the old. Suppose pain and suffering were greater negatives than mindlessness following normal life. Then the lowest end point on the graph might be present only in the old aged and in neither Benjamin's aged beginning as represented in the story, nor in his qualitative infancy preceding death.

In general, it at least seems that there is more predictability in the qualitative character of the end of a life with Benjamin's trajectory and more variety possible in the end of an ordinary life. Most importantly, in terms of predictability, it might seem that a striking difference between Benjamin and the ordinary person is that if it is knowable at what age-stage Benjamin's life began, it should also be knowable what the limit of his entire life *must* be. That is, suppose that the qualitative stages of his life after its beginning are not imagined to last longer than they do in ordinary persons and the final stage of infancy (or through infancy to the point where the person Benjamin would disappear into a nonperson embryo lacking capacity for consciousness) cannot go on longer than it does now. Then it could be knowable by when Benjamin must end.[11] (Of course, there being this knowable limit does not mean Benjamin could not have died earlier at any point in his life from illness, accident, or suicide, and it does not mean that Benjamin must know his limit.) By contrast, being in an old aged phase does not seem to have as knowable a limit. It may not be knowable when one will get a terminal illness and whether a death predicted to occur within six months will occur. In Benjamin's case, infancy is like a terminal illness whose associated quality of life, time of arrival, and end point seem to be definitely knowable. So there seems to be a limit asymmetry.

In the story, Benjamin is represented as uncertain up to about thirty-five years whether he will continue to ungrow. He has some hope that by the time he has reached what he takes to be the halfway point in his life, he will start moving in the other direction. But this is consistent with (and indeed implies) that he must die in another thirty-five years (if thirty-five is his halfway point). He would then die as an aged person having traversed the same qualitative life stages in reverse that he has already experienced.[12] What if he had not assumed thirty-five was the halfway point, but only that he would re-verse direction after thirty-five years? Then he could think he would traverse most of the same life stages twice but might have a much longer life than seventy years if there was less certainty in the limit of an ordinary life than in an ungrowing one. This might be one of the attractions of this change in direction.

C. Limit lessons and the badness of death

In his classic article on death, Thomas Nagel says some things that may help us further evaluate the significance of someone knowing in advance the limit of his life. He said:[13]

> The question is whether we can regard as a misfortune any limita-
> tion, like mortality, that is normal to the species. Blindness or near-
> blindness is not a misfortune for a mole, nor would it be for a man,
> if that were the natural condition of the human race. The trouble is
> that life familiarizes us with the goods of which death deprives us. We
> are already able to appreciate them as a mole is not able to appreciate
> vision. . . . [T]he question remains whether death, no matter when it
> occurs, can be said to deprive its victim of what is in the relevant sense
> a possible continuation of life. . . . Observed from without, human
> beings . . . have a natural life span and cannot live much longer than
> a hundred years. . . . A man's sense of his own experience . . . does

not embody this idea of a natural limit. His existence defines for him an essentially open-ended possible future. . . . [H]e finds himself the subject of a life with an indeterminate and not essentially limited future. . . . If there is no limit to the amount of life that it would be good to have, then it may be that a bad end is in store for us all.

There are several things that seem odd about what Nagel says here. First, consider his claim that it is only because "life familiarizes us with the goods of which death deprives us" that death is bad for us. Suppose we all have only had a painful existence for sixty years and then die right before we would have experienced twenty years of bliss such that we had been unable to imagine. Then Nagel's claim implies that our death at sixty is not bad for us. However, in the same article Nagel's explanation of the badness of death is a version of Deprivationism: death is bad for us if, because, and to the extent that it deprives us of more goods of life. It seems clear that on the Deprivationist account of the badness of death, loss of a wonderful future would make our death bad for us. Familiarity with goods is not necessary for interference with getting them being bad for us.

Now consider Nagel's claim that it is because people have a subjective sense of an open-ended possible future for themselves that death is always bad for them if their future would be good. Suppose Benjamin knows all along he is moving from a known age at birth toward being an embryo and because of this knows by when he must end. Could his trajectory be compatible with his subjectively having the sense of an open-ended future in the way that Nagel thinks is typical of ordinary humans? If it isn't compatible, does that mean Benjamin's death is not bad for him? If it is compatible, is his death not bad for him because continuing to be an infant would not be a good future it would be bad to lose?

Let us consider the second question first. Nagel's concern as a Deprivationist is that more goods must be possible for us in order for us to be deprived of them. He accepts that if someone has a natural limit to his life in a scientific sense, goods that would come to him if he didn't have the natural limit are not as a scientific matter possible for him. This is consistent with it being bad that he has this natural limit. However, if only not getting naturally possible goods made death bad, death itself would not be bad for the person on the Deprivationist view if it happened at the natural limit. To make his Deprivationist account of the badness of death consistent with his view that death can be bad beyond the natural limit, Nagel shifts to the subjective experience of limitlessness (i.e., the subjective experience of the possibility of going on). If more life would be good to have and it would be possible to have it in this new, nonnaturalistic sense, not having it would be bad for a person.

Deprivationism may not be the correct account of the badness of death or at least not the whole story. For one thing, simply going out of existence as a conscious person might be bad for someone independent of his being deprived of (other) goods.[14] My concern now is whether the badness of death (whatever accounts for it) has anything to do with the subjective experience of limitlessness (i.e., being the "subject of a life with an indeterminate and not essentially limited future"). Nagel's focus on this experience seems like a peculiar and unsuccessful way to support a Deprivationist account of the badness of death. To see this, consider an analogy. Suppose there is no scientifically natural possibility of a person flying without mechanical assistance but he has the experience of not being limited in this way. That his actual inability to fly unaided interferes with the fulfillment of his subjective sense that it is possible for him to fly unaided is not what makes his inability to fly unaided bad for him. That badness is accounted for by its being good to fly unaided which he cannot have due to natural limitations. Further, consider an animal that has no sense of itself as not essentially limited in the future. Suppose it doesn't die young in an accident but at the very limit set by nature for its species. Would its death cause it to lose out on possible goods of life? Nagel would wonder in what sense there are possible goods of which it is deprived. Since it had no sense of itself as limitless, he seems committed to thinking its death is not bad for it. But it seems that if it would get things that are good for it if it could live on, then not living on is bad for it; and if its nature makes it unable to live on (by causing its death), this is a bad aspect for it of its nature. We might reasonably be motivated to change this aspect of its nature because we thought it would be good for it to live on and better for it than death.

Similarly if there are goods for a person that she could have if her nature allowed her to exist longer, then not existing longer is bad for her; and if her nature makes it impossible for her to exist longer, then this is one way in which her nature is bad for her. This is close to what Nagel himself claims in saying, "If there is no limit to the amount of life that it would be good to have, then it may be that a bad end is in store for us all." This claim seems to have nothing to do with his preceding claims about familiarity with goods or one's having a subjective sense of an unlimited future. (It also leaves it open that one's ending is bad for one even if this ending is not identical with death [e.g., time ends] and so it is not death that is bad for one.)[15]

At the very least then, even if Benjamin's knowing about his fate made it impossible for him to have a sense of himself as "not having an essentially limited future," this alone would not mean that death was not bad for him even according to Deprivationism.

Now return to the first question. Would Benjamin's knowing of his trajectory make him lack the subjective sense of limitlessness that Nagel thinks ordinary people have? Earlier we focused on the seeming determinateness of the end in a backward, by contrast to a forward, trajectory of human life. But a difference in trajectory alone does not necessarily imply this difference in determinateness and ground a possible difference in the subjective sense of indeterminateness. For suppose that each forward-trajectory, ordinary person came into life with a sign on him of his maximal expiration date. Then there would be as much determinateness as in Benjamin's life. If these people knew their maximal expiration date as much as Benjamin does, then we could ask of them too whether they could find themselves "the subject of a life with an indeterminate and not essentially limited future."

Nagel believes that knowing that one is a member of a species that cannot live much longer than a hundred years is consistent with the subjective sense of no time limit. So he may think that an individual knowing his definite expiration date is also consistent with it. But then why should Nagel not also think that the sense of limitlessness remains for someone who correctly believes he is on his deathbed? Perhaps what Nagel means by a sense of indeterminateness is merely that people sense about themselves (the truth) that it is not essential to one's personal identity that one not live longer than one actually will and indeed that one not live forever. For example, even in the realistic realm, science might succeed in extending individuals' species-specific expiration dates without this changing anyone's personal identity. It might be only the awareness that time of death is a nonessential property of a person that contributes to the sense of a limitless future. Indeed, in a discussion preceding the above quotes, Nagel says (8):

> Given an identifiable individual, countless possibilities for his continued existence are imaginable, and we can clearly conceive of what it would be for him to go on existing indefinitely. However inevitable it is that this will not come about, its possibility is still that of the continuation of a good for him, if life is the good we take it to be.

Why could Benjamin not also conceive of himself going on indefinitely in this way?

However, is scientific life extension for someone like Benjamin *conceptually* impossible in the way such an extension of a forward-trajectory life is not impossible? If there were this asymmetry in the scientific possibility of life extension, this would be a reason to think that the different trajectories per se, given knowledge of them by those whose trajectories they are, might give people different senses of the limits of their lives even if hypothetical extension was compatible with retaining personal identity.

I think the belief in the existence of this asymmetry is an illusion due to assigning a given age to Benjamin (seventy) at birth. For suppose science could reduce the amount of cell energy needed to survive and this would ordinarily, in forward-trajectory people, extend someone's life by ten years. Imagining such a physical possibility for Benjamin too tempts us to think that we couldn't say he was really aged seventy when he was born since he could last for eighty years. Alternatively, if we correctly said he was seventy at birth, there is no way he could live eighty years. What may mislead us into thinking that scientifically extending his life is impossible and his life has a determinate limit is thinking that we must not only hold the *age* assigned at birth constant but that this implies how *old* he will be when he dies. But later scientific research could, in retrospect, lead us to change how long he lives without changing his age as a *qualitative* matter assigned at birth. If his birth "age" refers to quality of life associated with ordinary people who have lived seventy years, then his age at birth would not need to change in retrospect simply because he lived eighty years, and his age at birth would not limit the number of years he could live.

But now we come to the third question: Could Benjamin conceive of the possibility of his going on limitlessly as being good for him? Only if he could conceive of his future life being good. For this to be true, perhaps he would also have to conceive that it is not essential to his personal identity that he is doomed to become an infant and beyond to an embryo after, for example, seventy years even if in fact this will certainly happen to him. For going on indefinitely as an infant or near-embryo does not seem like a good prospect. Could Benjamin also believe that it is a realistic possibility that science could not only extend his life but change its continuing quality? Why could not scientific research extend the period Benjamin spends in a qualitatively mentally mature stage before becoming an embryo? This would not be the same as his dying later but only involve retaining qualitative characteristics of an adult stage for a longer time.

Hence, though it may seem that there is a determinate limit of Benjamin's life as a conceptual matter and a determinate quality of his last stage, neither is true even if Fitzgerald's story suggests otherwise. This opens the way for Benjamin's death to be bad for him even on a certain Deprivationist view of the badness of death.

Section II

Realistic discussions of getting old and aging assume that one qualitatively ages as one adds years and becomes old. So these discussions also assume that the goods of life decrease and the bads increase when one is old (given our earlier assumptions about aging). Gawande emphasizes that many are subject to the illusion that they will continue on the plateau achieved in adulthood and from there drop down to death. By contrast, as we noted in Chapter 3, he says there is overall decline within life from the plateau though it can come by way of multiple declines that are only partially reversed.[16] We will here briefly speculate on alternative ways in which human life could proceed and what would be the best distribution of goods and bads in life.

A. Various distributions with control and known total of goods and bads

To begin, assume we know how long a life would last and what goods and bads for a person there would be to distribute. The best distribution would probably not be the one in either Figure 5.1 or in the modified version of this suggested by Gawande, with multiple declines and partial reversals after the high point. One suggestion for the best is that we should aim for an equal distribution of goods and bads over time periods so that old and young years are equally good. This implies that if for some reason we could not control one period having more bads than another, more goods could be distributed to the worse period in order to maintain equality of goods and bads in the different stages. Since there is a diversity of goods, if goods coming from creative activity will unavoidably be over (or not have begun) at a certain stage, more goods of a material or relational sort might be added to that stage if this would keep the level of goods the same with stages that have more creative activity.

Another suggestion is that we distribute goods and bads so that there is an incline from less overall good to more overall good. This moves life in accordance with rational change: don't move unless to a better position. Then the years before one's death (the oldest one would be) would be the best in one's life, all or most bad being behind one. If one includes as a good the expectation of better times that will come, there might be a limit on how bad the earlier bad times would be, though that could depend on how good in absolute terms the better times to come would be. Similarly, if there were memories of past bad times, that could put a limit on how good the good times could be.

If the best times were right before death, this might seem to make the ending of one's life particularly "senseless" since there would be no stage right before death so bad that death would be a reasonable move away from it. However, just as goods could be arranged in any given stage to compensate for bads in the same stage, one very good stage near death could be understood as compensation for a past or future bad stage or event. This would be diachronic rather than synchronic (partial) compensation, with compensation including goods that precede a bad. Hence, if death would deprive the person of life that would be good if it went on, then in an egalitarian spirit, we could understand inclining to an extremely good end of life as compensation for the coming loss. (This would be analogous to condemned prisoners getting a great meal before execution.) Thus, an egalitarian ethos could be consistent with the view that life should incline at least for some time before its very end so that the way life comes to end should compensate to some degree for its ending (even if its ending is bad for non-Deprivationist reasons).[17]

A third option is for the distribution of goods and bads to be on a decline, so all goods would be at the start with a decline to all bads at the end. If one includes as a bad the expectation of worse times that will definitely come, there might be a limit on how good the earlier good times would be though that could depend on how bad in absolute terms the worse times would be. If there were memories of past goods, that could also put a limit on how bad the forthcoming bad times could be. (Since we are here assuming a fixed number of years and a fixed set of goods and bads, the assurance that there will have been goods in one's life can be equally obtained whether one has the goods as soon as possible or later on an incline.) If one's decline would be to a level worse than death if life continued, this would make death a reasonable next step and not senseless. Further, since we here assume that a fixed set of goods present in the life will already have been had, we would not be deliberately reducing the set of goods in the period before death merely in order to make the move to death "more sensible."

Some complications for this decline proposal are that it is not possible to have many of the greatest goods of life early (e.g., one can't have creation of artistic beauty as a neonate) and that many goods require nongood means to precede them (e.g., hard work that is not intrinsically good but a mere means to achieve worthwhile things).

A fourth proposal for the best distribution of goods and bads aims to have a period in life in which all goods are maximal. For example, it favors there being a point where one has maximal physical, creative, and financial capacities. The aim here is to experience the best life has to offer which (it is thought) one cannot do if a set quantity of goods is distributed more evenly or even on inclines or declines. Aside from the problem that other periods of life will be barren of goods and may contain only bads, this option may be self-defeating. The idea behind it seems to be that a composite of diverse goods could contain (i) each good at its pinnacle and (ii) the composite simultaneously be at its pinnacle. But it may be that, for example, the highest exercise of creative capacities will leave one with little need for using extraordinary physical achievements or great riches (defeating [i]) and these may in fact interfere with reaching maximal creative achievement (defeating [ii]). It is only if, for example, great riches or physical achievements were necessary to enable creative achievements (or vice versa) that there would be no waste of goods or interference with goods that were otherwise possible.

B. Distribution without control and known total of goods and bads

There are many other possible distributions, given control over a known total of goods and bads for a person, that involve a mix of inclines, declines, and plateaus. Rather than examine these I will drop the artificial supposition that we have knowledge of how long we will live, how much good and bad there will be for us in our lives overall, and control over distribution of these over time. In circumstances of great uncertainty concerning these matters, it might be reasonable to take whatever goods one can get as soon as possible. This is because one may not live to have another chance at them (including no longer being capable of enjoying them). A problem for this proposal has already been mentioned: one can't have some of the greater goods very early in life and mere instrumental goods often have to precede goods valuable as ends. Also, taking only easy-to-get goods that do not require much preparation (e.g., sensual stimulation) as soon as possible might reduce the overall goods possible in one's life.

What if the probability (if not certainty) of long-term survival increases and the probability (if not certainty) of certain goods being accessible so long as we are alive increases? It then could become more reasonable to try to either distribute goods and bads equally, on an incline, or in some other way rather than taking what goods one can get as soon as possible. Further, since there is no given (and known) total amount of goods and bads to be distributed and no given (and known) length of life, it is important to consider how the distribution of goods could affect length of life and overall quantity and quality of goods to be distributed. For example, suppose equal distribution reduced the total quantity and quality of goods to be distributed. Then it might be better to have an unequal distribution that allowed for a better total. This is especially so if doing this increased the absolute level of goods and reduced the absolute level of bads of the worst period in a life over what would be present with an equal distribution. This is comparable to "incentivizing" some periods of life so that the worst periods may not be as bad in absolute terms even if there is more inequality between life stages. This is analogous to Rawls' allowing inequality due to incentives in a just social order in order to maximize the absolute position of the worst off people, a policy known as maximin. However, in a social order one is dealing with separate people, whose good may not justly be sacrificed for the greater good of others because the sacrifice in one person is not compensated when others benefit. By contrast, within a single life a much greater sacrifice of goods in one stage can be reasonable for the greater good of other stages given that the same person benefits as suffers and so he is compensated for his suffering.

Furthermore, suppose inclines are preferable to declines if total goods and bads in the life are held constant. This is consistent with living in a decline being better if the total level of goods is greater than in an incline and if the worst periods in a decline are much better in absolute terms than those in an inclining life. (For example, one might go from great riches to upper middle-class economic status on a decline by contrast to going from poverty to lower middle-class existence on an incline.) Note that when total goods and bads are not predetermined (or known), eliminating goods at the end of life so that death is not as bad by comparison, would interfere with increasing the total goods in one's life. Since a good ending period may also compensate for the bad of life ending, a "senseless" death that prevents more good life would be preferable to one that is a reasonable move from a life that is worse than death.

C. Character

Aside from having and doing good and bad for oneself, determining the best distribution of goods and bads in a life should take account of being a certain sort of person (having a good or bad character), and this may be the result of (and cause) the goods and bads in one's life. The earlier one has the things, whether good or bad, that make one a good type of person, the longer one could have to be that sort of person assuming it is not the sort of thing that has an expiration date within life. The later one has the goods or bads that could make one a bad type of person, the shorter the time one will have to be that sort of person, though if this too has no expiration date within life, one may end as a bad person. How long one will have been a good or bad person seems to matter more than what sort of person one ends up being.[18] The goods and bads of being a certain sort of person at different stages in one's life have to be added to the combination of the other goods and bads in one's life at that stage and to a decision about when to have the goods and bads that make one be a certain type of person. (The earlier discussion of goods and bads in life might have to be modified to take account of this factor.)

D. Deliberately ending life and quality/quantity tradeoffs

Knowing with certainty or high probability the upper limit of someone's time alive is consistent with his deciding to exit earlier. (To simplify, I shall here assume that there are not any moral barriers to such an exit.) The possibility of a self-chosen exit also bears on what is the best distribution of goods and bads in a life. For example, consider the significance for this issue of Bernard Williams' distinction between conditional and categorical desires that we have discussed in earlier chapters.[19] Suppose one could not leave life before its naturalistic upper limit. Then at least some goods one seeks to distribute are likely to be objects only of conditional desires, namely those desires one will have only *if* one will go on living. For example, if one will go on living, one will (and even reasonably should) desire money for living quarters. However, one could also reasonably desire that no stage lack things that could be objects of categorical desires. These are things that one desires (even reasonably) to continue living to get, not just things that one desires conditional on one's being alive. One could reasonably desire that there be some objects of categorical desires even though these things would not be needed to make one decide to go on living given that exit was not possible. This is because they would make the life one *had* to lead a life one would want to lead even if one had the option to exit. The goods of mere, even reasonable, conditional desires would not do this, and thus would diminish the worthwhileness of the period of life in which they dominate. However, if one is unalterably continuing in life, one might have to sacrifice acquiring at least some objects of categorical desires in order to ensure the objects of mere conditional desires. For example, one might have to save for expensive help in old age rather than spend the money on a world tour in one's prime.

By contrast, suppose one knew one could choose to exit before the limit. It might then make sense to give up on some period of life that would unavoidably have only objects that satisfy (even reasonable) conditional desires to provide to a greater extent for objects of (at least reasonable) categorical desires in other periods.[20] Of course, one might also move resources from a period in which there are more than enough objects to satisfy categorical desires to a later period in order to secure objects of categorical desires for that stage so that one would have no reason to exit from it.[21] Notice that the fact that one would seek objects for which one would have categorical desires at different stages of life suggests that there is a prior desire to go on living independent of the one that results from the need to go on living to attain objects of existing categorical desires. That is, if one is not indifferent between having and not having categorical desires, this could indicate a desire to go on living that is antecedent to categorical desires for particular things. This is something that Williams does not emphasize. It is also not captured by his recognition of a "brute desire to go on living" since it focuses on finding things to be objects of categorical desires, suggesting that without them there might not be a brute desire sufficient for going on.[22]

Let us consider in more detail a case in which one may exit life at will. Start by supposing that Benjamin had come into existence at sixty instead of seventy and died at three instead of as a neonate, holding constant qualitative age features of these (and in-between) years. How good would his life have been by comparison to his actual life in the story? How great is the loss of seventy–sixty and three–zero by comparison to any possible gains if resources that would have been used in those years were redistributed to the remaining parts of his life? This is a question about doing an intrapersonal tradeoff before the person actually exists (ex ante) between quantity and quality of life. It is comparable to intrapersonal tradeoff questions asked about quality and quantity of life of people already in existence such as, "How many years of life as a quadriplegic would you sacrifice to live life fully mobile?"[23] In Benjamin's case, it seems that loss of his aged (young) phase would be more significant for him than loss of his (old) infancy since the aged phase was not mindless and so had some intrinsic value and also had instrumental value in the acquisition of knowledge of use in later stages. This suggests that for someone with Benjamin's trajectory, losing three to zero by arranging for death at three in order to move resources to improving seventy to three could make sense. Though some redistributed resources could go to satisfy conditional desires that would exist between seventy and three, that period is also more likely to provide opportunity for goods that are objects of reasonable categorical desires. In addition, once Benjamin starts to live at age seventy he could not decide to lose all of seventy to sixty without dying at seventy, but he could end his life by three.

In the trajectory of ordinary human life, (young) infancy has greater instrumental value than the (old) aged phase. However, if the old aged phase is not mindless, it may have more intrinsic value than infancy. Hence in the case of the ordinary human trajectory, the intrinsic and instrumental values may point in different directions with respect to arranging ex ante to lose a phase in order to move resources to the sixty-to-three period. Since humans with the ordinary life trajectory can't have high quality of life from three to sixty without going through ages zero to three, there is no option to cut ages zero to three even ex ante. This all suggests that to move resources so as to maximize satisfaction of categorical goods, those on an ordinary trajectory would more likely choose to exit at age sixty, while those with Benjamin's trajectory would more likely choose to exit at age three—given a (defeasible) assumption about where more categorical and conditional goods are located temporally.

From what perspective are we best able to answer these intrapersonal tradeoff questions? We have assumed that we are best able to evaluate the goods and bads of different stages of life from an imagined point outside and prior to the life (this is the ex ante perspective) rather than from a point inside the ongoing life, unless the latter involved ignorance of one's current temporal location. For example, judging from within a life with knowledge of one's temporal location there may be a tendency to discount distant goods, sacrificing them for ones that will come much sooner. However, the view from outside will not capture the attitude expressed in the quip "Who would want to live to a hundred? Someone who is ninety-nine." This quip expresses the desire of a person not to be all over as a conscious person; it rates the value of another year at least partially in terms of the good of mere consciousness and self-consciousness in it but also, perhaps, in having a temporary buffer against being all over as a conscious person.[24] The question is how many greater goods possible only in a shorter life would it be reasonable to sacrifice to get the additional benefits of mere consciousness and self-consciousness for a longer time and putting off being all over as a conscious person?[25]

Notes

1. See his *Being Mortal: Medicine and What Matters in the End*, chapters 1-3.

2. On this use of "aging" it could apply to someone who ages from being immature to being mature. On yet another use of "aging" it would only apply when someone was approaching being "aged." The first use goes along with the idea of the "ages of man." On the second use, one could say someone was "getting aged" rather than aging (analogous to "getting old" versus getting older).

3. In F. Scott Fitzgerald, "The Curious Case of Benjamin Button," in *The Curious Case of Benjamin Button and Other Stories*, New York: Penguin Books, 2008, 318-342.

4. In some ways the story is reminiscent of Tolstoy's "The Death of Ivan Ilych." Ivan is an ordinary human who is dying. His condition is seen as a burden by his wife and children (with the exception of his son). Benjamin's unusual life-trajectory is seen as an embarrassment and burden by his wife and family (including his son). Ivan's wife chastises him for not doing what will make him recover, thinking incorrectly that this is under his control. Similarly, Benjamin's wife and son think Benjamin should start behaving properly and stop ungrowing before things get ridiculous, suggesting this is under his control. Ivan's exit is aided by a sympathetic servant (whose merit Ivan appreciates) and Benjamin's exit is aided by a caring infant's nurse (whose merit Benjamin cannot appreciate). I discussed Tolstoy's novella in my "Rescuing Ivan Ilych," reprinted in my *Bioethical Prescriptions* (Oxford University Press, 2013).

5. In "Death" in his *Mortal Questions* (Cambridge University Press, 1979).

6. Is it because an ordinary infant has occurrent neurological properties that ordinary old people lack giving it the potential for a better future that we should not pity it? Suppose an infant had no such properties and outside intervention caused it to predictably have a better future. We should still not pity it as we

would the ordinary old person who also lacked potential-giving properties but had no comparable future. This is an example within life of the Asymmetry Problem, Deprivation, Insult, and a good being All Over (discussed in Chapter 1).

7. It is not only that he objects at a certain point to having a wife who is aging but that she objects to having a husband who is becoming increasingly less aged.

8. In this respect the movie *The Curious Case of Benjamin Button* (2008) differs radically from the story. The female movie character played by Cate Blanchett has an ordinary life trajectory and yet she is a constant friend at points throughout Benjamin's life. Her affection takes appropriate forms over the years, starting as a child's affection for an aged man, sexual intimacy when they have lived equally long, and maternal-like love when he becomes a child.

9. He would also answer to the complaint that youth is wasted on the young since youth would be given to the old.

10. After his work life is over Benjamin goes to college, then to prep school and kindergarten. Interestingly, this part of his trajectory may overlap with those among today's adults who have to go to work before getting an education and in retirement go to school, not to prepare for a vocation, but merely to learn for its own sake.

11. One way indeterminacy could be introduced is by not being sure at what "age" Benjamin was born were it not settled by Fitzgerald in the story. One would have to decide on age by qualitative signs. If it were possible that Benjamin's qualitative characteristics of an ordinary seventy-year-old might appear, for example, in someone who actually had only fifty years to go before he completely ungrew, then it wouldn't be knowable what the limits of his life actually were. I shall ignore this possibility.

12. It is interesting that his hope to go in a normal direction with its prospect of having the types of goods he has already had outweighs the prospect of experiencing new types of goods in life stages between thirty-five and the end of infancy.

13. See "Death," 9.

14. See Chapter 1 on this.

15. Michael Rabenberg makes this point in his *Matters of Life and Death* (2018 dissertation, unpublished) and distinguishes different versions of Deprivationism on the basis of the alternative with which they compare one's actual death to determine what one is deprived of: (a) when one would actually otherwise have died; (b) the species-limit of one's life; (c) the metaphysically possible extension of one's life. Nagel compares one's actual death with the metaphysically possible extension of which one has a subjective awareness which differs from (a)–(c).

16. See his *Being Mortal*, 36-9. For a review of some scientific attempts to reduce aging as one gets older see the entire *MIT Technology Review* 122(5), 2019.

17. For the possible different grounds of the badness of death, see Chapter 1. Suppose one didn't independently know when one would die but knew the limit on how good any stage in one's life could be. Then on this inclining model when

having the best time in one's life, one could deduce that the next step would be death.

18. This is consistent with ending up a good person being more important than having been one earlier holding amount of time spent as a good person constant. For some discussion of the possible importance of how one's character ends up, see my "Rescuing Ivan Illych." See also Chapter 3, this volume.

19. We introduced this distinction in Chapter 1 and used it again in Chapters 3 and 4. There we noted that many would speak instead of conditional or categorical goods or at least reasonable desires of each type rather than merely desires.

20. This is an additional point that Ezekiel Emanuel might have made to support his argument for ending life at seventy-five (which we examine in Chapter 6). That is, if life will not go on beyond seventy-five, there is less need to deny oneself satisfaction of reasonable categorical desires before seventy-five in order to satisfy later merely conditional desires.

21. This could be one way to interpret those who emphasize having meaningful activities continue in old age and who see this as an alternative to exiting life because there are no meaningful activities. This option of moving meaningful activities into old age does not exist in the opinion of some (like Ezekiel Emanuel). They think that old age makes it very unlikely that one can achieve things worthy of being objects of categorical of desires. We will consider this view in Chapter 6.

22. I also discuss this in Chapter 6. However, wanting to have reasonable categorical desires could also indicate a desire that there be things possible in human life that are truly worth having and doing and that one can appreciate them, independent of whether these things are instrumentally useful in fulfilling a preexisting desire one has to go on living.

23. A more neutrally-phrased question would ask, "Are there any years of life as a quadriplegic you would sacrifice to live life fully mobile?" On the difference between neutral and nonneutral questions see Chapter 4.

24. That these are separate (possible) goods is shown by what I call the Limbo Man Case (described in Chapter 1). It is meant to show that going into a coma-like limbo state for a long period and then returning to conscious life would not increase (or decrease) one's time as a conscious person; it would only put off the end of oneself as a conscious person. Yet there might be a reason to go into limbo.

25. I am grateful for comments on an earlier version of this chapter to Richard Arneson, David Brink, Gila Sher, and the audience at the University of California San Diego Philosophy Department.

Chapter 6

Death Wish

Beyond End-of-Life Care

How bad is normal human aging? What are the problems it raises? Is death a good answer to these? This chapter continues the examination of views in Chapters 2 to 4 about when it could make sense to die. It focuses on these questions for people who are not terminally (or even seriously) ill (unlike the focus in Chapters 2 to 4) but are qualitatively aging (in the sense described in Chapter 5) as they get older. I take as an example of one type of view about this issue Ezekiel Emanuel (EE)'s position as expressed in his 2014 article, "Why I Hope to Die at 75" (henceforth, 2014).[1] I first outline EE's position, where to better understand his type of view (as held by him or others), I make use of the views of philosophers Susan Wolf and Bernard Williams. I then critically examine whether EE in particular successfully defends this type of view. I also compare what he says about aging, loss of capacities, and continuing in life with the views of Atul Gawande, B. J. Miller, and Douglas MacLean. Finally, I consider some possible implications of views like EE's for public and personal action as well as whether those who share this view should sometimes favor suicide, assisted suicide, or euthanasia. (In Chapter 4, I briefly considered this question with regard to those end-of-life care specialists who emphasize having a good life until death.)[2]

I. What Is EE Saying?

1. According to the title, EE hopes to die when he is 75.[3] However, according to EE the title was constructed by an editor over his objection,[4] so we should not see it as crucial to his position. What he

Almost Over. F. M. Kamm, Oxford University Press (2020) © Oxford University Press.
DOI: 10.1093/oso/9780190097158.001.0001

(tentatively) commits to is not using any procedures that would extend his life beyond 75 (or save his life at 75 so he can live on), even if these procedures are in themselves easy, unobjectionable, and certain to work, when the only reason for using them is that they would extend/save his life. However, he refuses to use suicide (S), physician-assisted suicide (PAS), or euthanasia (E) to have his life ended. (He agrees that 75 is an arbitrary number but thinks it is in the right ballpark for reasons we consider later in this chapter. I will continue to use it.)

EE also begins by saying (in the subtitle of 2014) that he will present "an argument" that everyone would be better off if people died at 75 (with the exception of some "outliers" who would not be better off if they died at 75). (Call this the Strong Position.) As such, the article presents an argument relevant to population-level bioethics rather than to clinical ethics; that is, it is about what all people (and hence society) should consider worthwhile and should do regarding lifespan rather than what is worthwhile merely for patients under medical care. He presents his view as a contrast to the ideal of what he calls "the American immortal" who is "obsessed" with exercise and diet and in "manic desperation" tries, he says, to "endlessly extend life."[5]

However, at the very end of his article EE weakens his claim and says that he is "not trying to convince anyone I'm right," which would be the point of the argument that he first said he would present. He seems to retreat to claiming that what he has been talking about in his article is only what he wants for himself and that others should merely consider it a not-unreasonable alternative to the view represented by the "American immortal." This implies that the considerations he lists in favor of his view would at least be an argument for it not being an unreasonable option (possibly for all or, even weaker, only for him). (Call this the Weak Position.) The Strong Position implies there is a decisive reason not to go on beyond 75 (unless one is an outlier), whereas the Weak Position implies there could be at least sufficient reason for some not to go on but there may also be sufficient reason to continue.

At 2014's end EE also says that he does not think that those who try to live beyond 75 are doing something morally wrong and he would support them in their choice. These last two points, however, could be consistent with the Strong Position that not living beyond 75 would be better for everyone, so long as (1) one does not have a moral obligation to always bring about what is better for everyone (a typical position among nonconsequentialist philosophers) or for one-self, and (2) one should support people's autonomous decisions to do even what is not prudentially best for themselves. (This is a form of nonpaternalism that goes beyond merely not interfering with their choices.)

Some philosophers (such as Bernard Williams and Ronald Dworkin) have distinguished between the "ethical" question of how best to live one's life and the "moral" question of respect for rights and obligations. EE says that ultimately he is concerned with how best to live one's life, a question that would arise even if there were no so-cial scarcity of resources and no moral concerns about how to allocate life-extending means. If so, in wanting the general population to at least be aware of an alternative to the "American immortal" view, he is presenting an argument for an alternative view about how best to live. If enough people sought out this alternative good life, this too could have implications at a population level for society (as he himself brings out).[6]

2. There are three reasons EE gives for the Strong Position: (A) having had a complete life by 75, (B) losses due to further life, (C) and bad effects on posterity of further life.

A. Complete life. EE says that by the time he is 75 he will have lived a "complete life" (e.g., "loved and been loved," "made whatever contributions he is going to make, important or not," and "had rich relations with his children and grandchildren"). By a "complete life" he does not mean that his life is already at an end or coming to an end anyway. Rather, he means a life that will have been an overall satisfac-tory human life if it ends at 75 and does not go on further. It is against the background of having lived a complete life in this sense that he argues that death at 75 would not be a "tragedy" and uses this to sup-port the wisdom of dying at 75. (Note that one might agree that death at that age would not be a tragedy without arguing for the wisdom of dying at 75, so these are two separate claims.)

B. Losses. EE says that death is bad because it involves the loss to us of everything we value. This is like one version of what is known as Deprivationism: death is bad for those who die if and because it deprives them of valuable things that they would have had if they had gone on living. As discussed in Chapter 1, this view is consistent with death involving nonexistence and containing no bad experiences for the person who dies; on this view if death is bad, it is by comparison to what one would have had if one had lived on.[7] (Death itself is to be distinguished from a possible period of dying leading up to it, as discussed in Chapters 3 and 4, which may or may not involve bad experiences.) However, in emphasizing that death is not a tragedy if one has had a complete life, EE seems to also be claiming that how bad death is does not depend only on how much one loses out on. It can vary with how much one will have had in one's life by the time of death. (This is like the view that I called Willhavehadism in Chapter 1.) It is unlike a Deprivationist view that how bad death is varies only with the degree to which it deprives us of further good things.

EE further argues that living on past 75 will also involve loss of things we value without adequate compensatory gains and hence involve a decline within life even though, he says, the life with these losses isn't (necessarily) worse than death. If we assign zero to nonexistence (for argument's sake assumed to be) involved in death, his view implies that it is possible for the post-75 years to be either at zero or have a positive value relative to zero (e.g., +20). One question this raises that EE does not explicitly discuss is why one should move (or not resist moving) from even a low positive number to zero. (If someone's life is at zero—that is, no better or worse than death for her—there might have to be some tie-breaking reason to make sense of her seeking death but not for her omitting to do what would keep her alive.) As we saw in Chapter 2, some (e.g., philosopher Shelly Kagan) suggest it makes no sense to end life (including refusing easy life-saving means) when life still provides some positive value relative to death. We discussed alternatives to this view (in Chapters 2 and 3), and I shall return to this issue later in connection with a view such as EE holds.[8]

EE describes two general types of losses within life: The first type of loss involves physical disability, dementia, and other chronic illnesses which eventually lead to death and which, he believes, therefore involve "an extended dying process." Call this Disastrous Loss. He thinks that medical science recently has mostly lengthened life by keeping people alive longer in such extended dying. His way of characterizing the entire period involving these types of losses contrasts with an approach that distinguishes (a) conditions that require advanced care (AC) and that may in several years' time lead to death from (b) the same conditions when they have advanced enough so that a person is expected to soon die (e.g., within a year) and needs end-of-life care (EOLC).[9] On this alternative view, which we considered in Chapter 4, merely because a condition will lead to one's death does not mean that living with it for many years involves undergoing an extended dying process. It only involves living with what will eventually lead to a dying process when EOLC might begin. While this seems a reasonable alternative, it is not EE's view.

The second type of loss involves ordinary mental and physical decline (e.g., hearing loss, reduced creativity) that requires us to accommodate to restricted capacities and expectations. Call this second type of loss Diminishment Loss. EE first notes that these losses limit the "vibrant," "vital," and "vigorous" (terms he often uses)[10] activities that earlier made someone a creative contributor to a profession and an important member of a community. He points to scientific research that identifies age 45 as the beginning of such decline from a peak. He agrees that even with Diminishment Loss it is possible to mentor others, have avocations (e.g., pottery, reading, doing puzzles), and for one to be happy with a "slower" and "sluggish" way of life. (Indeed, he describes his father as living such a slower life after a heart attack and being happy.) EE considers the view that avocations might be valuable aspects of life even if they are a decline from creative contributions made at one's peak. In response, he emphasizes that avocations just show that we accommodate to restricted capacities; someone who does puzzles or reads most of the time has reduced expectations for his life by contrast to what he did at his peak.[11] EE finds the prospect of these accommodations to restricted capacities "unappealing."

EE emphasizes that even if many of those past 75 avoid Disastrous Loss for a long time almost everyone (except some "outliers") will have Diminishment Loss. He also emphasizes that Diminishment Loss in the absence of Disastrous Loss is sufficient (presumably absent countervailing considerations) to justify people not going on after 75. On the Strong Position it provides decisive reason for everyone not to go on after 75, and on the Weak Position it provides at least sufficient reason for some not to go on.

This emphasis on Diminishment Loss is important, in part, because at the very end of his article EE points to a different reason to think it would be good to die at 75 that he has not previously mentioned in the article: "to avoid the physical pain of elongated dying."[12] While he characterized Disastrous Loss as "extended dying," it's surprising that he says elongated dying causes physical pain. This is because he says that he would accept palliative care if he happened to live beyond 75 and this would, I surmise, mostly eliminate physical pain. One reason he may conclude 2014 with "to avoid the physical pain of elongated dying" is that, at least in the past, surveys have shown that the general public does not see Diminishment Loss (or being a burden on others) as justification for PAS or E. They see relief of irremediable physical pain as alone able to justify PAS or E.[13] Hence, EE may ultimately point to avoiding physical pain as the reason not to go on living because he thinks that the public would also reject his view that avoiding Diminishment Loss on its own justifies refusing easy life-saving means after 75. This is consistent with the public thinking there is a right not to use even easy life-extending treatment and wrong to require people to use such treatment. One may sometimes have a right to do an ethically or morally wrong act (e.g., if one engages in racist free speech).

C. Posterity. EE considers whether connecting with posterity (e.g., one's children and grandchildren) makes life worth living beyond 75. He claims such connection is worth having up to a certain point but not beyond 75 because: (i) One can become a burden to posterity (consuming more than one contributes and requiring aid from one's children); (ii) One continues to "shadow" one's children with expectations for them that intrude on their independence (he thinks that it is only when their parents are dead that children can really live their own lives); (iii) So long as their parents live, children can never really be the heads of families; (iv) One wants to be remembered by posterity as "vibrant, engaged, funny, astute," not as stooped and hard of hearing. He thinks the "real tragedy" is not death at 75[14] but leaving loved ones with final memories of oneself with various infirmities.[15]

EE goes on to describe what he thinks are further implications of these views for personal action and public policy. I shall present and discuss them in Section V.

II. Why Avoid a Future Not Worse Than Death?

To begin considering whether the reasons why EE prefers to die at 75 support the Strong and/or Weak Positions, consider whether they help deal with the seeming puzzle mentioned in I.2.B, namely that EE prefers to die even when the losses imposed on him by future life will not be greater than those imposed by death and his future life would not be worse than death (i.e., it would not have a negative value relative to zero). We discussed this type of view first in Chapter 2. Here we will mine the claims of some philosophers for help in further understanding and evaluating this type of view, whether held by Emanuel or merely as a possible view that could be held by others.

1. Life overall. This view might appear less puzzling if it were possible for a positive future to make one's life overall worse than if it had ended at 75.[16] The degree to which a decline relative to one's past life might make one's life overall worse could outweigh any additional goods post-75. For example, suppose that having lived a sophisticated and productive life until 75, after 75 one was demented but getting pleasure caused by artificial neural stimulation. It may be that one would have had a better life if one had died at 75. This is consistent with a version of Deprivationism according to which death is bad only when it deprives one of time alive that would have made one's life better overall. In this version, death is good when it deprives one of time alive that would have made one's life worse overall. In this case, going on is not necessarily worse than death in terms of the future alone, but it is worse than death in the sense that the zero of death does not diminish the value of one's life overall, whereas continuing on would.[17] Though EE does not explicitly say so, taking this perspective of what one's whole life will look like may lie behind and best explain many of his particular views.

As we have already seen (in Chapter 2), this perspective might be said to go along with a certain approach to the distinction between "me" and "my life overall."[18] For I may be doing acceptably during additional time alive, while my life overall may actually be getting worse because of this additional time alive. For example, the end continues to involve achievements and nonillusory happiness on balance but represents a decline from my past and so makes my whole life less uniformly exemplary. This life overall perspective is also exhibited in the view that a life is like a novel or story. An ending of a novel can be good but not as good as the brilliant parts that went before, and so it might be a better novel without the last merely good chapter. The question is whether it is correct to treat a person's life like a novel or story.[19] (We shall return to this issue later.)

2. *Worse than death.* A second approach to eliminating the appearance of a puzzle accepts that one's future life could be worse than death even if losses involved in declining years will not be as great as losses involved in death. (EE seems to accept the contrary view since he says that one's life need not be worse than death after he points out that the losses involved in living on may be less than those due to death.) For example, it may be worse than death for a once-rational person to be demented even though she can still exercise the capacities (that would be lost in death) to understand a few words, enjoy peanut butter and jelly sandwiches, and be in a good mood.[20] This period may be worse than death because (a) dementia is a perversion of thought that one would live through whereas the loss of thought due to death is not a perversion but a cessation and (b) retaining some other capacities that would also be lost in death does not compensate for the perversion.

3. *Interpersonally worse than death.* It might be suggested that a third way to eliminate the appearance of a puzzle is to compare intra- and interpersonal effects. That is, suppose living past 75 would not make one's future life worse than death or one's life overall worse in a narrowly self-interested way. It could still make the lives of relevant others worse than they would otherwise be to a degree greater than any benefits one accrues. Continuing in life would not be worse than death intrapersonally, but that life in combination with the harm done to others could be worse than one's death. However, eliminating the appearance of a puzzle in this way is not compatible with the Strong Position, which claims that it would be better for *everyone* if people died at 75 and this should include the person who would die (i.e., be intrapersonally better).

4. *Dignity.* A fourth possible way of dealing with the apparent puzzle is that even though one's future life would not be worse than death for one it would still be better if one were to die because "better" is understood in virtue-laden terms. Someone might argue that he morally must reject a certain end of life as a condition unworthy of him as a person and so sacrifice what would still be "good *for* him" (and even good for his life overall) in order to act in accordance with the "good

of him" (e.g., a person worthy of only respectful conditions).[21] It could then be true that it would be better of him to refuse more goods for himself. Similarly, one might turn down a monetary offer that is Pareto optimal (everyone is better off due to it than they would otherwise have been) because it is exploitative and so treats one in an inappropriate manner. Though EE says he does not think that nonoutliers who choose to live beyond 75 do anything morally wrong, this is consistent with it being "better of them" to die, designating ethically superior conduct.

This view may be related to the idea that at a certain point only death is consistent with the "dignity of the person" because it is the only way to escape states that are inconsistent with that dignity. Such states need not make the dignity of the person disappear but they treat inappropriately someone who retains the dignity of a person. Jeremy Waldron has argued[22] that in one sense retaining one's dignity has to do with being capable of certain achievements worthy of respect (e.g., retaining one's calm in the face of bad news). In this sense, one may lose one's dignity when one is not capable of the achievement. However, he argues, in another sense of dignity one retains one's inherent dignity as a person no matter what one's capacities for achievements are and even if one is not treated in accord with one's dignity (e.g., one is treated in a manner intended to humiliate). In this sense, dignity is what I have elsewhere referred to as a status; it implies (roughly) how it is permissible or appropriate to treat someone, and one retains that status even if one is actually treated impermissibly or inappropriately.[23] Nevertheless, even if nothing that actually happens undermines one's dignity as a status (and so one need not die to preserve one's dignity as a status), certain natural states or ways in which one is treated can be states one should not be in or ways one should not be treated given one's status. One might need to die to avoid those states or treatment. When people say they must die to retain their dignity, they can be understood to say either that they can no longer engage in achievements worthy of respect or (more likely) that the conditions in which they would live on do not befit the inherent dignity they retain. When the latter occurs, life might not be worse for them than death and yet it might not befit them to go on living.

5. *Meaning in life.* Another possible way to eliminate the appearance of a puzzle focuses on the necessity of "meaning in life" if one is to

go on (on the Strong Position) or the sufficiency of its absence for not going on (on the Weak Position). Meaning in life could be important independently of whether its absence affects the goodness of one's life overall or makes one's future life worse than death for one. It can be related to the concern with dignity insofar as one thinks that continuing in a life that lacks meaning might be unworthy of a being with human dignity. Further, an important aspect of EE's support for the Strong (and even Weak) Position is that he seems to think that there can be an objective evaluation of the worthwhileness of activities. Feeling happy or fulfilled[24] in an experiential sense with an activity is not sufficient to show that the activity is worthwhile; one could have these feelings due to or about something that was not objectively worth either being happy about or feeling fulfilled in doing. (This is probably what is behind his rejection of living on as a happy pig.) The claim that only a life with pursuits of sufficient objective worth can provide meaning in one's life and give one a reason to go on living resonates with EE's view. It is the focus on the objective worth of what gives one happiness that seems to distinguish EE's position from Gawande's about retaining meaning in life. (In Chapter 3, we considered Gawande's view of meaning in life as merely a particular type of pleasure. We will consider a different view of his further in this chapter.) While some might criticize this emphasis on objective worth of activities as judgmental, many philosophers will find it attractive because of its concern with what is truly valuable versus what merely seems valuable.

Furthermore, though happiness itself is often thought to be objectively valuable, it may not suffice to make an otherwise worthless activity that gives rise to it worth engaging in; the happiness itself may then fail to be objectively valuable since it is in response to something bad or worthless. A classic example is getting happiness from even the false belief that someone is being tortured. In any case, EE does not think that happiness like his elderly father's is a good sufficient to make it worth extending one's life.

A. Susan Wolf. In several respects Wolf's view of meaning in life seems to connect with this understanding of EE's views. She considers a Fulfilled Sisyphus[25] whose feelings of fulfillment come from rolling his rock endlessly up a hill from which it always falls again. Wolf suggests that finding happiness or fulfillment in such a worthless activity, even accompanied by the false belief that it is valuable, cannot provide meaning in life; it might even be worse than engaging in the activity while recognizing it as truly worthless and without positive feelings. EE might likewise have more respect for someone who, though "condemned" to make pottery or do puzzles (rather than roll a rock), would not feel happy or fulfilled by that avocation if it did not merit happiness or fulfillment.

Wolf argues that having meaning in life involves (i) being attracted to and (ii) positively engaging with what one (iii) correctly believes is something (iv) objectively valuable and outside of oneself.[26] (The attraction and positive engagement may not involve happiness; distress and concern can be involved in fulfillment found in dealing with an objective good.) On her view, engaging in a valuable activity without being attracted to it, even while believing it is valuable, also does not suffice for having meaning in life. Therefore, she says, her view is one in which subjective response meets objective value giving rise to "fitting fulfillment."[27]

It may be helpful to think of the concerns of EE and others about going on after 75 even when life is not worse than death as connected with whether there is still meaning in one's life in Wolf's sense. In EE's case in particular, this is because he rejects going on in life to do activities to which he is not attracted and that (he thinks) lack sufficient objective worth. However, Wolf accepts that not everyone is (or need be) attracted to the same things among those worthy of attraction (the objective goods). This implies that different people can find meaning in different things without thereby making a mistake. Hence, the things EE finds "unappealing" (e.g., reading all the time) could have sufficient objective worth to support meaning in life and others might not be making a mistake in being attracted to them, even while he may not be making a mistake in not being attracted to them. On the other hand, her view also implies that EE's finding certain activities unappealing is important because, according to Wolf, engaging in worthwhile pursuits without finding them appealing is not enough for having meaning in one's life.

It might be said that the fact that someone now, as a person much younger than 75, finds activities he thinks will be available to him after 75 unappealing does not show that he will find them unappealing after 75. This may be true, but the fact that he would later find them appealing also does not show that they have sufficient objective worth to provide meaning in life. Indeed, EE's support for the Strong Position suggests that he believes that he now finds the post-75 activities unappealing because he now correctly sees that they lack objective worth; later he may find them appealing because he will merely accommodate to reduced capacities and even attribute objective value to what really lacks it. Judgments now about the objective worth of later activities and the worth of later happiness from them could be correct even if they are made before one finds the activities appealing. This is an implication of these judgments being part of a theory of objective worth. However, if something can be objectively good even if it doesn't appeal to everyone, that post-75 activities lack worth is not the only possible explanation of EE's now finding them unappealing. If they were sufficiently worthwhile, his finding them appealing in the future could give him a reason to go on past 75.

One suggestion Wolf offers about the possible source of objective values might put her at odds with Emanuel. She originally locates value in the properties had by the object of one's attraction and positive engagement. However, in responding to Nomy Arpaly's commentary,[28] she hypothesizes that even when something is not in itself valuable (e.g., throwing a ball through a hoop), "it can provide an opportunity for much that is of value . . . cultivation and exercise of skill and virtue, . . . building of relationships, . . . value emerged from the interests and commitments of people . . . who agreed to . . . structures . . . just for fun or challenge" (129). She even gives as an example doing puzzles, the activity that most irritates Emanuel. She thinks it can go from being "a solitary daily ritual" (and, as such, a mere harmless pleasure) (130) to having objective value when done at a high level of achievement with others of comparable skill. She further suggests that the exercise of whatever capacities one has to their highest extent and the opportunity this gives for interacting with others may create objective value. So a normal adult who would exercise very few of her intellectual and social capacities in building her life around care of a goldfish would, on this view, not thereby have meaning in her life, but an intellectually disabled child who exercised his capacities to the fullest in building his life around care of a goldfish could get meaning in his life from this.[29]

A problematic implication of Wolf's revised view is that a person with great capacities exercising them to the highest degree in activities that have objective value in themselves and to which she is attracted, correctly believing them to be of great objective value, could have the same degree of meaning in her life as the aforementioned disabled child or as an aged adult whose capacities have declined to the level of the disabled child's and who exercises them to their limit, for example, in the care of a goldfish. But this last type of life is exactly the sort that EE would reject on the ground that one is then only capable of interacting positively with an object of low objective worth (i.e., care of a goldfish). The danger in Wolf's response that relativizes objective value to an individual's capacities is that it gives us no explanation, at least in terms of meaning in life, of why we should want to have greater capacities so that we can positively engage in pursuits that have greater objective value in themselves. Wolf says (108–9) that she is not concerned with ranking degrees of meaning in life, for example, on the basis of greater or lesser objective worth of the object to which one is attracted and with which one positively engages so long as there is some objective value present. But then the concept of meaning in life in her sense may not capture another aspect of what we (and Emanuel) want in life—greater capacities that allow us to positively engage in more valuable ways with objects (including activities) of greater value.

B. *Bernard Williams.* Revisiting a view of Williams' can further clarify the "meaning in life" answer to the seeming puzzle of preferring death to a life that is not worse than death. As already noted in earlier Chapters (1, 3, 4, and 5), Williams described two types of desires in life, the conditional and the categorical. Conditional desires are those whose satisfaction one would pursue *if* one were staying alive; for example, given that one remains alive, one would pursue alleviating one's pain or boredom. Categorical desires are those that one would stay alive in order to satisfy; they are not merely conditional on one's staying alive but rather give one a reason to stay alive. It would be odd for someone to stay alive merely in order to pursue alleviating his own pain or boredom.[30] Hence, these ends are not the objects of categorical desires. The use of "categorical" to modify desire may be misleading; Kant uses the term to denote things one must do under all conditions and so the term seems to suggest that one *must* have a certain desire and stay alive under all conditions to satisfy it. Williams does not mean that categorical desires are ones that must be had, but merely that if one is to decide to go on living, when the issue of whether to do so arises for one, there must be some desires that one does not have merely because one will remain alive. In that sense, they are not conditional on being alive. (Of course, if it were a given that one will soon die, categorical desires one had would not be satisfied.)[31]

Since the only means that EE is willing to use to help himself die at 75 may not always result in his dying then (e.g., he may not need life-saving treatments that he can refuse), there are certain desires he may have *if* he lives on longer. For example, rather than be completely bored he would no doubt engage in avocations, and he says that he would use pain-relieving drugs. Furthermore, he hopes that medicine will eliminate Disastrous Losses (e.g., dementia) and this would also benefit him if he lives on past 75. Some of these things would help make life be not worse than death, and yet as objects of conditional desires they need not be sufficient to ground a desire to go on living to get them.[32]

While Williams speaks in terms of desires, one might transfer his distinction to goods per se and also take the goods to give one reasons to pursue and desire them. So conditional goods would be ones that would reasonably be the objects of conditional desires and categorical goods would be those that could reasonably be the objects of categorical desires. One could then claim that there are categorical goods that give one at least a sufficient reason to stay alive to get them. Other goods are merely conditional goods that give one no such sufficient reason to stay alive to get them even though they are objective goods (e.g., no pain and low levels of pleasurable sensations). Hence, being an objective good to which someone is reasonably attracted is not sufficient (even if it is necessary) to make it be the object of a reasonable categorical desire.[33] Williams himself did not hold that there are objective reasons completely independent of one's actual "motivational set" (which includes desires) to come to have desires. However, the model of objective categorical goods fits with Wolf's and EE's views, that there can be objectively correct answers about which things are worth desiring so that they can provide meaning in life and reasons to go on living. Yet since Wolf and (it seems) EE focus not only on objective worth but on personal attraction to what has objective worth, the role of desire would not be completely eliminated as it would be in a theory that focused only on the objective worth of one's life independently of whether one desired to go on living it.

Suppose one holds that going on in life requires that there be possible objects of categorical desires and (even) that only things having objective value can be such objects. This still need not imply that only things that can provide meaning in life can be objects of categorical desires. Wolf herself says that "getting pleasure from an activity is a perfectly good reason for engaging in it" (126) and "in a multifaceted life, not every activity need contribute to meaning . . . in order for a commitment to it to be justified" (127). "Multifaceted" may suggest that when merely pleasant activities are temporarily interspersed among projects that provide meaning in life, engaging in them is all right, but it is the awareness of the projects that will follow that provides the objects of categorical desires and reasons to go on living a life. Figure 6.1, where M = meaning in life, P = mere pleasurable activity,[34] represents such a life.

But the view that "harmless" pleasures could be worth pursuing might also open the way for a concluding period of life involving only sufficiently pleasurable activities grounding categorical desires without their being followed by projects that could give meaning in life. Such a life is represented in Figure 6.2.

EE, however, seems to seek more than the life in Figure 6.2 (given his rejection of his father's happy "sluggish" life).[35] So support of his Strong Position may require claims that (1) objects of categorical desires must be things that give meaning in life and (2) there will be no such things for anyone (except outliers) past 75. Support for the Weak Position would hold that it is not unreasonable for someone (1) to require that all objects of categorical desires provide meaning in his life and (2) to judge that he will lack such objects past 75. On these views, happiness from activities may not

Life $\underline{M \quad P \quad M \quad P \quad M \quad P...}$
$ t_1 \quad t_2 \quad t_3 \quad t_4 \quad t_5 \quad t_6$

Figure 6.1

Life $\underline{M \quad M \quad M \quad P \quad P \quad P...}$
$ t_1 \quad t_2 \quad t_3 \quad t_4 \quad t_5 \quad t_6$

Figure 6.2

meet the threshold required of goods that provide reasons to go on living (categorical reasons), even if happiness has positive objective value (unlike the mere absence of an objective bad, like pain) and is worth having if one lives on. Table 6.1 shows some distinctions among objective (O), nonobjective (N), categorical (Ca), and conditional (Co) goods, and their possible combinations that we have been discussing.

Suppose having meaning in life is sufficient but not necessary to ground a reasonable categorical desire. Is having a meaningful life, which involves objective goods that are not "appealing" to a person or whose objective worth he does not recognize (such as discussed in endnote 27) similarly sufficient to support a reasonable categorical desire in the absence of meaning in life? Consider the following hypothetical: Someone who cares about producing great art is told that if he comes to believe the art he produces is not worthwhile, he will actually produce greater art. If he cares about producing great art and not about having meaning in his life, he will accept such a life. Arguably, such a person still has a meaningful life, though not meaning in life as he lives it (a contrast discussed in endnote 27). At the decision point, he would not exchange the meaningful life for a life which is less meaningful because he produces less good (but still worthwhile) art. This is so even if he would correctly believe in the worth of the less good artwork, be fulfilled by it, and so have meaning in his life (had as he lives it).[36] At that decision point having the (more) meaningful life can be the object of a categorical desire. Nevertheless, it is hard to see how the artist in this case could have a categorical desire to continue on in life beyond the decision point if great art is all he cares about. This is because he would have no desire to produce what he would think (beyond the decision point) is worthless art. This is so even though objectively there is a categorical reason for him to live on (i.e., to produce great art). If he had moral objections to suicide,

Table 6.1 Goods

	Nonobjective (N)	Objective (O)
Conditional (Co)	NCo	OC
Categorical (Ca)	NCa	OCa

others prevented his death, or other duties kept him going, he would remain alive. But others might have to force him to work since he would not get any incentive from producing the art itself in the case where he thinks it is worthless and for this reason finds creating it unappealing. While having the most meaningful life can be inconsistent with having meaning in life, it is unlikely that one will achieve the most meaningful life without at least categorical desires of some sort during one's life which the mere meaningfulness of one's life may not provide.

In sum, according to approach (5) it sometimes makes sense to end life that is not worse than death because it is not unreasonable to think that (a) Diminishment Losses endured post-75 will mean that there are no more pursuits to which someone (not an outlier) could be attracted that are objectively good enough to be the source of meaning in life (or meaningfulness of life) and (b) only such goods can provide reasons for going on in life that ground categorical desires. This is so even if conditional goods still make life not worse than death, and unavoidably having to continue in life gives one a reason to seek these conditional goods.

III. Some Comparisons

We have considered whether the reasons EE gives for preferring to die at 75 suggest the reasonableness of dying when life will not be worse for someone than death. Let us now compare the views about values and reasons for going on in life that I argued might ground views like EE's with some other views that have received much attention in public media. This will also allow us to reconsider an aspect of Williams' views.

1. *Gawande*. The view of meaningful activities and meaning in life that involves objective evaluation of goods contrasts with an experientialist view of meaningful activities and meaning in life that Atul Gawande presents in discussing the dying stage of life in his *Being Mortal*. As we saw in Chapter 3, in that discussion Gawande says that meaningful activities are ones that give us a particular sort of pleasure, and he also says we are willing to suffer even greatly to get a small amount of that pleasure. This experientialist view does

not critically examine what gives rise to the pleasure; it attributes importance only to an effect on one's mental state independently of the objective value of what gives rise to the pleasure. It also could ignore intentionality; that is, whether the pleasure comes from appreciating or engaging with something. To illustrate this point, suppose someone is in a vegetative state. There would be a difference between causing him to have pleasurable sensations and making it possible for him to get pleasure from thinking or doing something again. Holding amounts of pleasure constant, it is the latter way of getting pleasure that seems like a distinctively important route to improving the person's life.

Nevertheless in the section of *Being Mortal* devoted to aging (rather than dying) what Gawande says makes it seem as though he agrees with points made by EE and Wolf. For example, Gawande agrees with EE that decline in capacities is inevitable in aging, a reality most people do not acknowledge (36-7), and he emphasizes the importance of continuing to find meaning in old age even at the expense of security and safety. Furthermore, he cites with approval Josiah Royce's view (in his *Philosophy of Loyalty*)[37] that in focusing on things outside of oneself and ascribing value to them so they are worth making sacrifices for, we give our lives meaning. However, at least as Gawande presents Royce's view, it is unlike Wolf's original view both in not emphasizing that we be *attracted* to the valuable thing outside ourself on which we focus and in not requiring that we be *correct* in ascribing value to it because it really is valuable. Hence, to the extent that Gawande accepts such a "Roycean" view, he could hold that meaning in life requires focus on something that is objectively outside oneself (not something one merely believes to be, or experiences as, outside oneself) and still be an experientialist insofar as it is enough to believe that the object has value even if one is mistaken. Wolf and EE would not be satisfied with this.

At one point (127) Gawande adds to what he sees as Royce's conditions that the object outside of oneself on which one focuses should be "something greater" than oneself (e.g., a family, a community, a society of which one is a part). He says this is "the only way death is not meaningless" and it is not true that "mortality is only a horror." The contrast to valuing such greater objects is, he thinks, valuing only oneself. He may think that if one values only oneself, everything one values ends when one dies and this is a "horror."

Such a horror will not occur if what one values survives one's death. However, Wolf points out that one's life can have meaning in it if one cares only about one other person besides oneself and the person need not be or be thought to be greater than oneself. I would add that such a person need not even survive one. For example, if the person who makes there be meaning in one's life lives only so long as one does, the entire length of one's life will have meaning in it. In addition, insofar as one's own expected survival provided meaning in another person's life, fulfilling their past hopes by staying alive can provide meaning in one's life, as does keeping a memory of them alive. None of these sources of meaning in life require a focus on things that survive one.

The examples Gawande himself gives of things on which elderly people can focus outside of themselves and that, he thinks, can provide meaning in their lives, are a parakeet to take care of, a dog to walk, a plant to water, and meeting with young children (115–25). These things, he says, can "provide them with reasons to live" and so in his view, they can be objects of categorical desires. Yet they are not necessarily greater than those elderly people or longer-lived. He says about interaction with these things (125): "Even residents with dementia so severe that they had lost the ability to grasp much of what was going on could experience a life with greater meaning and pleasure and satisfaction," and (128–9, 130) "how much more worth people find in being alive . . . could anything matter more?" Indeed, Gawande thinks the good news is that (146–7) "as people become aware of the finitude of their life, they do not ask for much . . . only to be permitted . . . to make choices and sustain connections to others according to their own priorities" and this, it turns out, might be easy to provide (e.g., with a parakeet). When Gawande realized this, he says about a 94-year-old man, "it struck me that, for the first time . . . I did not fear reaching his phase of life" (146).

However, those with views like Wolf's or EE's may think that it is important to ask if commitment to a parakeet or a similar activity (such as goldfish care) is objectively worthwhile and, if not, can it really provide meaning in life or (if these differ) a reason to live on? They may conclude that the *feeling* that these activities provide meaning in life and the *feeling* that there is a reason to live on for these things is just a feeling with no basis in reality. In answer to

Gawande's question—"could anything matter more?"—EE and Wolf could say that what matters more is that the activities really have sufficient objective value. We have already seen that Wolf discusses the case of someone who devotes herself to a pet goldfish (16) when she could be doing something else, and Wolf takes this as an example of someone who does not have meaning in her life even if she feels personally fulfilled. However, we have also seen in her response to Arpaly that Wolf comes to accept that an intellectually disabled child's care of the goldfish may provide the objective value necessary for a life to have meaning in it because it is the best he can do and involves all his limited capacity for creativity and excellence. If she would say the same about an aged adult whose capacities have declined so much that they too are fully exercised in goldfish care, her revised view might have some implications that are closer to those of Gawande's view than the view I think EE holds.

The view that I think EE holds would probably imply that those who are satisfied with commitment to a parakeet or a goldfish that fully exercises what capacities they have left after a complete life have made a mistake, an extreme version of which would be Sisyphus finding meaning in endlessly rolling a stone and finding worthwhile autonomy in the decision to do so. (At the least, the view would imply that it is not unreasonable to think they have made a mistake.) The very thing that Gawande sees as good news and that takes away his fear of growing old is the *very thing* that EE fears about growing old—that he would become someone whose capacities are so limited that he would be satisfied with, think he has found meaning in life in, and be motivated to go on living by, interacting with a parakeet. I think part of a view like EE's is that we should take an objective view of the value of particular activities and maintain our standards by not relativizing the objective value of activities to reduced capacities (as Wolf eventually seems willing to do). A false belief about the value in one's life may keep one living on but if one's belief is false, living on may be a mistake.

2. *Miller.* B. J. Miller presents an even starker contrast to a view that insists on the importance of the objective value of one's pursuits and its role in giving one reasons to have categorical desires. Miller discusses disability in general and also disabilities due to aging and imminent death.[38] On the one hand he tells us to recognize that loss

and suffering are not disruptive of the way life is supposed to be but a part of life that everyone undergoes to some degree. He thinks that those who lose and suffer significantly should not see themselves as different from others but on a continuum (e.g., he says some suffer from losing their keys and some from losing their legs). On the other hand, he thinks that much suffering is unnecessary because one can take a perspective on a loss that stops the suffering due to it for, he claims, it is "always possible to find beauty or meaning in what's left." It might seem that this directs us to focus on the value still possible with one's remaining capabilities. However, Miller's discussion of the perspective to take on loss also involves "getting into" one's disability and designing life around it. This is different from focusing on the capabilities that remain despite the disability. His examples of "getting into" one's disability are his appreciating the ragged edges of the stump of his arm in the way he might appreciate a ragged stump in a broken sculpture and finding "sexiness" in his metal prostheses that replace the legs he lost. (Designing one's life around this positive view of the disability itself is like the approach he says he took to a cancer-scare and possible death: on the bright side, he thought, he would no longer have to work.)

These may be coping strategies, but are they based on truths? Here are some reasons to think they are not:

A. Being on a continuum with respect to loss and suffering does not mean that there cannot be qualitative differences between different points on the continuum. There is a big difference between black and white paint samples though they are on a continuum, and there is a big difference between how losing one's keys affects one's life and how losing one's legs affects one's life. Similarly, there is a big difference between losing a few brain cells in one's thirties and losing a large percentage of them in one's eighties, even if the losses are on a continuum. Miller emphasizes that the dying are living and the living are dying in order to make them seem less different. It is clearly true that those commonly referred to as "the dying" are not yet dead and so are still living, while those referred to as "the living" are getting closer to their deaths all the time. But since the dying have only a short period of life left to them it makes sense to distinguish them from those expected to go on living much longer by saying the latter are not yet dying.

B. While Miller suggests focusing positively on the disability it-self, in using prostheses he is trying to approximate the mobility he would have without the disability. Really "getting into" the disability would involve finding value in and designing a life around crawling or not being able to run (e.g., slowness is beautiful), but Miller does not do this. And the fact that an inanimate object can be admired for its shine or ragged edges need not imply that the appropriate standard for beauty in a person is the shine or ragged edges of his parts.

C. A positive focus on disability or death in itself as well as on abilities that are left raises questions for value theory. For example, even from the perspective of (what one took to be) an objective value theory that one held before one lost an arm, the value of capabilities that remain will probably be greater than the one lost. This is so even if before suffering the loss one did not notice these other valuable capabilities because one was focused on the value of the capability now lost. Nevertheless, it may be that for some losses, the value possible after (or to be found because of) the loss is extremely small according to the objective theory of value one had all along accepted. (For ex-ample, by comparison to all Miller would have lost due to death by cancer, not having to work is a relatively small benefit.) When there is very little of value possible with what remains, focusing on this small good is what EE would find objectionable because considered objec-tively this good may not outweigh bads or give one sufficient reason to go on.

Of course, focusing on the small good is not the same as claiming it is a large good or equal to the ones lost. Focusing on it is consistent with accepting objective truths about its size in absolute terms and relative to bads. However, Miller's view seems to involve revising one's theory of value so that the capabilities that remain or the dis-ability itself have great value, perhaps even as great or greater than what one had before the loss. But then the value of what remains would depend on whether one could or could not avoid the loss. And this has the peculiar implication that if one doesn't lose one's legs, it's valuable to have them, but if one loses them, there's no disvalue (or even positive value) in not having them. Miller seems to accept such a "value flipping view" when he says, for example, that if you can't have knowledge about what a dying person is going through, then you should love not knowing (though he might love knowing more than not knowing if he could know). Here we begin by assigning positive value to knowing (as shown by pursuing knowledge), but if we cannot know, we should love not knowing.[39] If love involves belief in the value of what one loves, then one will have to believe in the change in value of an option depending on its availability. Otherwise one will wind up loving something that one thinks doesn't merit it.

An alternative to this flipping of value might be to hold that there was always equal value to life with and without the loss. But then what reason (aside from the value of continuity) would there be to avoid losing the greater part of one's capabilities if one would only go from one equally good state to another?

D. After the accident in which he lost his legs and part of his arm, Miller credits himself with doing one thing right: he saw a good way to look at his situation and committed to taking that perspective (2–4). (The good way, as described earlier, involved seeing himself on a continuum with others and finding beauty or meaning in what's left.) He says, "This positivity was still mostly aspirational." He didn't really believe these things but "resolved to think" the good and "refused to believe" the bad. He was waiting for his "real self" to catch up.

Hence, Miller suggests that in dealing with loss of capabilities or other bad things one will initially have to "pretend" to believe that one is merely on a continuum with others and there is beauty and meaning left. He employs William James' idea of the Will to Believe. But why is he pretending at all? Presumably it is because he begins with some desire to go on living and wants to pretend that there are goods that make living on worthwhile. Importantly, this seems to diminish the role of categorical desires as Williams describes them since even before really believing there remain goods that one would want to stay alive to get, one has a desire to go on living that gives one a reason to look for and even pretend such goods are present. (This is a point we also made in Chapter 5 in discussing those who arrange to have projects in later life so that they will have reasons to live on.)

Without something in his life that has meaning and beauty (or at least the belief that it has) perhaps Miller could not go on, but the desire to go on seems to precede and so be independent of living on being needed in order to have such goods. If one is not indifferent between there being or not being categorical goods in one's life and seeks things to be objects of categorical desires, it is likely because there is an independent desire to go on.[40] This can be true even if the desire would not be sustained were no categorical goods found. Further, the more one would engage in self-deception in concluding that remaining capacities make it worth going on in life, the more something other than the worth of exercising these capacities is really carrying one forward.

As we noted in Chapter 5, Williams recognizes that a "sheer reactive drive" to go on can be present independent of categorical desires, but he says it cannot be what makes one go on when the bare drive is not present. (We also referred to this in endnote 31.) He says:

> But the questions might be raised . . . as to what the minimum categorical desire might be. Could it just be the desire to remain alive? The answer is perhaps "no." In saying that, I do not want to deny the existence, the value, or the basic necessity of a sheer reactive drive to self-preservation: humanity would certainly wither if the drive to keep alive were not stronger than any perceived reason for keeping alive. But if the question is asked, and it is going to be answered calculatedly, then the bare categorical desire to stay alive will not sustain the calculation—that desire itself, when things have got that far, has to be sustained or filled out by some desire for something else, even if it is only, at the margin, the desire that future desires of mine will be born and satisfied. ("The Makropulos Case," *Problems of the Self*, 86)

However, that this happens when "things have gone that far" does not show that when one does unthinkingly desire to go on (i.e., the question of whether to do so has not arisen), having the bare desire to live could not be functioning as a categorical desire. After all, if one has the bare desire to live on, then living on will be needed to achieve the object of that desire. Whether we call this a categorical desire or a reactive drive is less important than showing that there could be something other than categorical and conditional desires as Williams uses the terms leading to the desire to live on. Furthermore, insofar as this mere desire to live on leads one to search for other goods to be objects of categorical desires, and insofar as it would wither if none were found, it is hard to call the antecedent desire "a sheer reactive drive to self preservation."

Suppose Miller's pretending to believe that there is something positive in what happened to him is a response to a simple desire to go on living. Sometimes a pretense can keep one going until one can cope with a truth that is different from what one pretends to believe. By contrast, Miller is suggesting that what he is pretending to believe is something he should eventually come to really believe is true. But if the content of the belief is false, coming to really believe it in the way he is suggesting would involve self-deception. To engage in self-deception merely because it leads to felt satisfaction suggests an experientialist (even hedonistic) theory of value. But what if the felt satisfaction helps one to live on and so satisfy the desire to live on? Then self-deception may be instrumental to something in addition to felt satisfaction. Either way, it would not be the case that true "beauty or meaning" had been found and could provide objects of categorical desires. Rather, with the help of self-deception about these being present, felt satisfaction can be found and life can continue. And indeed, in discussing those who are dying (for whom finding a reason to go on living long-term is beside the point), Miller describes the possibility of making the end "a series of beautiful moments" that even the demented can have. He denies that his aim is for dying patients to have transformative, meaningful experiences rather than a series of happy moments that might consist simply in watching videos and playing the guitar. This suggests that in these cases felt satisfaction is the aim without further value as its source.

Despite what I think are their very different views about the importance of objective value in our lives, one similarity between EE's position and Miller's is the passivity with which they approach death. Both ask us to "wait for death to take us." Miller does not mention suicide or assisted suicide and EE refuses to use either. However, Miller seeks to make waiting for the end pleasant and lowers the standards for evaluating the sources of pleasures so that they could even serve as objects of categorical desires. By contrast, at least after a complete life, EE would, I think, see these types of experiences as nothing but conditional goods needed when one cannot yet die. Hence, he might think it contrary to self-respect (on the Strong Position) or at least not unreasonable to think it contrary to self-respect (on the Weak Position) to accept a last stage of life as Miller imagines it when one could instead die by means he (EE) considers acceptable, such as omitting even easy life-saving treatments.

IV. Does EE Prove His Strong or Weak Positions?

Now assume that support of the Strong Position stems from the following two concerns: (a) Diminishment Losses endured post-75 will mean for everyone (excluding outliers) that no more pursuits are objectively good enough to provide reasons for categorical desires (part of the approach described in II[5]) and (b) going on will diminish the overall value of one's life (the approach described in II[1]). Let us assume that support of the Weak Position stems from the view that it is not unreasonable to hold (a) and (b) modified to apply to some (not everyone) though they may not be the only reasonable views to hold. Are either or both of the Strong and Weak Positions true? To help answer this question I will first consider whether it is true that goods possible post-75 (to nonoutliers) are either not objectively good enough to provide reasons for categorical desires or on account of one's past it is reasonable not to be attracted to them. In this connection I will consider further the idea of a "complete life." I will then consider whether going on with post-75 goods would diminish the overall value of one's life and have bad, even tragic, effects on posterity.

1. *Value of future goods.* It does not seem true that possible (nonoutlier) goods post-75 lack sufficient objective worth to provide reasons for categorical desires. In response to the claim that there are goods beyond being a leader in one's profession and community, EE says that engaging in avocations demonstrates diminished abilities and expectations. But showing that abilities and expectations have diminished does nothing to prove that avocations such as art, music, and reading are not (nonrelativized) objective goods at all and not good enough to be worth being the object of anyone's categorical desires after a complete life. (This need not yet imply that they can provide meaning in everyone's life since, on Wolf's view at least, achieving such meaning requires that one is capable of being attracted to and positively engaged with such activities.) What EE's response may show is that he thinks that these goods are not as important as those earlier in one's life because they are open even to those with reduced capacities and they also indicate one is in decline. (He also thinks that engaging in them involves a "slower," "sluggish," "nonvibrant," and "nonvigorous" life, though taken literally one could imagine a decline to vigorous exercise from a poet's life of slow composition.) However,

this need not mean that the goods post-75 have value only when value is relativized to one's capacities. They could have the same degree of objective value even when done by people with higher capacities who are capable of even greater objective value.

These various claims raise the question of whether EE is concerned to show that what possibilities usually remain post-75 (i) fall below an acceptable threshold in absolute terms (call this the Threshold View) to justify going on or instead (ii) are intrapersonally comparatively unacceptable relative to what one has done previously and for this reason cannot justify going on (call this the Intrapersonal Comparative View).

The Threshold View does not require us to know about someone's past life in order to say that her life would contain no objects worth living on to get. On the Threshold View, the complaint about a life involving only avocations, such as reading and doing puzzles, is a complaint that these alone (or even in combination with some relationships) cannot provide sufficient reason to go on living. I do not see why this is true. I do not see why reading good books or being with friends could not be a reason to go on living. Admittedly, these activities may not add to the significance of one's life, though whether they do so could be a function of the life one has already lived and so would require intrapersonal comparison. (Hence, I will discuss this concern later.) Considered on their own, they do not seem unworthy of a human life or even unworthy to be the full content of a human life especially since in EE's discussion they are imagined to occur after someone has already lived a "complete" life, understood as having achieved the (supposedly) greater human goods of which one was capable. (This is a minimally comparative judgment.) It may be that when one was younger and involved in other (perhaps better) pursuits one ignored the value of the activities that can occupy one in old age. But it would be a mistake to deny their objective value and if one had to decide when young whether to live on in old age, one should consider the objective value of things one is currently not doing. Hence, the Threshold View does not seem to be true.

Nevertheless (as noted in Chapter 5), suppose one's personal resources in life are not unlimited. A reason to reduce chances of living beyond 75 is that one's resources might be better spent on objectively more worthwhile activities if they are only possible before

75. Furthermore, if one's resources would be increasingly spent on merely conditional goods in older age (e.g., nursing home), it would be better to entirely avoid those expenses and shift resources to categorical goods in time periods that don't require as many merely conditional goods as well.

2. *Comparative value of goods.* Let us now examine the Intrapersonal Comparative View.

A. This first requires considering further what is meant by certain goods coming after a "complete life" and so being judged relative to it. A "complete life" does not mean for EE that there is literally no more room for anything else; only that all the most significant goods that a particular human life is capable of containing have occurred. However, common length of a human life today is already much longer than it was in the 1800s or even early 1900s. Suppose it has gone from 30 to 80 years. Would it have been correct for someone to say in the 1800s that there was no point in going on to 50 years because one had already lived a complete life by the time one was 30? Saying this would ignore the possibility that the additional goods that could be achieved in the years 30 through 50 would come to be part of a "complete life" once the possibility of achieving them opened up because human life could be longer. Consider the analogy with a picture: If a canvas has dimensions x by y, then it is complete when that area is dealt with as well as possible. But suppose we add more canvas to the original canvas (as artists often did) so the dimensions are $2x$ by $7y$. Then the picture will not be complete until we add more significant elements. It would be considered an "unfinished" picture if this were not done. (Of course, it is possible that the smaller complete picture would be better than the larger complete one since "completeness" is not the only measure of goodness.) Whether a life is complete may have to be relativized to its length and the significant possibilities available at various lengths. EE himself includes having relations with grandchildren as part of a complete life, but this would not have been accessible to most people if people lived only to 40. Either one would then not have included it as a component of a complete life or one would have done so and taken its absence as a reason to extend life.

Suppose EE thinks it was not a mistake to lengthen human life from 30 to 50 but it would not be a mistake not to lengthen it beyond 75 (for nonoutliers). This must be because he assumes that no significant possibilities open up for people in virtue of living much longer than they currently do. For if humans had the capacity to talk with animals but it was only between 75 and 80 that it could be exercised, EE would probably think dying at 75 would leave one with an incomplete life. He might also agree that advances in brain chemistry and/or the creation of new forms of achievement could mean that in the future human life would not be complete when it is now. But then it is the assumption that either (a) no more goods needed to make one's life complete will come in the future or (b) no more goods of the right type (even if not the sort needed to have a complete life) will come in the future that is doing most of the work in his argument. It is not the idea that there is an unchangeable, fixed set of components to a complete human life and one will already have had them (or had one's only chance to have them) in the years before 75 that is crucial to his argument.

B. Now the question arises whether intrapersonal comparative decline due to Diminishment Losses is enough to imply that no remaining goods could reasonably be of the right type to be the object of categorical desires (even if they are not needed for a "complete life").

Suppose that after a long life as a genius in physics Albert Einstein declines so that he is only capable of doing high level bioethics and is as smart and productive as EE at his peak. Do the goods that Einstein is then capable of give him no reason to continue in life though they would give EE a reason after what he would now consider to be a complete life to continue as a productive "outlier"?[41]

The Einstein example shows that a decline after what would now be considered a complete life could leave one person with the option of getting the same set of goods (in absolute terms) that are had by someone else at his peak and which could provide that other person with a reason to go on living.[42] Is it how good they are relative to one's own past peak that determines whether they can provide reasons for categorical desires or what they are in absolute terms or some combination of these? The Einstein example also shows that people with a certain past who can no longer do or have all the types of goods that were in their past, at least when they wish they could still have them, may face what I will call the Substitution Problem. This is roughly the problem of seeing if anything can be an adequate substitute or follow up to what they had. Substitution is not the same as replacement; the latter suggests one is looking for something as much like what one had as possible, whereas "substitute" or "follow up" need not imply this. Hence, substitution may be possible when replacement is not. Would continuing to do physics but at a less outstanding level be a replacement or a substitute for physics at an outstanding level? Since it involves continuing to do what one has always done (physics) but less well, it seems to be neither a replacement nor a substitute strictly speaking though it is a "follow up."

It is possible that "remaining oneself" in the content of one's life is very important. That would mean that whether a good of some particular objective worth could reasonably be a substitute and the object of a categorical desire, at least after what would now be considered a complete life, could vary between people for this reason alone.[43] However, note that if going from a long life containing highly valuable objective goods to a part with lesser goods is inconsistent with remaining oneself content-wise, this must also be true of going from a long life with goods of one type to a different, but equally valuable, type[44] and going from a long life with lesser goods to a life with highly valuable goods (e.g., going from a long period being of average intelligence to being a genius). But in the latter case, at least, not remaining oneself content-wise would not, I think, be a reasonable objection to living on. So the importance of remaining oneself content-wise should probably be understood to put more limits on a content decline than on a content incline, thereby allowing that a big incline which was inconsistent with remaining oneself content-wise could still justify a categorical desire to go on living.[45]

It is also possible that what one has done in one's past life actually makes one unable to be attracted to and positively engaged with what one still recognizes is worth doing. Recall that attraction is one of Wolf's requirements for meaning in life. So given what Einstein has done, he may recognize that bioethics is a highly valuable field and yet not be able to get excited about doing it without claiming it lacks worth that could reasonably attract others.[46]

C. For some people, engaging in the sorts of activities EE identifies with Diminishment Losses in old age will not be a decline since they will have primarily engaged in such activities their entire lives. For example, they may have been disabled their whole life and only been able to do amateur pottery, read, and so on. EE does not want to imply that those who were disabled or not very capable even in their prime had no reason to go on living even before they became old. (I take this to be implied by his dealing with death after a "complete life" in which, he says, contributions already made can be "important or not.") And for some people the activities he describes as common in old age would actually represent an incline in some respects rather than a decline; for example, from back-breaking or boring labor to reading and creative avocations once there is physical diminishment. The question raised by these groups of people is to whom an argument like EE's is directed insofar as it is interpreted according to the Intrapersonal Comparative View. If it is applied only to those who will have been vibrant and vigorous leaders in their profession and community, then it could not be directed to everyone as the Strong Position claims. By definition, most people will not have been leaders and as a matter of fact most will not have had many of the other traits that EE associates with a peak. His saying that in a complete life one may not have made any important contributions suggests that his argument is directed to a wider group of people, but for many of these there may not be a very steep intrapersonal decline in old age (and, as noted, for some there might be an incline in some respects). What reason would these people have not to go on past 75 in the presence of only Diminishment Losses? Possibly, boredom with more of (close to) the same things they have always done (given that they have no extreme amnesia about their past)? Or unwillingness to continue doing things that were only objects of conditional desires or had only instrumental value to pursuing certain achievements in a "complete life" (e.g., be married, have children, etc.) but have no value after the achievements?

In sum, interpreted so as to apply to all sorts of people, a concern to avoid intrapersonal decline could imply that after what could now be considered a complete life some substitute goods can still reasonably be the objects of categorical desires at least if they are not too far (down) from satisfying the standards of value one has been able to live up to in one's past life. So when EE points to particular goods and says that he "finds them unappealing" this could make sense for him given his past life but be consistent with a general principle that implies it makes sense for someone else to find these same activities appealing (in part) because they are at least not too far (in value and even type) from her peak or past life. This provides a particular explanation of Wolf's claim that people can be attracted to different objective goods (i.e., because of the relation of these to different past personal peaks or past lives).

An implication of this concern with intrapersonal comparative decline seems to be that it makes most personal sense for those left standing beyond 75 with Diminishment Losses to be people whose earlier complete lives were not much better or even worse than their older years. This would be true even if the objective value of what they do post-75 is lower than what Einstein would do if he declined to do high-level bioethics. This is a worrisome conclusion (to which I shall return in D.).

D. Let us try to combine some of these points made about goods from the Threshold and the Intrapersonal Comparative Views. Suppose that in old age, whether in decline or not, one is engaged in a relatively slow pace of life, contributing in an amateur rather than a professional way to fields one did not have time to explore earlier in life (e.g., art) and even merely appreciating the creative outputs of others (e.g., in reading). I have already said that considered in themselves in absolute terms, I do not see why these things could not, as the total of the period at the end of one's life, provide reasons for categorical desires to go on past 75 (for example, there could reasonably be a categorical desire to live on merely to understand Shakespeare or read some good mysteries). This is especially so if one also has a sense of "remaining oneself" because the current activities are fulfillments of past wishes that one could not satisfy earlier (and so would provide some psychological connectedness between past and future). What seems sufficient to justify living on is that one is interested in things in which it is worth taking an interest. These things could reasonably be the objects of categorical desires even if they are not enjoyable (e.g., an interest in improving bad political events) or indeed not meaningful but just enjoyable. (As noted earlier, Wolf herself does not insist that only what gives meaning in life and not mere pleasurable activities can ground going on.)

Suppose doing only things that satisfy the Threshold View and that attract one were combined with being in a steep intrapersonal decline and change in content (e.g., old Einstein declines to enjoying good rock music). Should such decline due to Diminishment Losses always matter more than the absolute value (i.e., value neither compared with earlier pursuits not relativized to reduced capacities) of interests or goods to which one can be attracted during the decline? If so, it could be because of a refusal to live with the insult of having capabilities taken away from one, hurt pride, or an intrapersonally competitive attitude. If the primary problem were comparison with better things that others (e.g., younger people) are doing at the same time, then competitiveness with others would be crucial. I think it would be a shame for pride and competitiveness to deprive one of goods, perhaps connected with one's past wishes, with which one was able to positively engage and that considered in absolute terms could reasonably be seen as objects of categorical desires.

Indeed, the relation between (i) objective goods (including meaning) in what is now considered an already complete life and (ii) goods or interests after 75 could be a form of Willhavehadism within life: having contributed a great deal at one's peak and "justified" one's life one should not worry about finding categorical reasons in what (one recognizes) gives one merely "harmless" pleasure or satisfies some curiosity.[47] Then it could make sense for those left standing beyond 75 to also include many whose past lives were much better (contained more meaning in life, were higher in objective goods) than their declining years.

E. When EE discusses losses that occur after 75 (either Disastrous or Diminishment ones), he focuses on capacities to engage in various activities. It is striking that he does not at all discuss loss of important people in one's life as one ages. These losses may be disastrous (e.g., loss of a beloved spouse) or diminishing (e.g., loss of friends). Philosophers sometimes speak of persons as "nonsubstitutable," implying, for example, that killing one person does not compensate for saving another person because the person who is killed does not benefit from the gain to someone else. In this case, it is because of the personal perspective that individuals take to losses and gains (i.e., it matters to them whether it happens to them or to someone else) that people are not fully substitutable. However, in the context of the Substitution Problem, person A may be able to substitute friendship with B for friendship with C when the latter is no longer possible. This is compatible with person B not being a replacement for C insofar as seeking a "replacement" suggests evaluating persons on the basis of their properties and looking for someone with the same properties to fill the role of "friend." It has been argued that attachment to a person is to an individual not to a set of properties though we may come to value that individual by way of responding to her/his properties. Hence, forming a relationship with B once the relationship with C is no longer possible need not involve denying that there was a unique and irreplaceable commitment to C.[48] However, again, in virtue of her past relationships a given individual may not be able to form an attachment to anyone else (just as someone's past activities may rule out attraction to certain new ones). This does not rule out substituting activities for personal relations as the objects of categorical desires.

3. *Value of life overall.* How does all this bear on the view that if the value of one's whole life gets worse by what goes on post-75, one has sufficient or decisive reason not to go on? In considering this question, it is important to remember that a decline to a life phase of lesser value from what would have been a higher ending point if one had died soon after having a complete life need not necessarily make for a less good whole. We do not think worse of Churchill's whole life because he spent his later years painting only as moderately good amateur. Indeed, we may think better of it. Even in the case of a novel whose last chapter is a downturn from what went before, the whole might have been still worse without the only moderately good last chapter.

However, suppose that having goods at the end of life which only meet a threshold on objective value did lower the overall value of one's life. For example, they might reflect back on the strength of one's earlier commitment to the highest standards or make one's life less of a uniformly heroic enterprise. Love for one person that was strong for half a century might be shown never to have been inextinguishable if it wanes at the end or is supplanted by love for another person. These need not be decisive reasons not to go on to do things that considered on their own are worth doing. Living a good life (in the sense that contrasts with morally good) does not involve a person living as though she is constructing a novel or treating herself as a means to a good story. She need not eliminate an ending that would give her life a worse "narrative structure" or in some other way make her life overall less good. There is no duty fulfilled, or even virtue in, maximizing the overall goodness of one's life, let alone by sacrificing what would give one a good enough future.

This is especially so when events and achievements imagined to be true of the past do not vary depending on what is imagined to happen in the future (even if the meaning of past events and achievements changes somewhat due to what follows them).[49] That is, there are at least two different types of thought experiments in which giving up on a less good (but still good enough) future would be required to have an overall better life. In the one we have been considering, what events are imagined to have truly occurred in the past (though maybe not their meaning) stays constant regardless of the future. The second type of thought experiment asks us to consider the following question: You do not know what the past was like. Would you prefer that it be true that it is now (a) after you have lived a long productive life but you have only a few days to live or (b) just after you have come into existence (with adult capacities) and you have a few years ahead of you with moderate enjoyment but no productive achievements?[50] On option (a) by the time you die you will have had a long productive life, while on option (b) by the time you die you will have had a short nonproductive life. In this case, I think it makes sense to prefer that you will end sooner rather than later even though you will then lose a good enough future. This is because the worse future is (by hypothesis) necessarily connected both with there already having been a better past and yielding a better life overall. Here one's preferences for one's future are determined by a concern with one's overall life because the past that will truly have been yours varies with the future that is truly yours. But this is not true when, regardless of one's future, the events and achievements of one's past will have been the same (though their meaning might change in light of one's future). Furthermore, even when what is true of one's past becomes worse as what is true of one's future gets better, one's preferences about what is true needn't follow a principle of maximizing the value of one's life. One might, I think, not unreasonably prefer a third option (c) in which it will be true that one's past has had some fewer achievements in order for it to be true that one will have more merely enjoyable future time.

Parfit asks us to consider whether we would prefer it to be the day after great pain with no future pain or the day after no pain but with future moderate pain.[51] Our life overall would have less pain and (other things equal) be a better life in the second option, but Parfit noted that most find it reasonable not to prefer it. (From the point of view of narrative structure, the first life overall may be in one way preferable since things get better whereas in the second option they get worse. However, this good aspect of the first option cannot outweigh a great difference in amount of pain in judging the life overall. It is also hard to believe that the improving narrative structure is the reason why the more painful life overall is preferred in Parfit's case. After all, one would not prefer the more painful life with the improving narrative structure if one had to choose between the lives at a time when the pain in both lives was still to come.) A point of my example involving different achievements was that these do not follow the model of pain (as Parfit himself realized); it does not seem as reasonable to give less weight to greater past achievements than to lesser future ones as to give less weight to greater past pain than to lesser future pain (or to greater past physical pleasure than to future lesser pleasure). Now recall the distinction between "me" and "my life" that Kagan initially drew by contrasting the mental/physical states that make up a person with the relation of these to the world (e.g., a person's belief vs. whether the belief is true). Parfit's pain example shows that a different distinction—between me and my life overall—can arise completely within the realm of mental/physical states when some such states are in the past and others will be in the future. In Parfit's pain example, it will be true that my life is worse in having more pain in it overall if my future will be better. Yet it seems I could reasonably prefer it to be true that my future will be better and I will have the worse life overall experientially because my future but not my past will still affect me experientially. In the achievement case, I could reasonably prefer that my life overall go better at the expense of how my future will affect me experientially (or nonexperientially). (Of course, this is only when one will really have had achievements in the past, and so there is some veridical relation between any "achievement-experiences" I have and the world containing my achievements.)

4. *Summary.* In sum, I suggest that the correct position on losses and goods post-75 will have as components: (i) Not just any good above zero need reasonably provide the object of a categorical desire; (ii) Not just any activity that could give one happiness and/or seem meaningful need actually provide meaning or even be something worth living on for; (iii) It is not unreasonable to think that goods

that do not provide meaning in life (or contribute to meaningfulness of life) could give one reason to live on (e.g., some very enjoyable activities), and neither is it unreasonable to think that only goods that provide meaning could give one reason to live on; (iv) That the terms "nonvibrant," "nonvigorous," "slow," and "decline" characterize a set of goods and the shape of their occurrence is not enough to make them insufficient to give one reason to live on; (v) Which goods can give one reason to live on could vary for different persons in relation to the goods they have had in their past and possibly already "complete" life; this could be because of both the importance of "remaining oneself" content-wise and the effect of one's past on one's capacity to be interested in different things. In some cases, not being attracted to a true good might be a mistake (as enjoying a bad is) but not always; (vi) That going on will reduce the value of one's life overall (without varying the nature of past events and achievements) can be less important than the nature of the future life itself.

Hence, while what EE says about Diminishment Loss is not enough to support the Strong Position, there seems to be enough to support the Weak Position that it is not unreasonable for some people to reject post-75 life with only Diminishment (not Disastrous) Loss. One philosophical ground for this might be the view that it is not unreasonable for a particular person (i) to reject further life whose contents do not provide meaning in life and (ii) to believe that meaning in life can only be provided by engaging positively with things of sufficient objective value given by the properties of these things themselves.[52] Note that one could deny the truth of this view without denying that it is not unreasonable to hold it.[53] To continue to support the view, one could further argue that (it is not unreasonable to think) the view has not been shown to be false.

5. *Offspring and tragedy.* Now consider whether EE's positions on one's relation to posterity and the nature of tragedy (as described in I.2.C.) are correct.

A. Despite what EE says, there are alternatives to requiring aid from offspring besides death at 75. These could include increased public assistance and better financial planning by parents. It is also not clear why being (or there being) a "head of a family" is desirable or even what it amounts to if one is not the Monarch or the Godfather who inherits power and authority over others. Presumably it is more important that being the "head" of a family should not give one in-appropriate power or authority over others than that one should be able to have such a position once a parent dies (if one's sibling does not get it).

EE's concern about "shadowing" can be reduced if children know that parental love is (mostly) unconditional and if parents have a "hands off" approach to their adult children. (An incentive to doing this is that one's children will not wish one dead.) If shadowing does occur, it will probably have started before parents are 75. If it was not a sufficient reason for parents to die before 75, then it is probably only in combination with EE's view of the reduced value of parents' pursuits beyond 75 that it would support their not living on. After all, EE does not mention shadowing as a reason for productive "outliers" to die at 75 (even though such parents may continue to shadow and even outshine their offspring, and this may be hard for children to take). Furthermore, by the time a parent is 75 their children should be old enough to be less susceptible to parental expectations. An adult who is still so susceptible that he wishes for the alternative in which his parents die (when this is not good for them) needs to develop more autonomy. Otherwise he may find that psychologically even a parent's "death does not us part."

B. Lacking autonomy (or being excessively vain) may also lead to giving too great importance to how one is seen and remembered by significant others. EE says that a parent wants his children to re-member him only as he was in his prime, but this will probably already not happen if, for good reason, the parent lives until 75. Moreover their remembering him in decline does not mean they will not also remember him as he was in better days.[54] EE says that leaving one's children with memories of one's decline is "the real tragedy." Does he mean that it is one's own tragedy that one will be remembered in decline? Or does he mean it is a tragedy for the children to have been given such memories so that the earlier loss of their parent is less bad for them by comparison? I don't think the latter claim could usually be true when children love their parent. The former interpretation raises the concern already mentioned about being too dependent on the opinions of others (though concern for one's after-death reputa-tion is not unreasonable merely because one does not experience the reputation). In saying that death at 75 is not a tragedy for the person who dies, but leaving one's children with memories of one's decline is, EE may also be assuming that one should choose a non-tragic option if given the choice. But this does not seem true. For example, it may be tragic for a young person to lose his leg and not tragic for a post-75 productive "outlier" to die. Yet it is not true that the outlier's only reasonable choice is to give up his life when this is necessary to prevent the tragic loss to his child. Tragedy is a way of characterizing some bads, but it need not imply that they are always to be avoided by contrast to non-tragic bads.

These factors relating to posterity and tragedy, like those concerning losses considered earlier, fail to prove the Strong Position. They also seem to provide less support for the Weak Position than does Diminishment Loss.

V. Another Comparison

We have considered the claim that it is not unreasonable to prefer death if one's future would make one's life overall worse or if one's future life does not provide sufficiently worthwhile activities. These are different from the claim that future goods must improve or add value to one's life overall if getting them is to provide a reason to go on living. On this alternative view, while not adding value need not be a reason to die, it involves absence of a categorical reason to continue living. Douglas MacLean defends this alternative position at least for older people in his "Longevity" (unpublished).[55] His concern is with research efforts to extend life beyond its current length, which he takes to be 80 years. (He recognizes not all people now live this long.) He thinks that 80 years is an improvement over an average life span of 50 in earlier times but wonders whether immortality, radical life extension (e.g., to 1,000 years), or even adding another 25 years would be good for people.[56]

MacLean thinks one could have a "reasonable interest" in living on (even if one is demented) if one continues to have positive relations with family or friends and enjoys leisure or work activities. He considers these things "worthwhile" and "meaningful" (8).[57] But he thinks it is good for one to have this reasonable interest in living on satisfied only if living on contributes to the value of one's life. This is because he thinks it is only when future goods would add to the value of one's life that one can reasonably have categorical desires for them. Furthermore, he has a distinctive view about what can and cannot add value to a life. He rejects the view that one more or less pleasant or even meaningful experience always changes the value of one's life (as an additive aggregative view would hold). He also thinks that one does not add value by continuing on at one's former level (high or low) of achievement. For example, he thinks that if Rembrandt had lived longer and made additional paintings equal to but no greater than his earlier ones, this would not have added to the value of Rembrandt's life. This makes it true, he thinks, that making these paintings could not have been the object of a categorical desire of Rembrandt's and provided a reason for him to go on living. His living on wouldn't have been bad for him, but it wouldn't have been good for him either. By contrast, adding a new "dimension" to one's achievements—he thinks Manet's last flower paintings are an example—could provide the object of a categorical desire and be a reason to go on living even if one did not form the desire to do so. Possibly Einstein doing good bioethics for the first time after physics would be adding a new dimension to his achievements, even if good bioethics was not as great an achievement as his past work. (Perhaps if value would be added in this way, one cannot even say that one had yet had a "complete life" on MacLean's view.)

MacLean and EE's positions differ in several respects. Unlike EE, MacLean does not propose that living on in various Diminished or Disastrous states (such as being demented but happy) provides a sufficient reason to prefer death. He thinks that activities during years with Diminishment Loss can be worthwhile and have meaning for the person engaged with them. However, unlike EE, MacLean thinks the work of productive outliers could not be the object of categorical desires and give them a reason to go on living if their work were only more of the same excellent work they had done in the past.

I disagree with MacLean's view in several ways. First, I think his understanding of categorical desires and their possible objects is too narrow. Consider, for example, the desire to go to the beach to smell ocean air. MacLean takes this to be something one could have a reasonable interest in doing given that one will be alive (and so it is the possible object of a conditional desire). But in his view, unless interacting with that part of nature is (or should be) an important goal in one's life, it cannot add value to one's life since one more or less pleasant experience cannot add or detract from the value of one's life. Hence, he thinks it cannot be the object of a reasonable categorical desire to go on living. By contrast, it seems to me that a trip to the beach that doesn't add to the value of one's life in MacLean's sense (and doesn't even provide meaning in one's life) could reasonably be the object of a categorical desire. For example, I might appropriately offer going on this trip as a reason to go on living to someone who had lost interest in life. It is not that MacLean thinks that only great human achievements (such as Manet's flower paintings) can add value to someone's life. He describes going to St. Petersburg to connect with his family's roots as an important goal in his life whose achievement added value to his life. Other projects may have even greater personal significance—the sort that Bernard Williams called "ground projects" and which he says are so crucial to one's life that without them, someone can think he might as well be dead.[58] However, Williams himself says in describing objects of categorical desires[59] that "the propelling concerns may be of a relatively everyday kind such as certainly provide the ground of many sorts of happiness," and of the ground projects, he says[60] "in general a man does not have one separate project which plays this ground role, rather this is a nexus of projects and it would be the loss of all or most of them that would remove meaning."

My second disagreement with MacLean is that I think something can be "good for" a person without it increasing the value of his life (accepting a non-additive aggregative view of the latter). It seems to me that Rembrandt and EE would have a reason to stay alive (even after what at the time would be considered a complete life in EE's sense) in order to continue to produce new instances of the sort of valuable work that they have produced in the past. This is so even if we consider only what this work would contribute to their own life in living it (independent of its effect on others or on our evaluation of Rembrandt's or EE's life overall). Furthermore, if Rembrandt and EE correctly believe the work is objectively valuable and they love doing it, their life would have meaning in it (in Wolf's sense). This would be good for them as they are living their lives, even if it doesn't increase the overall value of their lives. Being good for them in these ways as they live their lives would be enough to provide the object of a categorical desire.[61]

My third concern is that MacLean's standard for when it is good for someone to go on living longer might also have ruled out extending most lives from 60 to 80. He says that he will just assume our current length of life and see if extending it is worthwhile. But to have confidence in his standard for extension we should consider its implications for having extended life from 60 to 80 or even for reducing the length of life from its current level. It seems that most of the experiences and activities past 60 (as MacLean himself describes them) do not add to the value (in his sense) of people's lives especially if the activities of those EE calls outliers are excluded from adding to such value. Is MacLean willing to say there are few categorical reasons for most people to go on beyond 60? If not, then perhaps factors other than increasing the value of someone's life should determine whether further extensions are considered.

VI. Further Implications for Personal Conduct and Public Policy

From his views about life post-75, EE draws implications both for personal action and public policy. Consider the latter first.

1. He thinks public policy should: (A) focus on reducing Disastrous Loss (described previously as involving disability, chronic illness, dementia, etc.); (B) no longer rank a country's success in health by how long its population lives beyond 75; and (C) instead invest in reducing infant mortality.

With respect to (B), recall that it was EE's view that Disastrous Losses condemn people to an "extended dying process." Hence, if such losses are eliminated, fewer people will die from this process and more will be able to live beyond 75. If they accommodate to and are happy despite Diminishment Loss, many will probably not choose to die from easily curable diseases. Hence, eliminating Disastrous Loss will probably increase those who live post-75. Suppose many would be mistaken in choosing to do this. Then even though getting rid of Disastrous Loss would be a conditional good if one must stay alive, it might have overall negative effects if the Strong View were correct.

With respect to (B), it is true that longevity (understood as life past 75) does not necessarily imply healthiness during the extended life. But EE's main point is that even improving health post-75 may not make it worthwhile to live if non-health-related capacities (such as creativity) fade. Giving a country higher marks for health if its people live on when they shouldn't would be like giving a country higher marks for more use of cars when they shouldn't be driving. But it is not clear why Diminishment as well as Disaster Loss could not be reduced sufficiently to undermine EE's objections to living beyond 75. Then he might agree that there is again reason to rank a country's success in part by how long its population lives beyond 75.

It is also worth noting that (C) (reducing infant mortality) differs from EE's earlier recommendations for rationing scarce flu vaccine.[62] There he argued that since very little has been "invested" in infants, their deaths are not as morally significant as the deaths of people aged 13 to 50 in whom more has been invested and who are at the stage of life in which "repayment" (in achievement) of the investment is maximal. He ranked saving infants and saving the elderly (whose opportunity to repay on investment in them is mostly past) as morally equivalent and below those aged 5 to 13 and 50 to 70. Given what he says in 2014, infants may now be distinguishable from those beyond 75 in having the potential for future achievement which provides a reason (though they don't know it) for them to go on living. Other things equal, 2014 would imply, contrary to his earlier view, that infants should have priority in receipt of scarce life-saving resources over those beyond 75.

However, EE also says in 2014 that he would support the decision of the aged (even with Diminishment Loss) to keep on living (e.g., they will not refuse flu shots at 75). Does this position imply that public policy should not give those over 75 who wish to live on lower priority than infants in distributing scarce life-saving resources? Not necessarily. For with or without elimination of Diminishment Loss, other factors could still favor one of these groups over the other in rationing despite its being in its members' interest, or a reasonable object of their desire, to be saved. For example, is it fair that those who will have had many years of life if they die at an advanced aged should get additional life (even of high quality) before we save infants who would die having had much less life? Is an infant a person who has a claim on others for help in getting its future (or, some might ask, sufficiently content-connected to its future so that getting that is a benefit to it)? Questions such as these would have to be answered to reach a decision about rationing.

2. Now consider the implications for one's personal way of life and actions that EE draws from his views about living beyond 75.

A. EE thinks that a benefit of trying to set a limit to one's life at a definite time is that it will force one to think about deep "existential issues," such as what makes a life worth living and what, if anything, follows death. He thinks that trying to extend life beyond 75 is a way to avoid thinking about these questions. However, it seems that it is EE's thinking about life's worth that has led him to try to set a limit to his life rather than his setting the limit that has led him to think about life's worth, and so it may be with others. Furthermore, thinking about the existential issues could as well lead to the conclusion that life can be worth extending much beyond 75 even with Diminishment Loss (as I have argued). There may also be dangers in setting a time limit. Gawande describes (*Being Mortal*, 94–99) researcher Laura Carstensen's conclusion that it is not age per se but distance from the end of one's life that causes one's perspective to change from doing, achieving, and expanding personal networks to "being" and a focus on close personal relations. If this is true, EE faces a dilemma: in trying to set a limit at 75 to his life, he risks triggering a shift before 75 away from achieving new things of which he is still capable to simply being and engaging in close personal relations. Setting the limit may reduce the time in which he will achieve, and increase the time in which he will do the nonvibrant, noncreative things that he now finds unappealing and of lesser worth.

B. EE says at the very end of his article that he reserves the right to change his mind at 75 about the overriding merits of his ending at 75. However, the reason he endorses for his changing his mind is his developing at 75 a good counterargument to the 75-year limit since that would show he was still creative. Suppose that at 75 he gave continuing creativity as a reason for rejecting a 75-year limit. This would indicate that he hadn't changed his mind about the standard he must meet in order for it to be worthwhile for him to go on in life (i.e., being creative). However, I suspect that if he did change his mind at 75 about ending his life, it would more likely be because he had, willy nilly, come to accommodate himself to reduced capacities and expectations. Either he would find objects of worth appealing that he now finds unappealing, or he would revise, correctly or incorrectly, his current views about what objects have sufficient worth. And if he is happy in his life, this alone is likely to make him want to live on. The fact that his standards may change at 75 should give him pause now about allowing his future self to be in control of things at that point rather than in some way binding that future self to act on standards that will not have been tainted by the sort of accommodation he now rejects. Ronald Dworkin argued for the right to make decisions when mentally competent for ending one's life in the future when one would be incompetent (e.g., demented) but resist dying.[63] If EE chose to control his future self, he would face a harder problem: binding himself in the future when he will (by hypothesis) still be competent and not the victim of Disaster Loss. (One way to do this is to not treat now a disease that will become incurable by the age of 75, on the supposition that one is more likely to evade death at 75 through accommodation to lower standards than because of continuing to meet higher standards.)

C. As we have already noted, the most important implication EE draws for his personal actions is that he should and will refuse or terminate any interventions that prevent "natural" causes of his death once he reaches 75. (This includes not taking measures years before 75 that would interfere with what would cause his death at 75).[64] He would do this because he wishes to avoid Diminishment Loss after a complete life even if he would not undergo Disaster Loss. However, he will not refuse or terminate purely palliative interventions that improve the quality of his life before it ends nor will he use S, PAS, or E to end his life. Let us now consider why he will not use S, PAS, or E and whether his views actually imply that he should use at least one of them.

(i) It is crucial to realize that the life-saving interventions he would refuse are not extraordinary measures that are burdensome in their own right and that have only a small chance of saving his life. (The latter are the sorts of interventions that Gawande believes people should decline at least when they interfere with good quality of what is probably remaining life.) It is easy to take an antibiotic that will certainly save one's life, but EE says he would refuse it after 75 if the only reason given to take it is that it will save his life. If he *foresees* his death will come and despite this refuses treatment that is in itself unobjectionable, must he be omitting treatment (or prevention) because he *intends* his death? It might seem so, and yet (in conversation 5/5/17) he denies that he would omit life-saving treatment with the intention to die. If he lacks the intention to die, he presumably also lacks the intention that he not go on further in life since not going on further involves dying.[65] Could it be true that his omissions lack these intentions?

We have already noted (I.1.) that he objected to the use of "hope" in the title of his article, but even if he hoped or wished to die at 75 this need not mean he would do any act or omission intending to get what he hoped or wished for. One way to explain the absence of his intention to die is that when one's living on further provides no reason at all to use life-saving assistance, failing to do so could be fully explained by the lack of a reason to act without there being an intention to avoid what acting would achieve (i.e., living on). (Analogously, something being red can give me no reason to eat it without my having an intention to avoid eating something red.)

However, suppose EE refused life-saving aid *because* the aid would save his life. This implies that he thinks living on is to be avoided. Must he then be intending his death in refusing easy life-saving means? I have argued elsewhere that doing something (including omitting) because (or on condition that) what we do will have some effect should be distinguished from doing something in order (intending) to bring about that effect.[66] For example, we might have a party only because we know that guests will clean up the mess afterwards, but that does not mean we have the party in order to get them to clean up. In this case, however, there is some other reason for having the party which is the object of one's intention (e.g., having fun) which could be defeated if the condition (of others cleaning up) is not met. Such an additional intention is not present if EE refuses easy life-saving means only because living on is to be avoided. A closer analogue to EE's case would involve our refusing to give the party because having the party would cause people to clean up (as he refuses to take treatment because it would cause him to live on). Here our original intention in having the party to have fun would be defeated by people cleaning up which we take to be a bad effect of our having the party.

The question this raises is whether the (now perceived) bad effect of "others cleaning up" is something whose nonexistence we would intend in refusing to have the party? Or could it be that we merely intend *not to be involved* in causing the cleanup by having the party? Suppose it is the latter. Then a possible explanation for why EE might not be intending his death in refusing easy life-saving treatment because it would save him is that he merely intends not to be involved in causing his continued life when, he thinks, going on in life is more to be avoided than death. This is like the intention not to be *complicit* in bringing about something bad without doing anything with the intention that the bad thing simply not come about.[67] This explanation coheres with the fact that EE has not just been arguing for there being no reason to live on after 75 but for there being sufficient (or decisive) reason at least for some people not to go on. However, given that there is such an all-things-considered reason not to go on, it is puzzling why EE should not go further than not being complicit in causing his further life. Why should he not also refuse life-saving assistance *intending* the lesser bad of dying to prevent what he sees as the greater bad of going on living?

(ii) After all, in other cases when something is the most preferable option for oneself, it is reasonable to intend it in order to prevent what is a worse option for oneself.[68] For example, it is reasonable and permissible to omit an easy way to save one's limb, intending that it wither (not merely intending that one not be complicit in interfering with its natural withering), if its withering is a necessary means to preventing one's death when life is worth living. Some (such as Justice Neil Gorsuch) have argued that one morally must not intend the elimination of an intrinsic good either as an end or as a means to some other end, and that the life of a person is such an intrinsic good.[69] But why then is it reasonable and permissible in other cases to intend the elimination of an intrinsic good to avoid a worse option (or to achieve a better option) intrapersonally? For example, we can agree that sight is an intrinsic good. Yet it would be permissible to omit an easy way to save one's sight, intending that it wither away, if its withering is a necessary means to prevent the worse option of death when it would be worth living on even without sight.

Furthermore, in this case (where one allows one's sight to wither with the intention that it do so), it need not be continued sight itself that threatens the preferable option of living on. The withering of one's sight could just be a necessary means to stop something else (e.g., a tumor) that presents a threat to the preferable option (in this case, living on). By contrast, in the case where death is preferable to living on (as shown by someone not wanting to use easy means to save his life because these means would save his life), the person's continuing alive *itself* threatens him. Hence, intentionally omitting to save one's life with the intention to die would be a case of (what the philosopher Warren Quinn called) "eliminative agency"[70] in which we aim to eliminate the very thing (in this case, one's continuing to live) that presents a threat to one. Quinn contrasted eliminative agency in interpersonal contexts with "opportunistic agency," which can involve intentionally not saving something (such as sight, in our intrapersonal example) because its withering is the means to preventing a threat that it does not itself present. So the question is why it is not reasonable for EE to omit life-saving treatment intending to stop what he sees as the greater threat of going on living past 75 with Diminishment Loss. Call this the Eliminative Argument for Non Treatment.[71]

(iii) Suppose, given other things he says, EE should be willing to omit easy care with the intention to die. Does this imply that he should be willing to actively kill himself with the intention to die or intend that others kill him with the intention that he die? EE says in 2014 that he will not commit suicide (S) (which involves intending one's death and actively bringing it about by killing oneself including intentionally putting oneself in harm's way). He also says he would refuse to use physician assisted suicide (PAS) (which involves intending one's death and bringing it about by killing oneself with a substance provided by a physician other than oneself) or euthanasia (E) (which involves being killed by someone else who acts with the intention to cause one's death for one's own good). He argues that PAS and E tend to be sought by people who "suffer . . . from depression, hopelessness, and fear of losing their dignity and control" (2014). He thinks they need help to die a good death instead of being given PAS or E. It has been a long-standing (and empirically supported) contention of EE's that PAS and E are not typically sought by people who want to end severe physical pain.

Several crucial issues are raised by what he says (and does not say) in 2014 relating to S, PAS, and E. First, it has been argued by nonconsequentialists that in interpersonal contexts there is often a moral distinction between killing someone else and letting someone else die (even apart from whether one intends the person's death). In killing, one often imposes on and takes from someone else life he would have had independently of one's help. In letting him die, one refuses to make an effort to help him get more life by way of one's help. In such an interpersonal killing case, one takes from someone else what is his (his own life), but in the intrapersonal case one either takes from oneself what is one's own (one's own life), as in suicide, or one waives one's right against someone else that she not take what is one's own (one's life), as in voluntary euthanasia.[72] Destroying what is one's own (or directing its destruction by someone else) is not morally problematic in the same way as destroying what is someone else's without that person's permission.

Second, it might have been thought that EE resisted intending his death even when it was just a matter of refusing life-saving treatment because he supports the Doctrine of Double Effect (DDE), which implies that it is morally impermissible to either let oneself die or to kill oneself with the intention that one die.[73] (The argument I presented earlier for why it is sometimes reasonable and morally permissible to refrain from doing what will save one's life with the intention that one die is essentially an argument against the DDE in intrapersonal contexts. I discuss this further in Chapter 7.) However, EE has said[74] that S, PAS, and E are always morally wrong. In cases of severe, irremediable physical pain in the terminally ill he thinks these procedures (at least when voluntarily requested by someone who is informed and mentally competent) would be morally permissible and even the right thing to do. (This is so even in the absence of the person killed having lived a complete life.)[75] Hence, EE is not always morally opposed to killing innocent people with the intention that death come about, and so he cannot be considered a supporter of either the DDE (at least in its absolutist form) or of the view that killing the innocent by contrast to letting them die is always morally wrong. His support for some killings intending death is consistent with the view that, first, undergoing irremediable physical pain can be the greater bad and death the lesser bad and, second, that it is permissible for someone to cause himself (or allow another to cause him) a lesser bad (death) with the intention to bring it about when this is necessary to prevent a greater bad to himself (of irremediable physical pain). This is on the model of intending to actively cause oneself the lesser bad of temporary pain or permanent blindness (or have someone cause it) if this is a necessary means to save oneself, respectively, from the greater bad of falling into a permanent coma or dying when continuing conscious life would be a greater good.[76]

However, in the case of severe irremediable pain, it seems that death is not only the preferable option by comparison to living on in pain but that living on would be worse than death. That is, suffering the pain would be a negative by contrast to the zero of nonexistence. By contrast, EE claimed that Diminishment Loss need not make life after 75 worse than death even for nonoutliers (and we have already discussed the puzzle of why he might still let himself die if this is the case). Hence, it is possible that his support for the moral permissibility of the particular means of S, PAS, or E is limited to cases where he thinks living on *is* worse than death.[77] Furthermore, in the case of terminally ill persons, there is also an alternative explanation of EE's thinking that intentional killing is morally permissible: even if death were a greater bad than long term life with severe irremediable pain, when death is soon to come in any case, it could make sense to speed it up somewhat in order to avoid severe pain. Somewhat analogously, suppose being blind is worse than being deaf but one will soon be blind in any case. It would make sense to intentionally cause the blindness and lose a short period of sightedness if this were necessary to prevent permanent deafness.[78]

We can sum up (i)-(iii) as follows: EE says that he would not be intending his death when he refuses or ends life-saving means because living on would involve Diminishment Loss post-75. But I have argued that given other things he says, he should be willing to so intend. He also says that active killing intending death, as in S, PAS, and E to avoid irremediable severe pain could sometimes (perhaps only in the terminally ill) be right. He is not willing to engage in and does not morally endorse actively killing intending death, as in S, PAS, and E, to end only Diminishment Loss in those who are not terminally ill. This is so even though such killing would also cause what he believes is the preferable option (death) in order to avoid the worse option (living with Diminishment Loss).[79]

(iv) Put to one side an objection to intending death per se when it is combined with not saving or killing (in the light of my earlier argument against the objection). Consider killing on its own. Perhaps EE considers actively causing (or permitting someone else to cause) his death to be a more extreme measure than merely letting himself die of an event he did not cause (e.g., the flu). Perhaps he considers the active measures "too extreme" to take in order to avoid only Diminishment Loss when he is not terminally ill. This would be to rely on the killing/ letting die distinction rather than the intention/foresight distinction to defend his position against S, PAS, and E. (What if he were terminally ill? Might he accept the permissibility of speeding up death, given that it will soon occur anyway, by intentionally causing it with S, PAS, or E in order to shorten his time living with Diminishment Loss? Unlike severe pain endured even for a short period, perhaps he would think that enduring a short period with Diminishment Loss is not a sufficiently worse option than death to justify killing himself.)

In connection with focusing on opposition to killing to avoid Diminishment Loss, note that when describing in 2014 what he would and would not do, EE does not consider another possible way of avoiding life past 75 with Diminishment Loss when he is not terminally ill. (He may not have considered it because this way is not yet a realistic option and considering it requires imagining a hypothetical case.) Suppose that at the point when EE would decline to a life he finds unacceptable after 75, he could use a treatment that would keep him functioning at a personally acceptable level. However, this treatment has the foreseen side effect of causing a quick death (e.g., heart attack) after a short time of additional creative and productive life. (Call this the Artificial Outlier Case.) In this case, the treatment would kill EE much earlier than he would otherwise be expected to die and in using it he would actively do what causes his death, at least foreseeing if not intending that death. This can be classified as killing himself since as a conceptual matter killing does not require intending death (e.g., we can kill someone as a foreseen, unintended side effect of bombing a military facility). In one way the Artificial Outlier Case is analogous to taking morphine for pain relief foreseeing but not intending that it will cause one's death. Even DDE proponents may justify giving morphine to stop pain when one foresees (but does not intend) that it will also certainly cause death if in the circumstances death is a lesser bad and avoiding pain is a greater good.[80] (This is usually done only in terminal cases because the loss of only a short period of life is judged to be a lesser bad.)

Considering the Artificial Outlier Case is important because if EE would not morally object to using this treatment, this would show that he does not always morally object to doing what *kills* him for the sake of avoiding only Diminishment Loss when he is not terminally ill. This would be consistent with his thinking that death is preferable to undergoing Diminishment Loss.[81]

It is true that in the Artificial Outlier Case EE would not only avoid decline that he finds unacceptable; he would also get some personally acceptable time alive before his death. This contrasts with merely avoiding unacceptable life without getting any positive benefit, as would occur if death itself (caused by S, PAS, E, or allowed to occur by omitting life-saving aid) prevents personally unacceptable life. But the shorter the period of goods achieved by taking the Artificial Outlier treatment that causes his death, the closer the treatment comes to doing what kills him when this prevents Diminishment Loss but provides no other goods. For example, suppose the only way to keep someone from expressing boring and repetitive thoughts that someone like EE wants to avoid producing past 75 involves a treatment that will put him to sleep but foreseeably also cause death much sooner than it would otherwise have occurred. (Call this the Sleeper Case.) In this case, he would merely sleep without getting additional goods before death.

Suppose EE would accept doing what foreseeably will kill him in the Sleeper Case because he thinks sleeping and death are preferable to his being boring and repetitive and remembered as such. I have already argued that it is reasonable and morally permissible to intend preferable options for oneself to avoid worse ones for oneself. Given this, if EE accepted doing what would foreseeably kill him in the Sleeper Case because this is the preferable option, why should he not do what will intentionally kill him because even without additional benefits before death it is the preferable option to staying alive? This combines (a) doing what kills him (not merely omitting to do what would save him) with (b) intending death (that I already argued he should accept in omitting treatment cases). Then he could accept S, PAS, or E to avoid personally unacceptable life due to Diminishment

Loss even when he is not terminally ill. Analogously, suppose one would take a treatment necessary to save one's life even if it caused one's blindness as a foreseen side effect because living on is the preferable option. Then it would also be reasonable to intentionally cause one's blindness if only this will save one's life.[82]

It is important to see that the argument I have presented does not merely move from (1) the moral permissibility of someone letting himself die even when he intends his death and (2) the moral permissibility of his doing what kills him despite foreseeing his death to (3) the moral permissibility of his killing himself with the intention to cause his death. This three-step argument is not correct for the following reasons: Step (1) might be true even when one thinks the intention to die is itself morally wrong. This is because the alternative to someone with this intention could be his having to take a treatment to which he reasonably objects just because of what it is itself and requiring this would be wrong. Hence, Step (1) does not show that the intention itself is not wrong and so someone might reasonably still object to joining it with killing in Step (3). For if intentionally killing himself were impermissible, the alternative would not be his having to take a treatment to which he objects because of what it is in itself.[83] In my argument, for S, PAS, or E, by contrast, I noted that EE does not object to the life-saving treatments for any reason other than that they will save his life. I further independently argued that in itself the intention to die is sometimes reasonable and morally acceptable when death is the less bad option that helps avoid a worse option. Given these additional claims, there is no obvious moral objection to joining intending death with killing in order to avoid a worse option, once killing oneself is shown not to be objectionable in cases such as Artificial Outlier or Sleeper where death is only foreseen.

D. We have provided an argument for someone killing himself intending his death to avoid the bad to him (as EE and others see it) of Diminishment Losses after a complete life even when the person killed is not terminally ill. But EE also emphasizes the losses to others (such as financial burdens) of caring for post-75 people. Can we incorporate someone's desire to avoid imposing losses on others (an interpersonal consideration) into the argument? Suppose that EE had a choice between two medical procedures post 75, one of which would save his family a great deal of money in caring for him. However, only the cheaper procedure will as a side effect foreseeably cause his death, and he will also die much sooner than with the other procedure. Suppose that he was right that his death at 75 is less bad for everyone than his financially burdening his family and that he seeks to avoid the greater bad to those he cares about. Then this would be a reason for him to favor using the cheaper procedure that foreseeably will kill him. It would also be a reason for his intending the preferable option (his death after 75) to avoid what he thinks is the worse option of financially burdening his family. So why does it not give him a reason for killing himself (or having someone do this) intending that he die (the preferable option) in order to avoid financially burdening his family (the worse option)? Of course, it may be wrong to think that burdening his family financially is the worse option by comparison to his death, and it may not be true that he is seeking to avoid the worse outcome for others as he might seek to avoid the worse outcome for himself. The argument I have just given merely begins with these assumptions (the first one being provided by EE) and shows what is implied by them.[84]

E. EE claims in 2014 that currently those who seek PAS and E tend to be depressed and hopeless, and he may think this is reason to oppose those people intentionally killing themselves. He also says the reasons commonly given by people seeking PAS and E are the meaninglessness of their lives, the insult of decline, and being a burden to their family. He also thinks that instead of PAS and E these people need to be helped to have a good death. This suggests that the conditions that make them seek PAS and E could be corrected by other means that are better for them. Perhaps he still thinks this is possible for those not yet 75. However, in 2014 EE argues that for most people beyond 75 Diminishment Loss cannot be avoided by means other than death, and the reasons he gives for refusing easy life-saving aid after 75 are exactly the reasons he says are given by those seeking PAS and E: to avoid meaninglessness, decline, and being a burden on one's family. If he were right that these bad things cannot be avoided if one stays alive past 75 (with the exception of outliers), then it would be impossible for someone past 75 to receive help to have a good death by EE's 2014 standards. That is, a "good death" is understood to be "a good life while (or before) dying," and as traditionally sought by palliative care and hospice professionals this amounts to a life without suffering. But this is not enough to constitute a good life before death for EE according to 2014. He requires such things as meaningful activities and not being a burden. Even if the good life after 75 while (or before) dying would involve what someone like Atul Gawande thinks of as meaning in life, this would not (I have argued) satisfy EE's 2014 conception of meaning in life. Hence, the life that he thinks is possible for most post-75 and especially for those in "elongated dying" does not provide a better alternative to death by EE's 2014 standards, at least for someone like himself (according to the Weak Position).

Furthermore, suppose one has no illness or other event that threatens death for which one can refuse life-saving aid. One will then have to go on living with Diminishment Loss whose avoidance EE thinks could justify refusing even easy life-saving aid. Would it be unreasonable to then become depressed and hopeless if one shares EE's views about what sort of life is worth living beyond 75 and if these views are not unreasonable? Hence, it may not be true even of those who now seek PAS and E that their depression and hopelessness are unreasonable. Indeed, these might be the responses EE would eventually have if he did not die at 75. Psychiatric or other treatment would not be appropriate for responses that were not unreasonable unless it could also eliminate the grounds for them (e.g., in EE's view provide sufficiently objectively worthwhile activities, eliminate being a burden on others, etc.). If it cannot do this, it would not be an alternative to death as a way to avoid the problems that EE sees in life past 75.

Of course, while those past 75 who seek PAS and E may share EE's view about what sort of life should be avoided, they are willing to use means to avoid that sort of life that EE rejects. Might he think that willingness to use those means to avoid problems other than extreme irremediable pain is what is unreasonable and shows that they need some sort of helpful treatment? But suppose the argument I provided earlier for S, PAS, or E is correct. This implies that one accepts certain premises, such as (i) the moral permissibility of one (or one's physician) sometimes doing something helpful that kills one as a mere foreseen side effect when death is preferable to living on in a condition without that help, and (ii) the moral acceptability of one (or one's physician) sometimes intending one's death when it is preferable to living on in that same condition. Given this, it can be shown that PAS, E, or S to avoid certain problems is no more or less unreasonable than refusing life-saving aid for the same reasons and with the same intentions. Hence, one could not conclude that wanting to use S, PAS, or E in particular shows that people are unreasonable and need treatment for this. Suppose this is so. Then it seems more reasonable to use these methods once one is actually in a condition that makes death preferable rather than not treat or prevent some life-threatening condition at an earlier time based on the likelihood that one will not be an outlier. The latter sort of means that EE suggests using may unnecessarily lead one to lose out on many good years of life.[85]

Notes

1. Ezekiel J. Emanuel, "Why I Hope to Die at 75," *The Atlantic* (October 2014). https://www.theatlantic.com/magazine/archive/2014/10/why-i-hope-to-die-at-75/379329/ (All citations to Emanuel in the text and endnotes refer to the digital version of this article unless otherwise noted.) Emanuel (EE) is a prominent bioethicist and architect of public health policy, and so attending to his view and how he argues for it makes sense. I was prompted to do so by participating in a debate with him on this topic at the thirtieth anniversary of the Edmond J. Safra Ethics Center at Harvard University on May 5, 2017 (henceforth 5/5/17). I am grateful to him for discussion on that occasion.

2. Chapter 8, "Death and the State: Public Policy of Suicide, Assisted Suicide, and Capital Punishment," considers EE's earlier and also more recent views on suicide (S), physician assisted suicide (PAS) and euthanasia (E) simply as matters of public policy and also in connection with what he says in his 2014 article.

3. Saying one hopes to die is different from saying "I have hope that I will die at 75," which implies that there is some reason to believe that one will die at 75. Merely hoping to die at 75 need not imply there are any such reasons, though it implies that one wants to die at 75 and does not believe this is impossible.

4. I learned of this on 5/5/17.

5. EE's conservative tone here is reminiscent of Michael Sandel's in his *Atlantic* article "Against Perfection" (2002), in which Sandel argued against what he saw as hyperactive parents trying to improve their offspring. For my discussion of Sandel see "What Is and Is Not Wrong with Enhancement," reprinted as Chapter 17 in my *Bioethical Prescriptions* (Oxford University Press, 2013).

6. Larry Temkin in his "Is Living Longer Living Better?" *Journal of Applied Philosophy*, 25:3 (2008), 193-210, claims that if we live well, we may not want to live many years longer (207). But this claim does not necessarily imply that to live well one should not live longer than 75, which is EE's Strong Position.

7. We examined this view in more detail in Chapter 1. There I discussed a second version of Deprivationism that is concerned with how the future we would have affects our life overall.

8. See Kagan's *Death*, 332-4. Jeff McMahan pointed out to me a similarity in (a) my view expressed in Chapter 2 that the threshold for going on living is above just any overall positive condition relative to the zero of nonexistence and (b) my view that the threshold for creating a person is above just any overall positive condition relative to the zero of nonexistence. (I described what is required for creating a person as the "minima." See my *Creation and Abortion*, Oxford University Press, 1992, and a shorter version, "Creation and Abortion Short," in my *Bioethical Prescriptions*.) If Kagan thinks someone's overall positive condition implies there is no sense in her dying, should he think an overall positive condition of someone one would create means there is no reason deriving from that person's expected condition not to create her? Not necessarily, because it could be that one threshold is needed to make sense of someone's not continuing to exist once he exists and a different threshold is needed to make sense of creating someone at all. This could be true on either Kagan's view or mine.

9. This distinction is drawn by the Coalition to Transform Advanced Care (C-TAC). See Chapter 4.

10. See for example 2, 6, 12, 14.

11. He has even said that doing these things all the time is "not a life" (5/5/17).

12. This is another way, in addition to weakening the strength of his argument (as already discussed), that he leaves the reader with a conclusion that does not represent the dominant themes of the article.

13. Even though, according to EE, data show that this is not why most people seek PAS or E. He discusses this in articles from 1998 and 2016, which I discuss in Chapter 8.

14. It is interesting to compare EE's view of what is not tragic with that of Thomas Nagel in his "Death" (reprinted in his *Mortal Questions* [Cambridge University Press, 1979]). Nagel says (9–10): "Observed from without, human beings . . . cannot live much longer than a hundred years. A man's sense of his own experience, on the other hand, does not embody this idea of a natural limit. His existence defines for him an essentially open-ended possible future. . . . Viewed in this way, death, no matter how inevitable, is an abrupt cancellation of indefinitely extensive possible goods. Normality seem to have nothing to do with it. . . . If the normal lifespan were a thousand years, death at 80 would be a tragedy. As things are, it may just be a more widespread tragedy. If there is no limit to the amount of life it would be good to have, then it may be that a bad end is in store for us all." This passage allows us to note several differences between EE's and Nagel's views on the whether death at 75 is a tragedy. (1) Nagel's view depends on the possibility that there will be more goods of life past 75 and, as we have seen, EE denies that there will usually be goods that make it worth going on. (2) The difference in (1) is a result of Nagel not restricting his view to

what biological data tell us about human lifespan and continuation of distinctively human goods; he is concerned with what is metaphysically possible for a human person to have. This may also mean that we can imagine that we would be the same people even if we went on (counterfactually) to unending good into the future. (I discussed this in Chapter 5.) By contrast, EE restricts his view to what science says is probable for him. Even with respect to those who would be outliers, it is not clear that he thinks their deaths at 75 would be a tragedy. This may be (in part) because they couldn't go on to have many more years of good life as a matter of biological (rather than metaphysical) possibility. (3) Nagel's view is based on what (in "Death") he took to be the correct account of the badness of death, namely Deprivationism. As discussed in Chapter 1, this view may focus on what we would lose out on if we die, and the more we would lose out on, the worse the death. Combined with the metaphysical possibility of more good life, this implies that we would be losing a lot of good life in dying and this may be tragic. (4) As also earlier noted, one might hold a different view that I called Willhavehadism. It decides how bad death is by considering how much of good and bad one will have had by the time of death. If one will have had a lot of good, then even if one loses out on a lot by death, one's death might not be tragic. In emphasizing that the people he is discussing will have had a complete life at 75, EE might be interpreted as emphasizing the factor that Willhavehadism rather than Deprivationism emphasizes. This would be another reason why his view about tragedy differs from Nagel's. As already noted, it would also mean that he is not completely a Deprivationist about the badness of death. (5) Nagel supports his claim that even if one will have had 80 years of life, death would be a tragedy by saying "If the normal lifespan were a thousand years, death at 80 would be a tragedy." However, if tragedy were tied to what is biologically normal, then one could not move from the context of normal biological possibility to the context of metaphysical possibility in determining what is tragic. (This is consistent with it being better for a person to abnormally go on to a thousand.)

15. EE makes this point by describing how he wants to be remembered by his offspring. However, one reason it is hard to read his article is one's awareness that what he says bears on his view of his own father (whether or not EE consciously recognizes this). Since he describes his father as having slowed and his life as sluggish, the implication of C(iv) is that EE wishes his father were not leaving him with such memories. Similarly, if EE thinks that his living beyond 75 will prevent his children from living their own lives, this suggests that his own parents living on are preventing him from living his. In general, everything he thinks his children would believe about him but would be unwilling to admit to him could be taken to be something he believes about his parents but is unwilling to admit to them. As we have seen in Chapter 3, in *Being Mortal* Atul Gawande also discusses his father, describing how he tries to find and balance still meaningful activities with medical treatments and hospice care as he approaches the end of his life. Gawande (like EE) is concerned that his father not suffer or sacrifice meaning in life for the sake of merely living on. However, unlike EE,

Gawande never speaks of a burden or shadow that his father casts on his son's life in continuing to stay alive, and he never doubts that some of his father's activities remain meaningful even though they are far from the peak activities of his past.

16. As we saw in Chapter 2, Ronald Dworkin seems to have held such a view according to which an ending period that is not bad in itself can ruin the "narrative structure" of one's life, like a merely good ending chapter to an otherwise brilliant novel can make it overall worse than if it had ended sooner.

17. Possibly continuing on alive at zero (e.g., in a complete coma) might also make one's overall life worse than the zero of death. I will not explore this issue here.

18. As noted in Chapter 2, when Kagan first discussed the distinction between "me" and "my life," he thought that the things that happen to me are those that affect my experiential and physical states and those that happen to my life can go beyond these. For example, I may be getting pleasure because I believe I am finding new truths when in fact this is an illusion, though its being an illusion never affects my experiential or physical states because I never know my beliefs are false. Kagan eventually changed his position so that things extrinsic to my intrinsic (experiential and physical) properties could bear on how I am doing at a given time. Hence, I could be doing worse if I am not finding new truths even though I continue to get pleasure from falsely believing I am. However, as also noted in Chapter 2, his new position is still consistent with another distinction to which I am now pointing, namely that my *life* overall is getting worse when *I* am doing better (including having good experiences that reflect good reality) or my *life* overall is getting better when *I* am doing worse (including having bad experiences reflective of bad reality).

19. This is an issue we also raised in the discussion of Gawande's views. However, though Gawande thinks how one's "story" ends matters, he focuses only on the quality of the ending period in itself rather than the contribution it makes to the whole story. Hence, he doesn't consider that an end that is not bad in itself could still make the whole story worse.

20. Like Margo in Ronald Dworkin's *Life's Dominion* (Knopf, 1996), discussed in Chapter 2.

21. In the 5/5/17 conversation, EE referred to not wanting to live on as a happy pig. This is stronger than J. S. Mill's claim that it is better to be Socrates dissatisfied than a pig satisfied; Mill's claim is consistent with it being true that if one doesn't have the option of being Socrates dissatisfied, being a pig satisfied is better than death.

22. In his "The Dignity of Old Age," *NYU School of Law, Public Law Research Paper* No. 17-41. (2017). Available at SSRN: https://ssrn.com/abstract=3048041 or http://dx.doi.org/10.2139/ssrn.3048041.

23. See my discussion in, among other places, Chapter 10 of *Morality, Mortality*, vol. 2 (Oxford University Press, 1996).

24. Fulfillment is a positive feeling but is not to be identified with happiness because it may involve anxiety and concern that interfere with happiness. Susan

Wolf gives the example of someone who finds meaning in helping a disabled child. See her *Meaning in Life and Why It Matters* (Princeton University Press, 2012). All references to Wolf are to that book (henceforth, *Meaning*).

25. See *Meaning*, 17. The case was originally given by Richard Taylor in his *Good and Evil* (New York: Macmillan, 1970), Chapter 8.

26. See for example *Meaning*, 9, 24, and 27.

27. That the object of one's engagement is outside of oneself is meant to show that having meaning in life is distinct from satisfying self-interest, though it doesn't require the impartiality that Wolf thinks is part of morality. Among my concerns about Wolf's view are that it seems to counterintuitively imply that someone could reasonably wonder whether, and hope that, his life has meaning in it even though as he lives it he feels it has such meaning. On her view, he could wonder because it is possible that he is mistaken about the worth of what he is doing. Also, someone who loves doing something whose objective worth she does not recognize could fail to have meaning in her life as she lives it since she lacks the belief in the objective worth of what she is doing that is part of Wolf's account. Should we encourage this person to switch to a different activity whose significant but lesser objective value she could engage with while believing in its true value? I doubt it. This suggests that being attracted to and engaging with objective goods is more important than having the belief that one is engaging with such goods. In addition, Wolf does not initially distinguish having *meaning in life* as one is living it from one's *life being meaningful* (or one's living a meaningful life). In response to Robert Adams (whose commentary is part of her book), she says she is focusing on the former. Indeed she says that she thinks "such overall assessment of the meaningfulness of people's lives are of limited interest" (115). Yet in discussing (106–7) those who fail in the worthwhile projects about which they care she seems to focus on the meaningfulness of their lives. For example, she says of the scientist whose project fails that there are values to be found in negative results helping science progress. But even if the scientist can recognize the value in negative results, that value would not have been sufficiently attractive to support her positive engagement with science. So it could not have satisfied Wolf's conditions for meaning in the scientist's life. Further, in discussing the general whose plot against Hitler failed she speaks of the objective value of his life that comes from the vision and courage which his attempt showed. But having these qualities of character could not have been the object of his positive engagement since his aim was overthrowing Hitler not developing his own character. A good character is also not something objectively valuable that is outside of oneself and so would not meet another one of Wolf's conditions on what can give meaning in life. It is possible that what we most want is not to have meaning in life but to have a meaningful life, where the latter is compatible with never believing that what one loves has objective worth (though it does) or never feeling attracted to an activity one engages in that has objective worth (even if one recognizes its worth). She says that having meaning in life is an answer to the "common and deep" (123) desire to have a life that is admirable from an

objective view. However, a meaningful life that does not provide meaning in life as one lives it is also admirable from an objective view. So it would also satisfy the desire for an objectively admirable life. It is certainly a live question how much meaning in life one should sacrifice to have a more meaningful life without as much meaning in it (and how much meaningful life without meaning in it one should sacrifice to have more meaning in life). (See this chapter in text for more on this.) Despite my concerns about these aspects of Wolf's view—others will be discussed in the text—I find her view useful in understanding a position like EE's in part because it emphasizes that positive feelings about something one engages in and belief in its worth are not enough in the absence of its actual worth to give meaning in one's life.

28. In *Meaning*, 127–32.

29. On the other hand, Wolf's account seems not to give enough weight to the fact that the adult who does not exercise many of her capacities loves the goldfish. Possibly certain attitudes like love and caring attention, at least when not directed to bad things, can be valuable in their own right and give meaning in life.

30. I put to one side seeking scientific progress that involves pursuing these ends. I have already noted (in Chapter 1) that while Williams speaks in terms of desires, those who are realists about value think it better to speak of something giving us conditional or categorical reasons independently of what we desire and to speak of conditional or categorical goods or pursuits. I shall return to this point in the text.

31. As we noted in Chapter 5, Williams says (in the Makropulos Case, 86) that he does "not want to deny . . . a sheer reactive drive to self-preservation" but he thinks this cannot be "the minimal categorical desire." This is, he says, because when the question whether to go on gets asked, the reactive drive is already shown not to be enough by itself to sustain life. I shall consider this response of Williams and the issue of desires besides the conditional and categorical below in III (2) when discussing B. J. Miller's views.

32. It is possible that some Americans' "manic obsession" with diet and exercise may be directed at ensuring the objects of conditional desires (i.e., a good quality of life *if* they live on). This is by contrast to its being directed at extending life beyond 75 per se, as EE interprets it, and so in the service of either achieving categorical desires or the sheer drive to self-preservation. (It is unlikely that dieting and exercising are in themselves objects of categorical desires.)

33. James Goodrich has suggested that one might also distinguish between goods that give one "decisive" rather than "sufficient" reasons to go on living. However, it is rare that one could say one had a decisive reason to go on regardless of what else might transpire (e.g., great pain and suffering) that might give one sufficient reason not to go on even if not a decisive reason not to.

34. To be distinguished from, for example, neural stimulation creating some pleasant sensations.

35. Though he may think this is a case in which an unworthy source of happiness (e.g., doing puzzles) even undermines the value of happiness itself.

36. This case suggests that it is not correct for Wolf to say that the overall assessment of the meaningfulness of people's lives is of "limited interest" (115), as it may be that it is meaningfulness that truly responds to the "common and deep" desire to have a life that is admirable from an objective view.

37. Josiah Royce, *The Philosophy of Loyalty*, Macmillan, 1908.

38. See his "One Man's Quest to Change the Way We Die," *New York Times Magazine*, January 3, 2017. Citations to Miller with page numbers in the text are to this article.

39. Is this reminiscent of the fox in the fable who convinces himself that the grapes he can't have are sour and it is good not to have them? It seems more like the attitude of the person in the song who says that when he can't be with the girl he loves, he loves the girl he's with. This is a less extreme view than the fox's because the person doesn't say that he no longer loves the first girl and Miller does not say having legs is no good.

40. See Chapter 5, endnote 22, for another possible reason to seek objects of reasonable categorical desires.

41. Note that I am here assuming along with EE that continuing on at the same high level (as his outliers do) could be a reason to have a categorical desire to go on. Some, such as Douglas MacLean, disagree with this assumption, and I will discuss that position in section V.

42. It is also possible that decline after a complete life could leave a person with the possibility of the same goods he had before reaching his own peak. In our example, this would be so if Einstein had happily done bioethics before discovering his genius for physics. As we have already seen (in Chapter 5), Thomas Nagel (in his "Death") claims that we do not pity a baby for being in diapers, but we do pity an old person who is in the same situation. So the fact that Einstein's early period as a bioethicist was not bad for him or his life overall need not automatically imply that ending up in this position is not bad for him and his life overall. Stephen Darwall seems to ignore the possible relevance of this point about asymmetrical value within life when he said (in oral remarks) that it is sweet to see how young children find meaning in playing card games, and so it may also be possible to find meaning in such games if one's capacities are limited in old age. Darwall may have had in mind a form of meaning that is either purely experiential and does not rest on evaluating the objective worth of what one is doing or that locates objective worth in exercising whatever capacities one has to a high degree and building social networks around this (as Wolf's revised view suggests). Playing games can also bring enjoyment and having enjoyment, whether it gives meaning in life or not, might reasonably ground a categorical desire to go on living (though EE seems to disagree). An implication of Nagel's point is just that the game having been a satisfactory component of life for a child does not alone imply that it is such in old age.

43. As pointed out in the previous endnote, one's decline may be content-wise like one's life before one's peak. Hence, I shall assume that "remaining oneself" refers to the more recent stage with which one identifies.

44. When goods are of different types, it has been argued that they are more often on a par rather than equal. This is because some improvement in one of the goods (e.g., making slightly better music) might not make the good of making music more valuable than doing physics if the two activities were originally on a par. However, it would if they were originally equal in value. On this see Ruth Chang's introduction to her *Incommensurability, Incomparability, and Practical Reason* (Cambridge: Harvard University Press, 1998).

45. We also pointed this out in Chapter 2 in connection with Kagan's concern about content-connectedness.

46. An additional comparative measure of decline could be interpersonal: one is no longer at least as able as everyone else (or some subset that is the appropriate comparand). But if one has been a genius or a physical "superwoman" and one declines to normality or considerably above, then one will not have declined relative to everyone else (even the up-and-coming young). Should this be relevant to whether the goods remaining after Diminishment Loss could reasonably be the objects of categorical desires?

47. This does not include enjoying what is bad (e.g., violent pornography).

48. It also need not involve refusing to sacrifice what one knows would be a future satisfying relationship with B by giving up one's future life altogether to save C's life.

49. In Chapter 2 we considered someone who when demented overpaints their earlier masterpieces. When achievements require continuing existence of a produced object, as in this case, destruction of the object should, I think, be classified as varying the past not merely its meaning by future events. This is so even though there is no literal undoing of prior existence of the object or events that produced it.

50. I first discussed a case involving preferences among pasts with different achievements in my *Morality, Mortality*, vol. 1, and I also referred to it in Chapter 1 this volume. The case was in response to, and making use of, the structure of Derek Parfit's famous case involving pain. (See his *Reasons and Persons*, Oxford University Press, 1984).

51. See *Reasons and Persons*.

52. A view that relativizes meaning in life to full use of whatever capacities one has would be more often compatible with staying alive even if one held that having meaning in future life were required.

53. Mingyang Xiao emphasized this.

54. Despite the fact that EE reports that decline begins at 45, he says that he wants to be remembered as he was at 70 "in his prime." One would have thought that he will then also be beyond his prime.

55. I thank MacLean for permission to discuss his paper. All citations to MacLean refer to this paper.

56. Radical life extension is not my concern in this book. So I will discuss MacLean's view only as it relates to adding another twenty to fifty years to a life of 80 (10) and what this implies about life to 80.

57. He describes his mother's final years in this way.

58. In his "Person, Character, and Morality" (henceforth PCM), 13, reprinted in his *Moral Luck: Philosophical Papers 1973-1980*, New York: Cambridge University Press, 1981.

59. See his PCM, 12.

60. PCM, 13.

61. Is it possible that some objects of categorical desires give one a sufficient reason to go on in life, but only doing what adds value to one's life gives one a decisive reason (as James Goodrich suggested to me)? But sufficient suffering or a reasonable lack of interest in increasing the value of one's life (given that maximizing value is not imperative) could count against increasing the value of one's life as a reason to go on, making it not decisive.

62. See E. Emanuel and A. Wertheimer "Who Should Get Influenza Vaccine When Not All Can?" in *Science* 312:5775 (2006), 854–855. Their views are reminiscent of Dworkin's in his *Life's Dominion*.

63. *Life's Dominion*, 237.

64. Theoretically, he might also not resist other persons causing his death (e.g., not self-defending against being murdered).

65. I am here ignoring the difference made by intention being an intensional context that does not preserve identity. That is, even if $x = y$, intending x need not imply intending y.

66. See my "The Doctrine of Triple Effect," reprinted in my *Intricate Ethics* (Oxford University Press, 2007).

67. This explanation, however, may fail to explain not allowing others to prevent his death unless failing to stop them would itself be complicity in their effort to save him.

68. I assume other things are equal. I say "most preferable" because if death were preferable to staying alive with Diminishment Loss but there was an option preferable to death that was also preferable to staying alive with such loss, it could be prudentially and (possibly) morally wrong to choose death. Henceforth, when I say death (or any other option) is preferable, I will assume it satisfies the "most preferable" condition.

69. I discuss his views and those of others on intending elimination of one's life in Chapter 7. Note that it is consistent with a person's life having properties that make it an intrinsic good for it to have other properties that make the continuation of his life be overall bad and bad for him. We discuss this in Chapter 7.

70. See his "Actions, Intentions, and Consequences: The Doctrine of Double Effect," *Philosophy & Public Affairs* 18 (1989), 334–51. I am here including refraining as a form of agency even if it is not causation.

71. I discuss what I call the Eliminative Argument for Assisted Suicide and other arguments for intentionally causing the death of persons in Chapter 7.

72. Waiving a right is different from alienating it. The latter but not the former involves giving up the right or transferring it to another so that one can no longer change one's mind about exercising it.

73. Though supporters of the DDE might tolerate letting oneself die with the intention to die because it would be morally problematic to require people to use life-saving treatments against their will whenever they would refuse them with what the DDE implies is the wrongful intention to die.

74. In Ezekiel Emanuel's "The Future of Euthanasia and Physician-Assisted Suicide: Beyond Rights Talk to Informed Public Policy," *Minnesota Law Review* 82 (1998), 983–1014 and in his "What is the Great Benefit of Legalizing Euthanasia or Physician-Assisted Suicide?" *Ethics* 109 (1999), 629–42.

75. EE has (1998, 1999) argued against the legalization of PAS or E even for irremediable severe physical pain in the terminally ill not on grounds that it is morally wrong but on grounds that the harms of legalization would probably outweigh the benefits. However, these are not his reasons in 2014 for not using these means to avoid only Diminishment Loss. In any case, I am here concerned only with what his moral and ethical views imply about S, PAS, and E. I discuss his view on PAS and E as public policy (including the law) in Chapter 8.

76. See Chapter 7 this volume and my "Four-Step Arguments for Physician-Assisted Suicide and Euthanasia," reprinted in my *Bioethical Prescriptions* (2013) for a more detailed argument in favor of the moral permissibility of PAS to eliminate pain.

77. Note that even if further life is not worse than death, the *option* of living on could be *worse* than the option of death.

78. See my "A Right to Death?" in *Boston Review* 22 (1997), "Physician-Assisted Suicide, the Doctrine of Double Effect, and the Ground of Value" in *Ethics* 109 (1999), and Chapter 7 where I refer to this as the Terminal Four-Step Argument for PAS. Also see Chapter 7 for why the analogy is not perfect.

79. EE does not discuss whether S, PAS, or E is morally permissible if someone has Disaster Loss (what he calls elongated dying) but is not yet terminally ill (in the ordinary sense). Nor does he discuss S, PAS, or E for those with only Diminishment Loss who are terminally ill. Presumably, he would think it not unreasonable to refuse to use life-saving aid past 75 if one had Disaster Loss, perhaps even if it did not also involve Diminishment Loss (e.g., total paralysis but undiminished creativity) when one is not terminally ill.

80. It is important to emphasize "certainly cause death" because the distinction between intending and merely foreseeing an effect is not a matter of the effect being only probable in the latter but certain in the former. One can intend something that is uncertain to occur, and one can merely foresee an effect of one's action certainly occurring. The distinction between intention and mere foresight is better (though imperfectly) captured by the Counterfactual Test: if an effect would not occur if one acted (or omitted to act) but all else remains constant, would this give one a reason not to act (or not to omit)? If the answer is yes, then the effect is intended; if one has no reason to change one's behavior, then the effect is merely foreseen. One reason why the Counterfactual Test is imperfect is that it fails to distinguish acting with the intention to produce an effect and acting on condition that an effect occurs. I mentioned this distinction in VI(2)(C).

For further discussion see my "The Doctrine of Triple Effect" (reprinted in my *Intricate Ethics*) and Chapter 7.

81. It is worth pointing out a possible additional public policy implication of EE's position if he accepts the permissibility of taking treatment in the Artificial Outlier Case: in developing, approving, or using drugs to treat various conditions in those past 75 who have Diminishment Loss, the risk of death as a side effect can have reduced significance by comparison to the significance it has in a younger population.

82. In "A Right to Death?" in *Boston Review* 22 (1997) and "Physician Assisted Suicide, Euthanasia, and Intending Death" in M. Battin and R. Rohdes, et al., eds., *Physician-Assisted Suicide: Expanding the Debate* (Routledge 1998) I argued that if someone could permissibly do what killed him as a side effect of acting for some other end, then it should be permissible for him to intentionally kill himself as a means to that same end. The current argument follows that pattern. For more on such arguments, see Chapter 7.

83. The Washington Court's reasoning in the Glucksberg case when it decided in favor of PAS in terminal cases included steps somewhat like (1)–(3), only involving the role of third parties. That is, assuming patient consent, its view could be analyzed as: (1) it can be legally permissible for doctors to allow a patient to die (e.g., omit or stop his treatment) when the patient intends his death; (2) it can be permissible for doctors to do what will kill a patient despite foreseeing his death (e.g., give morphine for pain relief); therefore, (3) it is permissible for doctors to give a prescription that assists a patient in his suicide that involves his intention to die. I criticized this argument (in my "Theory and Analogy in Law," reprinted in my *Bioethical Prescriptions*) because the Court's claim (1) might be true even though one thinks the patient's intention makes his omitting or stopping treatment wrong. This is because the alternative to letting someone refuse treatment is forcing it on him and if he is mentally competent he has a right that we not do this. But if the person is not permitted to intentionally kill himself in (3) because he is not given the means to do so by others (as in denying PAS), no treatment need be forced on him.

84. I discussed a case like this in "Physician Assisted Suicide, Euthanasia, and Intending Death" in M. Battin and R. Rohdes, et al., eds., *Physician-Assisted Suicide: Expanding the Debate* (Routledge 1998). I there put the point in the negative: Suppose one shouldn't take a cheaper drug that would foreseeably kill one because avoiding the financial burden on one's family is not a better outcome relative to one's death. Then one cannot use an argument that claims intending the preferable outcome of one's death is acceptable and from this derive the permissibility of intentionally killing oneself to avoid being a financial burden.

85. I am grateful for comments on an earlier version of this chapter to Shelly Kagan, Jeff McMahan, and Larry Temkin as well as to students in my graduate and undergraduate classes at Harvard and Rutgers Universities.

Chapter 7

Five Easy Arguments for Assisted Suicide and the Objections of Velleman and Gorsuch

I.

At the end of Chapter 6, we tried to deduce from the moral permissibility and reasonableness of someone's willingness to omit easy means of saving his life, the moral permissibility and reasonableness of his taking his life by suicide (S), physician-assisted suicide (PAS), or having euthanasia (E) done to him. In this chapter we return to different moral arguments for PAS[1] and E. These arguments are "freestanding" in that they are not concerned with deriving conclusions from the views that some particular thinker already holds unlike the moral argument in Chapter 6. In Part I, I first present two arguments for the moral permissibility of PAS and E and one argument for a duty of a doctor to engage in PAS or E, all to eliminate physical suffering. I then present a fourth argument for PAS and E on grounds other than eliminating suffering. In Part II, I consider several objections to these arguments including those that have been or might be raised by philosopher David Velleman and by Neil Gorsuch, now a U.S. Supreme Court justice (and so in a position to affect public policy on PAS and E). In the course of that discussion, I present a fifth argument for PAS and E. (I assume throughout that a patient's free and informed consent to PAS or E or other procedures I discuss is required and present).[2]

A. The Four-Step Argument

1. Doctors are morally permitted to relieve physical pain[3] in a patient by administering morphine to him or by providing it for his use, even if they know with certainty that its use will cause

Almost Over. F. M. Kamm, Oxford University Press (2020) © Oxford University Press.
DOI: 10.1093/oso/9780190097158.001.0001

his death as a foreseen side effect. They may do this when and because death is a lesser bad and pain relief is a greater good for that person (both objectively considered and in his own view) and only the morphine can stop the pain. This is the Morphine for Pain Relief (MPR) Case.[4]

2. Doctors are morally permitted to intentionally cause or assist in the intentional causing of other lesser bads to a patient when these are the necessary means to his medically relevant greater good (e.g., a doctor might permissibly assist a patient to intentionally cause the patient temporary pain if only this would keep the patient from falling into a permanent coma, or permanently eliminate his sight if only this will save him to still live an overall good life).[5]

3. When death is a lesser bad for a person, it is not morally different from other lesser bads for a person.[6]

4. Therefore, when death is a lesser bad and pain relief a greater good for the same person (just as it is in Step 1), a doctor is morally permitted to intentionally cause death, or assist in its being intentionally caused, when it alone can stop pain. For example, a doctor could give morphine, which itself no longer relieves pain, in order to induce death. This is the Morphine for Death (MD) Case.[7]

B. The Terminal Four-Step Argument

The Four-Step Argument applies to terminal and nonterminal cases. The following Terminal Four-Step Argument applies only to terminal cases in which death is any way imminent.[8]

1a. Doctors are morally permitted to relieve pain in a patient by administering morphine to him or providing it for his use, even if they know with certainty that this will cause his death as a foreseen side effect. They may do this *even if death is a greater bad than pain* for the same person, when and because death is unavoidably imminent in any case (e.g., in a terminal patient) and only the morphine can stop the pain.[9]

2a. Doctors are morally permitted to intentionally cause or assist in the intentional causing of other even greater, unavoidably imminent bads to a patient when these are the necessary means to his medically relevant (even lesser) goods. (For example, suppose that it is worse for someone to be blind than to be deaf. If a patient will shortly be blind anyway, it would be permissible to intentionally cause the blindness or help it to be intentionally caused, if only this would prevent the patient from also going deaf.)

3a. When death is an imminent bad for a person, it is not morally different from other imminent bads for a person.

4a. Therefore, even if death is a greater bad and relief of pain is a lesser good for the same person, doctors are morally permitted to intentionally cause death or assist in its being intentionally caused when death is imminent anyway and intentionally causing it can alone stop pain.

In the Terminal Four-Step Argument, we need not assume that a shorter life with less physical suffering can be better for someone than a much longer one with more such suffering. We need only assume that it is in one's interest to die somewhat sooner when death would come soon anyway and only dying sooner can reduce physical suffering. (Admittedly the suffering would not last long if death were imminent.) One way to understand this is that even if death is worse for a person than long-term pain, the loss of short additional time alive were death to come a bit sooner can be less bad for the person than pain during that time.[10] (In the terminal by contrast to the nonterminal case there is also less chance of losing significant additional good time alive were it a mistake to cause a death.)

C. Clarification and elaboration of the arguments

1. The general structure of the two Four-Step Arguments is to show that in some carefully circumscribed cases if a doctor is morally permitted to kill someone or assist in causing his death as a foreseen side effect, the doctor is also morally permitted to kill him intending the death or assist him in intentionally causing his death as the means to his medically relevant good. Sometimes it is said that the PAS is inconsistent with the "value of life." But at least the comparative value for the person of life versus avoiding pain is the same whether

avoiding pain involves causing a foreseen or intended death, or is involved in a decision not to use life-extending treatment either because
extended life or the treatment itself would be painful. Might it be
objected that in MPR, by contrast to MD, morphine causes a period of
life without pain and this period is what has greater value compared
to death that will occur, not the mere cessation of pain per se? But if
the period of life without pain has no goods in it (e.g., the morphine
also causes unconsciousness), it must be the mere end of pain that is
the greater good relative to staying alive. In addition if one would not
avoid immediate death by using a painful life-extending treatment
one would also be comparing the value of no pain, not the value of a
pain-free period of life, with the value of staying alive.

Hence the question of the comparative value for a person of continued life versus avoiding pain has already been settled even when
one chooses to allow death to come by omitting treatment rather than
to allow pain to continue by living on for some period of time.

There are two ways of thinking of this comparison. In the first way,
one compares the shorter life without pain at the end with the longer
life containing pain at the end and decides that the first life is better
for the person to have. In the second way, one compares the future
stretch of life with pain in it to zero involved in being dead during
the same period and decides the negative value of the painful future
stretch of life is worse for the person than the zero involved in his
being dead. Hence, one can decide that avoiding the pain is better for
the person even though he does not go on existing in a pain-free state
(since he goes out of existence).

Nevertheless, the comparative values of outcomes for persons
do not always determine what it is permissible to do, at least for
nonconsequentialists who emphasize deontological distinctions.
Hence, one has to argue for the permissibility of intending to end life
to avoid pain (as in Steps 2-4 in the Four-Step Argument) even if one
has already morally accepted letting someone die or causing only his
foreseen death. (As we shall see, Gorsuch tries to derive such a deontological distinction from what he sees as the intrinsic value of life despite its comparative disvalue for the person by comparison to death.)

2. When a doctor gives morphine merely foreseeing that death
will (or even could) be a side effect, he can be said to kill someone
when death results. This is because it is possible to kill people without

intending to do so (even when there was only a risk of their being killed) as in collateral killings of civilians in war. Also, it is assumed in Steps 1 and 1a in the arguments that even when death can be foreseen to certainly occur, giving the morphine need not involve an intention that death occur.[11]

I believe that the doctor has a moral right to not be interfered with by third parties while carrying on in the ways described in the arguments. Why then do I not speak of a doctor's full right (a liberty to act and claim right against interference) rather than just a moral permission to act? The fundamental right is, I think, a person's right to seek a doctor to help her, to not be interfered with in doing so, and to give the doctor permission to act. Since she might withdraw permission, the doctor does not have a moral right to noninterference from her.[12] But the arguments so far considered also do not demonstrate that she has a moral right against the doctor that would give the doctor a correlative duty to her to perform PAS at her request.

These arguments take elimination of physical pain and suffering to be the particular medically relevant goods to be weighed against death. The structure of the arguments, however, allows that other goods can be substituted for elimination of pain. In fact, avoiding such pain is not the most common reason given for wanting PAS.[13] I focus first on the arguments using avoidance of pain because many proponents and opponents of PAS think it is the strongest (though in the case of opponents, still inadequate) justification for PAS and because it is a clear medically relevant good.

The arguments do not *merely* conclude that the doctors who rightfully give the morphine when only it relieves pain may do so even if they intend their patients' deaths, though I believe this is true. In such a case, the morphine they give would relieve the patients' pain and even if that is not the doctors' aim in giving them the morphine, the fact that relief occurs can make the act morally permissible. By contrast, the Four-Step Arguments are concerned in their conclusion with more than this; they are concerned with a doctor who (it is reasonable to think) could have no other reason for giving morphine besides killing or assisting in killing since the morphine itself no longer relieves pain but only causes the death that is the means to pain relief.

3. The two Four-Step Arguments are directed against the common use of the Doctrine of Double Effect (DDE) to argue for the permissibility

of MPR but rule out S, PAS, and E. The absolutist version of the DDE says in its shortest version (roughly) that one may never act or omit to act intending a bad as a means or end. However, suppose the same bad is merely a foreseen side effect and is proportionate to a good end, for example it is a lesser bad by comparison to the good end of preventing a much greater bad. Then its occurrence need not interfere with acting (or omitting to act) intending that good end and using some nonbad means to it. Merely foreseen bad side effects may be certain to occur and intended bad effects may have a low probability of occurring without this affecting the permissibility of acting with mere foresight to the bad and the impermissibility of acting intending the bad according to the DDE. It is because my aim is to deal with the DDE that I imagine a case in which morphine needed to eliminate pain foreseeably also causes death, even if this never occurs in reality.

In arguing against the DDE, one need not support the more radical claim that the distinction between intending and foreseeing bads never makes a moral difference to permissibility in order to hold that it clearly makes no difference in a case where the least lesser bad is A's pain and we have A's free and informed consent to cause the pain to achieve the greater good of saving A's life. We may act merely foreseeing the pain or intending it. As premise (2) in the first Four-Step Argument shows, the intention to cause something bad need not be a bad intention in itself when the same person who suffers the bad benefits more. A person's willing this can be an instance of Intrapersonal Rationality.[14] The Four-Step Argument says, in part, that the same is true when death is the least lesser bad available and pain relief is the greater good, a comparative valuation already assumed by premise (1) in the Four-Step Argument.[15]

D. The Doctor's Duty Argument

As already noted, the arguments so far presented are for a moral permission for a doctor to act protected from third party interference. This gives the doctor a protected option to act or not to act. It does not give the doctor a duty to act. However, another Four-Step Argument may be available for a doctor's duty to assist suicide or to perform euthanasia. Assuming that free and informed patient consent is required and present:

1b. Doctors have a moral *duty* to treat pain (e.g., by administering morphine or providing it for a patient's use), even if they foresee with certainty that it will make them cause or assist in causing the patient's death soon. This is so when death is the (least) lesser bad and pain relief is a greater good, or when death is unavoidably imminent (even if it is a greater bad than long term pain) and only morphine can stop the pain.

2b. Doctors have a moral *duty* to intentionally cause bads or assist in their being intentionally caused (e.g., pain, blindness) for a patient's own medically relevant good. This is so when the bads are (the least) lesser ones and the goods to be achieved by them are greater or when the bads are unavoidably imminent anyway and the bads are the only way to achieve a medically relevant good (including avoiding a medically relevant bad).

3b. When death is a lesser or imminent bad for a person, it is not morally different from other lesser or imminent bads for a person.

4b. Therefore, doctors have a moral *duty* to intentionally cause the patient's death or assist in its being intentionally caused when death is a (least) lesser bad and pain relief is a greater good for the patient or when death is imminent anyway and causing it alone can stop the patient's pain.

The Doctor's Duty Argument is important because some have claimed that doctors' *professional ethic*, in particular, implies that they may not engage in PAS or E. By contrast, this argument suggests that doctors' professional ethic sometimes calls for them to perform PAS or E. It is also important because it shows that while a doctor might, for example, sometimes permissibly raise a conscientious objection to killing (e.g., killing a fetus in abortion), the same type of objection may not apply to PAS or E. This is because harming people for their own greater good (an intrapersonal matter) may be morally different from harming one being (e.g., fetus) for the sake of the greater good of another being (e.g., pregnant woman). Hence, suppose a doctor might conscientiously refuse to intentionally cause such evils as blindness in a viable fetus who will develop into a person for the sake of saving the life of a woman in whose body the fetus grows. She could still be required to blind a person to save that person's own life, assuming the person gives free and informed consent. If one continues to believe that doctors may conscientiously refuse to assist in PAS or to perform E in the cases I have described, one will have to provide a different objection to the Doctor's Duty Argument.[16]

Notice that the Doctor's Duty Argument differs from the following one: "Suppose the Four-Step Argument is correct. Then, with a patient's free and informed consent, a doctor is morally permitted to intentionally kill or assist in the suicide of her patient when the patient's death is the (least) lesser bad for the sake of the patient's medically relevant greater good. If the doctor has a duty to relieve physical suffering, then she has a duty to do whatever she is morally permitted to do in order to fulfill her duty. Hence, she has a duty to kill or assist in the suicide of the patient if death is the lesser bad in order to produce the greater good of pain relief." This argument is unsatisfactory, since one does not have a duty to do whatever one is morally permitted to do in order to carry out another duty. Sometimes what one has a moral permission to do is still supererogatory (i.e., beyond duty). For example, a doctor may have a moral permission to give up all her money to save her patient's life, and she has a duty to save her patient's life, but that does not mean she has a duty to give up all her money to save her patient's life.

The Doctor's Duty Argument is a better argument because it begins by pointing to a doctor's duty to at least sometimes give morphine even though she has no duty to sometimes give up all her money. Further, this dutiful act is in some important respects like the one that the Four-Step Argument concludes a doctor has a moral permission to do, namely give morphine intending to cause death or assist in its being intentionally caused by the person who will die. The Doctor's Duty Argument then points out that a doctor has a *duty* to do analogous acts of intentionally causing other lesser bads for a patient's medically relevant good (such as causing pain when it keeps someone from falling into a coma or blinding when it keeps someone alive for a good life). It thus shifts the burden of proof to showing why a doctor does *not* also have a duty to give a drug intending to cause death or to assist in its being intentionally used by the patient if the doctor has a moral permission to do so (given that providing the drug can sometimes be a duty unlike giving all one's money).

E. A paradigmatic reasons argument

I have already noted that according to empirical data most requests for PAS or E are not for relief from physical suffering. Though I will not focus on these other cases, it may be helpful to review the motivation for these requests and show how the structure of the Four-Step Argument can be adapted to cases not involving relief from physical suffering.[17]

As noted in Chapter 4, many proponents of advanced care (AC) and end of life care (EOLC) emphasize that people should be able to decide what makes life near death acceptable to them. As we have seen, the philosopher Bernard Williams said that there are what he called "conditional desires," the objects of which one would want if one is alive and must remain so. For example, for many people this includes not being in pain. Then there are other desires that Williams called "categorical," the objects of which give one reasons to go on living in order to get them. Not being in pain is not something whose achievement in itself gives one a reason to go on living. Often when proponents of AC and EOLC talk about providing a life that is acceptable to a person until the end, they talk about continuing to have meaningful relationships and activities. These are the sorts of things that could reasonably be the objects of categorical desires.[18] An implication of this could be that a good end of life may sometimes only be achievable by actually seeking death before life becomes unacceptable because it lacks objects of categorical desires that give one a reason to go on living. Such a lack could also exist in nonterminal cases where someone faces the prospect of a long life with nothing in it that could support categorical desires. (This lack may even be due to side effects of palliative care given to stop physical suffering.) This lack is one of the "paradigmatic reasons" for seeking PAS.

Here is an argument for PAS done for these paradigmatic reasons that is modeled on the Four-Step Argument. It assumes a patient's free and informed consent throughout.

1c. It could sometimes be morally permissible for a doctor to give people who find their lives unacceptable a drug that alone would allow them to engage in meaningful projects again (or prevent their engaging in what they not unreasonably consider unacceptable behavior) even though this drug puts a strain on their heart and foreseeably will shortly cause death.[19] This could be permissible because (as when they would refuse easy life-saving treatment) earlier death is these people's least bad option relative to a life they not unreasonably find unacceptable even though it has no physical suffering in it.[20]

2c. It is ordinarily reasonable to intend (by action or omission) the least bad option for oneself in order to avoid a worse option for oneself. This is part of Intrapersonal Rationality. This helps make it permissible for a doctor to intentionally impose or assist in imposing the bad of temporary pain on us if only this will prevent us from falling into a permanent coma or to permanently end our sight if only this will save us for a still acceptable life.

3c. When death is the least bad option for a person (or imminent in any case) it is not morally different from other least bad options (or imminent bads) for a person.

4c. If it has already been decided (not unreasonably) by the person (as in the first step) that death is his least bad option relative to continuing what he finds an unacceptable life, it is permissible for a doctor to intentionally cause a patient's death or assist a person in intentionally causing his death in order to avoid what that person not unreasonably sees as the worse option of continuing life.

One reason this argument may be contentious is that it involves doctors helping people avoid conditions that are not ordinarily considered medical problems. Another reason for its being contentious is that in step 1c it may be the extra acceptable life achieved by the drug that is the greater good relative to death not merely the avoidance of the unacceptable life (as would occur with immediate death). But as the period of extra acceptable life caused by the drug shrinks, it is more likely that merely avoiding unacceptable life is being weighed against death. This would also be shown by someone's refusing easy treatment to prevent immediate death when the life he would have if saved would be unacceptable to him.[21] I shall not consider the Paradigmatic Reasons Argument further in this chapter (but do so in Chapter 8). Instead, I will consider objections to the arguments concerned with avoiding physical suffering.[22]

II. Some Possible Objections

A. The Four-Step Argument focuses on what is good *for* a person (i.e., life or death).[23] An objection to the argument might be based on the claim that this ignores the good or value *of* the person. For example, David Velleman agrees that death may sometimes be in a person's interest (good for him) because it is less bad *for* him than living on would be *for* him.[24] However, he argues that what is good for the person (by which he means the person getting what is good for him) has value (matters) only because a person has value (matters).[25] It is, he argues, irrational to sacrifice the *ground* of the value of what is good for him (namely his personhood) to what is good for him. Velleman has tried to defend this view, it seems to me, in several ways.

One way is analogizing the relation between a person and what is good for him to the relation between an end to be brought about and the means to it: It makes no sense to sacrifice the existence of an end so as to achieve the means to it, and so (he says) it makes no sense to sacrifice the existence of the person to achieve what is good for him. I think the analogy is flawed. If our goal in PAS were the existence of a person who is not in pain, it would indeed make no sense to eliminate the person to get rid of the pain just as it would make no sense to eliminate an end so as to achieve the means to it. But while the nonexistence of an end is not "good for it," the person ceasing to exist earlier and so having a shorter life without the pain could be better for him than his ceasing to exist later and so having a longer life whose continuation involves the pain.

Another argument that Velleman seems to offer is that (a person getting) what is good for a person has value (matters) only because the person has value (matters). However, if it were permissible to eliminate a person to stop his pain that would show he had no value, and so eliminating his pain (something that is good for him) would have no value. One indication that this argument is problematic is that an analogous argument would make it senseless (contrary to fact) to euthanize even a cat: Presumably a cat's avoiding pain has value (matters) because the cat has value (matters) to some degree in its own right. However, according to Velleman's argument if we may eliminate the cat to stop its pain, then the cat doesn't matter and so its avoiding pain doesn't matter either. This argument too seems incorrect. The pain of the cat matters, at least in part, because the cat matters in its own right and eliminating the cat to stop what is bad for it does not show that the cat does not matter, only that its continuing existence does not matter as much as eliminating pain that is bad for it. I think the form of Velleman's argument is also wrong when applied to persons: preventing the pain of a person could matter because the person matters and eliminating the person to stop what is bad for her (the pain) does not show that she does not matter. It shows only that her *continuing existence* sometimes does not matter as much as preventing pain that is bad for her. It is the value of the *person*, not the value of the *continuing existence* of the person, that grounds the value of preventing her pain.[26]

However, Velleman has gone on to explicitly argue[27] that the appropriate attitude to the value of a person (which he thinks grounds the value of what is good for the person) is to maintain the person in existence.[28] In response one might say that in the case of many other things that have value in themselves, the appropriate attitude is not necessarily to maintain them in existence but to appreciate them for a time (e.g., a beautiful sound need not be sustained). In the case of valuable things with an inner life (beings vs. inanimate objects), maintaining them in existence may be important because it is good for them. But there may be only a prima facie or pro tanto reason to maintain them in existence since an appropriate attitude to their value should take account of "what it is like" for them to go on existing. Hence, an appropriate attitude to their value could imply that one thing that is good for them (e.g., no pain) overrides something else that is ordinarily also good *for* them and that derives its value from their value, namely their continuing existence.[29]

Such overriding implies that we can compare the value of their continued existence with the disvalue of pain and other bad things that would happen to them if they continued to exist. This raises another possibly contentious point. One interpretation of the Kantian view that a person has unconditional, incomparable value is that one cannot compare the value of the person with the value of what is merely good or bad *for* the person. As already noted, this claim relating to the value of a person per se may not rule out PAS since a person could have incomparable value without it being true that the continued existence of the person has incomparable value. Hence, the continued existence of the person (which ordinarily has value for the person) could be compared with, and exchanged for, other things that have value for the person. One does such an exchange if one takes a medicine that will foreseeably shorten one's life by five years in order to live the shortened life unparalyzed. But if the appropriate response to the value of a person were always to maintain him in existence, one should not compare the value of his continuing to exist for the extra years with something else that is good for him (e.g., not being paralyzed). Ruling out such comparisons and exchanges would not only rule out suicide (i.e., intentionally eliminating oneself) in order to eliminate what is bad for oneself; it would rule out giving morphine in MPR[30] or refusing life-saving treatment because the treatment itself (or the life saved) would be painful. In doing these things one merely foresees and does not intend that death will result. Yet they would be ruled out because the decisions to do them also require comparing the value of the continued existence of the person with the elimination or prevention of pain to him.

It might be said that one need not go through painful treatments to save one's life because one need not pay all costs to maintain one's life. However, weighing the pain to oneself against the continued existence of one's person would involve *comparing* them and exchanging one for the other. Doing this seems inconsistent with claiming that the incomparable value of a person implies that his continued existence also has incomparable value. Terminal sedation which does not itself shorten someone's life but puts him in a state in which he does not feel pain until he dies of an underlying disease could also be ruled out. This is because terminal sedation would permanently interfere with the exercise of rational agency and perhaps even with the continued existence of the capacity for rational agency, a capacity that is said by Kantians to be the basis of the value of the person. One weighs loss of this capacity and/or loss of its exercise against continuing pain in deciding whether to use terminal sedation.

There may indeed be morally significant distinctions among alternatives to pain that all interfere with the capacity for rational agency (and possibly with other grounds of the value of the person). Death simply eliminates the person. Suppose (contrary to fact) that severe dementia, which is a perversion but not elimination of thought and agency, also stopped severe pain. It could be worse than death as a way to eliminate pain. Indeed, because it can strip away character-istics on which personhood and its value is said to depend, Velleman thinks that preventing or ending dementia could justify "hastening death" when the avoidance of mere bad things *for* a person could not. He says: "My own view is that hastening death becomes mor-ally appropriate only in the context of deterioration or suffering that compromises autonomy to an extent that can make talk of suicide inappropriate."[31] By contrast, many supporters of the moral permissi-bility of PAS typically think that only a still rational person who has consented on several occasions, at appropriate intervals, to PAS may have it done, and legal regulations follow this model. (Arguably, MPR that foreseeably will shortly kill someone should also require con-sent of a still-rational agent.) This implies that the person who dies in PAS or E should be someone who still retains the characteristics that ground the value of a person.

Velleman's position on hastening death suggests that only nonvoluntary killing of someone would be morally permissible since the person's autonomy must already be severely compromised for killing him or assisting his (at least behavior of) killing himself to be permissible.[32] However, what he has in mind need not be nonvoluntary *euthanasia* because that is death that is good *for* the person, whereas he is concerned with avoiding the degradation *of* the person. Perhaps it could be called "nonvoluntary dignitasia." From the point of view of a liberal legal order based on individual choice, bringing this about would be problematic unless advance directives by still rational people who asked for such future "dignitasia" were legally recognized.

B. Another type of objection to the Four-Step Argument focuses on step 3 insofar as it takes intending death to be different from in-tending other lesser bads for a person.

(1) Greater badness of death. One version of this objection claims that if death in particular is intended (and caused) by the person who dies, it will incur overridingly bad consequences such as eternal punishment in hell. These bad effects of death will make it overall a greater bad for the person than pain (or an otherwise unaccept-able life). This would make the Four-Step Argument irrelevant to concluding that PAS and E were permissible because the second step which speaks about intending lesser bads would not apply to death in-tentionally brought about in PAS. This view about the consequences

of an intended death is part of a particular religious perspective that some may accept as a matter of faith. But it would not be unreasonable for others to ask why intentionally causing one's death in particular is punishable in this way. After all, there could be a religion one of whose tenets is that intentionally destroying one's sight in order to stay alive is punishable by hell but not the intentional destruction of one's life to avoid suffering. There could also be religions in which one is rewarded with a good afterlife if one intentionally ends one's life to avoid great suffering. Suppose we have as yet no reason to think that intentionally causing what is otherwise a lesser bad (e.g., as when it is merely foreseen to result from what we do) turns it into a greater bad by attaching terrible consequences to it. Then there is no reason as yet to think the objection being considered makes the Four-Step Argument irrelevant to deciding about the morality of PAS and E.

More importantly, suppose death became a greater bad for a person due to the bad consequences of intentionally causing it. If these bad consequences come as punishment, then there must be some moral reason why intentionally causing the death is wrong independent of the death being overall a greater rather than a lesser bad for the person. This is because death would only become an overall greater bad because it was wrong on other grounds to intentionally cause it. Hence, the moral reason for not intentionally causing it would be whatever makes doing this wrong, not the bad effects of committing the moral wrong that would make committing it be against one's self interest. It is its being wrong that makes doing it involve a greater bad for one, not its being a greater bad for one that makes doing it morally wrong. Suppose death remained a lesser bad for one because the moral wrong of intentionally causing it did not get punished. It would be beside the moral point to show that what one should not do because it is morally wrong is in one's self interest (because it is a lesser bad for one). Of course, one would still need to be provided with a reason why intentionally causing one's death when death is a lesser bad for one is wrong.[33]

(2) Doctrine of Double Effect. Neil Gorsuch (now Justice Gorsuch of the U.S. Supreme Court) tries to provide such a reason (on nonreligious grounds) why intentionally causing one's own or another's death is wrong when he defends the DDE both as a moral doctrine and as the basis for distinctions in the law. Since the

DDE does not imply that the first step in the Four-Step Argument permitting MPR is wrong, Gorsuch need not object to it. Let us examine some of his views.[34] Before considering his reasons for thinking intention is morally distinctive (in [d] below) let us consider his views on when PAS occurs and how to identify intention in theory and practice.

(a) Defining PAS. Gorsuch defines PAS to require that the doctor intends the patient's death not necessarily as an end in itself but as a means to an end. Gorsuch specifically argues (72) against the attempt by courts to permit intentionally causing death when it is a mere means to another good end. Gorsuch says, "Assisted suicide cases have never distinguished between intended means and intended ends"; he is correct that the DDE rules out both.

Gorsuch's focus on the doctor's intending death as a necessary condition for the presence of PAS contrasts with many who would allow that PAS can involve a doctor who does not intend the patient's death but only intends that the patient have the means (e.g., a prescription for a lethal medicine) to autonomously decide whether or not he will end his life. In Gorsuch's view (64) this alternative conception would not be PAS according to the law. Furthermore, he argues that the law takes "individualism" seriously: It does not assume that merely because a person who takes a lethal medication prescribed by a doctor intends his own death, the doctor also intends the death rather than intends to give the patient an autonomous choice.[35] In addition, Gorsuch thinks that the legal prohibition should only concern the doctor's role and intention, not the act and intention of the person who uses the medication to commit suicide even though the latter may be an immoral act. Hence, surprisingly, the objections that Gorsuch raises to PAS do not apply at all to cases in which doctors prescribe medications with the intention of promoting patients' autonomy even if the patients intentionally cause their own deaths.[36]

(b) Locating intention in theory. Now consider how Gorsuch understands and locates intention. This is a purely conceptual matter. Even those who think intention will not make a difference to moral permissibility of an act can agree it is conceptually distinct from mere foresight. At one point (60) he refers to (but does not endorse) the view that if one knows one's act will cause x and one desires x, then one intends x in acting. But this is not correct since, for example, one could know that one's act of building a house will cause flowers to grow nearby and one desires such flowers to grow without doing the act intending to make flowers grow.

Gorsuch also refers (71) to a counterfactual test for intentions. He seems to think the test could be of use at least in determining the intentions of others. He describes it as asking, "if the questionable result at issue could have been avoided . . . but all the other positive events also occurred, would the actor still have chosen to act as he or she did?" He thinks the test implies that if the actor would still have chosen to act, the questionable result "is not required to achieve the wished for results," and so it is not an intended means but only an unintended side effect. However, this is not a correct counterfactual test for intention. After all one might have had several intentions and proceeding if one does not get the "questionable result" as an end or means does not show one did not intend it.

It might be suggested that a better counterfactual test for conceptually distinguishing intention from foresight asks: Holding everything else constant, if effect x would not occur as a result of your act, would this give you a reason (i.e., some but not necessarily a determinative reason) not to act? If one says no, then according to the test this indicates one did not intend x. However, note that while this test also shows that if one intends x, one would answer yes—the absence of x would give one a reason not to act—it may not show that if one says yes, one intends x. After all, one could do an act *because* this will produce x and have a reason not to act if it doesn't without intending x. This is so in cases in which the worth of acting on some other intention (e.g., to produce z) is conditional on one's act also producing some effect x though one wouldn't do anything merely to bring about effect x. For example, suppose I want to have a party for my guests' enjoyment but I will not have it if I have to clean up the mess. I find out that psychologists have shown that if guests enjoy themselves, they will clean up. I have the party with the intention of producing my guests' enjoyment, not with the intention of making them clean up, and would do nothing additional besides holding the party to get them to clean up. But I would not have the party if it didn't have the effect of making them clean up. Here I take advantage of an effect I do not intend in deciding whether to do the act for the sake of a goal I do intend.[37]

Gorsuch's ultimate reason for not relying on a counterfactual test is that "It does not . . . focus directly on the actor's actual intentions and state of mind but replaces the inquiry with a hypothetical construct" (71). One problem with this reason for rejection is that a counterfactual test is meant to help us find out someone's (even our own) *actual* intentions. In addition, as we will see, focusing on the importance of actual intentions conflicts with the way in which Gorsuch tries to distinguish the permissibility of ending life support from what he thinks is the impermissibility of PAS.

(c) Locating intention in practice. I will not here pursue the issue of how to properly identify intentions as a theoretical matter. Instead I will consider where Gorsuch and some others locate intention as a practical matter and the role this plays in their deciding whether to prohibit PAS for some if it has bad effects on others. Gorsuch presents (138) this as the problem of comparing "the interest the rational adult seeking death has in dying with the danger of mistakenly killing [other] persons without their consent."[38] He thinks this comparison involves "radically differing competing values" (138) whose comparison "is senseless in the way that it is senseless to compare . . . the virtues of apples to those of oranges." Gorsuch considers one way to resolve the competition offered by philosopher Margaret Battin (139), who (he says) argues that prohibiting PAS on grounds of it leading to mistaken or coerced killing of others would involve *intending* to impose suffering on some that PAS could end in order (i.e., intending) to prevent the bad side effects on others. According to Gorsuch, Battin says this involves using some people in a way that is bad for them to help others and this is typically not allowed morally or legally at least in nonconsequentialist morality.

My own view is that there are at least three problems with Battin's analysis (as presented by Gorsuch). One problem is that she equates not allowing the alleviation of suffering with imposing it. A second problem is that she may think that even the former involves violating the DDE's prohibition on letting bads (such as suffering) occur with the intention that they occur (as a means to help others). However, intending that no one use the only means available to help end suffering does not necessarily involve intending the suffering itself to prevent bad effects to others. A third problem is that if a legal right to PAS itself would cause the bad effects to others, prohibiting PAS would not be like a case in which we would intentionally not use means to stop someone suffering because this will help others avoid bad effects that would *not* be caused by those very means. It is this latter type of conduct that falls in the class of what is clearly typically not allowed.[39]

Gorsuch himself responds to Battin's argument in two ways. First, he denies that if we prohibit PAS we would be intending to let people suffer to prevent wrongful harm to others. Rather, he says (141, 160), the situation should be analyzed as one in which we intend to protect people from mistaken or coerced PAS merely foreseeing that we will then not be able to help end some other people's suffering by PAS. Second, he also argues (140) that this is analogous to the state's intending not to mistakenly execute one innocent person even though this involves releasing ten guilty people foreseeing that releasing them enables (by emboldening) criminals to harm other innocents.

I think there are problems with both parts of Gorsuch's response to Battin. First, consider his second argument. In the supposed analogy, the state refuses to itself intentionally and possibly mistakenly kill one person even if its refusal enables more wrong killings by others. This differs from refusing to permit other agents (doctors) to perform nonmistaken PAS because this (by hypothesis) would enable more wrong killings by other agents (not the state). (So a better if imperfect analogy would involve the state refusing to kill a known guilty person only because its doing so may enable others to engage in wrongful killings.) However, the use of his analogy shows that Gorsuch thinks it is right for the state to sometimes do (including omit to do) what enables others to wrongfully kill. In his analogy it is the state not intentionally killing someone that enables others to kill but it could be the state allowing PAS that enables others to kill. Yet according to his analogy, it need not be wrong of the state to allow this to happen.

Second, consider a problem with the analysis in his first response to Battin. If the state intends to protect some people by not permitting PAS to others, its intended means to protect them is not allowing PAS (the act which is hypothesized to have the bad effects). The fact that the state's intended end is protection of some people from abuse does not exclude that it also *intends* to allow some others to suffer (though not intending their suffering per se) as a means to that end. Gorsuch's alternative analysis is that intending to protect some people from mistaken or coerced PAS would involve only foreseeably not helping relieve others' suffering. This analysis would be correct if, for example, limited financial resources were spent on police oversight to prevent coerced PAS thus leaving no more money to support proper PAS. However, this would be a different type of case. (I shall further refine this analysis below.)

I conclude that neither Battin's nor Gorsuch's analysis is quite right. However, it is Gorsuch who goes wrong in determining that there need be no intention to allow people to suffer if PAS were disallowed in order to prevent its (hypothesized) bad effects on others.

A different argument from Battin's might criticize Gorsuch's view that harm to others could be a ground for prohibiting PAS by emphasizing the distinction between "enabling" harm and causing it. (This distinction has already been noted above in discussing the government's releasing possibly guilty people though this may embolden other criminals to kill.) Suppose laws that permit PAS (and also the legal acts of PAS) causally enable or prompt another intervening agent to wrongly or mistakenly do PAS. This is not the same as the law directing such wrong conduct or a legal act of PAS causing harm to others without any intervening agents who act independently. Monitoring those who would act wrongfully should arguably be the first line of prevention of such bad effects, by contrast to cases in which bad effects from someone's act do not depend on action by intervening agents.[40] The distinction between enabling and causing harm may play a role in the state's not prohibiting other joint activities that enable mistaken or abusive behavior by other agents. For example, legally protected sex between consenting adults is not prohibited even though it may enable rapes. Legally permitted sterilization is not prohibited even though it may enable mistaken or abusive sterilizations.[41] (Possibly weighing the number who would permissibly benefit, the importance of the benefit, the number who would be abused, and alternative ways of providing benefits or stemming abuse is also relevant.)

(d) Whether intending death is wrong. Now let us consider why Gorsuch thinks we should morally and legally care more about action or omission done from the intention to end life than about action or omission done with mere foresight to ending life (holding probability of ending life constant) so that the former could be impermissible when the latter is not.

(i) One reason he gives (55) for the moral significance of intention versus foresight that applies quite generally is that a person freely defines herself by her intentions. This seems true when we look at what people intend as ultimate ends. But is it clearly true that, holding ultimate ends constant, a person freely defines herself by intending something as a means to her end rather than tolerating it as a mere side effect of her act or the end it achieves? After all, it is the environment and not the individual that may determine what means can bring about her end as much as what the side effects will be. Furthermore, when discussing the moral significance of intending versus merely foreseeing, Gorsuch often contrasts acting while merely foreseeing a bad effect (such as death) with intending the bad effect as an ultimate end rather than as a means. He does this when he compares a driver who accidentally runs over a child and "a driver who intentionally hunts down the child with his car" (56). The driver in the latter case defines himself in intending death as an end, so it is not clear how this supports the self-defining role of intending death as a means.

Comparing these two cases is not a good use of the method of contrasting cases because it varies at least two factors between the cases at once: (1) intention of a bad versus no intention of a bad and (2) a bad ultimate intention versus no bad ultimate intention. So one cannot tell whether it is having a bad ultimate intention or intending a bad in any way that is causing a moral difference between the cases. (Arguably the accident case does not even involve foresight to the death that is caused.) To use contrasting cases to see if intention of a bad as a means versus no intention (but foresight) makes a moral difference to self-definition, one should hold all other factors constant, as one would do in a scientific experiment to see if nitrogen has a different effect than oxygen. For example, one could contrast (i) intentionally rushing to save 100 people foreseeing that fumes from one's car will kill someone on the road, with (ii) intentionally releasing fumes from one's car to kill someone on the road because his death is a necessary means to one's ultimate end of saving 100 other people.

Suppose one does define oneself distinctively by one's means as well as by one's ends. If the means are good or neutral, one will define oneself in a good or neutral way by choosing them. So the burden of the argument has to be on showing that intending death as a means is always bad or wrong. (Gorsuch tries to show this by providing a second reason (besides self-definition) why intending death is distinctively important. We discuss this in (ii) below.)

Gorsuch's first, "self-defining" reason to avoid certain intentions may also depend on a notion of duties to oneself not to be a certain sort of person. The legal enforcement of such a duty seems problematic. Note also that it is only by one's actual intentions (or those one would actually have if certain circumstances arose) that one could define oneself. One cannot define oneself by the intention that one could possibly have had for doing a certain act but that one would never have actualized even when one could have. (For simplicity I will refer to these contrasts as "actual" and "possible" intentions.) Yet (as we shall see) in defending the permissibility of discontinuing life-saving means, Gorsuch often emphasizes possible intentions that could lead to an act rather than the actual intention leading to it. Suppose the possibility of there being a good intention for an act makes the act permissible even if the agent defines himself by actually having a bad intention for the act. Then any role intention has in determining whether an act is permissible or impermissible will not be grounded in how that person's intentions define him.

Finally, could it be correct to ground the impermissibility of intending an effect in what the intention says about or does to the agent who intends, rather than in what it says about or does to the person (even himself) he would act on (the "patient" in the "passive" nonmedical sense of this term)? At least in interpersonal cases it seems that even an intention-based theory of impermissibility should focus on how the person whom it is one's intention to affect is mistreated in virtue of one's intention or how some inappropriate relation between an agent and the patient comes to exist in virtue of the agent's intention. For example, Warren Quinn suggested[42] that the DDE is sound insofar as it "distinguishes . . . agency in which harm comes to some victims, at least in part, from the agent's deliberately involving them in something in order to further his purpose precisely by way of their being so involved" (184). Intending involvement is broader than but can include intending the harm itself.[43] He characterized acting or omitting to intentionally involve others in a manner that foreseeably will be harmful to them precisely because their involvement is required to achieve one's ends as "opportunistic agency" and "opportunistic use" of others. Because one requires their involvement in order to achieve one's goals, one takes the fact that they will be involved as a consideration in favor of acting. Quinn thought that treating other people as available for our use in this way when it would harm them (whether or not the harm itself is useful) was distinctively wrong. By contrast, when one affects and harms others as a mere side effect one does not require their involvement—if their involvement didn't occur, one could just as successfully achieve one's aim—and one does not treat them as available for one's use.[44]

In the interpersonal case in which a doctor intends the death of a person who has voluntarily asked for assistance in committing suicide, the doctor does not treat the person as available for her purposes as opposed to the person's own purposes, and the person's own purposes whose achievement requires that he treat his death as a means are not overall harmful for him if death is his least bad alternative by comparison to going on living. Hence the doctor's action and the patient's action would not fall under opportunistic agency as Quinn understands it.

(ii) Gorsuch's second, more fundamental reason for thinking that we should care more about action or omission intending to end life than about action or omission merely foreseeing ending life is that he thinks human life is a basic, innate (by which I think he means intrinsic) good[45] and he thinks one may not intentionally act against a basic, innate good even for the sake of some other such good (163). He thinks this is because to intentionally act against it "is simply and necessarily to deny that it contains inherent, rather than instrumental, value" (164). Unlike his focus on the self-defining aspect of intending this explanation of the moral significance of intention tries to derive the importance of a deontological distinction from the value of the person whom an agent would affect, even when the agent acts on himself. He claims there are many such intrinsic, basic goods, and so we must choose which among them to promote and we may promote some even if we foresee (but do not intend) that other such goods will thereby not be preserved and even be harmed by our actions (163).

One objection to this argument begins by noting that there are other things that Gorsuch recognizes as innate, basic goods such as liberty, works of nature, and art (158) (and others I believe he would recognize, such as sight). Yet it seems morally and legally permissible to sometimes intentionally act against these things despite his claim

(177) that "intentional acts by private persons against basic goods, including life, are categorically wrong." For example, we may sometimes intentionally restrict liberty for the sake of promoting liberty overall or for the sake of other goods. (Private persons such as parents, not only the state, may permissibly do this.) We may intentionally destroy an art work to save human lives or even other art works. We may intentionally destroy someone's sight to preserve his life. The fact that we may for instrumental purposes sometimes act against such intrinsic goods does not imply that they are not intrinsic goods but merely instrumental ones. It only implies that they are not incomparable, nonoverridable intrinsic goods.[46] Hence, it could be consistent with someone's life being a basic, intrinsic good that it be acted against as a means to achieve a different basic or perhaps nonbasic intrinsic good for the same person (e.g., no physical suffering).

If Gorsuch held that the basic intrinsic goods were incomparable and nonoverrideable, then he would no longer be able to compare relieving pain on the one hand with doing what ends human life merely *foreseeably* on the other, and so he could not defend MPR as he and other supporters of the DDE wish to do. He might also not be able to claim, as he does in his book, that those who stop treatment, "learning to accept the inevitable end and to choose to die in a graceful way" (166), are reasonable in thinking that the value of a few more days of life as a person if they continue medical treatment can be compared and outweighed by the value of being at home (with family). Furthermore, even if one holds that a person has incomparable, nonoverridable value, this need not mean that a person's continuing to exist has incomparable, nonoverridable value, as I emphasized in discussing Velleman.

An additional problem for Gorsuch's "inviolability of life principle" (164) prohibiting intentionally acting against human life is the permissibility of killing in self or other defense when we must intend the death of the threatening person. Gorsuch argues (169) that in self or other defense one need not intend the aggressor's death but only that his threat be ended. But this does not deal with the case in which the aggressor's death is a necessary means to ending his threat.[47] Quinn offered one explanation of the permissibility of intending the death in this case while denying the equal permissibility of opportunistic agency. He classified it as a case of "eliminative agency," in one type of which we treat others as available for our use and intend harm to them but only to eliminate a threat they present to us or others.[48] He thought that in this type of agency, unlike what is true in opportunistic agency, we do not require their involvement and presence even though we intentionally use them when they are present. This is because if they were not present and involvable, they also would not be presenting a threat and we would not have to harm them to stop their threat.[49]

Quinn limited his discussion of the moral relevance of distinctions among opportunistic, eliminative, and mere side effect involvements and harmings to interpersonal by contrast to intrapersonal cases. Hence he did not distinguish morally between suicide and doing what one merely foresees will result in one's death. However, I believe that if one's own continued life constitutes the threat one faces (e.g., when living on would be worse for one than death), then one's suicide would be a case of intrapersonal eliminative agency.[50] (This contrasts with someone whose life is good committing suicide to help others. In this case intentionally killing oneself is not eliminating a threat presented to oneself by one's own continued life.) Further, a physician assisting with what I call "eliminative suicide" (or engaging in "eliminative euthanasia") would be assisting someone in eliminating a threat of his own continued life to himself and so, arguably, engaged in helping defend another person against that threat.

In step 2 of the four previous arguments for PAS it was said that doctors are morally permitted to intentionally cause a patient lesser bads other than death if doing this is a means to the patient's medically relevant greater good. An example given was eliminating sight to save a still worthwhile life. But in this example it need not be sight that is a threat to the patient. For example it may just be necessary to intentionally eliminate it as a means to getting rid of the cancer that is threatening someone's life. Here, eliminating the sight would not involve eliminative agency in Quinn's sense. It would involve making use of something that did not present a threat to eliminate a threat and thus be opportunistic agency in Quinn's sense. While Quinn argued that in interpersonal contexts eliminative agency could be justified when opportunistic agency was not, this need not be true in the intrapersonal case at all. It is just that seeing the life that PAS intentionally ends as itself a threat may help some to understand why PAS is justified.

Furthermore, the assumption in step 1 of the four previous arguments is that the elimination of the life is a lesser bad relative to the greater good that results. In interpersonal cases of justified eliminative agency it need not be true that a lesser bad occurs for the sake of a greater good. For example, it could be that the only way to stop someone who threatens to paralyze you is to kill him. Here the good to you of no paralysis is less than the bad to the other person of death and yet the killing is permissible. The steps of the four previous arguments for PAS that we have considered can be combined with the idea that they involve eliminative agency to produce a fifth argument for PAS (or E) that I call the Eliminative Argument for PAS or E:[51] In detail it is:

1d. Doctors are morally permitted to eliminate the threat of physical pain to a patient by administering morphine to him, or by providing it for his use, even if they know with certainty that its use will cause his death as a foreseen side effect. They may do this when and because death is a lesser bad and the threat of pain presented by continuing life is a greater good for that person (both objectively considered and in his own view) and only the morphine can stop the pain. This is the Morphine for Pain Relief (MPR) Case.[52]

2d. Doctors are morally permitted to intentionally cause or assist in the intentional causing of other lesser bads to a patient when these are the necessary means to eliminate greater medically relevant threats (e.g., a doctor might permissibly intentionally amputate a patient's cancerous limb in order to eliminate the threat it presents to the patient's life when life without a limb is a lesser bad and death is a greater bad).

3d. When death is a lesser bad for a person, it is not morally different from other lesser bads for a person.

4d. Therefore, when death is a lesser bad and the threat of pain presented from continuing life is a greater bad (just as it is in step 1), a doctor is morally permitted to intentionally cause death, or assist in its being intentionally caused, when it alone can stop the threat presented by continuing life. For example, a doctor could give morphine, which itself no longer relieves pain, in order to induce death. This is the Morphine for Death (MD) Case.

In sum, it seems that Gorsuch's two ways of defending a moral and legal distinction between intending death and only foreseeing it as a side effect, so that intentionally causing death is wrong when only foreseeably causing it need not be, do not succeed.

(e) Intention and permissibility. We have considered whether intending a person's death is a wrong intention to have. A second question is whether, if an intention is wrong, it can make an act impermissible. The DDE claims that it can. (This is so at least when the act or omission results in what is intended. It is these cases that concern us.) We will now consider how Gorsuch tries to defend the DDE as applied to PAS in particular. To do this we should return to his claim that "a doctor's intention that the patient die must be present in PAS with which the law is concerned" (54). The "must" occurs here only because of his or legislators' decision about what is to count as PAS. This is different from the claim that a type of act (identified independently of the intention with which it is done) that helps someone die *must* involve the intention that the person die because it is a type of act that could not reasonably be done without the intention that someone die. For example, suppose morphine could only cause death and not pain relief in a particular patient who is suffering. A doctor who knows this (i) gives a patient a prescription for morphine (ii) that she would not have given had she not believed he would use it to cause his death, (iii) when giving the prescription produces no other effect she intends or on which her act depends. It is reasonable to conclude that she must be intending the patient's death. In this case, one can infer the intention from the act (along with a counterfactual (ii) and the absence of other attitudes (iii)). However, in the case where the law defines PAS to require the doctor's intention that the patient die, one need not be able to infer her intention from other properties of her act. For example, a doctor might give a prescription for morphine that would relieve pain when it will also kill with or without the intention that the morphine kill the patient.

This has further implications. Gorsuch says (73) that terminating life-saving care at a patient's request need not involve a doctor's intending that the patient die since other possible intentions (e.g., not imposing unwanted touching) could reasonably account for the doctor's act even if this doctor *actually* acts because he intends the patient's death (and the patient does so as well). However, just as one can define PAS for legal purposes as (something like) "a doctor providing a lethal medication that a patient requests to end his life when the doctor intends that the patient die" one could define an act of interest to the law of a "doctor terminating life-saving aid at a patient's request because the patient intends to die when the doctor intends that the patient die." In this description of an act that includes the intention with which it is done, the doctor's intention that death occur "must" be present as much as in Gorsuch's view of legally defined PAS, and it too could be declared illegal. If the possibility that a doctor's giving a lethal prescription to a patient could be done without his intending the patient's death (e.g., only seeking patient autonomy) does not in Gorsuch's view block making some acts of giving lethal prescriptions illegal (those where the doctor actually intends that the patient die), then the possibility that a doctor's terminating aid could be done without his intending the patient's death should not block making some terminations of aid illegal (those where the doctor actually intends that the patient die). In other words, why does Gorsuch focus on actual intentions in delimiting and deciding on illegality of PAS but focus only on possible intentions in delimiting and deciding on the legality of terminating aid?

Here is a possible answer: There would be no point in making it illegal for a doctor to terminate treatment if he actually intends that the patient die because it would still be wrong to keep treatment going against the patient's wishes, and without treatment the patient would predictably die in any case. By contrast, when it is made illegal for a doctor to assist in suicide with a comparable intention, the patient will not predictably die in any case. I do not think this response is adequate. It is possible to interfere with and prosecute a doctor acting with the (supposedly) wrong intention in terminating treatment and still permit a patient to be freed from unwanted treatment by doctors who act without the intention that the patient die. Similarly, Gorsuch is not against a doctor giving a patient a lethal prescription when that doctor only intends that the patient has an autonomous choice. That is, he is willing to prosecute a doctor with the (supposedly) incorrect intention in giving the prescription and yet allow a patient to be helped to commit suicide by a doctor who does not intend the patient's death.

Gorsuch's alternating between taking (i) actual intentions and (ii) possible intentions as important for legality[53] has important implications for his attempt to defend the DDE. This is because emphasizing possible intentions actually undermines rather than defends the DDE and its claim that intentions can determine moral and legal permissibility. It does this in at least two ways. First, one of the implications of the DDE that its supporters have been concerned to emphasize is that when all factors besides intentions are the same, it is the actual intention of an agent that can make the difference between moral permissibility and impermissibility of an act. Consider the case where morphine will eliminate pain but also cause death, and pain relief is the greater good and death the least lesser bad. According to the DDE, whether it is permissible for the doctor to give the morphine depends on whether he actually intends the pain relief and not the death (either as a means or an end). This core implication of the DDE cannot be captured by an approach that emphasizes what intentions for an act (described independently of the intention for it) are possible. This is because the objective features and effects of giving the morphine are, by hypothesis, equally open to the intention to relieve pain with death as an unintended side effect and to the intention to cause death as a means or end. So if Gorsuch emphasizes possible intentions, the act of giving the morphine with the actual intention to cause death could not be judged morally impermissible contrary to what the DDE holds, for reducing pain without intending death could be some agent's possible intention for giving the morphine.

The second way in which the approach that emphasizes possible intentions undermines the DDE is that while it is phrased in terms of intentions, determining which intentions are reasonably possible for an act is done by considering the objective features of the act (e.g., those that are independent of an agent's intention). This suggests that we can omit the intervening step of speaking about "possible intentions" in deciding about permissibility and go directly from the objective features to determining the permissibility or impermissibility of the act independent of agents' intentions.[54]

Therefore, the focus on possible intentions yields implications about cases at odds with those of the traditional DDE. Further, its results overlap with the view that denies that intentions (actual or possible) rather than objective features of acts independent of intentions determine permissibility.[55]

(f) Equal protection. Aside from defending the DDE, one of Gorsuch's arguments (76) against legal PAS for the terminally ill is that equal protection grounds would dictate that PAS also be permissible for the nonterminally ill who suffer greatly in continuing alive. He thinks this implication is unacceptable. (Others, of course, may think this implication is acceptable.)

However, it is worth noting that the Terminal Four-Step Argument points to a possible ground for morally and legally distinguishing PAS in the terminally ill from PAS in the nonterminally ill: Because death is imminent in the former group, PAS would not result in loss of much life that someone would otherwise have had. This would not be true of PAS in the nonterminally ill. The Terminal Four-Step Argument claims that if suffering is a bad, then when death is imminent anyway, we can afford to lose a bit of life to prevent suffering. Gorsuch himself thinks that one might gracefully accept the inevitable death that is imminent and end treatments in order to spend remaining time with family (67). Presumably this is so even if one will have somewhat less time before death if one stops treatment. (This is also independent of its being wrong to force treatment on someone, for that could be wrong even if it were foolish and not graceful to allow death to occur sooner.) This suggests that Gorsuch might also think that the loss of some time alive when death is imminent rather than suffering painful treatment or painful illness is also not unreasonable or morally objectionable. (For example, one might refuse painless but only minimally life-extending treatments if the life extended would be painful.) He also accepts MPR even if it foreseeably hastens death in the terminally ill (67). What the Terminal Four-Step Argument adds to all of this is the permissibility of intentionally causing the somewhat earlier death and the somewhat shorter life to avoid pain. It does not imply helping the nonterminally ill by intentionally causing their deaths much before they would otherwise die.[56]

Note that accepting *only* the Terminal Four-Step Argument might also imply rejecting MPR for nonterminal patients if one foresees that they would die from the morphine. For they could lose many years of life, albeit years with accompanying suffering. If Gorsuch would permit MPR for nonterminal patients when it greatly hastens death because it is not unreasonable to think that death can sometimes be less bad for them than a long future of physical suffering, then the question will again arise of why those patients should not also have a right to PAS. There may be special reasons not to grant either MPR or PAS in the case where many years of life would be lost. For example,

it is more likely that a cure for either the pain or the underlying condition will be found in a few years than in a few months. It might be
worth living a hard life until a cure if it would make possible years of
good life afterwards. However, it might also not be unreasonable to
avoid a period of life that is very bad even if there would be a lengthy
good future beyond it.[57] In any case, it does seem more appropriate to
require repeated requests for MPR that would cause death or for PAS
in nonterminal than in terminal patients, given the difference in the
amount of life they stand to lose.[58]

Notes

1. Not all assisted suicide need be done by a physician but I shall focus on this
case. Debates over the definition of PAS are discussed in more detail in IIB(2) this
chapter and in Chapter 8.

2. The first two arguments were discussed in much greater detail in "Four
Step Arguments for Physician-Assisted Suicide and Euthanasia" in my
Bioethical Prescriptions (Oxford University Press, 2013) and my "Physician-
Assisted Suicide, the Doctrine of Double Effect, and the Ground of Value"
(henceforth "The Ground of Value") in Ethics 109 (1999). The latter built on
my "A Right to Choose Death?" in Boston Review 22 (1997); parts of my
"Physician-Assisted Suicide, Euthanasia, and Intending Death" (henceforth
"PAS, E, and ID") in Physician-Assisted Suicide: Expanding the Debate, eds.
Margaret P. Battin, Rosamond Rhodes, and Anita Silvers (New York: Routledge,
1998, 26–49); and part of "Ending Life," in The Blackwell Guide to Medical
Ethics, eds. R. Rhodes, L. Francis, and A. Silvers (Oxford: Wiley-Blackwell,
2007). I first presented an argument like those in my Creation and Abortion
(New York: Oxford University Press, 1992), and then in Morality, Mortality,
Vol. 2 (New York: Oxford University Press, 1996). The fourth argument is
based on one presented in Chapter 6. It was suggested, in part, in my "End-
of-Life Care and Assisted Suicide," Boston Review, October 5, 2017 and
mentioned at the end of Chapter 4. The fifth argument appeared in that same
article. An earlier version of a part of this chapter was presented as the 2018
Lanson Lecture in Bioethics at the Chinese University of Hong Kong, as the
keynote address at the 2018 Undergraduate Philosophy Conference at St.
Louis University, and as part of a Master Class at the Philosophy School of
the Australian National University, 2019. I am grateful to my commentator,
Dr. Chun Yan Tse at the Lanson Lecture and to audiences on all these occasions
for suggestions.

3. Henceforth, it will be assumed that pain refers to severe physical pain that
involves suffering.

4. It may be said that rather than being a lesser bad, death (a) is no bad at all if one's future will contain only bad things in it, and (b) is no bad at all if a few goods in one's life will be outweighed by great bads. By contrast, I am willing to say that death is a bad in (a) and (b). This is, in part, because I think that the elimination of the person is something bad in itself for him, even if it has as a part the elimination of the person's pain (whether or not it also eliminates some goods the person would have had in living on). I assume that in MPR (and the other cases I discuss unless otherwise noted) death is not only a lesser bad but the least bad of the alternatives in the circumstances. Saying that death is the lesser bad than pain suggests that it must not deprive the person of so many future goods (including just being a person) that the loss of them is a greater bad than the pain would be. However, it may be that some pain would be so bad that even if it would eventually be followed by an outweighing degree of good, it would not be unreasonable not to go through it. Hence, when I say that death is the lesser bad and overall in a person's best interests, I should be understood to include the possibility that it instead is the best alternative to pain (or other bad) that the person could reasonably wish to avoid regardless of an outweighing future good. I discussed such cases (e.g., the case of Dax) in Chapter 2 in criticizing Shelly Kagan's views.

5. We might also imagine a variant on these cases in which a doctor only assists the patient by giving him the means of causing the loss of sight to himself. I also assume that these lesser bads are the least bad alternatives to avoiding a greater bad (including losing out on a greater good) and the patient consents to them.

6. This does not mean it is not different in any way. For example, some lesser bads are only temporary, death is assumed to be permanent; one can go on experiencing things when one undergoes some bads but this is not true if death involves nonexistence. But these differences need not make death morally different from other bads. If death is not assumed to involve nonexistence (e.g., it is followed by heaven, hell, reincarnation, etc.), then it would have further effects that might make its occurrence instrumentally overall better or overall worse than life with pain. In neither case would it be treated as a lesser bad. Step 3 in this argument is an addition to the three step argument given in Chapter 8.

7. Note that in the MPR Case where the morphine relieves the pain, the foreseen death is more completely a bad since the elimination of the person does not involve as a part of itself elimination of pain as in MD, the pain already having been eliminated by morphine.

8. Elsewhere I have called this the Alternative Four-Step Argument.

9. I owe this point to Rivka Weinberg.

10. Notice that the analogy to causing blindness a bit sooner when it is imminent anyway to prevent deafness is imperfect. In the example, long-term blindness is assumed to be worse than long-term deafness and death is assumed to be worse than living on with long-term pain. It can make sense to say that bringing on imminent blindness a bit sooner (i.e., losing a short period of sight) is less bad than the long-term deafness that would otherwise ensue but it makes no

sense to say that bringing on death a bit sooner (losing a short period of life) is less bad than long-term pain that would otherwise ensue. This is because there wouldn't be long-term pain if someone did die sooner since his imminent death will make long-term pain impossible in any case. Given the assumptions about relative value, it also does not seem to make sense to say losing a short period of sight before its imminent end is better than being deaf during that same short period, which would be the analogy to losing a short period of life before life's imminent end being better than enduring pain during that short period. After all, if sightlessness is worse than deafness why would a short period of no sight be better than a short period of deafness? The disanalogy arises, I think, because in the blind/deaf case, we compare one quality of life with another quality whereas in the death/pain case we compare quantity of life with quality of life. Death that involves giving up a great deal of life quantity-wise to avoid long-term pain may not be good for someone but giving up a small quantity of life to avoid pain during that period might be an acceptable trade-off.

11. The distinction between foresight and intention is not a matter of different probabilities of effects. For possible ways to draw the distinction between foresight and intention that do not depend on differences in probability see this chapter, II(B)(2)(b).

12. In Chapter 8 the same basic argument for PAS is presented in terms of a patient's right to give a doctor permission to assist her in suicide.

13. We discuss this in Chapters 6 and 8. For more on this see Emmanuel, E. et al., "Attitudes and Practices of Euthanasia and Physician-Assisted Suicide in the United States, Canada, and Europe," *Journal of the American Medical Association*, 2016, 83–84.

14. This does not imply that it is permissible to cause lesser harm either foreseen or intended to one person for the greater good of another person (interpersonally).

15. Here is an additional reason why it can be important to show that sometimes a patient or a doctor's intentionally causing a patient's death is not morally wrong. In actual cases (by contrast to my hypotheticals) there may be alternatives to PAS or E as a way to stop suffering such as induced comas or terminal sedation. Such ways may involve letting die rather than killing and foreseen rather than intended death. (However, if they are combined with not providing nutrition at a patient's direction and this causes death, the patient at least would be intending death by letting die.) The question is why these alternative means would be preferable if there is nothing morally wrong with intentional killing in PAS, especially since having to be maintained in a nonconscious, dependent state may itself provide reasons against using these alternatives. (I thank Walter Sinnott-Armstrong for suggesting I deal with these alternatives.)

16. One possible objection is related to the availability of possible alternatives such as terminal sedation. Suppose an alternative provided everything else PAS would provide for a patient except not being in a dependent state for months. Then one might consider whether achieving nondependency per se merits

requiring a doctor who finds it personally offensive to assist in intentional killing to perform PAS.

17. In Chapter 6 we considered an argument for S or PAS merely to avoid Diminishment Loss (which could be considered a paradigmatic reasons argument). In Chapter 8 we will also consider a paradigmatic reasons argument for PAS as legal policy.

18. We discuss Williams' distinction in greater detail in earlier chapters, including Chapter 6.

19. In Chapter 6 we investigated how a life could be unacceptable and death a better option without it being true that the life is literally worse than death. That is, if death is a zero on a graph, the life need not be in the negative region below zero.

20. For more details on step 1 in the argument see Chapters 6 and 8.

21. Notice that one can find the comparative value of death and something else by either (a) considering whether one would avoid that something else by a means that cause death or (b) considering whether one would avoid death by means that lead to that something else.

22. I consider objections to a paradigmatic reasons argument in Chapter 8.

23. I have considered other objections in articles cited in endnote 1.

24. Hence he need not disagree with step 3 in the Four-Step Argument, i.e., that when death is a lesser bad for a person it is not morally different from other lesser bads *for* a person. See his "Self Termination," in *Ethics*, April 1999.

25. This is by contrast to its not mattering if something that does not matter gets what is good for it (e.g., a blade of grass gets some water).

26. I raised these two objections to Velleman in "The Ground of Value."

27. Based on a suggestion by Connie Rosati. See J. David Velleman, "Beyond Price," *Ethics*, 118:2 (2008), 191-212.

28. He says: "Even if suicide promotes our happiness, it does so by destroying that whose value is registered in self-love and whose perpetuation self-love normally leads us to care about. Suicide therefore thwarts the concern out of which happiness is worth wanting in the way that entrenches it in our good. Self-interested suicide is therefore irrational" ("Beyond Price," 211).

29. Samuel Dishaw emphasized the fact that continuing existence is also something usually good *for* the person who has inherent value.

30. I also emphasized this point in "The Ground of Value."

31. "Beyond Price," 211.

32. A nonvoluntary killing is one in the absence of true consent. It could be a "guided" suicide. It is not an involuntary killing which is one despite true refusal to be killed.

33. Notice that even if having a particular intention is wrong (and even punishable) this may not be enough to show that the act done with that intention is impermissible. This is because one might do a permissible act (such as saving a life) with a wrong intention (e.g., to frighten one's parent when one takes a big risk to save a life). We shall discuss this further below.

34. As expressed in his *The Future of Euthanasia and Assisted Suicide* (Princeton University Press, 2006). All page references to Gorsuch in my text refer to this book.

35. What of the case in which a patient asks for morphine intending to use it only for pain relief but the doctor intends its foreseeable death-causing properties? Here the patient using the medicine would not commit suicide since he does not intend his death. Presumably the doctor's giving a prescription intending that the patient die is not sufficient to make this a case of PAS if the patient is not aiming to commit suicide, even if the patient takes the medicine prescribed and foresees he will die from it. If so, this implies that even on Gorsuch's view determining what the doctor does (PAS or not) is dependent at least in part on the intention of the patient; the patient's intention is a necessary if not a sufficient condition for whether the doctor performs PAS (on Gorsuch's view of what PAS is). This seems to place a limit on individualism. Henceforth, I shall ignore such a case in which the doctor but not the patient intends the death.

36. Gorsuch's view of PAS seems unduly narrow. Suppose I provide money to someone only so that he can have a realistic choice whether or not to go to college. If he chooses to go, it would seem reasonable to say that I assisted him in going to college. Something analogous could be said about a doctor who provides a lethal prescription to someone who uses it to commit suicide though the doctor only intends that the person have a choice. However, suppose the doctor gives someone a prescription because she believes having it will actually reduce the likelihood that the person will commit suicide (including by other means). In this case, the doctor may make possible a suicide that would otherwise not have occurred but if she reduced the probability of suicide occurring and aimed to do so, it seems problematic to say she assisted a suicide.

37. I discuss such cases in "The Doctrine of Triple Effect and Whether a Rational Agent Must Intend the Means to His End," reprinted in my *Intricate Ethics* (Oxford University Press, 2007).

38. That is, this adult may have an interest in dying but that need not mean it is morally correct for him to do what is in his interest regardless of its effect on others.

39. In discussing the limits of autonomy, Gorsuch notes that bad side effects of what we do may run afoul of Mill's Harm Principle. Interestingly, he argues (82) that autonomy, a value emphasized in the Supreme Court's Casey decision on abortion, can determine decisions about abortion but not PAS. This is because, he says, according to prior Supreme Court decisions "no recognized person" is affected by an abortion whereas with PAS misuse could affect other recognized persons. Abortion frees a woman of a pregnancy by often directly killing a fetus and so abortion could play a larger causal role in harm to another individual than does someone exercising a right to PAS which (we shall argue) only indirectly may, via another agent's act, lead others to be harmed. Gorsuch's view seems to be that if one accepts that a fetus is not a legally recognized person, one should not worry about direct harm to it.

40. See Chapter 8 for more on this issue and also why it is wrong to think the state causes what it enables or fails to prevent. The enabling/causing distinction bears on whether to outlaw vaping for some because others will self-harm in vaping.

41. Gorsuch notes (94) that one argument against enforcing voluntary slave contracts or allowing voluntary duels is that they may lead to mistaken or abusive conduct by others. The cases of sex and sterilization suggest that Gorsuch's cases of duels and slavery do not provide a sufficiently good argument.

42. See Warren Quinn, "Actions, Intentions, and Consequences: The Doctrine of Double Effect," in his *Morality and Action* (Cambridge University Press, 1994). Page numbers in the text are to that article.

43. Quinn's not requiring that one intend the harm itself for the intention to be problematic is one of his revisions of the traditional DDE.

44. Note that drawing a distinction between intending harm and intending involvement will still not imply that a state that does not permit PAS requires involvement of those who need but do not get PAS for the purpose of helping others (as Battin might claim). I do not necessarily endorse Quinn's views but am using them as an example of a different theory from Gorsuch's. For my criticism of Quinn's views see my "Intention, Harm, and the Possibility of a Unified Theory," reprinted in my *Intricate Ethics*.

45. It is not clear whether by "human life" Gorsuch wants to include anything with human DNA (e.g., also human cells, human fetuses, human anencephalics) or only human persons. Assume for the sake of argument it is the latter.

46. Gerald Dworkin makes this same point in his "No Exit," *The New Rambler*, 2017. Gorsuch himself discusses (166) restricting a person's liberty for the sake of his own greater liberty. He seems to think that the fact that one type of good is intentionally limited for the sake of more of the same type (where "type" includes the qualifier "the same person") implies that there is no instrumentalizing of basic goods. But this is not true: instances of the good are acted against intentionally for the sake of other instances of it. Furthermore, someone's liberty (e.g., to drive up a particular street) may be intentionally limited for the sake of the greater liberty of others (and for other goods). It is also not clear why he thinks the state may do some of these things when, Gorsuch claims, private persons may never intentionally act against basic goods.

47. Gerald Dworkin also raises this point in "No Exit."

48. We also discussed eliminative agency in Chapter 6 in connection with letting oneself die.

49. The distinction between eliminative and opportunistic agency bears on the debate between Battin and Gorsuch discussed earlier. Eliminating a threat, it might be said, is what is involved in refusing to stop suffering if helping would threaten others. In this case we do not opportunistically require that help not be given, contrary to what Battin's analysis implies. This is because if there were no person suffering to whom we could refuse aid, this would not interfere with a goal of stopping threats to others since there would then be no issue of threat arising from helping. Our intention not to aid can be presented as eliminative of a

threat not opportunistic. However, as noted earlier, permissible acts of PAS might only "enable" threats by others, and so in not allowing helping acts (of PAS) we would not be eliminating something that presents a threat to others without intervening agents' acts.

50. What follows elaborates on what was said in Chapter 4.

51. I first mentioned such an argument in my "End-of-Life Care and Assisted Suicide" as noted in Chapter 4. In Chapter 6 I presented an Eliminative Argument for Non Treatment.

52. For a response to a possible objection to the relevance of step 1d see I.C(1) and I.E. I shall not repeat it here.

53. Gorsuch mentions (170) that Supreme Court decisions show that the Court examines objective (in the sense of "public") factors of an act (i.e., nonmental ones) to see if it is possible for a reasonable person to have an upright intention in doing the act (objectively described). However, he notes that if they find out what the actual intention is, then that may take precedence. This is a combination of factors (ii) and (i).

54. I argued in this way against the "possible intentions" approach to permissibility in, for example, "Terrorism and Intending Evil," reprinted in my *Ethics for Enemies* (Oxford University Press, 2011). Jonathan Bennett, Judith Thomson, and Thomas Scanlon are among philosophers who have argued for the irrelevance (with some exceptions) of intention to permissibility. In addition, Christopher Fruge has argued that if an act can be permissible because it is possible to do it with a good intention (though it is actually done with a bad intention), why should the very same act not be impermissible since it is possible to do it with a bad intention? Hence, focusing on possible intentions might lead to contradictory conclusions: that an act is both permissible and impermissible. See his "Possible Intentions and the Doctrine of Double Effect," *Medicine, Ethics, and Public Health* 8 (2019), 11-17.

55. Those who hold this view do not deny that intention may alter the meaning and moral worth of actions but they argue that meaning and moral worth can be irrelevant to the moral permissibility of actions.

56. Though the Terminal Four-Step Argument does not imply that PAS is permissible in nonterminal cases, the form of the argument does imply that it could be permissible in such cases to intentionally bring about other imminent harms. For example, if someone with a nonterminal illness will soon be paralyzed no matter what is done, then it would be permissible both (1) to give him a drug to stop pain even though we foresee that the drug will cause comparable paralysis somewhat earlier as a side effect and (2) to intentionally cause such paralysis if (somehow) paralysis brought on in this particular way somewhat earlier were a necessary means to stopping his pain. This is because the loss of a short period of nonparalysis could be a lesser bad and the relief of the pain a greater good even if being paralyzed long-term were a greater bad than continuing pain.

57. We discussed this possibility in Chapter 2.

58. I owe this point to Iverson Zhou.

Chapter 8

Death and the State

Public Policy of Suicide, Assisted Suicide,
and Capital Punishment

This chapter concerns primarily physician-assisted suicide (PAS) and
euthanasia (E) as matters of law and public policy rather than as individual actions. It considers different views about what PAS and E are,
what a legal right to them would consist in, and what factors should
determine public policy about them. It does these things in part by
considering Ezekiel Emanuel (EE)'s positions on these matters because
he is a prominent architect of public health policy who has opposed
legalized PAS and E. Part I begins by examining different conceptions
of PAS and E and a particular view about how to decide on public
policy that concerns legalizing them. Part II begins the critical evaluation of this approach, focusing on the role of rights and equity. It is
in this part that we consider how some have reasoned about another
public policy concerning intended death: capital punishment. Part III
examines how to reason about harms and benefits per se. In conclusion, Part IV considers whether some past empirical predictions about
PAS have proven correct and whether views EE, in particular, now
holds should lead him to support legalization.[1]

I take EE's views to exemplify a type of position on the definition,
morality, and public policy of PAS and E that might be held by others,
and so my discussion has implications that go beyond those for EE's
position in particular. Furthermore, my discussion has implications
for other issues in public policy that EE does not discuss. It is in this
regard that I examine the particular way in which some debates about
capital punishment have proceeded.

Some of my major conclusions are the following. (1) In the absence
of a constitutional right to PAS and E, public policy about them need

Almost Over. F. M. Kamm, Oxford University Press (2020) © Oxford University Press.
DOI: 10.1093/oso/9780190097158.001.0001

not be carried on "beyond rights talk." (2) The potential "harms" of legalized PAS and E are often not harms or not only harms but wrongs that implicate rights. (3) Predictions about these wrongs and harms do not seem to have come to pass where PAS is legal.[2] (4) The reasons why people seek PAS and E are often the same as the reasons some give for wanting to avoid living into old age and for refusing or ending life-extending treatment.[3] (5) Hence, given (3), those who think public policy that allows refusal or termination of life-extending treatment is justified may also be committed to defending the legalization of S, PAS, and E for the same reasons.

Part I

1. Some conceptual issues. Before considering the substance of views about PAS and E, consider some contrasting definitions. Which of these definitions one accepts may have implications for public policy. There is a conceptual distinction between PAS and E. The former involves the person himself taking a lethal substance and intending his death with a physician providing access to the substance. This is consistent with thinking that in PAS the physician need not necessarily intend the death itself rather than, for example, intend the patient's autonomy in deciding for himself whether to live or die. However, as we saw in Chapter 7, Neil Gorsuch (now a U.S. Supreme Court Justice) insists that PAS as it concerns the law must involve the physician helping someone commit suicide when the physician intends that the person die. Hence, giving a lethal substance to a person, intending only that the person be free to decide for himself whether to live or die, is not PAS according to Gorsuch. (He argues that Dr. Timothy Quill was acquitted of PAS because Quill's intention to help cause death could not be proven.)[4] Although Gorsuch argues that PAS, as he thinks the law conceives of it, should be illegal due to the doctor's intention, his arguments do not imply that PAS should be illegal when it is under- stood as not requiring a doctor's intention that death occur.[5]

In E, someone other than the person who will die (typically a doctor) "actively and intentionally ends a patient's life by inducing it through some medical means" (2016, 80). This component of a defini- tion implies that there is no "passive E." (By contrast, it might be held that passive E would involve someone withholding or terminating another person's life-sustaining treatment with the intention that death occur.)

One difference between PAS and E not brought out by this component of a definition is that conceptually in PAS neither the physician nor the patient need aim at or succeed in achieving the patient's own good whereas E, by definition, aims at the person's own good (i.e., at this point death is the best available option with regard to the well-being open to the person). If a killing does not have this aim, it is not properly called E.

EE defines (2016, 80) involuntary E (IE) as occurring "when the patient is mentally competent but did not request" E and nonvoluntary E (NE) as involving someone who is not "mentally competent and could not request" E. But arguably IE involves a person who not only has not requested E but has specifically rejected it, so it is contrary to his expressed wishes if it is done. Also, arguably NE is done to someone (whether competent or not) who has neither requested nor rejected E. Hence, while EE considers "did not request" as sufficient for IE, on the alternative it is sufficient only for NE.[6] (I shall assume E refers only to voluntary E in what follows.)

EE's conception (1997) of legalized PAS is that "to have one's life ended by a doctor is a right."[7] By contrast, philosophers (such as Ronald Dworkin) think legal PAS need only involve a person's liberty right to seek a willing physician to do PAS and a claim right that he or she not be interfered with in seeking a willing physician. The willing physician is also to have a liberty right to accede to the request of the person and a claim against others (except the requesting person) interfering with this. (The combination of a liberty and claim right against interference can be considered a "full right," and henceforth I will assume that a full right is what is at issue when I speak of a right, whether it is a moral or a legal right.)[8] This conception does not imply a moral or legal right to have one's life ended that would give some doctor a duty, owed to the person with the right, to engage in PAS.[9] Rather it involves, as said above, a claim right against the state and others which gives them a duty not to interfere with the exercise of a person's and selected doctor's liberty (and a power granted by the state to a person and a doctor to make arrangements) to engage in a joint activity in which a doctor assists in a person's suicide.

EE has also said (1997) of legalized PAS that it would involve "routine interventions that can be administered without the need for a publicly acceptable justification. . . . Doctors who end patients' lives would no longer bear the burden of having to prove appropriateness of their action." However, in the very same article in which he says this he also (7–8) describes how Dutch law concerning PAS and E (at the time he wrote) required such public justifications as unbearable suffering, confirmation by a second physician, and facts being reported to a coroner. Further, in another article (1999, 631) he describes the safeguards proposed for U.S. law permitting PAS: a patient freely initiating a request for PAS, presence of unremitting pain only relievable by PAS, and a second physician's consultation. These conditions on PAS may not be the correct ones and in fact may not always be met, but this is not because the idea of legalization itself involves not "having to prove appropriateness."[10]

Despite recognizing a conceptual distinction between PAS and E, EE thinks that if PAS were legalized, the two couldn't be separated practically (1998, 1001).[11] One reason he gives for this (1998, 1002) is that PAS may fail and then the backup of a doctor administering a lethal substance will likely follow. Hence, he says (1998, 1003) that "the real choice is to legalize both PAS and E or to legalize neither." It might be counterargued that though there could be an increase in E as an effect of legalizing PAS, there is no reason to think that legalizing PAS *despite* such an effect commits one to legalizing that effect. Perhaps EE thinks that it would be wrong not to allow E as a backup when PAS fails and this would provide a justification for legalizing both or neither. However, it seems that it would be wrong not to have E as a backup only if failed PAS led to a condition so bad that had it occurred independently rather than due to failed PAS, it would be sufficient to justify legalizing E. If there were no such conditions, it is not clear why legalizing PAS would justify a follow up with E. Arguably, a mere legally unjustified, psychological propensity to follow up with E could be stemmed in other ways besides not legalizing PAS.

2. Morality, public policy, and legality: some general issues.
A. *Morality*. We have considered some differences in how PAS, E, and a right to them are understood. Hence, in considering someone's views about the morality and legality of PAS or E, we should keep in

mind that person's conception of these and whether an alternative conception of what they are and what a right to them involves would change his views about morality and legality. Some assert that sometimes PAS and E are morally right (e.g., to end extreme suffering not otherwise treatable). So, they are not always morally opposed to PAS or E on the ground that it involves someone intentionally causing or helping to cause someone's (intended) death. For example, EE says (1997, 12), "In any given case, it may be the ethical thing to do, whatever the law says, and should be done," endorsing even the moral correctness of sometimes disobeying the law. However, note that saying that an act is morally right or "the ethical thing to do" is not the same as saying that someone has a moral right against a doctor that gives the doctor a moral duty to do PAS or E. Emanuel also says[12] that the alternative to legalization of PAS and E involves "maintaining the current policy of permitting them in individual cases," suggesting that in doing the "right thing" the doctor could be acting in accord with an extant policy that sometimes allows violation of the law. While I am not sure this actually was or is our policy, the view supporting it is similar to one held by some about torture: it should not be legalized, but it might sometimes be morally right and legally excusable.[13]

B. *Public policy*. However, EE believes we should not be misled by even "a few thousand" such cases in which PAS or E is the ethical thing to do (1997) in deciding whether as a matter of public policy PAS or E should be legal. Let us now consider why he says this and on what he thinks public policy should depend. (Recall that EE conceived of legal PAS as involving a person's right against a doctor to have it done (1997), but we have noted that a weaker conception is a person's legal right to have a willing doctor do PAS.)

(i) Even before the U.S. Supreme Court decided in *Washington v. Glucksberg* that there was no constitutional right to PAS (1997), and certainly immediately afterward (1998, 1999), EE thought that in formulating public policy about legalizing PAS and E we should move "beyond rights talk" (as the title of his 1998 article asserts) and instead weigh the harms and benefits of legalization. He said (1999, 629) we should be concerned with "the ethics of having a particular social policy and practice but ultimately the ethical question . . . is . . . will legalizing—or permitting—E and PAS promote . . . or thwart a good death for the 2.3 million Americans who die each year in the U.S.?"[14]

He assumes that if there is no constitutional right to PAS (or E), rights talk should not be part of considerations from "ethics and political prudence" in deciding on legalizing PAS or E (1998, 983). He also holds that "the perspective is no longer first person, but third person. And the justifications no longer appeal to autonomy and beneficence" because putting rights to the side "shifts the discussion away from abstract, first-person arguments of principle and toward third-person interest-balancing and the empirical assessment of the utility of protections and regulations" (1998, 994).

To clarify, though EE believes that the Supreme Court was correct to decide that there is no constitutional right to PAS (1998, 983), he also seems to believe that if there were a constitutional right, it would play a major role in formulating public policy, reducing the role of weighing social harms and benefits. Presumably, this is because respecting a constitutional right is thought to take priority over preventing harms or pursuing benefits except in extreme cases, and in those cases there should be what is called "narrow tailoring" of infringements of the right. In general, rights are often side constraints that stand in the way of producing the best balance of harms and benefits, though it need not be the case that they are absolute and can never be overridden.[15] Since a constitutional right would belong to individuals, EE associates it with what he calls the first person point of view.

(ii) (a) In the absence of an individual's constitutional right, EE thinks that the public policy perspective on whether to legalize PAS or E changes. He says (1998, 994) that "Citing the wishes of . . . even a few thousand suffering individuals . . . no longer becomes dispositive" since, he thinks, they have no rights to PAS or E that protect their interests; rather, they have only mere interests that should be weighed against the interests of others. He says "the real issue is . . . the care for terminally ill patients generally." (Note that EE here assumes that legalized PAS or E would be limited to its use for the terminally ill, a position not all accept.) So, for example, if more terminally ill patients would be harmed due to legalizing PAS or E than would be benefited by it, there could be a public policy case against legalizing PAS and E.

(b) In addition, EE thinks that in developing public policy we should be concerned with risk. He says (1998, 1003): "Legalization would inevitably result in abuses . . . The real question is . . . whether . . . benefits of legalization outweigh its acknowledged risks."[16] One way to "inevitably" get abuses from only risk of abuse is for the risk to occur in each of very many people since, according to the so-called Law of Large Numbers, abuse will inevitably occur in some of them.

(iii) Finally, EE seems to think that public policy should depend on public opinion about the legalization of PAS or E for the paradigmatic type of patient who would request it. What is the paradigmatic type of patient? He says (1998, 1000) that the "wisdom of [legalized] PAS or E should turn on the rule rather than the exception . . . the proper paradigmatic case of a terminally ill patient who desires PAS or E is the depressed person who requires a great deal of care from his or her family, not one suffering from unremediable (sic) pain" (as shown by empirical evidence). Yet he notes that in 1998 public surveys (reported in 1998, 996) showed that people were favorable toward legalized PAS or E only for cases of irremediable pain and not for dealing with depressed persons who are a burden on their family. EE also notes (1999, 630) that public opinion does not support autonomy alone as a justifying reason for PAS.

These reasons against a legal right to PAS or E seem to apply not only to a patient's right against some physicians that would give the physicians a duty to these patients but also to a (full) right to have a willing physician perform them. So substituting this alternative conception of a legal right to PAS or E would not make EE's objections to a right disappear. However, the concern about abuse might be greater on his view that a legal right implies that no public justification would have to be given in exercising the right, by contrast to a view that a legal right is consistent with requiring public justification in exercising the right.

Part II

1. Evaluation. Are these views about how to decide on public policy regarding legal PAS and E correct? Consider them in turn.

Are rights irrelevant? It might be argued that while there is no currently recognized U.S. constitutional right to PAS or E, there really is such a right to be found in the U.S. Constitution. I will put this issue of constitutional interpretation aside. However, it should be noted that while Justices Breyer and O'Connor agreed that there was no free-standing constitutional right to PAS, they claimed that if patients in extreme pain were not given relief for it even when this hastened death, they would reconsider whether these patients had a constitutional right to PAS.[17] If they did have such a right, EE could not just weigh their interests against possible harms to others.

My focus will be on the fact that constitutional rights are not the only rights of individuals that could be relevant to public policy. EE himself says there is a recognized right (1997) for a patient to discontinue life-saving treatment, but at the time he wrote this it was a part of common law and the Supreme Court had only suggested it would find the right to be constitutionally protected; it was not strictly recognized as a constitutional right. Subsequently this has changed.[18] However, perhaps moral rights that would not be constitutionally protected could also be relevant to deciding what should be legal. Moral rights are not discovered by examining the U.S. Constitution (or the common law) but by moral reasoning. For example, such reasoning could be used to show that a patient has a moral right to give informed consent before medical treatment even if he lacks such a constitutional right. This moral right could then be a ground for arguing that patients should have a legal right (e.g., in legislated state law) to give informed consent to treatment. This could be so even if granting a legal right to give informed consent before treatment led to less good and did not prevent more harm. This might be so, for example, if more people refused consent to beneficial treatment than would have been harmed by treatments to which they did not consent. Some other moral rights, such as the right to have promises kept, are not usually grounds for legal rights except (arguably) in the law of contract. Even if a moral rights-based argument does not succeed in generating a legal right, perhaps it can appropriately be part of the conversation in addition to costs and benefits about whether a legal right should exist.

Could one counterargue that in a diverse society we are unlikely to get agreement on a moral right to PAS? That we cannot get unanimous agreement is consistent with getting majority agreement on such a moral right; could this be a ground for majority support for a legal right which would suffice for legislation? According to some theories of the sorts of reasons that one may give for coercive legislation about constitutional issues and basic justice, it can be contrary to liberal neutrality toward contentious moral theories and ways of life to legislate on the basis of the majority's view of a moral right even when the reasoning is accessible and secular. For example, John Rawls' view of "public reason" requires that when legislating on such issues, we present only reasons that we could reasonably believe that reasonable others could see as reasons without having to change their particular way of life or conception of a good life (assuming these ways of life and conceptions of the good are at least consistent with liberal democracy). People can see these "public reasons" as reasons even if they don't think they are the best reasons or good enough reasons for creating a law.[19] Some of the acceptable public reasons Rawls considers are drawn from the conception of a liberal constitutional democracy under which all agree to live and legislate. However, Rawls does not insist that these public reasons are all to be found in the rights guaranteed by the U.S. Constitution. Other public reasons might be ideas that are part of empirical sciences or that rely on common knowledge and use of ordinary logic. On Rawls' view, even moral reasoning based on contentious secular moral theories such as Kantianism or Utilitarianism must be backed up by reasoning using moral notions either inherent in the idea of constitutional liberal democracy or more generally accessible through ordinary reasoning. If the majority argue in this way in legislating, Rawls holds that the majority that supports a law will have abided by their civic duty in treating their fellow citizens as free and equal and not merely subject to the majority's view of moral correctness.

Are autonomy or pain relief such "public reasons" so that they could be the reasons given for a legal right to PAS in a liberal democracy? Rawls notes that insofar as autonomy in personal life is a value only on some views of a good life, it would not be a public reason. (For example, someone's view of the good life could involve his acting on a guru's directives, not his own judgment.) But insofar as autonomy is about persons as free and autonomous citizens, it is a public reason. As already noted, Justices Breyer and O'Connor views suggest that avoiding unrelieved severe pain might also be such a public reason.

Would the following argument that I have presented elsewhere pass the test of public reason?[20] First, with patients' permission, doctors are morally and legally permitted to provide pain relief even if it is foreseen that the patient will soon die as a side effect of appropriate use by himself or a doctor of a necessary drug.[21] This is because it is judged that sometimes pain relief is more important for a person than continuing life. Second, with the patient's permission, doctors are also morally and legally permitted to intentionally cause patients or assist in patients causing themselves what would ordinarily be considered harms (e.g., pain, loss of sight or limb) in order to save their lives or for some other benefit considered to outweigh the harms. This is an example of intrapersonal rationality in which an individual intentionally suffers a lesser harm to achieve a greater benefit or avoid a greater harm to himself. From these two steps that involve recognized facts, it seems we could use ordinary logic to conclude that if pain relief is sometimes more important for a person than continuing life (as assumed in the first step of the argument), doctors should also be morally and legally permitted to intentionally bring about or assist in bringing about loss of life (judged to be the lesser harm in the first step of the argument) in order to avoid pain that has been judged (in the first step of the argument) to be the greater harm. I believe this argument does rely only on public reasons (in the Rawlsian sense).[22]

It seems then that, at least on the Rawlsian view of public reason, there are four possible routes to bringing moral and already recognized legal rights into arguments for a legal right to PAS. One is that legislating about a right to PAS is not legislating about a basic part of justice and hence we may introduce even contentious moral reasoning about it to ground legislation about legal rights. However, that legalizing PAS is not legislating about a basic part of justice might conflict with the views of many of its supporters and opponents. A second route is to identify elements in a conception of liberal democratic relations that support PAS. This might, for example, be a right to "pursue happiness" and live without interference according to one's preferred conception of the value of life and the things in it. A third route related to the second is to argue negatively: Values inherent in liberal democracy rule out the state enforcing one contentious moral view that does not satisfy the standard of public reason (e.g., a purely religious view) about how life may permissibly be ended for those who are terminally ill.[23] While alternative views may not themselves be supported only by public reasons (e.g., they are based on contentious views about what is a good end to life), they are consistent with liberal democracy (e.g., they do not rule out respect for persons as equal citizens and do not require all citizens to use PAS). A fourth route is to present what might be called "minimal moral" arguments that do not rely on contentious theories but take moral views that are already legally accepted and logically argue from that. (This is the route followed in the argument for PAS I presented above.)

Finally, it is worth remembering that not all conceptions of public reason are Rawlsian and, on some conceptions, there may be a more direct route from ordinary moral reasoning to legislation. For example, in arguing for aid for disaster relief to other countries or against deporting undocumented long-term resident aliens brought to the U.S. as children, legislators have freely spoken of doing what is morally right without drawing in any explicit way on specifically "public reasons" in the Rawlsian sense. This need not mean that public reasons could not be found that support the same actions, but on a non-Rawlsian view finding them might not be necessary.

Since moral rights and existing legislated legal rights also provide what EE would call a first-person rather than a third-person justification for public policy, first-person justifications need not disappear from public policy in the absence of a constitutional right. Moral rights that are legalized, or with which interference is legally prohibited, can also be legal side constraints on achieving the best balance of benefits and harms. Furthermore, arguing for moral rights to PAS or E need not involve attending to what EE calls "heart-wrenching" cases involving irremediable suffering (1998, 874), since rights can also protect people from suffering lesser harms.

In sum, an initial question is whether moral reasoning can show that people have at least a moral right to seek a willing physician and have her perform PAS. A further question is whether a version of the argument satisfies conditions of public reason (perhaps because existing legal rights confirm parts of it) or if public reason prohibits interfering with acting on reasons support the moral right. If the former, the argument can be directly introduced to support legislating a protected, nonabsolute, and regulatable legal option to engage in PAS.

2. The possible existence of moral and already recognized legal rights that ground or prohibit interfering with a legal right to PAS or E is merely one reason why absence of a constitutional right to PAS or E does not imply that we should move "beyond rights talk" (1998) in formulating public policy, as EE claims. As we shall next see, there is another reason. Though EE says that in the absence of

a constitutional right to PAS or E we must balance interests, weigh harms and benefits, and consider overall utility, many of the possible problems of legalizing PAS or E that he lists involve rights violations rather than mere harms, setbacks of interests, or reduced utility.

A. Harm and benefit. To help make this clear, consider as background standard conceptions of harm and benefit. Roughly, to harm is to make someone worse off either than they were or would have been (depending on one's theory of harm); to benefit is to make someone better off either than they were or would have been (depending on one's theory of benefit).[24] What if one must choose between harming only person A or harming (equally) both persons B and C? In not harming B and C is one benefiting them, even though one doesn't make them better off than they were or would have been independently of one's harming them? Not on the standard notion of benefit, and yet in social policy doing less harm (by only harming A) might have to be weighed against not doing more harm (by harming both B and C). In doing social policy, it might not be unreasonable to consider this too as a form of weighing a harm to A and "benefits" to B and C. What if one must choose between improving (equally) the condition of only A or both B and C? Arguably, in social policy providing the greater benefit might have to be weighed against providing the lesser benefit. It would not be unreasonable to consider this a form of weighing costs (to A of not benefiting him) against benefits (to B and C). However, the "cost" in this case could not reasonably be considered a harm to A even in the way that not harming B and C (in our earlier case) might be considered a benefit to them (if we stretch the term benefit).

As we saw in Chapter 1, death is thought by many (though not by all) to be an event that overall harms someone only if it interferes with his having a future that would have been overall better for him than his nonexistence (assumed to be involved in being dead). (On this view, in order for death to be a harm rather than merely a failure to be benefited by getting more good time, it seems one has to conceive of death interfering with a good course of events that would otherwise have occurred.) A slightly different view is that one is harmed by death at t_1 if it prevents one from having a longer and better life overall than one will have had if one dies at t_1. By contrast, death is thought by many (though not by all) to be an event that overall benefits a person (even if it involves the harm of his extinction as a conscious person) if it interferes with his having a future that would have been overall worse for him than nonexistence. A slightly different view is that one is benefited by death at t_1 if it prevents one from having a longer but worse life overall than one will have had if one dies at t_1.[25]

EE does not always adhere to standard conceptions of harm and benefit. For example, as an effect of not legalizing PAS and E he points to (1998, 1012) "the harm caused to . . . 25,000 people who endure needless pain and who might be helped by having their lives ended." But not helping people avoid pain by legalizing PAS or E seems to be failing to benefit them rather than causing them harm. (This is so even if their pain is considered a cost to be weighed.) However, interfering with those who would have helped someone has been referred to as "preventative harming" (in preventing a benefit that would have been given), and it does make people worse off than they would otherwise have been. Nevertheless, it is not clear that it is morally the same as causing harm to the people not helped.[26] Possibly EE thinks the state in particular can harm people by not making it legal or making it illegal to help them. I shall return to these issues below.

As further background, note that violation of rights can occur even when people are not harmed or denied benefits. For example, paternalism is a case in which someone's right (to noninterference) may be violated though the person is overall benefited.[27] Hence, philosophers distinguish between wronging someone by a rights violation and harming her. Many rights violations may be serious because of the harms caused or the benefits lost, but then the concern is for how both rights and interests are affected, not just for the interests per se. Indeed, even philosophers who say harming someone is morally more serious than not benefiting them (other things equal) may think this is true only in cases where there is a right not to be harmed, so that harms that violate no rights (e.g., those due to competition) need not be morally problematic.

B. *Wrongs and rights.* With these points as background, consider EE's list of particular possible problems with legalizing PAS and E. He says (in 1998, 1003), "Legalization would inevitably result in abuses: patients coerced into ending their lives, patients given PAS or E without having received all palliative care . . . patients ending their lives for economic reasons, nonconsenting patients having their lives ended." Speaking of E without consent or PAS under pressure, he says (1998, 1010) "that 7,000 or so people might be given E in the U.S. without their consent." He also says (1998, 1012): "with at least one million people per year facing a dying process, the numbers of those at risk would dwarf the numbers of those helped,"[28] and (1999, 635) "86,000 to 240,000 patients impose significant financial burdens, while 160,000 to 340,000 impose significant caregiving burdens on their families. If just a few percent of these . . . are coerced to . . . E or PAS. . . . [T]he number of patients who might be harmed by legalization begins to equal or exceed the dying patients who might benefit from legalization."

As we can see from these quotes, to a significant degree EE's discussion of possible problems with legal PAS or E does not focus on possible harms per se (as earlier defined) but rather possible harmful *wrongings* including violations of rights. IE is a clear violation of a right. (These problems would, arguably, be recognized as "public reasons" against a practice not based on contentious moral views.) Coercion and abuse are wrongings and arguably there is often a right against each. Not getting palliative care as an alternative to PAS might be a violation of a positive right. Indeed wrongful coerced PAS or E could overall benefit and not harm a person to whom it is done (or at least be a lesser harm by comparison to living on). This could be so, for example, if death will not interfere with the person having any forthcoming goods of life (or not make his life go worse overall) and will prevent bads worse than death that are not otherwise preventable. In this case concern about coercion and IE would be concern only about wronging and rights violations, not about harms. Indeed, an act could only be IE or NE if the act at least aimed at benefiting someone overall. On the other hand, PAS or attempted E that is not a wronging because it is voluntary and noncoerced could sometimes be a mistake and overall harm someone, for example if death deprived the person of an overall good period of life he could otherwise have had.

Hence, some of EE's own arguments against legalizing PAS or E are concerned with violating the rights of individuals and violations could occur with or without overall harm. Additional evidence that some of his concern is about violating rights is that, as we shall see, he does not include on his list of benefits of PAS or E (to be weighed in the balance against the risk of coerced PAS or IE) reduction in relatives' financial or caregiving burdens. This may be because benefits brought about by rights violations (such as coerced PAS or IE) are typically not counted (i.e., they are nullified in a moral calculus).[29] These are further reasons to think that EE is wrong to say we should move "beyond rights talk" in formulating public policy in the absence of a constitutional right to PAS or E. Is it possible that in his argument the rights that may be violated are not functioning as strong side constraints and he merely attaches some additional negative weight to their violation (in addition to harms) and balances these against benefits?[30] Though this would involve a weaker conception of the significance of rights, we would still not be "beyond rights talk."[31]

3. The possibility that there are rights on both the pro and con sides of the legalization debate raises several questions related to rights that I shall mention but only briefly discuss here.[32]

A. Minimizing rights violations. First, should public policy aim to minimize rights violations, for example, by weighing numbers of rights violated by legalizing PAS as opposed to not legalizing it? Some philosophers argue that we should not always aim to minimize rights violations because we should not deliberately violate someone's right in order to minimize even comparable rights violations in others, especially when these violations would be carried out by agents other than ourselves. However, the cases discussed in this connection usually involve violating someone's negative right not to be killed to prevent someone else from independently violating the same negative right of a greater number of other people. If there is a moral right to PAS, not granting a legal right to it could interfere with someone getting help from a willing physician and this seems closer to interfering with a positive right (for help unrelated to warding off violations of negative rights) rather than interfering with a negative right.[33] Further, granting the right to PAS is the very thing that is said to cause the threats to the rights of others. If this were so, then this would not be a case of interfering with someone's right to be helped because this stops threats to others that arise independently of his being helped (in receiving PAS). It might be counterargued that these differences would also be present if we interfered with someone's positive right to have a doctor perform a sterilization (for birth control) because allowing this procedure led to an even greater number of people receiving involuntary sterilizations. Should we also not grant a legal right to have such a procedure if it had such a further bad effect?

B. *Pre-existent rights.* Second, are these issues complicated by the fact that some of the moral rights (e.g., not to be coerced to suicide or euthanized involuntarily) are already recognized legally? That is, should limiting the threat to already recognized legal rights be grounds for not recognizing any moral right (should there be one) as a new legal right? Why should a moral right that would have merited legalization had it been recognized earlier always lose out to (even less significant) moral rights merely because they were recognized sooner as meriting legalization?

C. *Enabling rights violations.* Third, is it significant that laws permitting PAS or E (or sterilization) would only as a side effect *enable* others to violate some rights (e.g., by making it easier for them to coerce PAS)? The laws would not direct that such violations occur or even cause them without further acts of other intervening agents. Note that the sense of "enable" here is something like "causally increase the probability" of a rights violation. Such laws need also only enable others to satisfy permissible requests for PAS or E rather than direct the satisfaction of requests or engage the state in carrying out the request.[34] However, in this case a different, noncausal sense of "enabling" is also involved when we say "laws enable." Here what is meant is something like "provide a legally protected option to arrange for and do something." It is an important and, I think, unresolved issue whether (i) not doing what enables (in the mere causal sense) others to wrongfully harm by violating negative rights should take precedence over (ii) doing what enables (in the causal and legal sense) benefits to be provided by others who accord positive rights, even if not doing harm would ordinarily take precedence over benefiting. To take another example, in legally permitting development and use of drugs for pain relief in a few people we may enable (as a matter of causality rather than of legal empowerment) illegal use of the drugs by other people. (Such enabling of harm differs from using drugs that release a powerful fume into the air that, without intervening voluntary acts of others, would cause drug intoxication in some people.) Should it not nevertheless be permissible to develop the drugs, causally and legally enable doctors to benefit people (at least if the people have a moral right to get the benefits from willing doctors), and limit harm enabled in some other way?[35]

Consider other examples that raise comparable issues. EE recommends suicide as opposed to PAS from a public policy perspective. This would require changing current law to prevent interference with suicide in certain cases (so the option to commit suicide would be protected). But this may lead other people to be coerced into suicide. Would the numbers at risk of such coercion be less (or more) than those at risk of being coerced to PAS? A legal right to refuse or terminate life-saving treatment, which EE recognizes is well established, may have led to a greater number of people being coerced into terminating their treatment.[36] In allowing doctors to give morphine for pain relief to a few, even if the dose necessary to stop pain would (hypothetically) hasten or certainly cause rapid death, we open the door to many others being abused by overdoses of morphine. In this last case, EE is willing to rule out the legal permissibility of treatment for pain in some if as a side effect it does causally enable more numerous wrongful deaths. For he says (1998, 987) only a "sadistic state" would interfere with palliative care "Unless . . . palliative care created or substantially contributed to . . . drug addiction, elder abuse . . . [and] murder." Then "The state might have good reason to balance the interests of dying patients against other state interests." Here his account seems to be entirely about balancing interests rather than about overriding a right to palliative care by other interests or rights. In the case of a right (positive or negative), not merely any bad that is slightly greater than the good provided by the right is sufficient to override it—that is one of the points of saying that (even nonabsolute) rights are side constraints—whereas a slightly greater bad could determine an outcome in ordinary balancing of interests.[37]

However, suppose there were a moral right to pain-terminating treatment, PAS, and E, and suppose that this was a ground for a legislated legal right. Then it might be better to accept such treatment, PAS, or E as a legal default and interfere with abuse they causally enable by means other than denying the legal right (e.g., heightened surveillance to stop coercion or misuse). This is the way we ordinarily deal with effects of essentially self-regarding acts when harm from them to others results by way of an intervening agent who acts wrongly (either in how he treats others or himself). Further, EE accepts the permissibility of giving pain relief when it is requested as the legal default until overriding bad effects on others are shown to occur. So why does he not similarly accept the legal permissibility of PAS (especially in cases where he thinks it is ethically right) as the default until overriding bad effects on others are shown to occur?[38]

D. *Rights vs. no rights*. Fourth, what if there are only rights on one side of the equation? For example, if there were no moral right to PAS or E that could ground a legal right, but there were moral and legal rights not to be coerced into PAS and against IE. Then the question seems to be whether the state should interfere with doctors providing the benefits of PAS to which there would (by hypothesis) be no right if this involves their using means that only *enable* (in a causal sense) rights violations by others? Certainly, if I want to provide someone with an important benefit to which she has no right, I should be permitted to leave my current location (given that I have no duty to be there) even though this enables a villain to reach and harm another person. However, in this case my going to help someone only removes the protection against a villain that my presence provides to someone else; my helping someone does not introduce means with which a villain becomes able to harm others (as use of drugs to stop pain might). It might be further argued that the state has a duty that I do not have both to protect people from villains and abuses such as coercion and to not grant legal rights that could (causally) enable wrong acts by others. Its fulfilling these duties could have greater significance than its enabling or not interfering with the provision of benefits to others not covered by moral rights that could ground a legal right.

E. *The state's harming*. Fifth, having raised the issue of the special role of the state, we should consider what might be true if only the state could provide PAS (e.g., if there is a government monopoly on health care). In this case, in not permitting PAS, the state could more clearly be interpreted as failing to provide a benefit rather than interfering with others providing a benefit. Some believe that in the case of the state the distinctions between (a) not benefiting and causing harm and (b) causing harm and enabling it do not apply. For example, in arguing for capital punishment, Sunstein and Vermeule[39] represent the state as a special sort of moral agent that is always acting rather than merely omitting.[40] This is supposed to imply in the case they discuss of capital punishment that the state faces a choice between

(i) killing in capital punishment and (ii) killing those whom it fails to protect by not introducing deterrent measures (assuming capital punishment deters). Another of their views is that even if the state is omitting in not deterring killers, it would be failing in a duty to deter. This is a culpable letting die (a form of not aiding) and, on Sunstein and Vermeule's view, as morally serious for a state as killing. Therefore, they think, the state should do life-for-life tradeoffs, essentially weighing lives it would take in capital punishment against those it would "take" when innocents are killed because it did not deter murderers.[41]

I already noted that EE speaks of the harm done to those who cannot have PAS rather than of the failure to benefit them by PAS. He might be interpreted as thinking the state engages in a preventative harm. A second interpretation is that he accepts a view like Sunstein and Vermeule's that there is no significance to the harm/not benefit distinction in the case of the state; when the state omits to make PAS legal it would harm those without PAS (or at least culpably fail to aid them), especially in the case where only the state could provide PAS. Similarly, when it does legalize PAS it harms (not merely enables harm to) those who are victims of coerced PAS (as the state is said by Sunstein and Vermeule to "kill" those who die because it does not deter murderers).

Some, such as Carol Steiker,[42] do not object to thinking of the government as either acting no matter what it does or as possibly failing in an important duty to aid if it does sometime omit. But she notes that in capital punishment the government intends to kill whereas (on the first Sunstein-Vermeule view) if it does not deter killers, it foreseeably but not intentionally kills (even if those not deterred intentionally kill). Steiker thinks that this difference interferes with doing a life-for-life tradeoff analysis because ordinarily one cannot kill someone intentionally to avoid one's merely foreseeably killing others. She thinks this intention/foresight distinction lies at the heart of deontology (which would accord with the view that the Doctrine of Double Effect (DDE) is crucial to deontology).[43] Steiker claims the tradeoff model only works when the deaths on either side of the ledger will be equally foreseen (or intended).

I have concerns about both Sunstein-Vermeule views about the state as well as Steiker's counterargument. First, while Steiker is right that the state does not intend the murders it does not deter, the murderers do intend to kill. Hence, Sunstein and Vermeule might claim that the state should minimize intentional killings, not giving special weight to the killings it would intend versus the ones that others would intend. Steiker's objection would then have to rest on an argument against minimizing intended killings. Such an argument would justify an agent (such as the state) giving greater weight to avoiding its own intended killings than it gives to preventing those of other agents. (In the case of legalized PAS, whether by private or government physicians, there would be intended killings on both sides of the ledger—instances of permissible PAS and instances of impermissible assisted suicide. When private physicians do PAS, the state need not itself be intending any killings, but this would not matter if it should not distinguish intended killings on the basis of who does them.)

Second, in focusing on whether the state intends a killing or only foresees it, Steiker might be showing that she agrees with Sunstein and Vermeule that foreseen killings *can* be weighed against each other and that the state's failure to prevent a foreseen killing should be treated as its having foreseeably caused it. Then this killing by the state can be weighed against foreseen killings that it causes in the ordinary way. A worrying implication of this view is that the government's not deterring killers would be no different from its dumping lethal chemicals that it foresees but does not intend will kill. But it seems wrong to morally equate these types of acts. To do so might imply that since the state foreseeably kills people when it doesn't deter criminals by capital punishment, it should be free to dump the lethal chemicals when the same people would only foreseeably be killed whichever way *it* kills them and dumping has some additional social benefits.

Furthermore, suppose the state had to save a large number of lives. In one case, it would have to do this by leaving a smaller group of other people to die. In another case, it would have to use means to save the larger group that as a foreseen side effect dumps lethal chemicals, thereby killing a different smaller group of people who would not otherwise have soon died. In these cases the state does not omit to prevent killings but it still either omits to save one smaller group or harms another smaller group. The view that the harm/not benefit distinction does not have moral significance applied to the state, combined with life-for-life tradeoffs, implies that there is no moral difference between the state saving the larger group instead of the smaller group in the first case and its saving the larger group by using means that foreseeably kill people in the smaller group in the second case. I think it is wrong to morally equate these courses of action; the first could be permissible when the second is not.

Similarly, suppose that with limited resources the state must choose between saving the lives of a large number of people or stopping a company from dumping chemicals that will foreseeably kill a small group of other people. It might permissibly choose to do the former without this implying that it could use means to save the large group of people that involve its dumping chemicals that will foreseeably kill a small group of other people. This is because its not preventing the company from killing people does not involve its killing but its dumping chemicals does involve its killing. This is true even though it only foresees and does not intend killings in either case.

I conclude that we should reject the view that the state is killing in failing to save lives or in failing to deter killings. Similarly, we should reject the view that the state is causing suffering in not preventing it. Hence, in defending legalization of PAS, proponents should not rely on the view that there is no moral difference between, on the one hand, the state not allowing or not providing PAS that would stop some from suffering and, on the other hand, its causing suffering. Nor should opponents of PAS rely on there being no moral difference between the state allowing or providing PAS for some when that enables others to wrongfully kill different people and its wrongfully killing those different people.

Now consider Sunstein and Vermeule's alternative view, that the state at least has a strong duty to aid, and suppose it would omit a very important duty of protection in not deterring murders. Philippa Foot noted that even if one has a strong positive duty, such as a doctor has to save the lives of her patients, the doctor should not use a gas to perform needed surgery on them if it would seep into the room next door and thereby foreseeably kill some innocent bystander. The prohibition on doing what foreseeably kills someone, not only the duty not to intentionally kill someone, is usually more stringent than a duty to aid others.[44] On Foot's view, one may not trade off (i) letting people die by failing in a duty to aid and (ii) causing even the unintentional deaths of fewer people because, she thinks, letting die is morally preferable to killing. She is thus also denying Steiker's view that it is the intention/foresight distinction that is at the heart of deontology and that we may do life-for-life tradeoffs when all the deaths are foreseen whether they are due to killing or to our not fulfilling a strong duty to aid.

Finally, here is another reason to doubt that intentionally causing death, at least on its own, should ground the objection to capital punishment. For suppose that to save his victim it is necessary and sufficient to intentionally kill a criminal when he is in custody after his crime.[45] In this case it may be morally permissible to intentionally kill the criminal because there is a debt owed by the criminal to his victim, if it is certain that the victim will die if he is not helped and will not die if he is helped and killing the criminal is something one could have permissibly done to stop his criminal act. By contrast, suppose a criminal is intentionally executed to deter other potential criminals from killing other victims in the future. Here there may be no special debt he owes to those other potential victims. Further, there may be no certainty that a particular person will die as a victim if the criminal is not executed and be saved if he is. There is only the small chance had by each of many people in the society of being a person who would be killed by other criminals if they are not deterred and only a small chance had by each of many people that he will be helped by capital punishment. It is these points, not Steiker's focus on intended killing alone, that may be important in arguing against capital punishment.[46]

4. *Equity.* Continuing our discussion about factors besides harms and benefits in reasoning about PAS as a matter of public policy, consider that EE also lists (1999, 641) lack of equity as a possible bad effect of PAS and E. Concern about equity need not be a concern about rights but it is also not a concern about harm and benefits per se. It is a concern about fairness in distribution of both harms and benefits. EE describes advocates of PAS or E as "relatively educated, well-off, politically vocal people . . . white, under sixty-five years of age. . . . If E or PAS were legalized they would receive the benefits" and, he continued, be "protected from the harms of legalization. They tend to have good health insurance, intact, supportive families." He says (1997, 13) "those most likely to experience abuse and coercion [are] the old, the less well off, and minorities." So he is concerned about unfairness in the distribution of benefits, rights-violations, and harms.

Suppose the amount of abusive harm is held constant and just shifted away from those who would not benefit from PAS or E and to the group whose members would benefit.[47] Then the inequity with which EE is concerned would disappear without reducing abusive harms. It is even theoretically possible that abusive harms would increase as their distribution and the distribution of benefits became more equitable. This could happen if benefits were extended to the communities more likely to suffer abuse when presented with the option for PAS or E. The point is that EE's concern about equity in public policy would also not simply be about weighing harms against benefits.

Part III

I have argued that many of EE's concerns are about possible violations of rights, wrongings, and equity rather than about harm per se. This may be true of others' concerns as well. But EE *is* also concerned with benefits and harms per se of PAS and E. In further evaluating his views, consider the specific benefits and harms per se that EE expected from legal PAS or E in his writings in 1997–1999, and how he thought they should be weighed.

1. *A. Benefits.* In those writings, EE focuses on the following supposed benefits of legal PAS or E not achievable (at the time) in any better way: ending irremediable physical suffering and providing patients with reassurance that they can end such suffering if it occurs. Though many think the biggest benefit of PAS today is avoiding dependence on others and lack of meaning in life, EE did not list these as the most significant benefits achievable *only* by PAS in his articles written in the 1990s. (We shall return to this issue below.)

With regard to the first benefit, EE agrees (1998, 1003) that "some terminally ill patients who want to end their lives suffer needlessly" without legal PAS (though in footnote 72, 1003, he notes that PAS is sometimes done contrary to law, and so fewer than one might think actually suffer).[48] However, he estimates (1998, 1009; 1999, 635) that "under 25,000 patients per year would utilize PAS or E to relieve excruciating pain refractory to optimal treatment" and expanding on this (1999, 633), he says "approximately 5,000 to 25,000 might have a distinct dying process with significant and unremitting pain, desire

E or PAS and be competent to repeatedly request and consent to E or PAS." (He here seems to recognize that regulation might exist that required repeated requests.) He concludes (1998, 1012), "We should not deceive ourselves into thinking that improving the last few days of life of 5,000 to 25,000 . . . constitutes a substantial intervention to improve end of life care in the U.S. where 2.3 million die each year." He also notes (1998, 1007, footnote 83) that based on relatives' reports "in the last three days of life about 55 percent of patients experience significant pain," suggesting that PAS or E would relieve only about three days of pain. So, his view is that though the benefit would be real, it would not be great if PAS or E were done for pain relief alone.

EE's second objection to emphasizing the benefit of pain relief (1997, 6; 1998, 984) is that most don't request PAS or E to end physical suffering but rather when they are depressed or have general psychological distress, fear loss of control, dignity, or being a burden and dependent, or have no good social supports. (It is possible that some means of pain relief themselves result in the loss of autonomy and states that some find inconsistent with their dignity, e.g., being in a stupor or totally sedated until death.) In an update in 2016 (2016, 12), he reiterates that data about PAS show that the "dominant motives are loss of autonomy and dignity and being less able to enjoy life's activities" and (2016, 20) "other forms of mental distress." Hence, the benefit from PAS would be the absence of these bads. In past work, he considered such sorts of reasons (1997, 12) as "symptoms" for which we should give psychiatric intervention, not life-ending drugs, suggesting that PAS or E for these reasons was not necessary and would interfere with providing such benefits by other better means.

Combined with EE's view that "the wisdom of [legalized] PAS or E should turn on the rule rather than the exception," (1998, 1000) the fact that *most* don't seek PAS or E for pain relief would imply that any benefits of pain relief are excluded as reasons for a law. The other reasons for which PAS or E is commonly sought, he thought in 1998, provide justification only for psychiatric or hospice intervention. Furthermore, he also thinks that benefits such as no more pain and not being dependent gotten from PAS and E can be achieved by a person's own suicide without physician assistance (1998, 983–4), and, he says, thousands successfully commit suicide each year with readily available substances. On these grounds he argues that those who insist on PAS or E rather than suicide really want a different benefit, the approval of a socially respected authority figure (doctor) who endorses their death (something that he says even a nonphysician specialist in ending life could not provide).[49] Indeed, he suggests[50] that it is this that provides "death with dignity" because "social acceptance is essential to 'dignity.'" He thinks this also shows that granting legal PAS would not be about an individual right to do as one wishes but about providing the benefit from society of its approval. Hence, he says, "The necessity of society's approval transfers the proper fulcrum of the debate from rights to policy."

With regard to the second benefit of legalization that he initially lists, EE says that those who get reassurance from having the option of legal PAS or E are balanced by those who would lose trust because they fear they might be coerced into PAS or involuntarily receive E (1998, 1008; 1999, 635). (Note that this does not deny the real benefit but only claims it can be outweighed by a harm he thinks is associated with legalizing PAS.)

B. Responses. Let us now evaluate EE's views on benefits. First, it is unclear why public policy must deal with the rule rather than with the exception. Restrictive abortion laws typically permit abortion only in cases of rape or incest which are not the "paradigm" cases in which abortion is requested. Should states that refuse to allow abortion in paradigm cases not legally permit it in exceptional cases? If laws can cover exceptional cases of abortion, then relief of irremediable pain should not be excluded as reason for legalized PAS or E merely because it covers only nonparadigmatic cases.

Second, in the very same article in which he says that most benefits of PAS can be achieved by unassisted suicide he also says (1998, 1002), "Today, most suicide attempts fail" and notes that even many PAS attempts fail. In his most recent discussion (2016, 16), he also notes a "higher frequency of problems with PAS than with E," suggesting that even more problems would occur with unassisted suicide attempts. Additionally, while suicide itself is not a crime, it is not a legal right protected by a duty of noninterference by others and this may complicate the situation of those contemplating its use. It may be that EE and others opposed to legalizing PAS and E could be brought to support a full legal right (that could be regulated) to commit suicide (including a claim against interference) in certain cases. This would be a compromise acceptable to some. However, in 2016 (8) EE says of public opinion surveys that "when the question is changed so that the patient is in 'severe pain' and the term 'legalization' is added but the action is a patient's 'suicide' rather than a physician participating in ending the patient's life, public support is consistently lower by 10 to 15 percent." Public opinion favoring PAS over S should matter to EE since he thinks that public opinion should be considered in constructing public policy.

The public may be reluctant about suicide per se because the regulation and oversight provided by a physician would not be present if suicide were (sometimes) a full legal right. The public may also not yet conceive of a respectable profession besides doctors who would assist in suicide. This, rather than EE's view that what is sought is approval of one's death by an authority figure, could explain the focus on PAS. I have also previously argued against the view that physician involvement in PAS does provide social sanction.[51] I claimed that patients should interpret a physician's involvement as mere respect for patient autonomy (when a decision is not clearly against patient's interests), not necessarily endorsement of their decision. This is consistent with the view (held by many) that PAS need not involve a physician's intention that the person she assists die but only that he get what he wants. EE's view that seeking "death with dignity" amounts to seeking the benefit of social approval is also problematic.

In Chapter 6, we discussed the concern that one's dignity would be lost. We there pointed to two notions of dignity that do not involve society's approval: dignity due to accomplishments and dignity as a status inherent to being a person. Dignity in the first sense may be lost because, for example, one cannot maintain a dignified physical state (e.g., one is incontinent), and it may be maintained if, for example, one succeeds in being calm in bad circumstances. But dignity as a status inherent in a person is not lost simply because one cannot control one's bodily functions or because one does not remain calm. The dignity of the person as a status is also not lost merely because one is not treated in a manner befitting one's status (e.g., if one is abused). Indeed, it is because one retains one's dignity as a status that being treated in a certain manner does not befit it. This is the primary reason Jeremy Waldron thinks PAS is not needed to "die with dignity," since one retains the dignity inherent in a person even if one remains alive in a state that does not befit it or one does not achieve dignity as an accomplishment.[52] Nevertheless, even keeping in mind the second sense of dignity, it might make sense to give as a reason for PAS that it is no longer possible to live in ways that befit one's dignity as a person (i.e., it is being insulted, if not extinguished) or that one cannot achieve what gives one dignity in the accomplishment sense. (As I did in Chapter 6, I will here interpret those who say they want PAS because they have "lost their dignity" as having these complaints.)[53] Hence, those who seek PAS to have death with dignity may be seeking to escape conditions they think are incompatible with or do not befit their dignity, not seeking death with social approval.

Third, consider the common reasons for PAS and E themselves (i.e., loss of autonomy and dignity and being less able to enjoy activities). They are the sorts of reasons EE subsequently gave (in 2014) for preferring death at 75 and for planning to refuse easy and certain to succeed life-extending treatment at that age. Hence, 2014 shows that he thinks that avoiding loss of autonomy and dignity as well as avoiding living without enjoyment in worthwhile pursuits are real benefits that can sometimes be provided only by death. This is so whether or not such benefits justify killing oneself or even intentionally letting oneself die past 75. In addition, EE said (1997, 2) of the typical patient seeking PAS that he "wants to die because of concern about being a burden to family or because he finds a drawn-out dying process meaningless." These are also almost exactly the sorts of reasons he gives in 2014 to avoid living on beyond 75—once he classifies much of life after 75 as often being a "drawn-out dying process" even when one is then not literally terminally ill (i.e., expected to die within six months). Might these reasons he cites in 2014 not also sometimes apply at a younger age, especially when one is terminally ill?

Furthermore, suppose all these paradigmatic reasons for wanting PAS point to real benefits it would be worth losing one's life to get (if only by not using life-saving measures). Then not getting them might cause *reasonable* distress and depression, and so these bads would not best be thought of as symptoms requiring psychiatric intervention. This would especially be true if such intervention was *not* an alternative, better way to provide the benefits achievable by death (e.g., avoiding a life without enjoyment of worthwhile activities), as EE believes is true at least in those past 75.[54]

EE emphasizes that refusing or ending treatment (even when it involves assistance by a doctor to turn off life-sustaining machinery) is a "recognized right" of a patient (1997), and he thinks that its being done for reasons other than to end physical pain need not make it legally or morally impermissible (2014). Of course, dying from refusing treatment will likely be more "drawn out" than the "swift, not drawn out end of life" he recommends in 2014 that could be delivered by PAS or E. This again raises the issue of justifying a legal and moral difference between refusing or ending treatment and using PAS or E in order to get benefits other than pain relief. This is so especially given that there is less oversight required for refusing treatment than there would be for legal PAS (on conceptions of it that involve public regulation). We shall return to this issue.

2. *A. Harms.* Now consider the harms per se of legalization with which Emanuel is concerned. We have already pointed to many of them in trying to show that they often are conjoined with wronging and rights violations. In particular, EE warned (1997, 14) of the "possibility that E not only would be performed on incompetent patients in violation of the rules . . . but would become the rule in the context of demographic and budgetary pressures . . . around 2010. . . . The influence of ethical arguments, medical practice, demographic and budgetary pressures, and a social ethos that views the old and sick as burdens[55] would seem capable of overwhelming any barriers against E for incompetent patients." (I have earlier argued that coercion to PAS and nonvoluntariness or involuntariness of E, as well as inequity in the distribution of these abuses, can be wrongings that are not necessarily overall harms and can even occur when there would be overall benefits to the person acted on. Thus I shall henceforth refer to the combination of them and overall harms per se as "problems" or "bads.") The biggest harms per se of PAS would presumably be loss of still acceptable time alive and fear of this loss.[56]

Another bad EE sees in legalization of PAS and E is absence of incentives to improve end of life care (EOLC) (1998, 985). He says, "Ending a patient's life . . . quick[ly] and painless[ly] is much easier than this constant physical and emotional care. If there is a way to avoid all this hard work it becomes difficult not to use it." At the time of writing these words he favored a "good death" of the sort proposed at the time by the hospice movement. He said the "real objective [should be to] improve care of . . . Americans who die . . . [with] pain management, treatment of depression, or use of hospice" (1998, 985). He thought that "properly utilized E and PAS are 'last ditch' interventions . . . justified only after appropriate palliative options are attempted," though these are less likely to be available in the uninsured (1999, 641). He thought that such end-of-life care may prevent loss of still acceptable time alive to those who would die prematurely through PAS or E (even if voluntarily chosen) and also prevent the fear of many more people that this harm will come to them.

B. *Responses.* Let us first assume for the sake of argument that EE's concerns about bads and harms due to legalization of PAS or E were and still are well founded. Let us also assume for illustrative purposes that the benefit to be weighed against the harms is relief of suffering not achievable without PAS or E. Making this use of the nonparadigmatic reason for PAS or E is not unreasonable once we have argued that laws could be fashioned to deal with nonparadigmatic reasons and that according to surveys the public is most accepting of PAS for this reason. I will eventually move on to consider arguments concerning the paradigmatic benefits sought (in Part IV).[57]

(i) *Weighing harms and benefits.* How does EE weigh the harms and benefits per se in deciding on public policy? EE calculates that there are more people who are at risk of losing acceptable life from legal PAS than who need it to avoid irremediable physical suffering. When this risk to each of the many materializes in some definite people, he thinks the total harm of acceptable life lost through inappropriate PAS or E will greatly outweigh the total good of physical suffering avoided in the smaller number of people who stand to benefit. EE's way of reasoning to this conclusion may involve at least three morally contentious moves: (a) omitting to determine the relative significance of the harm and benefit per se, (b) weighing the benefits and harms that result from risks to each of many persons in the same way as weighing certain-to-occur benefits and harms to individual persons (sometimes referred to as the problem of equating statistical and identifiable victims or beneficiaries),[58] and (c) interpersonal aggregation of harms and benefits of different significance.

Consider the issue (a) by focusing on the benefit of relief from irremediable physical suffering worse than death. We would have to know how much time would be spent in this state if not for PAS or E to know the benefit of these acts to a person. Similarly, we would have to know how much acceptable time alive would be lost if someone died prematurely by inappropriate PAS or E to know the harm of this to the person. Suppose we had this information. How should we compare these benefits and harms per se, independent of how they come about and assuming the harms and benefits occur in different people?

Consider first only two people. Although the harm and benefit would actually be interpersonal (i.e., happening to different people), we could use what I call an Intrapersonal Choice Test to weigh the harms against the benefits per se by imagining them occurring to the same person. The test asks one individual whether he would prefer to have (or prefer to avoid) (a) the life in which he suffers severely for a certain period (e.g., for five days) before death or (b) the life in which he loses an equivalent period of acceptable life (e.g., five days) at the end of his life. In this Intrapersonal Choice Test the suffering neither causes nor is caused by the acceptable period of life. It might reasonably be suggested that it would take many more days of merely acceptable life lost to be as important as avoiding a day of extreme physical suffering. So one would rather have a life in which one lost more than five days of acceptable life at one's end rather than a life in which one went through five days of great suffering at one's end. This suggests that interpersonally as well, when considering one person who is harmed and another who is benefited (and abstracting from issues of rights), losing a few days of merely acceptable life to death is less of a harm to one person than avoiding the same number of days of irremediable pain is a benefit to the other person.[59] The problem is that EE does not employ such a procedure—the one I have described or another—to get the relative values of harms and benefits.

Now consider the second possible problem (b) and whether it arises in the way EE weighs harms and benefits per se. It has been argued that we should not treat statistical and (so-called) identifiable harms alike.[60] For example, it is said that we could justify saving one person who is otherwise certain to die at $time_1$ rather than preventing even a somewhat greater number of deaths that we know will occur at a not distant $time_2$, when we can do either only at t_1. This is because the deaths at $time_2$ will occur in a few of many people each of whom at $time_1$ has only a small chance of being one of these few who will die at $time_2$. ($Time_1$ is referred to as "ex ante" to the time more will die and time$_2$ as "ex post" that outcome). What may underlie this claim, it has been suggested, is a contractualist ethical theory such as proposed by Thomas Scanlon[61] that focuses on what we owe to each person as an individual (e.g., preventing one person's 100 percent certain death at time$_1$ versus preventing the small risk of death that each of many individuals has at the time we must decide what to do). Alternatively, what may underlie these claims is a moral view that favors dispersion versus concentration of risk.[62] These ways of reasoning contrast with just focusing on the total number of deaths prevented overall. Similarly, if we abstract from how harm comes about, it might be claimed that it is more important that someone avoid certain irremediable physical suffering than that each of many other people do not have a small risk of dying prematurely and so losing some acceptable life. This could be so even if that harm were comparable to physical suffering and even if that harm would eventually happen to more people once the small risks come to fruition.

However, suppose it is also uncertain which particular person will get relief from irremediable physical suffering, even though it is certain that some person will be benefited in this way by legalization. Then "statistical" effects would be present on both the harm and benefit sides of the calculation. And indeed when EE does his calculations of benefits and harms he seems to be considering the chances of each, thus avoiding problem (b). Hence, if EE were correct about relative numbers and possible harms, legalization of PAS or E could give each person ex ante a greater chance of losing some acceptable time alive than of benefiting by avoiding irremediable physical suffering. Nevertheless, suppose the more probable harm is less bad for the person who gets it than the less probable benefit is good for the person who gets it (as determined by the Intrapersonal Choice Test). Then the product of probability multiplied by the value of the outcome could result in the equality of expected harm and benefit or even higher expected benefit (of relief from suffering) than overall harm (of losing some time alive). After all, a small chance of a big benefit could outweigh a big chance of a small harm.

Thus, despite what EE says, we cannot decide whether the expected benefit or expected harm due to legalized PAS or E is greater just on the basis of numbers of people who have a chance of benefit or harm. We need to use some procedure to decide on the relative significance of the individual harm and benefit (such as the Intrapersonal Choice Test), apply its results interpersonally, and then combine this value with a figure for the probability of harm or benefit based on numbers of people who have a chance of harm or benefit in order to complete the calculation. EE does not do all this.

Now consider the third possible problem (c) with the way EE weighs harms and benefits per se: interpersonal additive aggregation. It may seem in what we have so far said that we have not adequately taken account of the total number of people who would be ultimately benefited or harmed. For example, we considered the number of people at risk of harm merely to determine the risk for any individual that he would be harmed. But should we also additively *aggregate* small harms to each of many who will actually be harmed which may make the total harm equal to or greater than the total benefit to fewer people who avoid a very bad state (e.g., avoid suffering greatly)? Or should we instead compare pairwise the harm or benefit each person would get? According to the latter procedure, if no one of the many harmed will lose something that is equal to or greater than the benefit that someone else gets (in avoiding very bad suffering), we should not additively aggregate the harms to the many and count the total against the total of benefits.[63] Suppose that each of many people would lose a few days of acceptable life at the end of his/her life and no one of these losses can outweigh the benefit to any one of fewer people of avoiding a period of great suffering. Then according to pairwise comparison combined with giving priority to helping the worst off, if it were a matter of harms and benefits per se independent of rights violations, we should give priority to preventing the great suffering in each person in the smaller group (even if it is only one person).[64] It is only once the loss that sufficiently many in the larger group will individually undergo is equal or sufficiently close to the suffering to be avoided in each person in the smaller group that we may additively aggregate some of the losses. Then (at least some of) the numbers of people on opposing sides of harm and benefit should count.[65]

In sum, when EE argues that more people stand to lose life prematurely than would benefit from relief of irremediable suffering if PAS or E were legalized, he does not consider how the value of what each in the larger group would lose compares with the value of the benefit to each in the smaller group. So his method does not tell us how many of the greater number are at risk of losing something comparable in importance to what beneficiaries of PAS and E would gain. In addition, he does not use pairwise comparison of harms and benefits combined with giving priority to the worst off, additively aggregating and comparing totals only when the harms and benefits to individuals are equal or nearly so. His not doing these things could be justified if he were really concerned not with harms and benefits per se but with the rights violations to those who would lose life prematurely. For even if the loss to each of these people is less than the benefit to those who are saved from suffering, one might think (correctly or incorrectly) that what matters most is their right not to have the loss imposed and to have the state not do what enables such a rights violation (with the right functioning as a side constraint or at least having added weight). In this way *not* giving priority to avoiding the worst outcome for individuals could be another indication that EE's view is not "beyond rights talk."

(ii) *Harms from ending treatment.* In examining how to weigh benefits and harms, we are assuming that EE was right in his prediction of harms and bads due to legalization of PAS and E. But would such harms and bads be uniquely due to such legalization? As noted earlier, all of the bads with which EE is concerned seem to also be possible effects of a right that he accepts to refuse or end treatment. For example, patients can be pressured to refuse or end treatment as well as to commit PAS and doctors could end treatment without or against a patient's consent just as they could perform NE or IE. Indeed, EE says (1998, 1009; 1999, 637) families may not want to maintain life-sustaining treatment for their dying relative and may put pressure on him to end his treatment. Despite this, EE does not deny the person's right to refuse treatment (even with the intention to die, whether it is morally appropriate or not). He also accepts as a default that doctors may sometimes legally give a patient drugs to stop pain, even if this has a lethal side effect for the patient until it is shown that this results in abuse (such as physicians or others giving pain killers that cause death against someone's wishes). There is no similar view that legal PAS should be the default until bad effects are shown.

EE does not tell us what could support the moral and legal distinction between the legal permissibility of refusing or ending treatment and PAS or E such that comparable possible harms per se (such as loss of still acceptable time alive) that weigh against benefits in a harm/benefit analysis stand in the way of legalizing the latter but not the former. Arguably, it could be the concern not to violate someone's bodily integrity by imposing treatment when he refuses it, something that would not occur if we do not assist him in PAS or do not induce his death in E.[66] In addition, of the people for whom losing additional time alive would be a harm, many fewer are attached to life support that could be inappropriately ended than are not attached and susceptible to coerced to PAS or E. However, suppose we did not treat severe pain in the terminally ill with drugs that are foreseen to kill the patient as a side effect. Then we would also not violate someone's bodily integrity. Further, the number who could be subject to inappropriate injection with lethal doses of painkillers does not seem to differ from the number who could be subject to inappropriate PAS or E. Hence, it is not clear why the good of providing such pain treatments should make it the legal default until evidence arises of actual bads but the comparable goods of providing PAS or E at least for irremediable pain relief do not make it the default.[67] So these drug use cases turn out to have distinctive argumentative significance because refusing the drugs would no more interfere with bodily integrity than would refusing PAS and yet drug use is legally permissible.

3. *Doing public policy in general.* The points I have made in considering EE's views in Parts II and III are relevant to formulating public policy in general and for that purpose can be summarized as follows:

(i) Reasoning based on moral and legal rights and for legislated legal rights can be relevant even in the absence of a constitutional right. Individuals may have both a moral right to do something (e.g., acquire PAS) and a moral right that things not be done to them (e.g., IE).

(ii) In weighing harms and benefits one should distinguish (a) when these per se are at issue and (b) when these are bound up with rights violations or other wrongings. The same degree of harm or benefit may have different significance depending on whether it is or is not connected with violating rights. For example, a smaller loss may be more important than a larger benefit just because bringing it about would violate a negative right.

(iii) When the state grants certain rights whose being acted on by others might threaten different legal rights of others, it is important to take account of how such threats would come about (e.g., via the unauthorized acts of intervening agents or more directly). This could determine whether to grant a legal right and control potential violations of different rights in other ways. Further, it is not true that where state behavior is concerned there is no moral distinction between its harming and its allowing or enabling harm .

(iv) It is not true that laws should never be formulated to deal with nonparadigmatic cases in which benefits could be provided.

(v) When weighing interpersonal harms and benefits per se (i.e., independent of how they come about) the following should be taken into account. (a) It is important to compare the relative significance of the harms and benefits. For this purpose, the Intrapersonal Choice Test can be useful. (b) It can be appropriate to consider the ex ante chance of harm or benefit to each person, not only the overall harm or benefit that can eventuate. (c) It could be right to do pairwise comparison of harms and benefits in different individuals giving priority to avoiding the worst states in individuals, and only additively aggregating over persons those harms and benefits that are comparable.

(vi) When there are goods that it is permissible to achieve by some legal means (e.g., stopping treatment), it is important to consider why the goods may not be achieved by legalizing alternative means. Check whether legally permitted activities have the same balance of harms and benefits as activities not yet legal and whether there is justification for a distinction among the legal statuses of the different activities (including a distinction based on an upper limit of allowable harms).

(vii) Consider the policies and laws already in existence and the views already held by others. Using these try to contruct arguments that could be considered variations of a freestanding ideal argument for or against a public policy or law.

Part IV

1. *Predictions and facts.* Let us now critically examine the assumption that the bad effects of PAS and E (harms, rights violations, other
wrongings, and reduced attention to end-of-life care (EOLC)) with
which EE was concerned are real. In his own most recent discussion,
he says (2016, 2) of PAS where it has been legalized that the "typical
patient is older, white, and well educated. . . . In no jurisdiction . . . [is
there] evidence that [the] vulnerable . . . have been receiving E and
PAS at rates higher than . . . [the] general population." Further, he
says (2016, 19): "In the U.S., the concern that minorities, the disabled,
the poor, or other socially marginalized groups might be pressured
to accept PAS does not seem to be borne out. The demographic pro-
file of patients in the U.S. who have received these interventions is
white, well-educated, and well insured. . . . In jurisdictions that have
legalized E or PAS, use of these procedures has increased but alleged
slippery-slope cases . . . appear to be a very small minority of cases."
His conclusion (2016, 1) is that "E and PAS are increasingly being
legalized, [and] remain relatively rare. . . . [E]xisting data do not indicate widespread abuse." In addition, he says (2016, 1) that a "large
portion of patients receiving PAS in Oregon and Washington reported
being enrolled in hospice or palliative care, as did patients in Belgium."
Hence they did not choose PAS because they lacked the other options.
Thus what EE says in 2016 implies that his earlier concerns and
predictions about bad effects of legalizing PAS have not so far come to
pass. (Possibly this is true because there has not yet been legalization
in areas where there are many uninsured vulnerable people.)

However, 2016 supports his earlier view that it is not for pain relief that PAS or E is paradigmatically sought. Rather it is because autonomy and enjoyment of life are felt to have been lost. As noted
above, these are the sorts of reasons he himself gives for not wanting
to use even easy life-saving measures beyond 75.

Since most who get PAS after being in hospice are well educated
and insured, this also suggests they have had optimal palliative care.
The fact that hospice and palliation usually precede PAS also suggests
that legalizing PAS has not depressed the development of this sort of
EOLC, at least for the insured. Furthermore, a concern that legalized
PAS and E could reduce attention to providing "a good death" via

hospice and palliation requires the assumption that what is provided by hospice and palliation would be good enough to make death a worse option. By contrast, EE's 2014 view is that a "drawn-out death," a phrase he applies even to advanced care of chronic conditions, is not good enough to justify staying alive, at least after 75. In 2014 he says a good death is to "go swiftly and promptly," and he would do this by refusing even easy life-saving treatment, though he would take palliative care if he didn't go swiftly. This implies that in 2014 he does not see the "good death" as he imagined it in 1998 as providing a positive benefit over death at least after 75. Rather it just provides a reduction in bads if the better option of death is not available. Hence, his current position implies that he thinks that at least for some palliation and hospice would not provide goods that provide sufficient reasons to stay alive rather than die—the sort of goods that could reasonably be the objects of what are called categorical desires to go on living. Rather, they would provide only goods by comparison with worse physical suffering and greater boredom if one must continue to live—the sorts of good that are objects of what are called conditional desires that one reasonably has *if* one unavoidably goes on living. For example, one does not (usually) desire to go on living merely in order to avoid being in pain or to avoid boredom even if these are reasonably objects of conditional desires.[68]

The types of goods that EE thinks are available at the end of life—whether they are reasonably possible objects of categorical or only conditional desires—should also affect EE's calculation of the harms due to premature deaths caused by PAS or E independently of, or connected to, rights violations. If the goods are only conditional, this would reduce the significance of dying earlier than one physically had to, at least in terms of goods lost. However, the fact that most who seek PAS or E are trying to avoid lack of autonomy and reduced enjoyment of activities rather than great physical suffering should also affect the calculation of the benefits of PAS and E. It seems more important to avoid suffering rather than reduced enjoyment, for example. Putting these two points together suggests that the importance both of benefits per se only achievable by PAS and harms per se enabled by legal PAS or E is less than previously surmised. This could still leave the relative weight of benefits to harms the same as when PAS is necessary to achieve relief of physical suffering and the harm threatened is loss of worthwhile time alive. Hence, weighing benefits against harms in paradigmatic cases might differ in absolute but not relative terms from the weighing of benefits and harms we considered earlier. It could still be necessary to separately consider the importance of the possible rights affected on either the benefit or harm side.

2. *Legalizing PAS*. Given what EE says in 2016 about the absence of the sort of bad effects that concerned him in the past, should he now support legalizing PAS to some degree? Let us consider a possible argument for this conclusion. Unlike the argument for legalization given earlier in this chapter that began with a premise about giving painkillers that foreseeably cause death, this argument is like the one discussed in Chapter 6 that began with what EE believes. The difference is that the conclusion now is about law and policy, not personal morality.

Consider the following points.[69] (a) EE's discussion suggests that the general public would not oppose legalizing PAS at least for relieving irremediable physical suffering in the terminally ill when palliative care has failed. EE could also support this, given his view that assisting suicide and even euthanasia in such cases is ethically right, if he would agree that legislation can cover nonparadigmatic requests. (Perhaps both he and the general public could also support PAS for those not terminally ill but with irremediable physical suffering on the ground that continuing long life in such conditions is worse than death.) If this is so, then EE could morally and legally endorse PAS and E sometimes with the intention that the person die. (b) EE also morally and legally endorses the right of doctors to give drugs necessary for pain relief in some cases even if their best use would foreseeably cause death as an unintended but foreseen side effect. This too constitutes killing (not merely assisting killing) since in many cases killing involves merely foreseen deaths (e.g., collateral deaths caused by bombing). He might limit the drug use to the terminally ill who would die soon anyway (but possibly extend its use to nonterminal cases when long life in severe physical pain would be worse than death). (c) EE also endorses the reasonableness as well as the moral and legal right of competent older persons (e.g., past 75) who have lived what he calls a "complete life" to refuse easy life-saving treatment (2014). (By "complete life" he means that if they die now they will have had life with the important activities or goods available to them.)[70] This is so when they find life unacceptable even if it involves no great physical suffering and no terminal illness (so they might live for many years with easy medical help such as a flu shot). Thus they would be offering reasons for omitting life-saving measures that have nothing to do with the intrusiveness of these measures and are like the paradigmatic reasons given for PAS. Indeed, EE thinks it is not unreasonable for people to think death is a lesser bad for them by comparison to living on in these cases.

Can we conclude from this that EE would endorse letting oneself die intending one's death in such a case? Possibly he only endorses the intention not to be complicit in keeping oneself alive after a complete life by taking life-extending treatments.[71] However, should his endorsement be this limited? After all, in other situations it is morally and legally permissible to intend what it is not unreasonable to think is a lesser bad to oneself in order to avoid what it is not unreasonable to think is a greater bad to oneself.[72] (For example, one may intend that a doctor intentionally cause one a period of pain as a means to keep one from falling into a permanent coma or destroy one's sight as a means to stay alive when life is still worth living.) Why should it not be morally and legally permissible to refuse easy treatment intending one's death if death is the lesser bad relative to living on?

On this view, we should legally permit refusing even easy life-saving treatment with the intention to die not merely because the alternative would involve violating bodily integrity by imposing treatment on someone, but because the *intention* not to live a life whose contents one (not unreasonably) finds unacceptable relative to death is not always unreasonable or morally wrong. We don't have to merely tolerate the intention, we can endorse it as sometimes not unreasonable and not morally wrong.[73] It is not clear why in some cases this could not also be true of those who have not lived a "complete" life if living on "unacceptably" would not help them live a "complete life" in EE's sense. (This is especially true if they are also terminally ill though they do not have great physical suffering).

The positions so far described involve several possible combinations of the factors of killing, letting die, intending death, merely foreseeing death, having/not having terminal illness, and having not having had a complete life (i.e., being/not being old), physical suffering/unacceptable life. It may help to lay some of these out in a table (see Table 8.1) before proceeding further.

Table 8.1

	Intend Death as Means (ID)	Foresee Death (FD)
	(a)	(b)
Kill (K)	K(ID) to Avoid Physical Suffering Terminal Nonterminal Old (-Old)	K(FD) to Avoid Physical Suffering Terminal Nonterminal Old (-Old)
	(c)	(d)
Let Die (LD)	LD(ID) to Avoid Physical Suffering LD(ID) to Avoid Un- Acceptable Life Terminal Nonterminal Old (-Old)	LD(FD) to Avoid Physical Suffering LD(FD) to Avoid Unacceptable Life Terminal Nonterminal Old (-Old)

As noted before, one big difference between EE's position and that of traditional opponents of PAS and E (such as some supporters of the DDE) is that EE does not always morally and legally oppose intending death as a means; for example, when one omits treatment for a terminal illness intending to die to avoid irremediable great suffering. He also is not morally opposed to a person himself or his physician (with the patient's consent) killing or assisting killing intending death as a means to stop irremediable suffering in the terminally ill.[74] I also suggested earlier that in the absence of abuse he should support legalization of this even if it is a nonparadigmatic case for suicide or PAS. The question now is whether there is an argument that should convince him to endorse the moral and legal right to PAS, involving a physician assisting a person in *killing himself intending to die* with the aim of preventing life unacceptable to that person though it does not involve irremediable suffering. This question can arise when life (i) will soon end anyway (terminal) or (ii) will not soon end anyway (nonterminal).

One such argument[75] first asks, would it be morally and legally permissible for doctors to give drugs that improve quality of life to a person who intends to avoid life that is unacceptable to him even though each foresees but does not intend that doing this will shortly also cause the person's death? One way drugs could do this is by maintaining strength and preventing diminished capacities and dependency when these are coming, though the drugs place a great burden on the heart. Crucially, in 2014 EE omits to consider whether he would be willing to take such drugs (if they existed) beyond age 75 to help him avoid life he finds unacceptable. It seems to me that given his views, he may be committed to taking such drugs and, in the absence of abuse, legally allowing doctors to provide the drugs at least to those beyond 75. (Hence, we could add K(FD) as morally and legally permissible in box (b) of the table at least sometimes to avoid unacceptable life (without physical suffering).) After all, EE sees death as less bad by comparison to adding years of nonworthwhile life whose low quality, he thinks, also reduces the overall value of his life and of remembrances of him.[76] It is this that leads him to say he would refuse easy life-saving treatments after 75. So he should be willing to use the drugs as another way to avoid the worse option to himself even though it foreseeably will cause his death (the less bad option). Possibly he would limit use of such drugs to those who have already lived a complete life if they are nonterminal but extend it to allow all who are terminal to use drugs that give them some higher quality life (beyond relief of physical pain) even if this also hastens death.

If this is true, should he also be willing to legally permit doctors to provide what he can use to *intentionally* kill himself to avoid life he not unreasonably finds unacceptable for him? I already argued that it is reasonable for him to *intend* his death to avoid such unacceptable life by refusing even easy treatment if he is willing to refuse such treatment foreseeing death, and both should be legally permissible. (Box (c) in the Table). This was because he (suppose not unreasonably) believes death is the less bad option for him by comparison to such a life. I have now argued that he should be willing to take drugs that will foreseeably kill him in order to sufficiently improve the quality of his life and it should be legally permissible for doctors to provide or administer such drugs. Why then should he not allow doctors to provide him with what he can use to *kill* himself when he *intends* his death to avoid the unacceptable life (i.e., PAS)? After all, it is intrapersonally rational to actively pursue the less bad option as a means to avoid the worse option for oneself. (Then we could fill in K(ID) to avoid unacceptable life that does not involve physical suffering in the Table's box (a) both for the terminal or nonterminal at least after a complete life.)

This argument moves from (i) the moral and legal permissibility of intending death (when it is a less bad option) by letting die in order to avoid unacceptable life (when such life is a worse option) and (ii) the moral and legal permissibility of killing that results from a physician providing or administering a drug that prevents such unacceptable life with mere foresight to death to (iii) the moral and legal permissibility of a person combining killing himself with intending his death (assisted by a physician) to avoid unacceptable life. I assume the moral and legal permissibility also yields a full right (including a claim against interference). Call this the Legal Paradigmatic Reasons Argument for PAS, since it focuses on what EE says are the paradigmatic reasons for PAS.

However, suppose EE would think that it is not an acceptable goal of doctors in particular to maintain high quality of life in nonterminally ill people, especially after a certain age, in a way that will foreseeably cause death. Then he could be limited to defending a personal moral and legal right (perhaps with the help of a nonmedical assistant) to do what will avoid unacceptable life but foreseeably shortly cause his death, and also what will intentionally kill him to avoid the same unacceptable life. However, what of those who are terminally ill and seek medical assistance to improve quality of life and avoid life that is unacceptable to them (though it involves no physical suffering but only lack of autonomy and enjoyment)? If death will soon occur anyway, would it be inconsistent with a doctor's mission for her to use drugs to help a patient achieve autonomy and enjoyment when this foreseeably will cause the patient's death sooner? Suppose it is not inconsistent. Suppose also such patients have a moral and legal right to refuse life-saving means intending death to avoid what to them is an unacceptable life because intending the less bad option to avoid the worse option to oneself is reasonable and not morally wrong. Why then should they not have a moral and legal right to a willing physician's assistance to engage in PAS, which combines the patient killing himself and intending the less bad option of death for himself, in order to avoid the worse option for him of unacceptable life?

An additional possible problem for the Legal Paradigmatic Reasons Argument for PAS is that in using quality-of-life-maintaining drugs, EE (or any terminally or nonterminally ill person) would not only avoid life he finds unacceptable, but would also get some personally acceptable time alive before his death. This contrasts with merely avoiding unacceptable life without getting any positive benefits, as would occur if death itself (whether by PAS, E, or omitting life-saving aid) prevents unacceptable life.[77] But the shorter the period of goods achieved by taking the quality-enhancing drug that causes his death, the closer the treatment comes to achieving only what is achieved by PAS merely to avoid unacceptable life. At the extreme, suppose that, instead of maintaining performance, the drugs put someone to sleep and this was the only way to keep him from expressing the boring, repetitive thoughts that EE thinks could make someone's life unacceptable for him past 75 (see 2014). Though it is foreseen that the drug will also shortly cause a deadly heart attack, it would seem to be worth taking by someone like EE who thinks death is a less bad option than such unacceptable life in old age. (This is the Sleeper Case already discussed in Chapter 6 in connection with purely moral conclusions that may follow from what EE already believes.) Suppose there were a moral and legal right to the drugs that will foreseeably kill [K(FD)] to avoid unacceptable life in the Sleeper Case. It seems reasonable to move on to killing intending death [K(ID)] to achieve the same good, given that intending a less bad option to avoid a worse option for oneself is reasonable. A moral and legal right to either suicide protected from interference, assisted suicide with nonphysician assistance, or PAS would achieve this.[78]

Notes

1. I shall move between work EE did on this issue in 1997–1999 and what he has said in 2014 and 2016.

2. See Ezekiel Emanuel et al., "Attitudes and Practices of Euthanasia and Physician-Assisted Suicide in the United States, Canada, and Europe," *Journal of the American Medical Association* 316 (2016), 79–90. doi:10.1001/

jama.2016.8499. Henceforth 2016. All references in the text to Emanuel 2016 are to this article.

3. See, for example, Ezekiel Emanuel, "Why I Hope to Die When I am 75," *Atlantic* (October 2014) and discussion of this in Chapter 6. https://www.theatlantic.com/magazine/archive/2014/10/why-i-hope-to-die-at-75/379329/. Henceforth 2014. All references in the text to Emanuel 2014 are to this article.

4. Neil Gorsuch, *The Future of Assisted Suicide and Euthanasia* (Princeton: Princeton University Press, 2006).

5. For more on Gorsuch's views, see Chapter 7, "Five Easy Arguments for Assisted Suicide and the Objections of Velleman and Gorsuch." A shorter version of that chapter discussing only Gorsuch was my 2018 Lanson Lecture in Bioethics and will be published elsewhere.

6. These alternative conceptions follow those in Philippa Foot's "Euthanasia," *Philosophy & Public Affairs* 6 (1977), 85–112. https://www.jstor.org/stable/i313715.

7. Ezekiel Emanuel, "Whose Right to Die," *Atlantic* (March 1997). https://www.theatlantic.com/magazine/archive/1997/03/whose-right-to-die/304641/. Henceforth 1997. All references in the text to Emanuel 1997 are to this article.

8. See Ronald Dworkin et al., "Assisted Suicide: The Philosophers' Brief," *New York Review of Books* 44 (1997), 41–45.

9. However, I elsewhere consider an argument for a doctor's duty to perform PAS. See for example "A Right to Choose Death?" *Boston Review* (Summer 1997) and Chapter 7 this volume.

10. A recent (2015) example of proposed law is provided by the Massachusetts End-of-Life Options Bill, which requires repeated requests at intervals by the patient as well as psychiatric examination and is limited to the terminally ill. However, it is instructive to consider this bill for some issues legislation in this area can raise. First, while repeated requests and mental examination are required to get a lethal prescription, if one changes one's mind nothing further need be done for one's wishes to be heeded. One need not undergo a mental examination or make repeated requests over a period of time to rescind a request to die. This is so though one's decision not to have PAS may not be as well thought out and be the result of a less sound mind than one had when making a decision for PAS. There seems to be a bias in favor of life. However, it may be said that since we do not, in general, have to make multiple requests to others or have mental examinations in order to go on living, not requiring these to revoke a decision for PAS merely treats a terminally ill person the way others are ordinarily treated. The crucial legislative point is that those who seek assistance in dying must have these examinations. However, they are not required to give reasons for wanting to die and this parallels not having to give reasons for wanting to live.

Second, the bill is meant to apply to people who are expected to die within six months "whether or not treatment is provided." Since people are free to refuse treatment, the bill's wording suggests that those who refuse treatment that would have kept them alive beyond six months would not be eligible for assistance in dying. This seems wrong.

Third (and perhaps most striking), the legislation denies that it is about "assisted suicide." The bill says that the person who takes the lethal drug will not be said to have engaged in suicide (15) and the cause of death will be listed as the underlying terminal illness (12). But if someone takes a lethal drug in order to kill himself and dies of this (at a time when the disease would not have killed him), he has committed suicide. Presumably the state wishes to protect the person from losing insurance coverage on account of suicide, but it might be better to change insurance policies than to deny that what is suicide is not. The bill goes on to say that the term "assisted suicide" should not be used in any state documents or websites to describe the practice of aid in dying. But if a doctor gives someone a prescription even merely to give a patient an option to take his own life, it seems he will have helped the patient to commit suicide if the patient uses that prescription to kill himself. (Similarly, if I give someone money that he can use to go to college if he chooses to and he does so, I will have assisted him in going to college. An exception may arise when one gives the option to do x because one believes it reduces the chance of someone doing x.) Finally in this regard, the bill says that doctors should counsel patients about the importance of having someone else present when the patient takes the lethal drug. However, it does not say what the role of this person is to be and whether they could be said to assist suicide if, for example, they actually give the patient the drug. The denial that what they do is assist suicide could follow from the legislators' view that the patient will not be considered to have committed suicide legally speaking. But the refusal to acknowledge such assistance in what really is suicide is also an oddity in the proposed law.

11. Ezekiel Emanuel, "The Future of Euthanasia and Physician-Assisted Suicide: Beyond Rights Talk to Informed Public Policy," *Minnesota Law Review* 82 (1998), 983–1014. All references in the text to Emanuel 1998 are to this article. Note that whether the two could be separated morally (by contrast to conceptually or practically) is another question.

12. In Ezekiel Emanuel, "What is the Great Benefit of Legalizing Euthanasia or Physician-Assisted Suicide?" *Ethics* 109 (1999), 629–42. Henceforth 1999.

13. It is also similar to the policy about PAS that the Netherlands at one time followed without officially legalizing PAS.

14. However, he also says at one point in this same article, "consideration of PAS or E as a matter of policy rather than right requires a shift of perspective, from the moral to the political." Unless he uses "moral" to mean something other than "ethical," this would also imply moving beyond the ethical to the political.

15. Constitutional rights may also stand in the way of preventing morally wrong acts, as rights may protect individual's options to do the morally wrong thing (e.g., exercising one's free speech rights to promote Nazi ideals).

16. Despite here using "inevitably," in the same article (1998, 1005) he also says only that "we can make useful educated guesses about likely actual

practices" and in 1997 (985) he says, "An adequate evaluation of benefits and harms requires much more information."

17. See *Washington v. Glucksberg*, 117 S. Ct. 2303 (1997) (O'Connor, J., concurring) and 2310 (Breyer, J., concurring).

18. According to Neil Gorsuch, it is part of the common law. *The Future of Assisted Suicide and Euthanasia* (Princeton: Princeton University Press, 2006), 83. However, in *Glucksberg* the majority opinion says, "We have also assumed, and strongly suggested, that the Due Process Clause protects the traditional right to refuse unwanted lifesaving medical treatment. *Cruzan*, 497 U.S., at 278–279, 110 S.Ct., at 2851–2852." *Washington v. Glucksberg*, 521 U.S. 702, 720 (1997). And, "we concluded that the right to refuse unwanted medical treatment was so rooted in our history, tradition, and practice as to require special protection under the Fourteenth Amendment. *Cruzan*, 497 U.S., at 278–279, 110 S.Ct., at 2851–2852; *id.*, at 287–288, 110 S.Ct., at 2856–2857 (O'Connor, J. concurring)." *Washington v. Glucksberg*, 521 U.S. 702, 722 n. 7 (1997). I thank Seana Shiffrin for guidance on this issue.

19. See John Rawls, "The Idea of Public Reason Revisited," *University of Chicago Law Review* 64 (1997), 765–807. https://www.jstor.org/stable/1600311.

20. See first in *Boston Review* (1997), and in more detail in *Ethics* (April 1999). Also see Chapter 7 this volume.

21. Even if proper use of pain-relieving drugs does not in fact have the certain side effect of death, the issue is whether use of the drugs would be legally permissible even if they did certainly have this effect.

22. We considered various objections to the four-step version of this three-step argument in Chapter 7. Note that this argument is similar to but also different from the one given at the end of Chapter 6 and from the one given at the end of this chapter. The argument in Chapter 6 began with what EE already believed (i.e., that he should omit easy life-saving aid foreseeing his death after a complete life). It then tried to show that this view, along with some other views he held, would imply that he should think PAS was morally permissible when sought for certain reasons. The argument in this chapter begins with moves from a widely endorsed social practice that involves unintended killing (giving the drug for pain relief that kills as a side effect). Hence, it entirely bypasses moving from letting oneself die (by omitting life-saving aid) to assistance in killing oneself. However, the two arguments share premises about intrapersonal rationality and foreseen killing and reach the same conclusion.

23. I believe Ronald Dworkin argues in this way in his *Life's Dominion: An Argument about Abortion, Euthanasia, and Individual Freedom* (New York: Knopf, 1993).

24. These conceptions of harm and benefit focus on *changes* in well-being rather than on, for example, so-called "harmed states" which involve extremely bad states of the person even if they are not a decline relative to some baseline. For defense of the latter conception of harm, see Seana Shiffrin, "Harm and Its Moral Significance," *Legal Theory* 18 (2012), 357–98.

https://doi.org/10.1017/S1352325212000080. One problem with using the "would have been" comparison is that it seems to imply that we will not harm someone if someone else would have caused the same loss to them anyway.

25. The slightly different views do not depend on comparing a possible stretch of future life with nonexistence occupying the same time period since they compare whole possible lives. These views also allow us to consider (1) the possible benefit of death at t_1 even when it interferes with one's having a good future that nevertheless would make one's overall life worse for one to have and (2) the possible harm of death at t_1 even when it interferes with one having a future worse than death that nevertheless would make one's overall life better for one to have. Notice also that while some accept the view that death is not overall a harm to a person when it interferes with a future worse than death others hold that an overall harmful death can sometimes merely be less harmful than the greater harm of living on. As Michael Rabenberg notes, torture for one hour can be a harm overall even if it interferes with the greater harm of being tortured for ten hours. See his *Matters of Life and Death* (unpublished Ph.D. thesis), 2018.

26. Matthew Hanser discusses these issues in "Interfering with Aid," *Analysis* 59(1), 1999: 41-7.

27. This allows that loss of autonomy due to paternalism can itself be a harm (in addition to interference with autonomy being a rights violation). However, that harm can be outweighed so that interference overall produces a benefit, and yet there could still be a rights violation.

28. The number of those at risk is smaller than the number who die because many die suddenly and do not face a "dying process."

29. I owe this point to Adil Haque. Rawls similarly argues that the loss of the benefit to the slave owners due to having slaves cannot be counted against the good of abolition of unjust slavery since the benefits arise from that injustice. See John Rawls, "The Idea of Public Reason Revisited," *University of Chicago Law Review* 64 (1997) 765. https://chicagounbound.uchicago.edu/uclrev/vol64/iss3/1.

30. I owe this point to Erin James.

31. Note, however, that Thomas Scanlon has argued that though we should not violate rights, this is not because their violation adds some greater negative weight to a state of affairs. To support this, he says that there is no additional reason to save one person rather than another from drowning merely because one person was wrongfully pushed into the water by an aggressor and the other was pushed in by a natural force. (See discussion of his view in Samuel Scheffler's *The Rejection of Consequentialism* [New York: Oxford University Press, 1982].) However, I suggest, it still seems more important morally to prevent an aggressor from pushing a person into the water in the first place, due to this being a rights violation, than to prevent the natural force from pushing the other person into the water. If this is so, one might give some added weight to such prevention of rights violation in a balancing calculation even if one was not focusing on rights as side constraints.

32. See Chapter 7 for more discussion of these issues, especially in the section where I consider the contrasting ways Justice Gorsuch and philosopher Margaret Battin reason about legalizing PAS for relief of suffering and avoiding abuse to others.

33. This is one reason why in this case a "preventative harm" may differ morally from harm which violates a negative right or from preventative harm that interferes with preventing violation of a negative right. It may be that a negative right of the doctor's to pursue his profession is being interfered with but I shall not focus on this.

34. Though, as Alec Walen pointed out, the state might pay for the PAS if it were covered by public medical insurance.

35. The earlier example of sterilization is relevant here too.

36. Gerald Dworkin emphasized this parallel in his "Physician-Assisted Suicide and Public Policy," Philosophical Studies 89 (1998), 133–41. https://www.jstor.org/stable/4320815.

37. As noted earlier, in the Supreme Court's PAS decision two justices, Breyer and O'Connor, said that they would reconsider whether there was a right to PAS if seriously ill people could not get pain relief even though it would foreseeably hasten their death. However, they did not discuss what to do if pain relief for some would causally enable unwilling deaths of others.

38. He may think it is the nonparadigmatic nature of these cases that stands in the way of doing this. We discuss this issue in III.

39. In their "Is Capital Punishment Morally Required? Acts, Omissions, and Life-Life Tradeoffs," Stanford Law Review 58 (2010), 703–750.

40. The act/omission distinction does not overlap exactly with the harm/not benefit distinction. I shall ignore this here.

41. Suppose it were found that the state doing capital punishment enabled murders by setting an example of deliberately taking the lives of people at a time when they do not present a threat. Then Sunstein and Vermeule would have a reason to oppose capital punishment.

42. In her "No, Capital Punishment Is Not Morally Required," Stanford Law Review 58 (2010), 751–89.

43. See Chapters 6 and 7 where we discussed the DDE.

44. That is why Foot initially found the permission to turn the trolley from killing five in the Trolley Problem puzzling as she didn't think she could explain it merely by morally distinguishing an unintended killing of one person that would occur if the trolley is turned, from an intended killing of one person to save the five. See her "The Problem of Abortion and the Doctrine of Double Effect," reprinted in her Virtues and Vices (Oxford: Basil Blackwell, 1978).

45. Jeff McMahan has discussed a case like this in his "Justice and Liability in Organ Allocation," Social Research 74:1 (2007), 101-24. I discuss such a case involving torture in my Ethics for Enemies: Terror, Torture, and War (New York: Oxford University Press, 2011).

46. For discussion of such an analysis applied to torture see my "Torture: Rescue, Prevention, and Punishment," *The Oxford Handbook of Ethics of War*, eds. S. Lazar and H. Frowe, Oxford University Press, 2016.

47. Given that PAS or E cannot be both an overall benefit and an overall abusive harm to the same person, we have to think of shifting such harm to the *group* likely to benefit.

48. Assuming pain relief is more effective and safer now than in 1998, the numbers who suffer now might be even fewer. However, the possibility that more people have extended dying periods (due to advances in medical treatments) than in the past raises the possibility that more might suffer.

49. 1998, 993, footnote 31.

50. See 1998, 993.

51. In my "Ending Life," in *Blackwell's Guide to Medical Ethics*, edited by Rosamond Rhodes, Leslie P. Francis, and Anita Silvers (Blackwell Publishing, 2008), 142–61. In particular, I criticized Dan Brock's contrary view in his "Voluntary Active Euthanasia," in *Intervention and Reflection: Basic Issues in Medical Ethics*, 5th ed., edited by R. Munson (Belmont, CA: Wadsworth, 1996), 180–87.

52. See his "The Dignity of Old Age," NYU School of Law, *Public Law Research Paper* No. 17-41, 2017. DOI: http://dx.doi.org/10.2139/ssrn.3048041 .

53. See also Michael Rosen's *Dignity* (Cambridge, MA: Harvard University Press, 2018) for discussion of different uses of "dignity."

54. In 1998 (998) he disputed the claim that requests for ending life by PAS or E come from a "growing number of terminally ill who die protracted and painful deaths." He there used the words "protracted and painful death" that he would use at the end of his 2014 article to describe what he wants to avoid by dying at 75. However, as I argued in Chapter 6, this does not accurately describe the reasons he gives throughout 2014 for wanting to die at 75 which involve reduced creativity, being a burden, and leaving bad memories of himself. Possibly, the way he ends 2014, I suggested, reflects his belief that just as (1998, 996) "public support for PAS or E drops dramatically when the scenario is not one of a patient in pain but of a bedridden patient, a patient worried about burdening his family, or a patient who just finds waiting for death purposeless," there will be little public support for the similar reasons he gives throughout his 2014 article for refusing easy and effective life-saving aid past 75.

55. An ethos, it is worth noting, he himself exhibits in his 2014 article.

56. Such harms would qualify as public reasons (in the Rawlsian sense) against PAS or E.

57. If other means of relieving physical suffering are available, the bad effects of using these rather than PAS would also have to be considered. For example, terminal sedation might have the bad effect for the person of being in a dependent state. Then PAS or E might be seen as providing the benefit of avoid dependency brought about in this way. This, in essence, would make a reason for PAS or E become one of the paradigmatic reasons.

58. We raised this issue when discussing capital punishment in II 3(E).

59. However, undergoing a smaller loss (a harm) can have greater disvalue that not getting a greater benefit according to Kahneman and Tversky's Prospect Theory. So it might be argued that losing some period of life one would otherwise ordinarily continue to have would have greater significance than not getting the benefit of relief of suffering (or even not getting the benefit of unexpected lengthy life extension). (I owe this point to Erin James.) However, presumably some loss could be outweighed by a big enough benefit. Also, in the Intrapersonal Choice Test, the significance of loss versus gain per se would be taken into account, since someone would have to decide whether it is preferable to lose additional life or gain relief from suffering.

60. See, for example, Johann Frick, "Treatment versus Prevention in the Fight Against HIV/AIDS and the Problem of Identified versus Statistical Lives," in *Identified Versus Statistical Lives: An Interdisciplinary Perspective*, edited by Glenn Cohen, Norman Daniels, and Nir Eyal (New York: Oxford University Press, 2015). https://scholar.princeton.edu/jfrick/publications/treatment-versus-prevention-fight-against-hivaids-and-problem-identified-versus.

61. In his *What We Owe to Each Other* (Cambridge, MA: Harvard University Press, 1999).

62. As argued for in Larry Temkin's *Rethinking the Good: Moral Ideals and the Nature of Practical Reasoning* (New York: Oxford University Press, 2012).

63. For a classic discussion about the contrast between additive aggregation and pairwise comparison see Thomas Nagel's "Equality" in his *Mortal Questions* (New York: Cambridge University Press, 1979), 106–27.

64. Problems can arise with the procedure I am describing in repeated decisions affecting the same sets of people. See Temkin, *Rethinking the Good: Moral Ideals and the Nature of Practical Reasoning*. However, this is not an issue in our cases since suffering before death without PAS or foreshortening of final days can only occur once in any person's life.

65. The less strict version of pairwise comparison would permit slightly smaller individual losses to be additively aggregated and outweigh the benefits to others of avoiding greater individual harms. On this see my *Morality, Mortality*, vol. 1 (New York: Oxford University Press, 1993), and T. M. Scanlon's *What We Owe to Each Other*.

66. Gorsuch emphasizes this. I argued in this way against "The Philosophers' Brief" when it equates doctors ending treatment even intending death and assisting suicide even intending death. (See my "A Right to Death?" *Boston Review* and "Problems with 'Assisted Suicide: The Philosophers' Brief'" in my *Bioethical Prescriptions* (Oxford University Press, 2013).) Gerald Dworkin agrees that this point may be relevant to deciding about the moral status of PAS or E versus terminating treatment. However, he argues that if PAS or E has been found to be morally permissible, then it is not clear why it should not be legally permissible just because no one will be subject to unwanted touching if it is not permitted. See his article "Physician Assisted Suicide and Public Policy."

A partial response might be that the different bad effects (i.e., imposing or not on someone's body against his will) of not legally permitting what is morally permissible might make it more urgent to make ending treatment legal than to make PAS or E legal.

67. It may be because EE thinks that laws for PAS should be made for the "paradigmatic" case and these do not involve relief of physical suffering that he thinks the threat of abuse is greater for PAS than in giving pain medicine. However, I have argued that laws for nonparadigmatic cases should not be ruled out and here the comparison with giving pain medicine that foreseeably hastens death seems to hold.

68. For more on the conditional/categorical distinction see Chapter 6, "Death Wish." For more on EE's negative views about the goods aside from pain relief that can be provided by EOLC at least past 75 see his 2014 and Chapter 6.

69. Some of the considerations I here raise as they bear on legalization and public policy were already raised in Chapter 6 in connection with moral permissibility of, and reasonable preference for, PAS as a matter of individual conduct.

70. See Chapter 6 for more on "complete life."

71. I discussed this issue in more detail in Chapter 6.

72. As noted in the 3-step argument in II(1) this chapter and in versions of the 4-step argument presented in Chapters 6 and 7.

73. I have criticized the Washington Court in *Glucksberg v. Washington* for its claim that once one may (1) give pain relieving drugs that one foresees will kill someone and (2) allow refusal of treatment when someone intends his death, it is hard to see why (3) one may not assist suicide intending a death (as in some conceptions of PAS). (See my "Theory and Analogy in the Law," *Arizona Law Review* 29 (1997) [relevant sections of which are reprinted in my *Bioethical Prescriptions*] and Chapter 6 on this.) But one may merely tolerate an intention to die when someone refuses treatment because the alternative is to impose treatment on him. This would not endorse the intention as permissible per se and that could be needed to justify assisting someone who is killing himself intending to die or assisting someone's suicide with the intention that he die. This is because there need be no imposition of treatment on someone if they are not assisted in suicide. That is why I argue specifically for the permissibility of such an intention.

74. See discussion of this in Part I, Section 2A.

75. A 4-step version of this argument is discussed in Chapter 6 in the context of the morality and reasonableness, not legality, of individual conduct.

76. For this interpretation of 2014 see Chapter 6.

77. We also discussed this issue in Chapters 6 and 7.

78. This chapter, like Chapter 6, was prompted by a debate between Ezekiel Emanuel and myself at the 30th Anniversary of the Edmond J. Safra Ethics Center at Harvard University, May 2017. I am grateful to Emanuel for discussion on that occasion. I am also grateful for comments on this chapter to Shelly Kagan, Jeff McMahan, Larry Sager, Seana Shiffrin, and Larry Temkin. Earlier versions were

presented as the A. I. Melden Lecture at the University of California Irvine, at the Law and Philosophy Colloquium at the UCLA School of Law, and as the Lecretia Seales Memorial Lecture in Law Reform, Victoria University of Wellington Law Faculty. I thank Matthew Vickers for inviting me to give the latter lecture and I am grateful to audiences at these events and to the students in my graduate and undergraduate philosophy classes at Harvard and Rutgers Universities for their comments.

Appendix
Cost-Effectiveness Analysis and Fairness

This appendix considers some different views of fairness and whether they conflict with the use of a version of Cost-Effectiveness Analysis (CEA) that calls for maximizing health benefits per dollar spent. Among the concerns addressed are whether this version of CEA ignores the concerns of the worst off and inappropriately aggregates small benefits to many people. I critically examine the views of Daniel Hausman and Peter Singer who defend this version of CEA, and of Eric Nord who criticizes it. I come to focus in particular on the use of CEA in allocating scarce resources to the disabled.[1]

Cost-Effectiveness Analysis (CEA) in medical care tries to maximize health benefits produced per dollar spent. Its use is recommended when society cannot afford every form of health care and must choose what to provide. Yet it is often taken as a truism that there can be deep conflicts between maximizing benefits and distributing fairly, in general. For example, the philosopher Robert Nozick imagined a "Utility Monster" (where utility is [roughly] experiential well-being) such that for any resource up for distribution, one always produces more additional benefit at less cost if one gives the resource to the Monster rather to others even though he is already much better off than they are. This would result in one person getting all the additional benefits while others get none. This seems unfair.

However, CEA cannot result in this most extreme form of unfairness because of limits that result from how it calculates benefits. Each additional year of very healthy life is given a value of 1; no one can get more than 1 per year. Still, it is possible that only those who are already very healthy can achieve many additional years at a value of 1 at low cost if they are saved from an otherwise fatal bacteria. Maximizing health benefits per cost would imply helping them rather than people who are not as healthy and can achieve only fewer additional years at a value of less than 1 and at higher cost if they are saved from the same threat. This too seems unfair.

Why does it seem unfair to help only the Utility Monster and the healthy people? Fairness is about how one person is treated relative to another. This is by contrast with a notion such as justice which need not be comparative; that is, we could decide what justice requires us to give a person in virtue of his characteristics independently of considering what anyone else is owed. Hence, we could treat someone justly in giving him what he is owed and yet increase unfairness if we treat him justly while not treating anyone else justly. (For example, we might punish some who deserve this even if we cannot punish all who do. This case also shows that fairness is only one moral dimension on which we can evaluate how we treat people or states of affairs we produce; it is possible that we should sometimes override fairness to be just or to achieve some other moral value.)

According to what measure shall we compare people to see if each is being treated fairly relative to others? Suppose we think that all that fairness requires in allocating benefits (via allocating resources) is that a certain amount of benefit be given the same value regardless of the person who will be benefited; no extra value should be assigned to a certain amount of benefit in person A rather than in person B. We could call this the Simple Standard. According to this standard, Nozick's Utility Monster and our Bacteria Case need not involve unfairness, for we could give the same value to a certain amount of benefit in the lives of everyone but it happens that more benefits can be produced in the Utility Monster and in the already healthy. These examples suggest that there may be more to fairness than the Simple Standard.

Indeed, there are different views about what fairness requires. I will consider whether, according to some of these views, problems of fairness arise in the medical context if we use a version of CEA that always emphasizes maximizing health benefits per dollar spent. Without pretending to settle the matter, I will raise some issues to consider. However, it is important to realize that problems with this version of CEA need not imply that it is never consistent with fairness to use some form of cost-effectiveness evaluation. For example, it seems fair and right to treat one hundred people equally well with a cheap drug rather than with an expensive one, other things equal. It would also be fair and right to use a drug with which we can save two hundred people rather than use an equally costly one with which we can save only one hundred of these people.

1. Chances in proportion to need. Some think that when we cannot help everyone, fairness requires that people get a chance for medical care in proportion to their need for it, regardless of outcome in terms of CEA. If this view were correct, someone who has a weak need for a scarce resource should get a small chance to get it. But does fairness really require giving a small chance to someone who needs the resource to cure his sore throat so that if against great odds he wins, then someone else who needs the resource to save her life dies? Would we be overriding fairness merely in order to achieve a better outcome if we did not give the person with a sore throat a chance? I suspect not for in other cases achieving a better outcome would not lead us to override what fairness really requires. For example, suppose a doctor and a janitor both equally need a scarce life-saving medicine. If the doctor survives, he can save someone else's life from another illness while the janitor cannot. Although we could achieve a better outcome if we save the doctor (two people saved rather than one), this may not be sufficient reason to deny equal chances to the doctor and janitor who both need the scarce medicine. If we would not override fairness in this case to achieve the better outcome, this suggests that in denying the person with the sore throat a proportional chance we are also not overriding fairness for the sake of a better outcome but rather we do not think fairness requires his having a chance.

What about chances in proportion to need of a group of people? Imagine that we can produce more cures per dollar if we treat six people who have one fatal disease rather than only treating five who have a different fatal disease. In this case the route to maximizing health benefits involves giving a life-saving benefit to more rather than fewer equally needy people. Hence, this case raises the question of whether it is unfair to save a greater number of people rather than to give each group a chance to be saved in proportion to the need of each member multiplied by the number of people in the group. Some think that fairness does not demand giving chances in proportion to need in the group but requires counting numbers of people, balancing one person of similar need (and, perhaps, expected outcome) against another and allowing the greater number to get the resource. On this view fairness does not require giving some chance to be helped to fewer people, when all suffer from equally serious problems.

Nevertheless, even on this view of fairness it may be right to give equal chances to be saved to the two groups if they each contain the same number of equally sick people when we only have enough resources to treat one type of fatal disease. But proponents of CEA should see no reason to give equal chances if outcome per dollar would be the same. It is only if we take seriously the personal perspectives of each person, and so recognize that each person is not indifferent to whether he or someone else survives, that we see why fairness could sometimes require giving equal chances to different people even when their need and outcomes are the same. (If we take seriously the perspectives of different people, we might even think it is wrong to deprive one person of his 50 percent chance to be treated merely because we would get a slightly better outcome if another person were treated.)

In sum, I have argued that while CEA does not necessarily contravene fairness in not giving chances to individuals in proportion to their need, it may fail to recognize an appropriate role for giving equal chances when need and outcome would be the same.

2. Priority to the worse off. Another possible fairness concern about CEA is that it is indifferent to whether an equally cost-effective benefit, such as relief from a certain amount of pain, goes to someone moderately ill or to someone severely ill. Some think fairness requires that the worse off be preferred. Indeed, it might be thought that fairness requires providing even a somewhat smaller benefit to those who are severely ill rather than a larger benefit to those who are moderately ill, holding cost constant. Such a "prioritarian" view of what fairness requires implies, roughly, that it is reasonable that the claim to benefits of those who are worse off should be weighed more heavily than the claim of those who are better off because it is right to give priority to improving the condition of a worse-off person before improving someone who is already better off than he is.[2] This view of fairness implies, contrary to the Simple Standard, that a given benefit in one person sometimes has greater moral value than the same benefit in another person. (However, giving priority to the worse off is not the same as always taking care of the worse off regardless of benefit that can be achieved.)

3. Anti-Additive Aggregation.[3] A third fairness concern about CEA is that providing minor, inexpensive health benefits (such as teeth fillings) in many people

may be more cost-effective than providing bigger, more expensive benefits (such as treating appendicitis) in a few, but fairness may require giving greater weight to the latter. This issue arises because CEA permits adding small benefits to each of many people to produce a large aggregate benefit that is then weighed against a smaller aggregate benefit composed of adding bigger benefits to a few people. The question is when it is fair to additively aggregate and weigh smaller benefits to some people against bigger benefits to others to decide how to allocate scarce resources.[4] This question about aggregation is sometimes related to the issue of giving priority to the worse off when the small benefits would go to many people already better off and the bigger benefits would to go to a few people more severely ill.

4. More on 2 and 3. Now consider the second and third concerns in greater detail by examining some responses to them. With regard to the second, some think that willingness to help the severely ill even when this produces fewer benefits per dollar need not depend on a prioritarian conception of fairness. Rather it can reflect compassion for those in dire straits. For example, Dan Hausman argues that CEA is the reasonable, rational, and not unfair way to decide how to allocate medical resources but we sometimes override it because of compassion for the severely ill. On this view, compassion can conflict with reason and it is compassion rather than a reasonable view of fairness that can lead us to help the severely ill when doing so conflicts with CEA.

One problem with this view is that it conflicts with the possibility that it is fair and reasonable to give priority to treating those who are only moderately ill rather than to those slightly ill even though compassion is not triggered for the former in the way it is for those in dire straits. Similarly, we do not now feel great compassion for 20-year-olds who we know will die in 30 years at age 50 by comparison with 20-year-olds who we know will die at age 65. Yet we might still think it is morally right to invest in research that will buy five more good years for those who would otherwise die at 50 rather than in research that will buy 10 more good years for those who will otherwise die at 65, even if this conflicts with CEA. Presumably, this is because it seems reasonable to help people who would be worse off when they die (in having had shorter lives) instead of people who would be better off (in having had longer lives) even without help. This reflects a prioritarian conception of fairness.

Another problem with the view that it is compassion rather than a reasonable conception of fairness that sometimes conflicts with CEA is that we often override compassion to do what is morally reasonable. For example, we may feel greater compassion for an incurably blind person who will also have to deal with a second problem if his arthritis is not treated than for a sighted person who will become (only) nearly blind if his eye problem is not treated. In this case, holding other factors constant, the blind arthritic will be the worst-off person if he is not treated. Yet it seems morally acceptable and reasonable to cure the more severe condition of near blindness rather than (what is here assumed to be) the less disabling condition of arthritis when we cannot do both. Suppose it is morally right to resist the call of compassion (as well as the call to help the person who would be worst off) in this case. Then perhaps in other cases when we do *not* give up on helping the worst-off person even though helping him conflicts with CEA it is because giving up would be contrary to reason and fairness rather than to compassion. This would imply that sometimes CEA is not the reasonable and fair approach.

Further support for the view that CEA does not necessarily coincide with what is reasonable and fair comes from the third concern about additive aggregation. That is, is it always fair to additively aggregate small health benefits to many people and weigh that aggregate against the smaller aggregate of bigger benefits to fewer people, when the benefits to each group cost the same? Suppose that each of many people has a mild headache and is otherwise already much better off health-wise than someone whom we can save from appendicitis. Suppose that none of the many people is a compassionate person and each would give up no more than the money for an aspirin that could cure his headache in order to help a dying person. But there are so many of these people with mild headaches that the additively aggregated harm of many headaches that would occur if each sacrificed his aspirin money is greater than the harm prevented in using the money to save the person with appendicitis. Though none of the people is rescuing the one person because of great compassion for him, presumably they would not refuse to give up the aspirin money for him on the grounds that the sum of losses to all of them is so enormous by comparison to one person's loss of life. No one has to be compassionate in order to realize that it would be a bizarre mistake of reason to treat the very large sum of small losses to each of the many people as if it had the same moral significance as a very large loss to a single person and allow him to suffer it to prevent a smaller loss to each of many other people.

Some suggest that the fair way to decide what to do in such cases, when the small harm (such as a headache) is occurring to each of many separate persons, is to compare in a pairwise fashion how much harm would be suffered and avoided by a severely ill person depending on whether he is helped with how much harm would be suffered and avoided by each of the many depending on whether they are helped. Fairness is comparative but, on this view, it requires comparing how individual persons fare one person at a time depending on what we do. Suppose that no one of the many will suffer anywhere near as great a loss as the single person would and they are already better off than he is. Then if our view of fairness combines pairwise comparison with priority to the worse off, curing a headache in each of many people would never take precedence over curing a much more serious condition in even one much worse-off person. A conception of fairness that involves these two components—pairwise comparison and prioritarianism—would support concerns about the fairness of CEA.

5. Singer. By contrast, Peter Singer, a philosopher who supports CEA, believes it is morally correct to additively aggregate smaller individual benefits to better-off people and weigh the aggregate against a bigger individual benefit to a worse-off person. For example, in a *New York Times Magazine* article on rationing,[5] he

considered how to compare the health benefit achieved in saving one person's life with curing a serious but non-life-threatening condition such as quadriplegia in another. He tells us to consider the trade-off each person would reasonably make in his own life between length of life and quality of life. Suppose every person (already disabled or not) would be indifferent between living ten years with quadriplegia or living five years non-disabled. This seems to indicate that people take living with quadriplegia to be half as good as living nondisabled.[6] Singer thinks that such data would show that using our resources to cure two quadriplegics is just as good as saving someone else's life when all three people would have the same life expectancy if helped (for example, ten years). His reasoning seems to be that if someone would give up five out of ten years of his own life rather than be quadriplegic, that would justify curing one person's quadriplegia rather than saving someone else's life for five years; the combined benefit of curing two people with quadriplegia would therefore justify not saving someone else's life when doing so would give her an additional ten years.

Several things seem problematic about this reasoning. First, in the trade-off between quality and quantity that a person might make in his own life, it is that person who benefits from the trade-off. When we make trade-offs between different people, the people who get the improved quality of life are not the same people who suffer the loss of more years of life. Hence, trade-offs between people may raise different moral issues than trade-offs within one life.[7] This is related to the point made earlier that fairness considerations arise when we take seriously that different people are not indifferent to whether benefits and losses fall in someone else's life or their own. Second, the conclusion that curing two quadriplegics who would live for ten years anyway is equal to saving for ten years someone else who would otherwise soon die depends on adding the benefit to *two* people to weigh it against the loss to the single person. We can see how problematic this is by considering the following example: Suppose that the trade-off test within one person's life showed that a small disability (e.g., a permanently damaged ankle) made life slightly less than 95 percent as good as a nondisabled life. This implies that a person would rather live nine and a half years without the small disability than ten years with it. On Singer's view, this implies that we should cure one person's small disability rather than save someone else who will otherwise soon die so that he can live for an additional half year. It also implies that we should cure the small disability in twenty-one people rather than save someone so that he can live for an additional ten years. This sort of problematic reasoning may have led to the rationing plan in Oregon many years ago in which resources were to be allocated to cap many people's teeth rather than save a few people's lives.[8]

A third concern about Singer's reasoning is that someone's imagined sacrifice of five years of life to avoid quadriplegia is imagined to leave him with five years of life instead of ten and he need not be willing to give up most or all of the remaining five years, thus dying immediately, to avoid quadriplegia. Yet if we choose to cure the two quadriplegics, the person who dies as a result of our choice will die immediately so that we may cure a condition whose victims, it is assumed, would not die immediately to avoid it.

Note that the problem with always additively aggregating small benefits can exist independently of aiming to give priority to treating those more severely ill. For suppose all patients have the same disability. We have a choice of making very small improvements in the degree of disability in each of a great many patients or providing a complete cure to one patient. It would not be morally unreasonable (and might not be unfair) to do the latter, for we then make a significant difference in this person's life rather than a barely perceptible difference to each of many others. This is so even though additively aggregating the many barely perceptible differences across persons creates an enormous total difference.[9]

6. Risk. Notice that in many of the cases we have considered if a particular person is not helped, he will *certainly* suffer a great loss and be worse off than others who will certainly avoid only small losses and be better off than he. But we may also consider the role of uncertainty and risk in deciding what is fair. We know that it can be reasonable for each individual to take a small risk of a large loss (such as losing many years of life) if this is the price of having a high probability of getting a smaller benefit. For example, someone might run a small risk of dying from an aspirin in order to get a high probability of relief from a nonlethal headache. If everyone in a community does this, in a large enough population it is certain that someone will die from an aspirin though each person had only a very small chance of dying. It seems morally permissible to allow individuals to expose themselves to such a small risk of the large loss for the sake of the small benefit. This is so even if we know that someone who took the risk that came to fruition will certainly die because there will then be nothing we can do to save him. However, when it is still possible to save this person whose risk of dying has gone from small to certain, or when someone was always known to be the person who would die, fairness may require aiding that person if we can, for example, with all the aspirin that would otherwise be used to prevent many people from each having a headache.[10]

Suppose there are a few people who will certainly die unless we treat them with a scarce resource. Should we do so or rather use our resource to prevent a small risk of death to each of many others when it is certain that eventually more than a few of these will certainly die? (Notice that to make sure it is only the known probability of any given person dying whose relevance to an allocation decision we are judging, we should hold constant the time at which those already ill and those who will become ill would die. Otherwise, we may be judging the relevance to an allocation decision of sooner rather than later deaths, not greater or smaller probabilities each person has of dying.)

On at least one view, fairness requires helping those with a higher individual risk of dying as ascertained by a pairwise comparison of the risks each person faces at the time we must allocate resources. This is because if we engage in pairwise comparison, we could justify to each person with the low risk of death our decision to not help him and instead help the person who it is known will certainly die. By contrast, it seems we could not justify to the person who it is known will certainly die our decision to leave him and instead help each of those who have a small chance of death. On this view, it is each individual's comparative risk at the time we must allocate, not whether in the ultimate outcome more rather than fewer people die, that should lead us to allocate the money. Hence we could have reason to favor the less-cost-effective treatment policy that saves fewer people. This is so even if fairness requires saving the greater number of people when these are all people who are known at the time we allocate to each face certain death at the same time if not helped.[11]

Except for the fact that time of death is not held constant, this is like the situation we may face when deciding whether to allocate scarce funds to combat AIDS by either treating those already ill or by preventing future cases. Suppose fewer people overall will die from AIDS if the money is put into prevention than if it is put into treatment, and so prevention is most cost-effective. Without prevention more people who once had only a small risk of getting AIDS will eventually face certain death. But at the time we must decide how to spend funds there is a smaller group of other people who already have a known prognosis of certain death if they are not treated at that time. It is not the case that there are already some people in the larger group who have a known prognosis of certain death if prevention measures are not taken now. Rather there are many people each of whom has a small chance of being a person who will face certain death. Hence, the treatment policy might be recommended on the grounds that we should help those who face known certain death rather than help any of those who as far as we know have only a small risk of death.[12]

7. Disability and discrimination. Another possible fairness concern is that CEA might involve discrimination against those who are poor or disabled. This is because it may cost more to treat these people by contrast to the rich or nondisabled, and the health benefits achieved may also be less. Peter Singer relies on CEA when he argues that if we accept that disability can make a person's life less good health-wise, and we want to maximize the health benefits we get with our resources, we should save the life of a nondisabled person rather than of someone whose disability cannot be cured if he lives on (other things equal).[13] In doing this, we maximize quality-adjusted life years (QALYs). The only alternative to this, Singer says, is to deny that disability per se makes someone's life not as good health-wise, and then there would be no reason to allocate resources to cure or prevent disabilities, which seems wrong.

I agree that understanding the issue of disability and allocation of scarce resource should not depend on accepting the view that disabilities make little difference to the quality of life. For if we hold this view, we may see little reason to invest in curing disabilities. We should also recognize that a satisfied "mood" that may be equally present in the disabled and nondisabled is not the sole measure of the goodness of one's life; one's objective capacities matter as well. Consistent with all this, one proposed response to a view like Singer's is offered by Eric Nord, Norman Daniels, and Mark Kamlet in their 2009 article.[14] They think it is important to distinguish two different questions. The first is: "Is a health state one we would prefer to cure?" A second question arises if we have this health state and it cannot be cured but life is still worth living, and we also have a life-threatening treatable condition but the medicine is scarce. The second question as stated by the authors is: "Should we defer to those who can be restored to more complete health than we can because they lack the untreatable condition?" The authors say we can reasonably answer "yes" to the first question—we would prefer a cure to the health state—and "no" to the second question. They do not say what explains the reasonableness of these responses.

Given the way their second question is phrased, it might be thought that one simple explanation is that the person with the untreatable condition does not have a duty to defer because he does not have a moral duty to sacrifice what is very important to him (his life) to produce the outcome that would be considered best from an impartial point of view. The fact that this view, which is standardly held by those who reject consequentialism, might explain the consistency of the first and second answers suggests to me that the second question as phrased by Nord, Daniels, and Kamlet is the wrong one to pose if we want to get to the heart of the issue in allocating scarce resources.

This is because it should be an impartial distributor who is allocating the resource, not a candidate for the resource, and the mere fact that a candidate need not defer to another candidate does not mean that the impartial distributor must give these people the same chance of treatment. Analogously, someone need not give up his medicine that will save his leg so that someone else may use it to save his own two legs even though the second person will be worse off without the medicine than its owner would be if he gives up his medicine. But if the drug is publicly owned and to be distributed by an impartial agent, that agent should prefer to help the person who would otherwise lose two legs. So a crucial issue in dealing with Singer's CEA-inspired view is whether, if an impartial distributor says yes to the first question ("Is a health-state one we would prefer to cure"), this distributor should also decide to treat the person who can be restored to more complete health. In my own past work (first in Kamm 2004),[15] I have been interested in the answer to these questions (which I shall refer to as the Impartial Questions).

Suppose I am the impartial distributor. When I imagine a case in which someone has a paralyzed finger, I can see that this can make life not as good in a small way, other things equal, and give us a reason to fix the disability. Hence, my answer to the first question is yes. But when I consider whether to save someone's life from pneumonia when I can save only one person, the fact that one of the people I would save has a paralyzed finger and the other has all his fingers working should, I think, make no difference to whom I choose, given the important benefit that is at stake for each person and that each person desires to be the one to live. Hence, I should answer "no" to the second Impartial Question. Part of the explanation for this, I have suggested, is that a factor (such as a paralyzed finger) could give us a reason to act in one context (curing it) while it is an irrelevant consideration in another context where the action in question (saving a life) is different. This is an instance of what I call "contextual interaction."[16]

It may be clear that small differences, like a paralyzed finger, should not affect who is chosen for a life-saving resource. But what is the explanation of this irrelevance? A possible explanation is that in this two-person contest for a scarce life-saving resource, either person would get the greater part of the best possible outcome that can be had by someone (i.e., a worthwhile life whether with or without a paralyzed finger). It is also the case that the alternative for each to being saved would be very bad (death) and each wants to be the one to survive. It is crucial to this explanation that we are dealing with separate persons and that as impartial allocators acting from a moral point of view, their different perspectives on an outcome (viz., each cares who survives) should influence what we should do. Otherwise, it would be clear that we should maximize QALYs as we would do if we had a choice with respect to one person of merely saving his life or saving his life and also unparalyzing his finger, holding costs constant.

But what of larger disabilities that bring down quality of life as far as 0.5 or somewhat below, so that it is not true that whomever is helped that person would get the greater part of the best possible QALY outcome that can be gotten by any candidate? I have suggested at least two grounds for why we should still give equal chances for a life-saving procedure to the disabled and nondisabled. Importantly, neither ground depends on the view that a disabled life is as good for someone as a nondisabled one, other things equal. First, each person can get what it is morally most important that people have, namely a worthwhile life, and each wants to be the one to survive. (Call this the Moral Importance Ground.) Second, when one's only option is to have a life at 0.5 quality rating, it may be reasonable to *care about* keeping it as much as it would be reasonable to care about keeping a life quality-rated at 1. (Call this the Only Option Ground.) Note that this is consistent with its being reasonable to *care to have* the life rated at 1 rather than at 0.5 and even with its being reasonable to risk death to get it, were this possible.

But now imagine two nondisabled patients. One could live for *twenty* years if he had a scarce life-saving surgery and the other could live for five years. The Moral Importance and Only Option Grounds also seem to imply the seemingly mistaken view that it would be wrong to favor the person who would live much longer. If we disagree, we will need an argument that allows significant differences in length of life, but not significant differences in quality of life, to count in rationing decisions. One argument I have suggested is that we should distinguish between the "type" of person someone is, constituted by the qualitative features of his life, and how long any type of life goes on. Respect for persons might often require ignoring types when rationing but not require ignoring big differences in how long any given type will persist. (Call this the Respect Ground.)

Now consider another case about which we ask the first and second Impartial Questions. Suppose we agree paraplegia is a condition that we should prefer to cure. Now imagine two people with paraplegia who each need to be saved from fatal heart disease. The only difference between them is that in one of the people the scarce heart disease medicine will also cure his paraplegia. This is a case in which one candidate has an untreatable condition (paraplegia) and a treatable one (heart disease) and another candidate lacks untreatable conditions (because both his heart disease and his paraplegia can be cured). I suggest that it might be right for the impartial distributor of a scarce resource to choose to save the candidate whose paraplegia will also be cured rather than the other candidate. However, I think that this is neither simply because a life with paraplegia is worse than one with full mobility (other things equal) nor because CEA would rate a treatment as more effective if a person is saved to a life of higher rather than lower quality. Rather, it has something to do with both how bad paraplegia is and, crucially, with our medical procedure *causing* the person to no longer have paraplegia. That is, suppose it is not unfair to treat the second person if and because we can also cure his paraplegia. This does not imply that it would be fair to treat the heart condition of someone who is and will remain unparalyzed quite independently of our treatment rather than treat the heart condition of a permanently paralyzed person.

These two different heart cure cases suggest that a possible problem with CEA is that it does not distinguish (i) the case in which our treatment is more cost-effective in one candidate because it saves a life and also *causes* the change in disability status from (ii) the case in which our treatment is more cost-effective in one candidate because it saves someone who is already nondisabled independent of our doing anything to cure him of disability. In the latter case, we maximize QALYs by "piggybacking on" (i.e., taking advantage of his independently held) nondisabled condition. However, the two heart cure cases need not imply that causation always matters. For example, suppose each of two people has a paralyzed finger and a scarce life-saving drug that each needs will unparalyze the finger in only one of the people. The two Heart Cases need not imply that we should give that one person the medicine. A condition that we would prefer to cure may not be serious enough in itself that our being able to cure it in one person but not another should make a difference to which person we give a drug that each needs to survive.[17]

8. Conclusion. I have considered several views about what fairness requires and allows in conditions of certainty and uncertainty and how CEA understood in its strongest form may conflict with fairness. It has not been my aim to decide which conception of fairness is correct or to decide how important fairness is relative to other moral considerations. Nor has it been my aim to deny that CEA should sometimes play a role in allocating scarce resources. However, if the value of maximizing good outcomes relative to cost is neither a preeminent value nor necessarily consistent with fairness, there are bound to be moral questions about limits on the use of CEA that will need to be resolved.[18]

Notes

1. This appendix pertains to issues discussed in Chapters 4 and 8. It is a revised version of the article of the same name printed in the *Journal of Practical*

Ethics 3 (2015) which was a response to Daniel Hausman's "How Can We Ration Health Care Fairly and Humanely?" (originally presented by him at "Bioethical Reflections: A Conference in Honor of Dan Brock," at Harvard Medical School, November 22, 2014). All references to Hausman are to that paper. Hausman focused on discussions in several of Brock's articles (including his "Ethical Issues in the Use of Cost-Effectiveness Analysis for the Prioritization of Health Care") about the problems of fair chances, priority to the worse off, aggregation, and discrimination. Hence, the order in which I discuss some issues in this appendix follows the order in which Hausman chose to discuss Brock's work.

2. There is a noncomparative view about giving priority to the worse off according to which the moral value of giving a benefit to someone varies with how well off in absolute terms that person is—the worse off, the greater the value. This view does not require comparing how well off someone is relative to others. (It should not be interpreted to imply the mistaken view that a world in which moral value is maximized because everyone was very badly off but is completely helped is a better world than one in which no existing person was very badly off and each got only the little help he needed.) I am focusing on the comparative prioritarian view in taking it to be an interpretation of fairness which is a comparative value.

3. Some use the term "aggregation" to include the idea of addition. Here the term is used to connote merely putting items together in some way and adding them is just one way of doing this.

4. It is not unfair to additively aggregate small benefits to a few and weigh these against an aggregate of the same small benefits to many others, other things equal. But I am concerned with additively aggregating and weighing smaller benefits against bigger benefits.

5. Peter Singer, "Why We Must Ration Health Care," *New York Times*, July 19, 2009.

6. I say "seems" because it is possible that as the absolute number of years to be lived not disabled decreases (e.g., from 5 to 2 even if the ratio of unparalyzed to paralyzed years in the choice does not fall below 1:2), people would no longer be indifferent.

7. In Chapter 8 I make use of an intrapersonal trade-off test to judge which of two possible outcomes is worse and then apply the result to see which of two people would suffer a worse outcome. Nothing I say there depends on ignoring the fact that if one person suffers the less bad outcome it is not so that he (rather than someone else) can avoid the worse outcome.

8. For further discussion of this see my *Intricate Ethics* (New York: Oxford University Press, 2007), chapter 2.

9. Larry Temkin has emphasized this point. See his *Rethinking the Good: Moral Ideals and the Nature of Practical Reason* (Oxford University Press, 2012).

10. One place I discuss this issue is in "Should You Save This Child? Gibbard on Intuitions, Contractualism, and Strains of Commitment," in *Reconciling Our Aims*, ed. A. Gibbard (New York: Oxford University Press, 2008).

11. A limited version of this view (and its application to cases like AIDS) is argued for by Norman Daniels (2012) and Johann Frick (2013 and unpublished) though they may not hold time of the relevant deaths constant. See Norman Daniels, "Reasonable Disagreement about Identified vs. Statistical Victims," *Hastings Center Report* 42 (2012), 35–45; Johann Frick, "Uncertainty and Justifiability to Each Person: Response to Fleurbaey and Voorhoeve," in ed. Nir Eyal et al., *Inequalities in Health: Concepts, Measures, and Ethics* (New York: Oxford University Press, 2013); Johann Frick, "Treatment versus Prevention in the Fight Against HIV/AIDS and the Problem of Identified versus Statistical Lives" in *Inequalities in Health*, ed. Glenn Cohen et al. (New York: Oxford University Press, 2015).

12. Frick proposes such an argument but also considers objections to it in his "Treatment and Prevention in the Fight Against HIV/AIDS."

13. See Peter Singer et al., "Double Jeopardy and the Use of QALYS in Health Care Allocation," in *Unsanctifying Human Life: Essays on Ethics*, ed. Helga Kuhse (Oxford: Blackwell, 2002).

14. See Eric Nord, Norman Daniels, and Mark Kamlet, "QALYs: Some Challenges," *Value in Health* 12, Suppl 1 (2009), S10–S15. Norman Daniels brought my attention to what was said in this article in his commentary on my *Bioethical Prescriptions: To Create, End, Choose, and Improve Lives* (New York: Oxford University Press, 2013) at a panel in February 2013.

15. Frances M. Kamm, "Deciding Whom to Help, Health Adjusted Life-Years, and Disabilities," in *Public Health, Ethics and Equality*, eds. S. Anand, F. Peter, and A. Sen (New York: Oxford University Press, 2004).

16. I first discussed contextual interaction in my "Killing and Letting Die: Methodological and Substantive Issues," *Pacific Philosophical Quarterly* 64, no. 4 (1983). Singer gives a counterargument that is meant to show that it is reasonable to connect the answer to the first Impartial Question to an answer to the second Impartial Question. The argument claims the morally right way for an impartial allocator to make his decision is determined by what any person would decide about his possible future treatment when he is ignorant of which particular person (disabled or not) he will be. Singer thinks such a person would want to maximize his chances of living in the better condition (e.g., with all working fingers). I do not think this argument is correct and argue against it in *Bioethical Prescriptions*. But it is useful to see an argument, aside from maximizing good outcomes, that has been thought to connect a "yes" answer to the first question to a "yes" answer to the second question.

17. I have considered the issues discussed in Section 7 in more detail in "Aggregation, Allocating Scarce Resources, and the Disabled," *Social Philosophy and Policy* 26 (2009), 148–97, and in "Aggregation, Allocating Scarce Resources, and Discrimination Against the Disabled," in *Bioethical Prescriptions*.

18. I am grateful to Julian Savulescu and a reader for the *Journal of Practical Ethics* for comments on an earlier version of this appendix.

Index

For the benefit of digital users, indexed terms that span two pages
(e.g., 52–53) may, on occasion, appear on only one of those pages